www.wadsworth.com

www.wadsworth.com is the World Wide Web site for Wadsworth and is your direct source to dozens of online resources.

At *www.wadsworth.com* you can find out about supplements, demonstration software, and student resources. You can also send e-mail to many of our authors and preview new publications and exciting new technologies.

www.wadsworth.com
Changing the way the world learns®

From the Wadsworth Series in Mass Communication and Journalism

General Mass Communication

Anokwa/Lin/Salwen, *International Communication: Issues and Controversies*
Biagi, *Media/Impact: An Introduction to Mass Media*, Eight Edition
Bucy, *Living in the Information Age: A New Media Reader*, Second Edition
Day, *Ethics in Media Communications: Cases and Controversies*, Fifth Edition
Dennis/Merrill, *Media Debates: Great Issues for the Digital Age*, Fourth Edition
Fellow, *American Media History*
Hilmes, *Connections: A Broadcast History Reader*
Hilmes, *Only Connect: A Cultural History of Broadcasting in the United States*, Second Edition
Jamieson/Campbell, *The Interplay of Influence: News, Advertising, Politics, and the Mass Media*, Sixth Edition
Kamalipour, *Global Communication*, Second Edition
Lester, *Visual Communication: Images with Messages*, Fourth Edition
Overbeck, *Major Principles of Media Law*, 2007 Edition
Straubhaar/LaRose, *Media Now: Understanding Media, Culture, and Technology*, Fifth Edition
Zelezny, *Communications Law: Liberties, Restraints, and the Modern Media*, Fifth Edition
Zelezny, *Cases in Communications Law*, Fifth Edition

Journalism

Bowles/Borden, *Creative Editing*, Fourth Edition
Craig, *Online Journalism*
Hilliard, *Writing for Television, Radio, and New Media*, Eighth Edition
Kessler/McDonald, *When Words Collide: A Media Writer's Guide to Grammar and Style*, Sixth Edition
Poulter/Tidwell, *News Scene 2.0: Interactive Writing Exercises*
Rich/Harper, *Writing and Reporting News: A Coaching Method*, Fifth Edition
Rich/Harper, *Writing and Reporting News: A Coaching Method, Student Exercise Workbook*, Fifth Edition
Stephens, *Broadcast News*, Fourth Edition
Wilber/Miller, *Modern Media Writing*

Photojournalism and Photography

Parrish, *Photojournalism: An Introduction*

Public Relations and Advertising

Diggs-Brown, *The PR Styleguide: Formats for Public Relations Practice*, Second Edition
Hendrix/Hayes, *Public Relations Cases*, Seventh Edition
Jewler/Drewniany, *Creative Strategy in Advertising*, Eighth Edition
Newsom/Haynes, *Public Relations Writing: Form and Style*, Seventh Edition
Newsom/Turk/Kruckeberg, *This Is PR: The Realities of Public Relations*, Ninth Edition

Research and Theory

Baran/Davis, *Mass Communication Theory: Foundations, Ferment, and Future*, Fourth Edition
Littlejohn, *Theories of Human Communication*, Seventh Edition
Rubin/Rubin/Piele, *Communication Research: Strategies and Sources*, Sixth Edition
Scheufele/Babbie, *The Basics of Media Research*
Sparks, *Media Effects Research: A Basic Overview*, Second Edition
Wimmer/Dominick, *Mass Media Research: An Introduction*, Eighth Edition

Global Communication

SECOND EDITION

Edited by
YAHYA R. KAMALIPOUR
Purdue University Calumet

Australia • Brazil • Canada • Mexico • Singapore • Spain
United Kingdom • United States

Global Communication, Second Edition
Yahya R. Kamalipour

Publisher: Holly J. Allen
Assistant Editor: Lucinda Bingham
Editorial Assistant: Meghan Bass
Senior Technology Project Manager: Jeanette Wiseman
Senior Marketing Manager: Mark Orr
Marketing Assistant: Alexandra Tran
Marketing Communications Manager: Shemika Britt
Project Manager, Editorial Production: Megan E. Hansen
Creative Director: Rob Hugel

Executive Art Director: Maria Epes
Print Buyer: Rebecca Cross
Permissions Editor: Kiely Sisk
Production Service: Kalpalathika Rajan, Integra
Copy Editor: Sara Dovre Wudali
Cover Designer: Qin-Zhong Yu
Cover Printer: Transcontinental-Louiseville
Compositor: Integra
Printer: Transcontinental-Louiseville

Library of Congress Control Number: 2005930875

ISBN 0-495-05027-X

Thomson Higher Education
10 Davis Drive
Belmont, CA 94002-3098
USA

For more information about our products, contact us at:
Thomson Learning Academic Resource Center
1-800-423-0563

For permission to use material from this text or product, submit a request online at
http://www.thomsonrights.com.
Any additional questions about permissions can be submitted by e-mail to
thomsonrights@thomson.com.

For Mah, Daria, Shirin, Niki

All the particles of universe,
Speak to you, day and night.
We see, we hear, we delight,
But to you strangers, we're blight.

Jalal ed-Din Rumi, the 13th century Persian poet

I don't know if evil and ignorance are in fact twins, but I can tell you this. Of all the people I have interviewed, and I have interviewed murderers - Charles Manson - and I have interviewed bigots and racists and presidents, and the one thing they have all had in common is profound ignorance about the world.

Diane Sawyer, *Broadcast journalist*

An education isn't how much you have committed to memory, or even how much you know. It's being able to differentiate between what you do know and what you don't.

Anatole France, *French novelist*

The central task of education is to implant a will and facility for learning; it should produce not learned but learning people. The truly human society is a learning society, where grandparents, parents, and children are students together.

Eric Hoffer, *American Philosopher*

Contents

Foreword

ITO YOUICHI

Ito Youichi is Professor of Policy Management at the Shonan Fujisawa campus of Keio University and a researcher at the Institute for Communications Research at Keio University in Tokyo. He served as a board member-at-large of the International Communication Association (ICA) and the International Council of the International Association for Media and Communication Research (IAMCR), and is currently Vice-President of the Political Communication Section of IAMCR and is also Vice-President of the Research Committee on Political Communication of the International Political Science Association (IPSA). He is the founding editor of the *Keio Communication Review* and an editorial board member of *The Journal of Communication, Media Culture & Society, Gazette, Global Media Journal, Political Communication, International Journal of Public Opinion Research,* and *The Asian Journal of Communication.*

The history of international communication and cultural interchange is as old as human civilization. A civilized society that has never been influenced by another culture does not exist. In ancient and medieval times, this was considered quite normal, and nobody complained about it. It is only since the beginning of the 19th century that foreign cultural influences have been regarded by some people as a "problem."

In the case of Japan, it was the middle of the 19th century and soon after World War II when Japanese intellectuals felt "cultural threats," including the loss of their traditional culture due to the overwhelming inflows of foreign cultures (specifically European and American). With the exception of these two periods, subjects such as cultural continuity or the loss of traditional culture have not been considered a serious problem in Japan.

When the New World Information and Communication Order (NWICO) was eagerly discussed at UNESCO and the United Nations in the 1970s and

1980s, Japanese political and intellectual leaders were practically indifferent to the subject. Japan at that time already exported more television programs (animations to all over the world and dramas to neighboring countries) than it imported. Although the news flow from the United States to Japan exceeded by far the flow from Japan to the United States, many research results confirmed that American mass media usually covered Japan more thoroughly than Germany, Italy, or Israel (although less than the United Kingdom and France). Under these situations, NWICO's slogans were not at all appealing to the Japanese.

In September 1995, large-scale international collaborative research on international news flows was conducted. A data set of 46 countries became available as a result. In analyzing the data, several criteria were set to judge the degree of "health" or "problems" in each region. Heavy dependence on specific powers, especially those outside the region or the power that colonized the country in the past, was judged to be "unhealthy." On the other hand, countries with exchange of news with neighboring countries or countries within the same region were judged to be "healthy." What was found that the situations in Latin America and Africa have much improved compared with the 1970s and 1980s. On the other hand, reflecting continued wars and conflicts, the situation in the Middle East was still poor. Only in the Middle East the "dummy variable" of "colonial past" judged to be statistically significant in the regression analysis. However, the worst region was Eastern and Central Europe, where dependence on the United States and Russia was more than Africa's dependence on the United States and the United Kingdom. Although the concept of "colonial past" was not statistically significant in Eastern and Central Europe as a whole, it was significant in Estonia and Ukraine. (The seven Eastern and Central European countries that participated in this collaborative research were all coded as "ex-colonies" of Russia.)[1]

Korea was a colony of Japan from 1910 through 1945. Partly because of this, flow of information and culture between Korea and Japan has been one-way (from Japan to Korea) since the late 19th century. However, the Korean government began strengthening the visual contents industry as a strategic export industry about 10 years ago. Korean movies and television dramas first succeeded in Taiwan and mainland China markets, and in the last two years, they have become very successful in the Japanese market as well. The kanryu or "Korean-style" boom in Japan arose from movies and TV drama series and extended to tourism, food, music, and many related areas.

These facts and experiences indicate that the problem of imbalanced flow of information and culture is basically a matter of economic conditions and policies. Also, as in the case of news flow in Africa and Latin America, the problems can be solved, or at least improved, by conscious efforts as economic conditions improve. The situation in Eastern and Central Europe at present is now improved compared with 1995 when our research was conducted.

---

1. See the following literature for details: Ito, Youichi (Spring 2004). The grass beneath two bears: News flows in Eastern and Central Europe, *Global Media Journal*, *3*(4). Retrieved from http://www.globalmediajournal.com or http://lass.calumet.purdue.edu/cca/gmj

On the other hand, however, our research on international news flow indicated that we cannot be too optimistic. What seems to be unchanged since the 1970s is the dominance of international news media in the United States, the United Kingdom, and France. The dummy variable indicating the existence of international news agencies was found to be the most important determinant factor in international news flows, which means that the volume of news flow from these three countries exceeded the "appropriate level", that is, the volume predicted by other general or common factors such as population, the GDP, per capita GDP, the volume of trade with them, geographical distance from them, and so on. The supremacy of international news media of these three countries is protected by their monopolistic languages, English and French; therefore, their hegemony is likely to continue long into the future.

I was intrigued by the following quotation from a paper by a Swedish American researcher: "Were it not for the reporting of various isolated crises, overall coverage of Scandinavia in the American media would be so scant as to be practically nonexistent . . . [therefore] the Third World has no exclusive right to complaints that the U.S. media largely overlook developmental stories in favor of spot crisis-oriented news."

Our research confirmed this fact. International flow of news, as well as popular culture, is strongly determined by scale factors such as population, the GDP, the defense budget, and so on. However, the dominant discourse in international communication research is "West versus non-West." As a result, small countries in the West, such as Sweden, Norway, Denmark, the Netherlands, and others, tend to be ignored or overlooked. At the same time, a highly developed country in the non-West, such as Japan, also tends to be ignored in this Western versus non-Western discourse. This discourse certainly includes many biases or even prejudices in some cases, which I suspect has something to do with "Western nationalism" or "Western narcissism"[2] held by Western scholars.

Our research confirmed that the existence of international news media protected by language monopoly (English and French) was found to be the most important factor determining international news flow. This finding is not at all new. However, in the traditional Western versus non-Western discourse, this phenomenon has been discussed as another example of Western supremacy, and the fact that this supremacy is protected by language monopoly has been ignored, especially by Anglo-American scholars. The reason for this might be the following: While the emphasis on the supremacy of Western news media gives them narcissistic pleasure, the emphasis on English language imperialism might bring them inconvenience in the future.

---

2. Ito, Youichi (2003). Globalisation and Western narcissism. In N. Chitty (Ed.), *Faces of globalisation* (pp. 131–150). Varanasi, India: Ganga Kaveri Publishing House.

Preface to the Second Edition

YAHYA R. KAMALIPOUR

The second edition of *Global Communication* is completely updated and expanded and promises to be more comprehensive, informative, and engaging than the first edition. The published national and international journal reviews of the first edition—including instructors' feedback—have been highly favorable and included several constructive recommendations that have been incorporated into this edition. Below are some of the highlights of this volume:

- All chapters have been updated to reflect major events that have impacted our global communication environment since the publication of the first edition.

- A new chapter on communication and propaganda has been added to reflect the global changes that have taken place since the 9/11 attacks on the United States and the subsequent wars on Afghanistan, Iraq, and so-called terrorism in general.

- A new chapter on the Internet and its global implications has been added.

- A new "Foreword" and updated "Suggested Readings" are included.

- End-of-chapter questions are comprehensive and intended to stimulate discussion.

- An expanded glossary of the many key terms used in the book is included.

- Helpful Internet links to information relevant to topics discussed are suggested throughout the book.

This book is intended to explore, analyze, inform, and provoke discussions about one of the major components of globalization: global communication. Global communication is a post–Cold War and post-Industrial Revolution phenomenon that is rapidly transforming economic, relational, social, cultural, political, and structural aspects of practically every nation of the world. Global communication, made possible by the marvels of telecommunication technologies, is a vast, diverse, dynamic, complex, interactive, and rapidly growing discipline and enterprise.

It is an essential component of another evolutionary and revolutionary process, called globalization, which has enveloped much of the world, particularly the advanced and many of the developing nations. Hence, from the communication standpoint, shifts in national, regional, and international media patterns of production, distribution, and consumption are a part of much larger shift prompted by globalization.

A noticeable consequence of globalization is that peoples, nations, and institutions of the world have become economically interdependent and socially interconnected—everything has a global dimension and everyone is electronically connected. In other words, the concept of the "global village," predicted by Marshall McLuhan in the 1960s, is now our shared reality.

DEFINITIONS

Due to its vast scope and complexity, no standard and universally acceptable definition for the concept of *globalization* can be formulated. Nonetheless, various experts define the concept in accordance with their worldviews and disciplines. "In the idiom of popular opinion," writes James H. Mittleman (1997), "globalization means that instantaneous telecommunications and modern transportation overcome the barriers between states and increase the range of interaction across international limits. The cliché is that people are exposed to the same global media and consumer products, that such flows are making borders less relevant" (p. 229).

Manfred Steger (2004) defines globalization "as a multidimensional set of social processes that create, multiply, stretch, and intensify worldwide social interdependence and exchange while at the same time fostering in people a growing awareness of deepening connections between the local and distant" (p. 2). On the other hand, critics of globalization define it as a "worldwide drive toward a globalised economic system dominated by supranational corporate trade and banking institutions that are not accountable to democratic processes or national governments" ("What Is Globalisation?" n.d.). They also argue that "Globalisation is an undeniably capitalist process. It has taken off as a concept in the wake of the collapse of the Soviet Union and of socialism as a viable alternate form of economic organization" ("What Is Globalisation?" n.d.).

Globalization has resulted in the integration of economies through increased interdependence among nations, decreased trade barriers, and the generation of open markets. Throughout this book, you will also read a variety of definitions posed by the contributing authors.

Likewise, the concepts of *international communication, global communication, transnational communication, transborder communication, world communication, intercultural communication, cross-cultural communication,* and *international relations* are multidimensional and highly complex. Hence, any attempt at formulating a simple definition would be incomplete and certainly debatable. Nonetheless, in terms of meaning, the aforementioned first five concepts are interchangeable—they all refer to information flow that crosses geographical boundaries of nation–states. A necessary distinction among the five terms is that while three (*international, transnational,* and *transborder*) recognize the geographical boundaries between nation–states, two (*global* and *world*) do not. On the other hand, while *intercultural communication* and *cross-cultural communication* refer to interpersonal relations among peoples of different cultures, races, and backgrounds, *international relations* mainly refers to political (government-to-government) and economic (business-to-business) relations and activities.

A GROWING FIELD

In tandem with the globalization process, an increasing number of universities in the United States and abroad stress what is commonly known as the internationalization of curricula, by offering new courses in international communication, international relations, international education, intercultural communication, and international business and marketing. At the same time, some universities have established global education centers in order to (1) attract international students, (2) promote student and faculty exchanges, (3) promote study-abroad programs, (4) foster cross-cultural awareness, (5) offer online (eLearning) courses, (6) organize cultural activities and seminars, (7) encourage research and scholarly activities, and (8) foster awareness of domestic and global issues. Accordingly, in the last decade or so, the demand for books dealing with global issues and globalization has been increasing rapidly. This timely book, along with the supplementary websites, fills the gap between the high demand for teaching material for global communication and the serious shortage of such material.

SCOPE OF THE BOOK

The speed of change in global communication is such that no textbook can be entirely current or adequate, nor can it include all the issues and concepts related to this complex, dynamic, and fascinating field of study. To the extent possible, in terms of content and scope, this book attempts to provide an up-to-date and comprehensive coverage of global communication.

In conceptualizing this book, I operated under the highly probable assumptions that upper-level undergraduate and lower-level graduate students enrolled in an international communication course have already taken some mass communication courses, possess the basic information and knowledge about the field, and are already familiar with at least some (if not most) of the fundamental issues and concepts.

A unique feature of this book is that it brings together diverse issues and perspectives from some of the world's most notable and accomplished communication scholars. In addition to covering the essential concepts of international communication, this book includes several emerging and controversial topics, such as international public relations and advertising, recent trends in media consolidation, cultural implications of globalization, international broadcasting, information flow, propaganda and persuasion, governmental and nongovernmental organizations, international communication law and regulation, the impact of the Internet, and trends in communication and information technologies.

STRUCTURE OF THE BOOK

The 14 chapters of this book are organized to evolve from theoretical paradigms to specific topics and issues. The order could be easily changed to suit the preferences of instructors who may wish to follow a topical or thematic pattern of instruction. The first two chapters offer students essential information about historical and theoretical aspects of global communication; thus, they should be assigned first. Thereafter, the order is not as important as tailoring the contents of the book to meet the particular needs of students.

Readers will note that the length of chapters varies, depending on the complexity of the topic. In brief, the book is organized according to the following broad themes: historical, theoretical, economic, legal and regulatory, news and information, broadcasting and the Internet, institutional and structural, political, developmental, cultural, and future prospects.

- **Chapter 1** (Following the Historical Paths of Global Communication). In this chapter, Allen Palmer provides a succinct background for studying global communication. History reveals the story of the amazing achievements that led to today's vast networks of global communication. Over the millennia, there has been a long and fascinating parade of communication devices and technologies designed to conquer distance. From the earliest myths and misconceptions of our ancestors in prehistory; to the rudimentary tools used by hunters and artists, the meditations of pilgrims and scientists, and dispatches of soldiers and diplomats; and finally, to developers of the electrical revolution of the past two centuries—our grasp of global communication has taken a long, circuitous road to our nearly transparent world today.

- **Chapter 2** (Drawing a Bead on Global Communication Theories). John Downing takes the term *theory,* fearsome to some, irrelevant and speculative to others, and sets out to unpack its importance and interest if, that is, we want really to understand media rather than just react to them unthinkingly. He begins by critically evaluating one of the longest-running sets of media theories we have, the so-called "normative" approach. He then proceeds to dissect a media system quite unfamiliar to Western media users but one with great resonance still in many countries across the planet, the now-defunct Soviet Russian system. This exercise helps to highlight the distinctive features of Western media systems, which many people in the West assume are natural and inevitable, the way media "just are." After this, Downing reviews varied attempts to understand the contemporary globalization of media and its impacts around the world. Finally, he briefly addresses the small-scale media of social and political movements around the world, once again throwing into question the frequent unthinking assumptions we retain about what "media" are. For Downing, the word *media* is always a plural, not a singular noun, because of their great diversity and because of the constant changes they undergo. This is the source of the difficulties we face in trying to get them clearly in focus—a task that we can only expect to achieve by carefully building and comparing adequate explanations (theories) of how media work in our complex world.

- **Chapter 3** (Global Economy and International Telecommunications Networks). Harmeet Sawhney examines the structural patterns of global telecommunication networks. The British imperial telegraph network, the first global telecommunications network, was highly centralized and had few lateral connections. All lines led to London. If two neighboring colonized countries wanted to communicate with each other, the message had to be routed via London, which was often thousands of miles away. Later, this pattern was carried over to the telephone network. After World War II, the center of the world moved across the Atlantic to the United States, and accordingly, global telecommunications networks were reconfigured. Now all lines led to New York. However, the overall structure of global telecommunications networks remained unchanged. They continued to be highly centralized networks with few lateral lines. Even today this pattern persists in telephone traffic, computer-to-computer communication, media flows, monetary flows, and other modes of global communication. This chapter examines the economic, political, and historical forces that have created and sustained this pattern. It also explores whether the seemingly unique qualities of the Internet will disrupt the long-established pattern and restructure global communications.

- **Chapter 4** (The Transnational Media Corporation and the Economics of Global Competition). Richard Gershon examines the status of transnational media corporations (TNMCs) and explains why they engage in foreign direct investments. The transnational corporation is a nationally based company with overseas operations in two or more countries. One distinctive feature of the transnational corporation (TNC) is that strategic decision making and the allocation of resources are predicated upon economic goals and efficiencies with little regard to national boundaries. What distinguishes the transnational media corporation (TNMC) from other types of TNCs is that the principal commodity being sold is information and entertainment. It has become a salient feature of today's global economic landscape. In Part I, Gershon examines the purpose of a global media strategy and why companies engage in foreign direct investment. In Part II, he focuses on the challenges of staying globally competitive in a world that is becoming increasingly more deregulated and privatized. Special attention is given to the subject of business strategy.

- **Chapter 5** (Global Communication Law). John Huffman, Denise Trauth, and Jan Samoriski explore the issues that arise when communication crosses national boundaries and becomes global. As the world becomes more interconnected, different approaches to freedom of expression are becoming more pronounced. The result is producing inconsistencies in the way different nation–states impose censorship and limit expression within their societies. In the absence of a satisfactory method of global Internet regulation, this leaves nation–states with two basic alternatives. They can either leave Internet communication alone or try to impose censorship. Both approaches bring with them implications that will have an impact on the free flow of ideas, information, and commerce in global society for years to come.

- **Chapter 6** (Global News and Information Flow in the Internet Age). In this chapter, Kuldip Rampal discusses the origins of major international print and broadcast news agencies, and their services for traditional media organizations and for online consumers. Opportunities offered by the Internet to facilitate the emergence of new international news agencies are also addressed. Finally, Rampal explores issues pertaining to the quality and quantity of the flow of news between the developed and developing countries.

- **Chapter 7** (International Broadcasting). Joseph Straubhaar and Douglas Boyd trace the history and development of international radio broadcasting from before World War I to the present, examine the growth of direct satellite television across borders by both governments and media companies, and examine the movement of international radio and television on to the Internet. It discusses the history of direct and cross-border broadcasting between countries. The chapter explains why nations and certain organizations aim their broadcasts at each other's populations and, at the same time, outlines some of the key concepts about propaganda and public diplomacy. The authors also examine why audiences listen to across-border and Internet broadcasts, and why governments are concerned about such broadcasts.

- **Chapter 8** (Global Implications of the Internet: Challenges and Prospects). In this chapter, George Barnett and Devan Rosen describe the global implications of the Internet, which links the members of the international community. Through their examination of the strength of the connections among the nations of the world, they predict the Internet's impact on national culture and the process leading to the formation of a global culture. In doing so, they begin by explicating the systems and network perspectives, and the structural model of intercultural communication, which may be operationalized using network analysis. Next, they review the results of a network analysis of international Internet flows. Based upon these findings, they draw inferences from cultural convergence theory to make a series of prognoses about the short-term and long-term impact of the Internet on global culture and national identity.

- **Chapter 9** (Milestones in Communication and National Development). Vibert Cambridge surveys the role of the international community and its organizations, especially the United Nations, in the evolution of communication for development practice since the end of World War II. Several terms are used to describe the deliberate use of a social system's communication resources to promote, support, and sustain planned social change. Among the terms are *communication and national development, development communication, communication and development,* and *communication for development.* In this chapter, the term *communication for development* is used to describe the systematic use of a social system's communication resources to stimulate, promote, and support human development.

- **Chapter 10** (The Politics of Global Communication). Cees Hamelink provides a brief history of the politics of global communication, focusing on the domains of telecommunication, intellectual property rights, and the mass media. The most important shifts that affect these domains are analyzed. The essential issues that will shape the future of global communication are discussed. Special attention is given to recent developments in the global governance of telecommunication and in the expansion and enforcement of intellectual property rights. The chapter concludes with a proposal for public intervention in global communication politics and a brief analysis of the United Nations World Summit on the Information Society.

- **Chapter 11** (Global Communication and Propaganda). In this chapter, Richard Vincent discusses propaganda as a long-established technique for public opinion manipulation and control. He argues that advances in communication technologies have made propaganda more pervasive than before and that propaganda is used in domestic and international spheres by both government leaders and nongovernmental entities. In modern times, propaganda has turned to more blatant use of public relations campaigns, sometimes labeled public diplomacy. Often used in support of war efforts by governments, propaganda has evolved as an information campaign to influence public opinion. Of more recent concern is the use of propaganda techniques by international terrorists. Vincent suggests that a solution to terrorism may rest in our willingness to address global inequities and international power imbalances. He suggests that it would also serve us well to engage in more straightforward communication with our global neighbors and among ourselves as we continue to expand the nature of communication in a global civil society.

- **Chapter 12** (Global Advertising and Public Relations). In this chapter, Dean Kruckeberg and Marina Vujnovic problematize potentials of advertising and public relations to adjust their philosophies and practices in the rapidly changing world. Can we argue that both advertising and public relations are becoming more "global" in their practice? If so, how is such globalism manifested in real life? Advertising and public relations have an arduous task to balance the need to be compelling for the numerous niche markets and at the same time to be global. The adjustment to the global conditions is partly in response to rapidly developing transnational media and global communication systems that are both becoming increasingly dependent upon global markets to sustain them. Partly, it is a response to a corresponding multiculturalism. These challenges have come about because of previously unimaginable technological advances that are changing how and why people communicate. This chapter provides a brief historical analysis and a prognosis of the continuing development—and role—of advertising and public relations worldwide, together with the implications of this development as well as of the future challenges in the mission, role, and function of both advertising and public relations.

- **Chapter 13** (Communication and Culture). In this chapter, Christine Ogan examines the role of culture in global communication. Following a discussion of the definition of culture and the ways it is transmitted in a society, the issue of how U.S. mass media products dominate the world's cultural industries is discussed. Cultural and media imperialism, concepts that were much debated in the 20th century, have not entirely disappeared from mass media flow discourse in the 21st century despite the lack of strong empirical evidence for cultural domination by the United States in the world's media markets. In hopes of achieving a level playing field, many countries try to adopt strategies to compete with Hollywood and U.S. television program production. Those strategies include the establishment of quotas, the provision of subsidies to producers, regional alliances for co-productions, adaptation of program formats, and resistance measures. Countries manage cultural conflicts in the media within their countries in a variety of ways. And because most countries have multicultural environments, they often have to address globalization with a process of "glocalization," or taking a global media product and making it fit into the local environment.

- **Chapter 14** (Patterns in Global Communication: Prospects and Concerns). In this concluding chapter, Leo Gher challenges readers to think critically about current and future prospects and concerns of global communication. In doing so, he (1) reviews the current status of the communication industry's global infrastructure; (2) examines issues of privacy and information warfare; and (3) explores the interdependent connections of global economics, transnational media corporations, and vanishing national culture in 21st-century media. Gher argues that the *information revolution,* at least this generation's information revolution, seems to have come to an end in the last decade of the 20th century. It has been called the driving force behind globalization, but of course all information revolutions have had a significant worldwide impact. That this revolution, or any of its forerunners, will have had a greater impact on humanity than Gutenberg's printing press is highly unlikely. But this generation's information revolution has indeed had profound effects on the world community, and recent changes in entertainment and information services have occurred at a faster pace than ever before. Global communities everywhere are now faced with four critical questions about the meaning of such change: Is humanity better off as a result of the transformation? Who are the winners and the losers? What immediate concerns should industry leadership address? And what are the prospects and concerns for the future development of media and communicatioin a new world order?

Undoubtedly, the information revolution has had profound effects on the world community and continues to alter the structure, speed, complexity, and nature of entertainment and information services at an alarming rate. Consequently, global communities and societies are faced with new challenges and opportunities as well as many questions and concerns about the impact of the communications revolution and consequences of globalization. Among such questions might be:

- Is humanity better off as a result of globalization?
- Are audiences more informed and educated about global problems/issues?
- Do the communication professionals become more or less responsible as a result of media concentration?
- Who are the winners and the losers in global transformations?
- What social concerns should industry leadership address worldwide?
- Will the gap between the "haves" and "have-nots" continue to widen?
- What are the prospects for the future development of media and communication in the new world order?
- What are the prospects for the achievement of relative state of global peace and harmony in the post–9/11 world order?
- What are the roles and responsibilities of individuals, educational institutions, and governmental and nongovernmental organizations in the process of globalization?

INTENDED AUDIENCE

This book is primarily intended for upper-level undergraduate and lower-level graduate students in such courses as international communication, comparative telecommunication systems, international broadcasting, international journalism, and intercultural communication. Students enrolled in international relations, international politics, international business, and the like will also benefit from the contents of this volume. In addition, this book will be a valuable resource for researchers, journalists, international agencies, international enterprises, and libraries. Individuals interested in globalization and global communication also will find this book highly beneficial.

RESOURCES AND WEBSITES

To keep students and instructors abreast of the ever-changing developments in the field of global communication and to supplement the contents of this textbook, I have conceived and developed an electronic publication, *Global Media*

Journal (GMJ), and two web portals, *Global Media Monitor* (GMM) and *My Global Village* (GMV). In addition, Wadsworth/Thomson Learning will give the users of this book access to a vast array of teaching and learning resources through their *Communication Café* and InfoTrac College Edition®.

- The GMJ (www.globalmediajournal.com) is published online bi-annually in Arabic, English, Spanish, and quarterly (in print format) in Chinese languages. It includes articles written by global media scholars and experts, book reviews, announcements, profiles, commentaries, and more.
- The GMM (www.globalmediamonitor.com) serves as an information portal for numerous issues related to global communication. It serves as an electronic media data bank that provides a wide range of information, including profiles of global scholars; links to journals and articles; links to international online radio and television stations; links to online newspapers and journals; and links to websites where instructors and students can obtain up-to-date cultural, political, economic, geographical, and other information about a specific country, region, or media corporation.
- The GMV (www.myglobalvillage.com) goes beyond the global media and communication and serves as an information portal on a variety of environmental, economic, political, social, and other issues/problems that impact—either directly or indirectly—all inhabitants of our global village.
- Communication Café (http://communication.wadsworth.com) gives users of this book access to an outstanding array of educational resources, including online quizzing and discussion forums.
- The InfoTrac® College Edition (www.infotrac-college.com/wadsworth) is an online electronic library that provides an online university library with access to more than 700 publications. Wadsworth offers this invaluable service to instructors and students who use this textbook for their courses.

INSTRUCTIONAL BENEFITS

This textbook, in conjunction with the websites and instructors' guidance, can aid students in undertaking a variety of interesting and informative case studies related to global communication. Students can easily access the websites and listen to broadcasts in many languages, including English (for example, Voice of America, Radio Free Europe/Radio Liberty, British Broadcasting Corporation, Radio Canada International, Radio Mexico International, International Broadcast Services of the Islamic Republic of Iran, Radio Beijing, and Radio Moscow). In the process, they become exposed to international broadcasting and learn about a wide range of issues, news, and global perspectives. Likewise, students can access numerous newspapers, journals, governmental and nongovernmental organizations, cultural centers, U.S. Central Intelligence Agency databases, United Nations databases, and others throughout the world. These comprehensive resources should collectively keep students up to date and also satisfy the needs of practically any instructor who wishes to include a case-study approach in the study of global communication.

QUESTIONS FOR DISCUSSION

To encourage classroom discussions and to promote critical thinking skills among students, each chapter in this book ends with several open-ended questions. Students may use these questions to debate issues, to assess comprehension of chapter contents, to prepare for examinations, to write research papers, or to develop case-study projects.

ADVANTAGES AND DISADVANTAGES

One of the key advantages of an edited volume, such as this textbook, is that it offers students, instructors, and researchers broad and multidimensional perspectives that typically are absent, or presented one-dimensionally, in a textbook authored by a single author. You will note that throughout this book several authors explain certain concepts (for instance, globalization, cultural imperialism, and information flow) in different contexts. Ordinarily, a given perspective depends on where (location) an individual stands (orientation/affiliation) and how (from what angle/through what lens) he or she looks (perspective) at a given situation (context). Hence, some authors may explain the same or similar concepts differently in different contexts.

Such explanations should be viewed not as redundancies but as efforts to explain or frame a point in different contexts and from different cultural orientations or perspectives. Education experts seem to agree that repetition, when used judiciously, becomes a key factor in the process of helping students learn, understand, and retain information better. I have attempted consistently to reduce redundancies while using repetition judiciously.

One of the major disadvantages of an edited volume is that the writing styles and approaches may be varied and inconsistent. In some cases, authors may even offer contradictory arguments. My own belief is that, in teaching and studying global communication, even such disadvantages may be turned into advantages.

Advantages and disadvantages, together, potentially can lead to lively discussions, critical analysis, further research, exposure to diverse thoughts, exposure to diverse writing/communication styles, and an appreciation of the complexity of the global communication field.

FINAL THOUGHTS

At this particular juncture in human history, regional unrest, political conflicts, wars, uprisings, and ethnic tensions threaten the unity not only of many nations but also of the entire world. The widely trumpeted promises of globalization have been certainly beneficial for global corporations; national economies of mainly industrialized countries; and the transfer of goods, services, labor, knowledge, information, and information technologies throughout the world. Territorial boundaries have become blurred or redefined in favor of regional cooperatives (such as the North American Free Trade Agreement, or NAFTA; the European Union; the Asia–Pacific zone; and others). Liberalization processes that often favor free market economies, consumerism, or capitalistic tendencies are on the rise. On the other hand, the economic and information inequities between haves and have-nots, "East and West," and North and South have been increasing rapidly, replacing the old bipolar East–West divide.

My hope is that this textbook provides a reasonable and sufficient framework for generating meaningful discussions that will result in an appreciation for the immense scope, disparity, and complexity of global communication. Furthermore, I hope that such discussions will ultimately lead to action and positive change—peaceful coexistence, mutual respect, less conflict, increased cultural sensitivity, and better cooperation among the peoples and nations of the world.

It seems appropriate to conclude my preface with one of my favorite quotations by the American writer and scholar, John Schaar (n.d.):

> The future is not a result of choices among alternative paths offered by the present, but a place that is created—created first in the mind and will, created next in activity. The future is not some place we are going to, but one we are creating. The paths are not to be found, but made, and the activity of making them changes both the maker and the destination.

I hope, through this book, you will experience an exciting and rewarding educational journey into the dynamic and fascinating field of global communication. Please feel free to send me your comments and suggestions for enhancing the future editions of this book at kamaliyr@calumet.purdue.edu.

REFERENCES

Mittelman, J. H. (Ed.). (1997). *Globalization: Critical reflections*. Boulder, CO: Lynne Rienner.

Schaar, J. (n.d.). Creating the great community. Retrieved from http://www.umsl.edu/rcew/gallup/schaar.pdf

Steger, M. B. (Ed.). (2004). *Rethinking globalization*. Lanham, MD: Rowman & Littlefield.
    What is globalisation? (n.d.) Retrieved from http://www.globalisationguide.org/01.html

ACKNOWLEDGMENTS

In updating, revising, and completing the second edition of *Global Communication*, I have benefited from the kind support and cooperation of many colleagues and friends throughout the world. My sincere gratitude goes to the contributing authors of this book, for without their genuine interest and continued support, this project could not have materialized. Furthermore, I am indebted to Dr. Dan Dunn, Dean of the School of Liberal Arts and Social Sciences, at Purdue University Calumet for his encouragement and cooperation. Dr. Sandra Littleton-Uetz deserves to be acknowledged for her careful indexing of this volume.

At Wadsworth/Thomson, I am grateful to my publisher, Holly Allen, for her enthusiasm and continued interest in this project. The excellent creative, production, and marketing teams at Wadsworth also deserve to be noted for their valuable contributions to the overall design, layout, structure, and promotion of this book. I would like to offer my thanks to Kalpalathika Rajan and her professional team for their careful typesetting and proofing—we were in constant communication, via the Internet, for several months.

Of course, I am indebted to my wife, children, and family members for their unconditional love, emotional support, and understanding throughout this project.

YRK

About the Editor

 An internationally noted scholar, Yahya R. Kamalipour is Professor of Mass Communication and Head of the Department of Communication and Creative Arts at Purdue University Calumet, Hammond, Indiana, USA. His areas of research include globalization, media impact, international communication, and new communication technologies. Kamalipour has over 10 published books, including *Bring 'Em On: Media and Politics in the Iraq War* (with L. Artz, 2005); *War, Media, and Propaganda: A Global Perspective* (with N. Snow, 2004); and *Globalization and Corporate Media Hegemony* (with L. Artz, 2003).

Kamalipour is the founder and managing editor of a rapidly expanding online publication network, Global Media Journal (www.globalmediajournal.com), which includes African, American, Arabic, Australian, Chinese, Indian, Mediterranean, Polish, Spanish, and Turkish editions. He is editor of two web portals, Global Media Monitor (www.globalmediamonitor.com) and My Global Village (www.myglobalvillage.com), and also coeditor of the Global Media Studies Book Series for the State University of New York Press.

Kamalipour has given presentations in Egypt, Canada, China, India, Iran, Kenya, Mexico, Slovenia, and the United States, and taught courses at universities in Ohio, Illinois, Missouri, Indiana, Iran, and Oxford (England). In addition to numerous mass media appearances and interviews, his articles have appeared in professional and mainstream publications throughout the world.

The recipient of numerous awards and recognitions, Kamalipour earned his PhD degree in Communication (Radio–TV–Film) from University of Missouri–Columbia, MA degree in Mass Media from University of Wisconsin–Superior, and BA degree in Mass Communication (Public Relations) from Minnesota State University. He has been at Purdue University Calumet since 1986.

For additional information, visit his personal website at www.kamalipour.com.

Following the Historical Paths of Global Communication

ALLEN PALMER

Allen Palmer (PhD, University of Utah) is director of International Media Studies in the Department of Communications at Brigham Young University, Provo, Utah, where his research is focused on international communication problems. He also has taught as a visiting professor in Namibia, Mauritius, Benin, the Philippines, and Kosovo.

> The global village is more than ever a turbulent place.
> KARIN DOVRING

GEOGRAPHICAL SPACE: A BARRIER TO COMMUNICATION

For at least 3,000 years, people have sought to communicate across great distances. Elaborate courier systems were used in ancient China and Egypt. The Greeks announced the fall of Troy by lighting signal fires on the tops of mountains. A Roman emperor ruled his empire by sending messages in reflected sunlight off polished metal shields. From its early beginnings, communication has evolved into today's elaborate technosystems and networks, transforming world communication. For the first time in millennia, physical space is no longer an insurmountable obstacle to human interaction in international communication.

For additional online resources, access the Global Media Monitor website that accompanies this book on the Wadsworth Communication Cafe website at http://communication.wadsworth.com.

What was once the "geography of space" has become the "geography of experience" (Wark, 1994). When rudimentary communication began, perhaps with simple symbols such as a mark on a wooden stick, there was no hint of the revolutionary changes to come on the distant horizon. How did global communication evolve from such modest origins? Even though historians have long been interested in oral and written language traditions and technologies, the broader concept of communication is relatively new. It was introduced for the first time as recently as 1979 by medieval historians who examined the cultural and intellectual history of the Middle Ages (Mostert, 1999). Communication history is not just a question of new technologies; rather, it involves questions of how those technologies arise from complex social conditions and, in turn, transform human interactions (see, for instance, Aitken, 1985; Beniger, 1986; Carey, 1989; McIntyre, 1987; Peters, 1999; Winston, 1986). With faster and more far-reaching communication, important social and political developments occurred at the margins of technology and ideology, each interacting and expanding the potential outcomes of the other (Gouldner, 1982). In the broadest sense, technologies are cultural metaphors for prevailing social and cultural conditions.

In this review, I examine some of the forces at work in how early cultures created the conditions for communication across great distances. I begin in prehistory with the mythical images of ancient life. The fate of people in ancient times was, as often as not, violent, uncertain, cruel, and short. Human encounters with enemies, animals, and nature were fraught with hazards. From a symbolic view, this ancient world was enchanted, filled with otherworldly spirits, creatures, and images.

In time, migrant populations turned to agriculture and commerce, with trade routes extending outward to distant and unfamiliar lands. Science eventually disproved and displaced myths about the outside world. By the late Middle Ages, the "age of discovery" saw explorers traveling the edge of the known world, mapping their paths for others to follow.

Communication strategies and devices of many varieties were used to gain advantage in warfare and trade. Military conquests and religious crusades often resulted in unexpected consequences, including the intermingling of cultures and ideas. The ancient Chinese art of papermaking was carried to Europe by Arab soldiers, eventually making it possible for a German printer to develop movable metal type to print multiple copies of the Holy Bible. The magnetic compass needle, similarly, was carried to Europe from Asia, leading to experiments on electric telegraph signals. The printing press and telegraph challenged the barriers of space and time, redefining individual identity and shrinking the world outside (Launius, 1996).

Scientists experimented with new devices to solve old problems, seeing every problem as just another closed door to swing open (Lindberg, 1992). These social processes, once begun, created the conditions in which technologies made sense at the moment they appeared. Collectively, they ushered society toward the industrial and electrical transformation of the late 19th century, and the information revolution at the close of the 20th century.

GEOGRAPHY AND THE MYTHICAL WORLD

Ancient people certainly must have regarded the world with a sense of awe and wonder, struggling to grasp—and control—the unexplained events of their lives. The Greeks used the word *mantic* to describe ideas, both mythical and supernatural, coming to people from somewhere beyond the immediate world, the "other" world, one not of their own making. These beliefs were part of the ancient mystification, more often implied in their worldview than expressed in their words, about the uncontrolled forces reaching beyond their mundane lives (Nibley, 1991).

Until relatively recently in history, perhaps within just the past century or two, most people knew life only as they saw it unfolding within a few square miles of their rural homes. Travel in most of the historical past was hazardous and unpractical. The vast world beyond one's immediate reach was grasped through magical or metaphysical images. Beliefs about the earth, heaven, and underworld were built around sacred and profane spaces (Eliade, 1987). Images of these ancient mythic worlds are in the ancient lore of history. The Greek historian Synesius reported on peasants in the Aegean islands who believed in the existence of the Cyclopes, one-eyed giants (Migne, 1857). Such images appeared in the work of early mapmakers, like the medieval cartographer Pliny, who illustrated his maps with fanciful creatures in strange foreign lands. Monster sightings reported by mariners were used to enliven ancient map illustrations (Edson, 1997).

Europeans believed that India and Africa were places where pygmies fought with storks and giant humans battled griffins, winged creatures that could carry an elephant in their talons. Foreign lands were believed to be the bizarre and frightening places where gymnosophists contemplated the sun all day, standing in the hot rays first on one leg and then on the other; where humans lived who had feet turned backward and eight toes on each foot; and where others who had only one large leg could run as fast as the wind. There were cynocephali, humans with doglike heads and claws who barked and snarled; and sciapods, people who shaded themselves from the sun by lying on their backs and holding up a single huge foot. There were headless humans with eyes in their stomachs, people who could sustain themselves just on the odors of food, and monsters that had the body parts of several animals (Wright, 1965).

Myths surfaced in many places during the Middle Ages about the travels and exploits of a fictitious Christian king named Prester John, whose tales were repeated in music and poetry throughout Europe. Rumors circulated in the 12th century that he had written a letter addressed to the rulers in Europe, describing both his piety and his formidable conquests. According to the historian Albericus, the text of this epistle, spread across the countryside by troubadours and minstrels, contained accounts of a kingdom "beyond India . . . toward the sunrise over the wastes, and . . . near the tower of Babel" (Baring-Gould, 1885/1967, p. 38).

Prester John was believed to rule over a land inhabited by men with horns, along with giants and curious creatures, like Cyclopes. What frightened many Europeans most of all was the threat conveyed in this epistle that Prester John could command his fearsome legions of soldiers, accompanied by cannibals and flesh-eating animals, to sweep across western Europe. Pope Alexander II in the 12th century even drafted a response to Prester John to be carried by his personal envoy. The messengers left Rome and never returned (Baring-Gould, 1885/1967, p. 39).

Attila, king of the medieval Huns (406–453), understood the psychological power of such mythical beliefs among his enemies and encouraged the circulation of such exaggerations in his campaigns throughout Europe in the 5th century (Cantor, 1999). Popular lore about dragons, sea serpents, and other creatures was repeated among different people throughout the late medieval age and early Renaissance, even though the stories were most prevalent among the poor and uneducated (Lecouteux, 1995). As historians have concluded, the metaphysical world was "no less 'real' to those societies than [was] the physical world of Western culture" (Harley & Woodward, 1987, p. xxiv).

The product of fear and imagination, these mythical ideas among ancient cultures were richly symbolic and were accompanied by expression in art, science, language, and ritual (Scheffler, 1997; Schuster & Carpenter, 1996). Art historians believe that even cave art, such as the 30,000-year-old drawings of prehistoric animals discovered at Vallon-Pont-d'Arc in the Ardennes region of southern France, were used for rituals associated with hunting. A small horse carved in mammoth ivory, only 2 1/2 inches long and found near Vogelherd, Germany, has a small marking deciphered by historians to be associated with animal killing (Marshack, 2003).

ANCIENT ENCOUNTERS OF SOCIETIES AND CULTURES

When Greek and Arab philosophers and mathematicians sought to rise above mythical beliefs and to construct rational models of knowledge, they saw the world as measurable, even suggesting the use of coordinates to divide geographical space. The earliest history of Western geography as a science began for the ancient Greeks of Ionia in the 12th century BCE, from whom both Plato and Aristotle inherited their vision of the physical world (Stahl, 1962).

The early Greeks regarded the remote islands to their west as the horizon of the known world. One of the momentous voyages of discovery in Greek history was recorded in the 4th century BCE when the Greek explorer Pytheas sailed around Spain into what must have been to him a strange and alien world, along the coast of Gaul (France), around Britain, and into the Baltic regions. His astronomical and mariner records were used in Greece for several centuries as the basis for the earliest writings on mathematical geography and cartography.

Alexander the Great stretched the geographical boundaries of the European worldview even farther in the 4th century BCE. His empire covered a vast region from Egypt through the Balkans, and Asia Minor, east to the Ganges River in India. Trade routes established in his empire brought geographical knowledge back to Alexandria from Southern and Eastern Europe, Africa, and Asia. The accumulation of knowledge on papyrus rolls in the renowned library of Alexandria, starting about 300 BCE, was a momentous achievement but one soon lost because of the fragility of papyrus and the political upheavals that swept across the region. The library, founded by Ptolemy Philadelphus, was built through Alexander's conquests of Europe, Asia, and North Africa and, in an ironic turn of history, was destroyed by fire in the first millennium. The library held half-a-million papyrus rolls, which constituted the largest library in antiquity (Thiem, 1999).

The learning of the Greeks survived the Roman Empire, being revived in Latin translations by the Byzantines in the 5th century. Arab translations of the Greek manuscripts appeared in the 9th century. Maimonides, a leading 12th-century Jewish scholar, also studied Aristotle's writing and helped spread his influence (Cantor, 1999).

GLOBAL EXPLORERS: MIGRANTS, HOLY PEOPLE, MERCHANTS

For ancient pre-agrarian societies in Europe, migration was a way of life. Changing climate conditions and food supplies required a nomadic life before 2000 BCE. Improvement of farming techniques and implements allowed many nomadic groups to settle on fertile lands, unless they were confronted by disease, invasion, or war. Except for trade caravans and emissaries on state business with armed escorts, travel was always considered hazardous and difficult. Asians, for their part, did not travel far. The cultures of the Far East, especially the eastern parts of Asia governed by the hereditary monarchy of China (which encompasses today's China, Japan, Korea, and Vietnam), were loosely united by a Chinese worldview, while the western region of Asia responded more particularly to India's religious influences of Hinduism and Buddhism (Sivin & Ledyard, 1994).

By the 9th century, Arab ships made regular trips from the Persian Gulf to China. A North African scholar, al-Idrisi, wrote a document in 1153 titled "Amusement for Him Who Desires to Travel Round the World." Records show that Egyptian merchants engaged in trade in India and the Spice Islands at the end of the 13th century. Lamenting the sketchy knowledge of the East, one Arab writer noted:

> Writers on the customs and kingdoms of the world have in their works mentioned many provinces and places and rivers as existing in China . . . but the names have not reached us with any exactness, nor have we any certain information as to their circumstances. Thus they are as good as unknown to us; there being few travelers who arrive from these parts, such as might furnish us with intelligence, and for this reason we forbear to detail them. (Yule, 1915, p. 255)

After the fall of the classical Greek and Roman empires, substantive knowledge and curiosity about China and India ebbed among Europeans. Historians puzzle over the 1,000-year gap in East–West contact from the end of the late classical Greek period to the 17th-century Renaissance. Even though the period has long been described as static, brutal, and benighted, some historians now suggest that the so-called Dark Ages instead was a dynamic period when social and intellectual life was in transition (Cantor, 1991).

> It is hard to believe that for almost two millennia people were any less curious about the construction of practical methods for long-distance communication . . . but the sobering fact is that throughout this period only occasional references were made. (Holzmann & Pehrson, 1995, p. 57)

The disappearance of Greek scholarship on geography left Europeans without many clues about the outside world, but their desire to explore would soon lead to the expansion of their knowledge of the shrinking world. Europeans were introduced in the 15th century to the Arab translation of *Geographia,* by Claudius Ptolemy, written in the first century BCE. Widely used as a reference by mapmakers despite its miscalculations and errors, it was a guide for Christopher Columbus in his search for a new western trade route to India. "The purpose of *Geographia* is to represent the unity and continuity of the known world in its true nature and location," Ptolemy wrote (Cosgrove, 1992, p. 66).

Among the known records of Jewish travelers are written accounts of the trade paths followed into the farthest reaches of the known world. Jacob ibn Tarik carried astronomical books from Ceylon to Baghdad in 820. Another traveler, Joseph of Spain, introduced Arabic numerals to the Western world from India. Jewish merchants from Persia brought goods from China to Aix-la-Chapelle (now Aachen, Germany) (Adler, 1966). Radanite Jewish merchants also traveled overland routes from Spain across Europe, as far north as Kiev and east to India and China. An Arab geographer, Ibn Khordadbeh, composed the *Book of Roads and Kingdoms* in 847, tracing numerous trade routes throughout Europe, stretching from Spain to Asia. In the book, he described contact with "ar-Rus merchants," early ancestors of Russian–Scandinavians: "They are a tribe from among the as-Saqaliba . . . [who] bring furs of beavers and of black foxes and swords from the most distant parts of the [land] to the sea of Rum [Mediterranean]" (Boba, 1967, p. 27).

Vikings, or Norsemen, were known to have plied sea routes in the northern oceans, raiding cities in Western Europe as far south as Seville and the Andalusia region in southern Spain in the 9th century (Thrower, 1996). The population centers of Europe were long plagued with raids and incursions by these nomadic tribes. These tribes also settled western regions of the north Atlantic, including the coastal areas of Iceland, Greenland, and Newfoundland.

When Marco Polo's caravan ventured from Venice to the kingdom of the Mongols, and then to the court of the great Kublai Khan about 1260, European traders speculated much—but actually knew little—about life in Asia. Traders had an interest in obtaining silk from the East for European trade. Scholars now have grave doubts that the Polo family actually merited their far-flung reputation for bringing down barriers between Europe and Asia and instead attribute their good fortune to storytellers' exaggerations. By 1340, trade with Asia was virtually cut off because of economic collapse in Europe and danger on the trade routes east (Larner, 1999).

MAPMAKERS IN THE MEDIEVAL WORLD

Mapmaking was an integral part of communication history. Maps were widely considered to be valuable keys to unlocking unknown worlds. Walter Ong (1982) describes how printed maps enabled exploration and discovery:

> Only after . . . extensive experience with maps . . . would human beings, when they thought about the cosmos or universe or "world," think primarily of something laid out before their eyes, as in a modern printed atlas, a vast surface . . . ready to be "explored." The ancient oral world knew few "explorers," though it did know many itinerants, travelers, voyagers, adventurers and pilgrims. (p. 73)

Maps were closely guarded by European royalty and considered to be state secrets. Maps and charts from Columbus's first voyage to the Americas were deposited for safekeeping in Seville's most secure vaults. This extreme secrecy probably accounts for how the original maps used by Columbus, Cortez, and Magellan, among others, were lost. The reliability of maps was, in any case, rife with uncertainty. Columbus thought he was making landfall on the coast of Asia, instead of the Caribbean isles.

Mapmaking spurred empire building by some European powers, especially after the introduction of gunpowder (Hale, 1985). The information on most ancient maps reflected the mapmaker's cultural and religious orientations, and much of the information was estimated, distorted, or just plain wrong.

Maps served many purposes in ancient times, including maritime navigation, religious pilgrimages, and military and administrative uses. In the more symbolic view, "maps make the invisible visible" (Jacob, 1996, p. 193). Asian maps were drawn as art. Tibetan maps, by contrast, led travelers along a spiritual path through one of many possible universes, vertically ordered, from an imagined world of "desire" to a world of "non-forms" (Smith, 1964). Because maps were an intellectual tool of the most educated in ancient Greece and Rome, travelers and military leaders probably seldom had access to them or practical reasons to use them. Maps were used instead as intellectual tools among the Greeks, as objects for meditation.

After the fall of the Roman Empire, Europe was roughly divided by Islam in the south, the Christian kingdoms in the west, and the Christian Byzantine Empire in the east. Medieval geographers depicted the world on rough maps divided among three continents—Asia, Africa, and Europe. In one version of these ancient maps, the world was contained within a circle, with Asia, the largest of the three continents, filling the upper semicircle. In the lower half is a "T" dividing Africa on the right from Europe on the left by the Nile River (Larner, 1999).

Because travel involved venturing beyond safe and familiar terrain, it was often regarded as an act of religious devotion. Religious belief systems were directly reflected in many medieval European maps. Such maps were centered, explicitly or otherwise, on Jerusalem and were meant to be interpreted like scripture, as a kind of "moralized geography" as much as an instrument of science (Cosgrove, 1992, p. 68). Such maps used a measured grid system that diminished in size around Jerusalem.

The relative isolation of the European populations in the Middle Ages between the 4th and 18th centuries was reflected in their incomplete road systems. According to a leading medieval historian, no real roads existed in 11th-century Europe other than the remnants of a few old Roman roads. Travel and commerce relied almost exclusively on a few navigable rivers, such as the Danube and the Rhine. Trade and commerce were hindered in France because of the lack of inland waterways (Cantor, 1991).

A new awareness of geography arose with the Christian Crusades, beginning at the end of the 11th century and continuing into the 15th century. The Crusades marked a new wave of exploration. During these military expeditions across Europe into the Balkans and the eastern Mediterranean, many Europeans became more familiar with distant languages, cultures, and locations (Constable, 1988; Riley-Smith, 1986). Crusaders developed a taste for goods they found during their travels, including goods from China and India. The Crusades constituted a major chapter in international communication, even though they had both complex and contradictory effects (Barnouw, 1989).

Ultimately, the Crusades ignited a chain of events extending the trading activity of European merchants, changing attitudes in Europe toward the outside world, and launching the "age of discovery" with 15th-century explorers like Columbus, Bartolomeu Dias, and Vasco da Gama of Portugal, and others. Commercial centers, including Venice, became trade centers linking Europe and the Middle East.

Muslims, for their part, observed for 1,400 years the sacred direction toward their holiest shrine at Mecca, the edifice that symbolizes the presence of Allah. In the Middle Ages, they used two traditions to determine the sacred direction, one that sought to locate certain stars and the equinox of the sun, and the other using the direction of a circle on a terrestrial sphere. The Muslims were also responsible for acquiring ideas and devices from many lands. An Islamic proverb offered this insight into their transcultural consciousness: "Allah has made three marvels: the brain of the Greek, the hand of the Chinese, and the tongue of the Arab" (Strayer, 1988, p. 661).

Islam's scholars recognized that the earth was a sphere, and they used Ptolemy's *Geographia* to improve their measurements until they employed longitude and latitude by the mid-9th century. Such grid coordinates became the basis of extensive and elaborate mapping of Islamic regions and cities (King, 1997). Only later did innovators like Roger Bacon (c. 1220–1292) blend insights of both Greek and Islamic science in his encyclopedia of medieval science, *Opus Maius*. European scholars, such as Bacon, began to weigh the value of advancements from other cultures, borrowing elemental ideas for development of a telescope, gunpowder, air flight, and maritime navigation.

INVENTORS: SIGNALS AND SEMAPHORES

The historical succession of technologies used for communication is lengthy. A time line tracking the emergence of information technologies shows a bewildering array of conceptual and material inventions. The chronology of innovations can be atomized to discrete events (Desmond, 1978) or viewed from evidence of cultural continuities. One review has categorized them by their domains: either alphabet and mathematics, or optical and audio media (Schement & Stout, 1990).

At their simplest, most information technologies were solutions to tangible and immediate problems. The earliest known communication use of a simple signal system over distances employed fires or beacons. Aristotle (384–322 BCE) described in *Peri Kosmon* an elaborate signaling plan in 500 BCE to inform the Persian king within one day about everything of significance that took place in his empire in Asia Minor. Three Greek writers—Homer, Virgil, and Aeschylus—described signal systems for military use. Aeschylus wrote in *Agamemnon* about the arrival of news of the conquest of Troy (1184 BCE) in Mycenae, a distance of 400 miles: "Yet who so swift could speed the message here?" The message was conveyed, the writer answered, "beacon to beacon" across mountaintops and "urged its way, in golden glory, like some strange new sun" (Oates & O'Neill, 1938, p. 177).

The Greeks attempted to develop a more elaborate torch signal system based on letters of the alphabet, but it proved to be too cumbersome for practical use, according to the historian Polybius (c. 200–c. 118 BCE) (Walbank, 1979).

Interest in signaling systems among the Greeks was based on potential military purposes. Homer wrote in *The Iliad* around 700 BCE:

> Thus, from some far-away beleaguered island, where all day long the
> men have fought a desperate battle from their city walls, the smoke goes
> up to heaven; but no sooner has the sun gone down than the light of
> the line of beacons blazes up and shoots into the sky to warn the
> neighboring islanders and bring them to the rescue in their ships.
> (Homer, 1950, p. 342)

Roman rulers adapted a type of heliograph, or visual signal system using reflected sunlight. The emperor Tiberius ruled Rome (26–37 CE) from the island of Capri, sending signals from a mirror of polished metal. No records have been found of the code used for the reflected messages, raising doubts among skeptics about the practical value of the attempt. The Moors also used a type of heliograph in Algeria in the 11th century (Woods, 1965, p. 151).

In-transit message systems employed couriers both on foot and on horse. In ancient Babylon, King Hammurabi (1792–1750 BCE) dispatched messengers on a regular two-day route to Larsa, riding continuously day and night. Egyptian scribes tracked the daily passage of messengers for military and diplomatic missions along the kingdom's Syrian and Palestinian border outposts. These messengers were wary of being attacked en route by Bedouin robbers, prompting the posting of royal guards at stations and the eventual use of fire-beacon signals on the frontiers.

Herodotus, a Greek historian, described in minute detail a pony express–style relay system during Xerxes' rule over Persia in 486–465 BCE, modeled after a torch race to celebrate the Greek ruler Hephaestus (Dvornik, 1974). King Cyrus the Great of Persia made significant improvements in the courier system.

> [Cyrus] experimented to find out how great a distance a horse could cover in a day when ridden hard, but so as not to break down, and then he erected post-stations at just such distances and equipped them with horses, and men to take care of them; at each one of the stations he had the proper official appointed to receive the letters that were delivered and to forward them on, to take in the exhausted horses and riders and send on fresh ones. They say, moreover, that sometimes this express does not stop all night, but the night-messengers succeed the day messengers in relays, and when this is the case, this express, some say, gets over the ground faster than the cranes. (Holzmann & Pehrson, 1995, p. 48)

The Greek historian Herodotus reported there were at least 111 courier relay stations between Sardis and Susa, a distance of about 1,800 miles. In the Battle of Marathon (490 BCE) near Athens, in which Greek forces withheld an invasion of the Persians, the Persian king Cyrus dispatched a message to his field commanders, using the words later adopted as a slogan by the U.S. Postal Service: "There is nothing in the world which travels faster than these Persian couriers. . . . Nothing stops these couriers from covering their allotted stage in the quickest possible time—neither snow, rain, heat, nor darkness" (Herodotus, De Sélincourt, & Burn, 1972, p. 556).

The Romans adapted the Persian courier and message systems, using the famous Roman highway system for moving troops, commerce, and communications. Both government and commercial services delivered correspondence throughout the Roman Empire. Messages were conveyed on papyrus, parchment, and wax tablets. The courier system used elaborate relay stations to sustain the rigors of overland travel. Each station maintained a stable of 40 horses and riders, known as strators, who carried special licenses from the emperor to obtain fresh horses. In this arrangement, mail could be delivered 50 to 100 miles per day. The system eventually collapsed over controversy about who would be responsible for supplying horses and provisions.

Throughout the Middle Ages, regional commercial postal services were maintained around merchant centers, such as Venice and Bruges. Charlemagne directed a courier system among France, Italy, Germany, and Spain. In 1464, Louis XI of France reintroduced a network of relay stations with mounted couriers for official communiqués. England began a comparable service in 1481. Private commercial systems, based on royal franchises, began as early as the 15th century in Venice.

Reliability and speed of delivery through the medieval postal systems were remarkably good. Historians have found evidence that some messages traveled up to 150 miles in one day from the 15th to the early 19th centuries in Britain. By 1900, the delivery service offered one-day service within 350 miles.

The Chinese developed extensive networks of messengers and couriers as early as the Chou dynasty (1122–221 BCE), but few historical details are known. Marco Polo described a relay system employed by the Mongols in the 13th century, dispatching everything from diplomatic messages to fruits from surrounding regions. Each station, separated at 25- to 30-mile intervals, was stocked with at least 400 horses. Messengers could travel as far as 250 to 300 miles per day when required by emergencies. The Venetian merchant Polo observed, "The whole organization is so stupendous and so costly that it baffles speech and writing" (Polo, 1938, p. 150).

The Mongol ruler Genghis Khan used pigeons in the 12th century for communication in his kingdom, which covered a vast area, including almost all of central Asia, from the Aral Sea on the west to the China Sea in the east (Woods, 1965). Carrier or homing pigeons were also used by Egyptian pharaohs to announce the arrival of important visitors as early as 2900 BCE. News of the outcome of the Olympic Games in ancient Greece was sent to Athens by bird carriers.

The kings of Mesopotamia in 2350 BCE gave a homing pigeon to each royal messenger to carry on dangerous routes. If the messenger was attacked, he released the pigeon to signal that the message had been lost and a new messenger should be dispatched (Neal, 1974).

The Incas in medieval South America, beginning about 1200, used an elaborate communication system with both smoke signals and a quipu, a cord with knots based on a numerical system, for messages. The numeric cord was sent by relay messengers as far as 150 miles in a day (Cantor, 1999).

Devices such as trumpets, drums, and even ordinary people's shouting were used by many different cultures to extend the reach of physical sounds. Diodorus Siculus, in the first century, described the use of stentors, or shouters, to pass news across open fields (Woods, 1965). Other communication innovations that were developed involved tapping codes on metal tubes with a hammer or blowing into cylinders to produce sounds. An Italian scholar, Giambattista della Porta, wrote in *Magia Naturalis* in 1553 about an acoustical device in which messages were shouted through so-called speaking tubes.

The magnetic compass was introduced to Europe from China at the end of the 12th century. By the 16th century, experiments succeeded in transmitting a cryptographic code using a crude system of magnetic compass needles, leading to eventual development of the electric telegraph (Strayer, 1988).

The enthusiasm of Renaissance inventors for various inventions intended to communicate over distances had detractors. Galileo wrote about his response to one such proposed delvice in *Dialogus de Systemate Mundi* in 1632:

> You remind me of a man who wanted to sell me a secret art that would
> allow me to speak to someone at a distance of 2–3 thousand miles, by
> means of the attraction of magnetized needles. When I told him that
> I would be delighted to purchase the device, if only I was allowed to try
> it first, and that I would be satisfied if I could do so from one corner of
> the room to another, he answered that at such a short distance the effect
> would be barely visible. At that point I said farewell to the man

and I told him I had no interest to travel to Egypt or Moscow before I could try the device, but if he wanted to move there I would be happy to remain in Venice and give the signals from here. (Galileo, 1953, p. 88)

A renewal of interest in signaling systems came in the 16th century as the French, Spanish, and Venetian navies began using flag-signaling techniques from their ships. Then the subsequent development of the telescope in 1608 by Dutch spectacle maker Hans Lippersley extended the range of observers.

Interest in optical signals resulted in experiments by the 18th century in Germany and Switzerland. German professor Johann Bergstrasser constructed an optical telegraph line that connected Feldberg, Homberg, and Phillippsuhe. A Czech musician, Joseph Chudy, devised a system of five lights that could be read by telescope at a distance, in effect employing a five-bit binary code, in 1786.

THE PRINTING PRESS, LITERACY, AND THE KNOWLEDGE EXPLOSION

Throughout the early Middle Ages, clerics were among the few literate people engaged in any task requiring writing. In addition to their religious duties, they drafted legal documents and letters for official dispatches. On occasions when written communication for diplomacy or commerce was necessary, the preferred means was through epistles.

The circulation of religious and diplomatic correspondence was an ancient practice but was expanded and refined in the high Middle Ages in the 12th through the 14th centuries, a time when western Europe exhibited dramatic changes in literature, as well as philosophy, government, and law. Literacy for the common public, however, required easy access to printed matter and the means to transport and circulate it widely; thus, a printing press and a postal service were prerequisites.

The complexity and diversity of the intellectual and cultural life created a marketplace ripe for information, stimulating the spread of literacy in Europe after the development of the printing press (McIntyre, 1987).

Printing presses had appeared in Asia as early as the 8th century, but the success of such presses was hindered by the vast collection of Chinese characters required to reproduce texts. When the Arabs defeated Chinese forces in Samarkand in 751, they captured Chinese papermakers and brought the innovative process to North Africa. Papermaking arrived in Spain around 1150, in Italy in 1270, and in Germany in 1390. France acquired the new process from Spain in the 12th century but did not produce paper until later in the 14th century.

Johannes Gutenberg's development of the press in Mainz, Germany, about 1450, stemmed from his concerted effort to print Bibles for use in local churches. Advances in metalwork in Germany made it possible for Gutenberg to fabricate metal type for only 50 letter characters. He also adapted his presses to allow printing on both sides of a sheet of paper and produced copies with much clearer print than had been possible with older block printing.

The social consequences of the printing press were far-reaching, eventually encouraging the practice of reading among common people and the reformation of medieval European institutions, religions, and governments (Eisenstein, 1979). Still, in 17th-century Europe almost nothing printed was trustworthy. The world of printing was notorious for its piracy, incivility, plagiarism, unauthorized copying, false attributions, sedition, and errors (Adrian, 1998). Books and other printed material eventually sparked social and political changes that gave rise to popular political consciousness and "public opinion" (Darnton, 2000).

The Industrial Revolution was not finished with printing technology with the advent of movable type. Even after Gutenberg's innovations, printers set type by hand for almost five centuries until the middle of the 19th century when Ottmar Mergenthaler introduced a machine, the Linotype, to set type in lines and columns with molten metal (Gardner & Shortelle, 1997). The changes set in motion by the printing press were profound. New literacy introduced new kinds of social relationships and networks among both learned and common people (Thomas & Knippendorf, 1990).

The postal service was an innovation patterned after older courier and messenger systems. Such a delivery regularized and routinized delivery of epistles and other correspondence at a cost accessible to a growing middle class, opening a market for pamphlets and newspapers (Robinson, 1953).

SCIENTISTS AND INTERNATIONAL NETWORKS

Technological innovations in travel and the changing role of international science in the mid-19th century brought far-reaching changes in relations between nations. The melding of cordial relations between previously isolated countries into a coherent global network resulted from intermingling both their shared interests and intractable differences through the means of technology.

Introduction of the first user-friendly electric telegraph in 1844 was a breakthrough in the longstanding dilemma over development of two-way information exchange (Hugill, 1999). It also marked a shift between transportation and ritual modes of communication and permitted the dissemination of strategic information over great distances (Carey, 1989). The electric telegraph was soon followed by the telephone and wireless radio. These instruments opened the door to the subsequent social revolution that accompanied the information age.

Beginning with the railroad and the telegraph, towns and cities were brought closer together within a nation, regardless of whether participants were reluctant or enthusiastic to embrace these changes. Railroad and telegraph companies were built upon the era's unbridled optimism in empire building.

Oddly, national governments were usually ambivalent about scientific initiatives through the middle of the 19th century. Government cooperation on science often hinged on the preconditions that such projects "did not cost too much, that the scientists themselves were prepared to do the work, and that nothing in the commitment trenched upon national security or sovereignty" (Lyons, 1963, pp. 228–229).

Because of the strategic importance of communication for military and diplomatic purposes, communication between nations was regarded in most 19th-century political circles as strategic and proprietary. Tensions between nation-states even prevented the rise of international organizations until about 1850. One of the first modern intergovernmental organizations was the Central Commission for the Navigation of the Rhine, organized by the Congress of Vienna in 1851 (Barnouw, 1989).

France was positioned to emerge in a central role in negotiation of new international standards of exchange among colonial powers but had a history of guarding communication systems for strategic military objectives. France maintained one of the best-organized visual signal systems, involving a network of towers across the countryside. The semaphore code used by the French was considered a state secret until about 1850. Eventually, scientists sought to bridge national interests and obtain increased intergovernmental cooperation and support, and a few intergovernmental science ventures were launched by the end of the 19th century.

One of the these projects was an initiative to measure the circumference of the earth, introduced in 1862 by the Prussian Institute of Geodesy, which changed its name to the International Geodetic Association in 1867.

The first standardization of a code of science occurred in 1860 when an assembly of chemists convened in Karlsruhe, Germany, to clarify the general usage of chemical symbols. Within a few years, similar congresses were convened to discuss international cooperation in the disciplines of botany and horticulture (1864), geodesy (1864), astronomy (1865), pharmacy (1865), meteorology (1873), and geology (1878). International agreements were being drafted to regulate postal and telegraph traffic. The International Telegraph Union was formed in 1865, and the Universal Postal Union was established in 1875.

By 1889, there were 91 international meetings held in conjunction with the Paris Universal Exhibition. By the late 1880s, the Paris-based Association for Scientific Advancement (Alliance Scientifique Universelle) issued an identity card, or passport, called the *diplome-circulaire,* which scientists carried during their foreign travels (Crawford, 1992). From such scientific assemblies, 37 international cooperative agreements were drafted between 1850 and 1880, including a compact for cooperative mail delivery issued by the General Postal Union in 1874 and a treaty for the International Regulation of Sea Routes in 1879 (Mattelart, 2000).

One of the earliest significant steps toward globalizing the world was adoption of a global time system (Macey, 1989). An 1884 conference on international standards of time reckoning was held in Washington DC to discuss reforming time standards and designating an international meridian.

The selection of Greenwich Observatory near London as the international meridian showed tacit acceptance among negotiators of a shift to a scientific center of global interests, in spite of France's objections to Greenwich because of French–British jealousy. French officials sought to barter an agreement, trading their acceptance of the proposal to make Greenwich the international meridian in exchange for British acceptance of the French metric system as the basis of international exchange. France promoted worldwide adoption of the metric system as early as 1792, calling the meter a "new bond of general fraternity for the peoples who adopt it" and the "beneficial truth that will become a new link between nations and one of the most useful conquests of equality" (Mattelart, 2000, p. 5). Officers in the American Metrological Society had accepted the challenge to promote the metric system. Their primary objective was universal adoption, especially in the English-speaking countries that had long resisted.

THE INTERNATIONAL ELECTRIC REVOLUTION

The scientific innovations of the 19th century launched the world on a path to electrification of industry and commerce. Steam power led to what had once seemed to be startling speeds of travel, first by steamboat and then by railroad. The *Savannah* was the first steamboat to cross the Atlantic Ocean, under power of both paddle wheel and sails, in 1819. The steam-powered railway system in England opened the first rail service between Liverpool and Manchester in 1830, reaching speeds of 45 kilometers an hour. Electrical experiments in England, Denmark, Russia, and Sweden led to the first use of a telegraph by Carl Friedrich Gauss and Wilhelm Weber in Göttingen in 1838. The railroad and telegraph systems were important in establishing international corporate empires that successfully brought technological innovations, linking the telegraph to the railway systems in England in 1839 (International Telecommunication Union, 1965).

Within 20 years of the general introduction of the telegraph in 1844, there were 150,000 miles of telegraph lines throughout the world, but mostly in Europe and North America. The transatlantic line eventually became a landmark step in bringing nations together in an international communication network.

One of the earliest proposals for a transatlantic cable line was mentioned in the *National Telegraph Review* in July 1853, but business promoters failed to attract sufficient backing. Cyrus Field and Frederick N. Gisborne considered the proposal again in 1854 and sought the backing by telegraph inventor Samuel F. B. Morse (Thompson, 1972). Consummating the project involved a series of difficult business agreements, including consolidation of then-independent U.S. telegraph systems into what would eventually become the American Telegraph Company.

Morse was anxious to see the expansion of telegraph technology and promised to allow the use of his patents without charge on a line from the British provinces in Canada to New York and to transmit telegraph messages at half price.

The first transatlantic line did not work, and other attempts to lay lines either broke or failed. Eventually a line was fully operational by 1866. Backers of the project were primarily motivated by their desire to reduce the time required for news to travel from Europe to America by as much as 48 hours (Thompson, 1972).

Before the transatlantic project was begun, another entrepreneur, business-man Perry McDonough Collins, began promoting his ambitious scheme to tie the world together by telegraph. Collins wanted to lay a telegraph line from the western United States through British Columbia, Russian America (Alaska), under the icy waters of the Bering Strait, and overland again through Siberia to connect to a Russian line in eastern Asia. The endeavor also included construction of telegraph lines to Central and Latin America. Collins had obtained approval of both American and Russian governments to begin work on the Alaska–Russia line, and he had dispatched George Kennan to begin surveying a route through the Siberian tundra. The project was aborted in July 1866, upon the successful laying of a transatlantic cable (Travis, 1990).

Alexander Graham Bell, who considered his true vocation to be a teacher of the deaf, stumbled across the electrical signaling process used by the telephone in his effort to improve the telegraph. Bell sought to devise a system to send several simultaneous messages over a single wire without interference (Pool, 1977).

When telephones were demonstrated at the Philadelphia Centennial Exposition of 1876, the public showed little enthusiasm for the device. Even some scientists, who saw the virtue of the science employed in the telephone, were ambivalent about its practical social uses (Gardner & Shortelle, 1997).

The telephone was a communication innovation that was adopted and managed differently in each nation. In the United States, the privately operated Bell Telephone Company oversaw its development. The company sought to sell the first phone patents to the Western Union Telegraph Company for $100,000, but the offer was refused. Later, Bell franchised rights to lease phones to private agents throughout the country. Governments oversaw commercial phone development in Germany, France, and England, creating state monopolies. Sweden and a few other countries began with open markets but eventually moved toward government control through regulation and licensing.

Once unleashed, the social uses of technologies follow their own paths of social and economic opportunity. One of the oldest news agencies, Reuters, began in 1850 when Paul Julius Reuter used 40 carrier pigeons to send stock market prices between Brussels and Aachen to compete with the inefficient European telegraph system. Reuters News Service eventually became a major source of international information because of its emphasis on the speed of information exchange, a value shared in other enterprises:

> Speed was prominent in the . . . growth of international wire services. But speedy information was most important for the military (because it meant the difference between victory and defeat, life and death) and international traders (because it meant the difference between profit and loss). International news agencies grew because they served this demand for speedy information. (Alleyne, 1997, p. 20)

Inventors of "aerial telegraphy," sending signals over the air without wires, filed for the first patent in 1872. Later, Thomas Edison and others developed the elemental ideas for wireless transmissions. Edison eventually sold his ideas and patents to Guglielmo Marconi and his Marconi Wireless

Telegraph Company. The first coded trans-Atlantic radio signal was received in 1901 (Dunlap, 1937).

Broadcast inventor Lee De Forest, who is now remembered as the "father of radio," made significant advancement in the clarity of sound with his triode vacuum tube, making the transmission of sound—voice and music—possible. De Forest's vision of the social use of radio was based on his idea that transmissions to mariners at sea would be a kind of musical beacon. He disliked proposals to commercialize radio, believing until his death that the technology was destined for some higher, more transcendent use (De Forest, 1950).

Interestingly, others who devised new technologies for communication also saw hope in the new information machines for ushering in an age of more authentic connections in society (Peters, 1999). Their dreams, however, were soon displaced by the commercial imperatives and the expanding public appetite for information.

SUMMARY: GLOBAL IMMEDIACY
AND TRANSPARENCY

Communication across great distance has been a catalyst for many changes in human relationships. Through a variety of mediated technologies, the cumulative effect of these changes was a redefinition of space and time, and increasing immediacy and transparency in global connections (Olson, 1999).

Echoes of continuity are found between what began in simple signal systems among the Greeks and Romans and the innovations in today's global society (Innis, 1950, 1951; Lasswell, Lerner, & Speier, 1979). Taken as a whole, these technologies accompanied the broad movement toward modernism and, later, its nemesis, postmodernism.

Communication is implicated in the sweeping social and political informationscape, including the shifting relations between capital and labor and the continuing struggle over old metaphysical symbols and obstacles. Others have placed these developments within predominant historical themes, such as war, progress, and culture (Mattelart, 1994). Global communication always has been bound up in "the geopolitical consequences of human power struggles" (Cantor, 1999, p. 7) or in the rationalizing of the marketplace through technoscientific networks of power (Mattelart, 2000). Significantly, one of the most penetrating studies of ancient communication practices is contained in a history of espionage (Dvornik, 1974). Deciding what is—or is not—distinctive about today's global communication calls for synthesis of historical evidence.

The challenge of understanding this kind of cultural transformation is only partly explained by technology. We fail to see otherwise: "That our history has been shaped by the form and use of our tools in ways totally unanticipated by their inventors is, as always, conveniently forgotten" (Rochlin, 1997, p. 5). The emergence of global communication imposes new frames of meaning about the winding path of historical change.

For more information on the topics that appear in this chapter, use the password that came free with this book to access InfoTrac College Edition. Use the following words as keyterms and subject searches: communicaton history, communication symbols, distance communication, medieval communication, visual signals, communication innovation, printing press, industrial revolution, communication networks, transnational line, international communication.

QUESTIONS FOR DISCUSSION

1. What strange images and myths did Europeans entertain about the people they believed lived in far-off places like India? Do such myths about strangers and distant lands persist in some form today?

2. How did exploration and conquests by people like Marco Polo and Alexander the Great stretch the boundaries of the known world? Who are today's explorers?

3. What role did mapmakers and traveling merchants play in unlocking unknown regions of the world in the Middle Ages? Do mapmakers play an important role in unlocking unknown worlds today?

4. Describe how the earliest known signal and messenger systems eventually evolved into modern communication across vast distances.

5. What were the consequences for international communication of the printing press? The telegraph? The clock? How might today's inventions change communication in the future?

REFERENCES

Adler, E. N. (1966). *Jewish travellers*. New York: Hermon Press.

Adrian, J. (1998). *The nature of the book: Print and knowledge in the making*. Chicago: University of Chicago Press.

Aitken, H. G. J. (1985). *The continuous wave: Technology and American radio, 1900–1932*. Princeton, NJ: Princeton University Press.

Alleyne, M. D. (1997). *News revolution: Political and economic decisions about global information*. New York: St. Martin's Press.

Baring-Gould, S. (1967). *Curious myths of the Middle Ages*. New Hyde Park, NY: University Books. (Reprinted from 1885, New York: J. B. Alden).

Barnouw, E. (1989). *International encyclopedia of communications*. Oxford: Oxford University Press.

Beniger, J. R. (1986). *The control revolution*. Cambridge: Harvard University Press.

Boba, I. (1967). *Nomads, Northmen, and Slavs*. The Hague: Mouton.

Cantor, N. F. (1991). *Inventing the Middle Ages*. New York: William Morrow.

Cantor, N. F. (1999). *Encyclopedia of the Middle Ages*. New York: Viking.

Carey, J. (1989). *Communication and culture*. Thousand Oaks, CA: Sage.

Constable, G. (1988). *Monks, hermits, and crusaders in medieval Europe*. Aldershot, England: Variorum.

Cosgrove, D. (1992). Mapping new worlds: Culture and cartography in 16th-century Venice. *Imago Mundi, 44*, 65–89.

Crawford, E. (1992). *Nationalism and internationalism in science, 1880–1939*. Cambridge: Cambridge University Press.

Darnton, R. (2000). An early information society: News and media in 18th-century Paris. *American Historical Review, 105*. Retrieved November 15, 2000, from http://www.indiana.edu/_ahr/darnton

De Forest, L. (1950). *Father of radio: The autobiography of Lee De Forest*. Chicago: Wilcox & Follett.

Desmond, R. W. (1978). *The information process*. Iowa City: University of Iowa Press.

Dunlap, O. E. (1937). *Marconi: The man and his wireless*. New York: Macmillan.

Dvornik, F. (1974). *Origins of intelligence services*. New Brunswick, NJ: Rutgers University Press.

Edson, E. (1997). *Mapping time and space: How medieval mapmakers viewed their world*. London: British Library.

Eisenstein, E. L. (1979). *The printing press as an agent of change*. Cambridge: Cambridge University Press.

Eliade, M. (1987). *The sacred and the profane*. New York: Harcourt.

Galileo. (1953). *Dialogue concerning the two chief world systems* (S. Drake, Trans.). Berkeley and Los Angeles: University of California Press.

Gardner, R., & Shortelle, D. (1997). *Encyclopedia of communication technology*. Santa Barbara, CA: ABC-CLIO.

Gouldner, A. W. (1982). *The dialectic of ideology and technology: The origins, grammar, and future of technology*. New York: Oxford University Press.

Hale, J. (1985). *War and society in renaissance Europe*. London: Fontana.

Harley, J. B., & Woodward, D. (1987). *The history of cartography*. Chicago: University of Chicago Press.

Herodotus, De Sélincourt, A., & Burn, A. R. (1972). *The histories* (A. R. Burn, Ed.). Baltimore: Penguin Books.

Holzmann, G. J., & Pehrson, B. (1995). *The early history of data networks*. Los Alamitos, CA: IEEE Computer Society.

Homer. (1950). *Iliad*. New York: Penguin Classics.

Hugill, P. J. (1999). *Global communication since 1844: Geopolitics and technology*. Baltimore: Johns Hopkins University Press.

Innis, H. (1950). *Empire and communication*. Oxford: Clarendon Press.

Innis, H. (1951). *The bias of communication*. Toronto: University of Toronto Press.

International Telecommunication Union (1965). *From semaphore to satellite*. Geneva: ITU.

Jacob, C. (1996). Toward a cultural history of cartography. *Imago Mundi, 48*, 191–198.

King, D. A. (1997). Two Iranian world maps for finding the direction and distance to Mecca. *Imago Mundi, 49*, 62–82.

Larner, J. (1999). *Marco Polo and the discovery of the world*. New Haven, CT: Yale University Press.

Lasswell, H. D., Lerner, D., & Speier, H. (1979). *Propaganda and communication in world history*. Honolulu: East–West Center/University Press of Hawaii.

Launius, R. D. (1996). *Technohistory: Using the history of American technology in interdisciplinary research*. Malabar, FL: Krieger Publishing Co.

Lecouteux, C. (1995). *Démons et génies du terroir au Moyen Age*. Paris: Imago.

Lindberg, D. C. (1992). *The beginnings of western science*. Chicago: University of Chicago Press.

Lyons, F. (1963). *Internationalism in Europe, 1815–1914*. Leyden: A. W. Sythoff.

Macey, S. L. (1989). *The dynamics of progress: Time, method, and measure*. Athens: University of Georgia Press.

Marshack, A. (2003). The art and symbols of Ice Age man. In D. Crowley & P. Heyer (Eds.), *Communication in history: Technology, culture, society* (pp. 5–14). Boston: Allyn & Bacon.

Mattelart, A. (1994). *Mapping world communication: War, progress, culture*. Minneapolis: University of Minnesota Press.

Mattelart, A. (2000). *Networking the world: 1794–2000*. Minneapolis: University of Minnesota Press.

McIntyre, J. (1987, Summer/Autumn). The Avvisi of Venice: Toward an archaeology of media forms. *Journalism History, 14,* 68–85.

Migne, J. P. (1857). *Patrologiae Cursus Completus: Series Graeca*. Paris: Migne.

Mostert, M. (1999). *New approaches to medieval communication*. Turnhout, Belgium: Brepols.

Neal, H. (1974). *Communication from Stone Age to space age*. New York: J. Messner.

Nibley, H. (1991). *The ancient state: The rulers and the ruled*. Salt Lake City, UT: Deseret Book Co.

Oates, W. J., & O'Neill, E., Jr. (1938). *The complete Greek drama*. New York: Random House.

Olson, S. R. (1999). *Hollywood planet: Global media and the competitive advantage of narrative transparency*. Mahwah, NJ: Lawrence Erlbaum Associates.

Ong, W. (1982). *Orality and literacy: The technologizing of the word*. London: Methuen.

Peters, J. D. (1999). *Speaking into the air: History of the idea of communication*. Chicago: University of Chicago Press.

Polo, M. (1938). *The description of the world* (A. C. Moule & P. Pelliot, Trans.). London: G. Routledge.

Pool, I. (1977). *The social impact of the telephone*. Cambridge: MIT Press.

Riley-Smith, J. (1986). *The first Crusade and the idea of crusading*. London: Athlone Press.

Robinson, H. (1953). *Britain's post office: A history of development from the beginnings to the present day*. New York: Oxford University Press.

Rochlin, G. I. (1997). *Trapped in the net: The unintended consequences of computerization*. Princeton, NJ: Princeton University Press.

Scheffler, I. (1997). *Symbolic worlds*. Cambridge: Cambridge University Press.

Schement, J., & Stout, D. (1990). A timeline of information technology. In B. Ruben & L. Lievrouw (Eds.), *Mediation, information, and communication: Vol. 3, Information and behavior* (pp. 395–424). New Brunswick, NJ: Transaction Publishers.

Schuster, C., & Carpenter, E. (1996). *Patterns that connect: Social symbolism in ancient and tribal art*. New York: Harry N. Adams Publishers.

Sivin, N., & Ledyard, G. (1994). *Introduction to East Asian cartography*. In J. B. Harley & D. Woodward (Eds.), *Cartography in the traditional East and Southeast Asian societies* (Vol. 2, Book 2; pp. 23–31). Chicago: University of Chicago Press.

Smith, C. D. (1964). Prehistoric cartography in Asia. In J. B. Harley & D. Woodward (Eds.), *Cartography in the traditional East and Southeast Asian societies* (Vol. 2, Book 2; pp. 1–22). Chicago: University of Chicago Press.

Stahl, W. H. (1962). *Roman science*. Madison: University of Wisconsin Press.

Strayer, J. R. (1988). *Dictionary of the Middle Ages*. New York: Charles Scribner's Sons.

Thiem, J. (1999). Myths of the universal library: From Alexandria to the Postmodern age. In M. L. Ryan (Ed.), *Cyberspace textuality: Computer technology and literary theory* (pp. 256–266). Bloomington: Indiana University Press.

Thomas, S., & Knippendorf, M. (1990). The death of intellectual history and the birth of the transient past. In B. Ruben & L. Lievrouw (Eds.), *Mediation, information, and communication:* Vol. *3, Information and behavior* (pp. 117–124). New Brunswick, NJ: Transaction Publishers.

Thompson, R. L. (1972). *Wiring a continent: The history of the telegraph industry in the United States, 1832–1866*. New York: Arno Press.

Thrower, N. (1996). *Maps and civilization: Cartography in culture and society*. Chicago: University of Chicago Press.

Travis, F. F. (1990). *George Kennan and the American-Russian relationship, 1865–1924*. Athens: Ohio University Press.

Walbank, F. W. (1979). *A historical commentary on Polybius*. Oxford: Clarendon Press.

Wark, M. (1994). *Virtual geography: Living with global media events*. Bloomington: Indiana University Press.

Winston, B. (1986). *Misunderstanding media*. Cambridge: Harvard University Press.

Woods, D. (1965). *A history of tactical communication techniques*. New York: Arno Press.

Wright, J. K. (1965). *The geographical lore of the time of the Crusades*. New York: Dover Publications.

Yule, H. (1915). *Cathay and the way thither*. London: Hakluyt.

2

Drawing a Bead on Global Communication Theories

JOHN D. H. DOWNING

John D. H. Downing (PhD, London School of Economics and Political Science) is John T. Jones, Jr., Centennial Professor of Communication at the Southern Illinois University–Carbondale. He writes on international communication; radical alternative media and social movements; and ethnicity, racism, and media. He teaches African and Latin American cinemas, media in Russia, and media theory.

A "bead," as the word is used in the title of this chapter, is the small piece of raised metal at the tip of a rifle barrel that enabled accurate targeting before telescopic sights were common. Theorizing has the same function, or it should. It is not an end in itself but a way of getting a phenomenon clearly in our sights—though hopefully not of killing it, which is where the analogy collapses.

This is why it makes sense to argue about different theories. It's one thing to have a "fact" staring you in the face. For instance, there are many times more telephones and TV sets per head in Japan than in the 50+ nations of the African continent—but how did that happen, and what does it mean? We need to attempt an explanation, a theory. What did it mean at the turn of the last century and into this one to have a single corporation—News Corporation—own one of the four major TV networks in the United States; Star TV satellite television, which beamed programs to China and India (accounting for more than 40 percent of the world's

For additional online resources, access the Global Media Monitor website that accompanies this book on the Wadsworth Communication Cafe website at http://communication.wadsworth.com.

population); a bunch of major newspapers in Britain and Australia; and a whole lot more media besides? Again, we need to attempt an explanation, a theory.

To answer such questions, someone has to produce a theory or at least spin some guesswork. Most of us would rather deal seriously with an idea that someone has thought out carefully than with guesswork. Careful, focused thinking is what "theorizing," properly speaking, means. Thinking carefully and with focus does not mean that a theory is automatically right or even mostly correct. That's one reason we argue about theories. But theorizing is a serious attempt to think connectedly and deeply about something.

There are better theories and worse theories, just as there are smarter guesses and stupider ones. If we are to understand international media, we have to train ourselves to think through these theories and evaluate them. What follows is a start on doing just that. We will begin by reviewing critically the first systematic attempt to analyze media across the planet. In the second and third sections, we will examine two different approaches to the same task.

"NORMATIVE" THEORIES

One of the earliest attempts to think about media internationally was a book published in the 1950s entitled *Four Theories of the Press* (Siebert, Peterson, & Schramm, 1956). Its authors set out to create what is sometimes called a taxonomy, which means dividing up all the various versions and aspects of a topic into systematic categories and sometimes subcategories as well. The taxonomy the authors proposed was that the world's various media systems could be grouped into four categories or models: authoritarian, Soviet, liberal, and social responsibility. It compared the systems with each other, which in principle makes it easier to see the differences and then to see each system's particular characteristics—all too often, familiar only with the media system with which we grew up, we assume it is the only imaginable way of organizing media communication. Comparisons are not just interesting for what they tell us about the rest of the world. They help us sharpen our understanding of our own nation's media system (see "Six Normative Theories" box, which cites a leading media scholar's summary of normative theories).

Authoritarian effectively meant dictatorial, and the authors had especially in mind the nightmare fascist regimes of Hitler in Germany and Mussolini in Italy. *Soviet* referred to the communist dictatorships at that time in Russia and its surrounding ring of client regimes in Eastern Europe, the Transcaucasus, and Central Asia. The prime difference between the Soviet bloc dictatorships and "authoritarian" regimes lay, the authors proposed, in the particular political ideology that undergirded the Soviet regimes, namely Communism, which claimed to show the way to construct a just and equal society.

By *liberal,* the authors meant not "left-wing," as in current American parlance, but free market–based, which is the sense of the term in current continental European parlance. The contrast with both of the first two categories was, clearly,

B O X 2.1   Six Normative Theories

Authoritarian theory can justify advance censorship and punishment for deviation. . . . the theory was likely to be observed in dictatorial regimes, under conditions of military rule or foreign occupation and even during states of extreme emergency in democratic societies. Authoritarian principles may even express the popular will under some conditions (such as in a nation at war or in response to terrorism). Authoritarian theory is generally designed to protect the established social order and its agents, setting clear and close limits to media freedom.

The second of the Four Theories . . . was labeled *libertarian,* drawing on the ideas of classical liberalism and referring to the idea that the press should be a "free marketplace of ideas" in which the best would be recognized and the worst fail. In one respect it is a simple extension to the (newspaper) press of the fundamental individual rights to freedom of opinion, speech, religion and assembly. . . . The nearest approximation to truth will emerge from the competitive exposure of alternative viewpoints, and progress for society will depend on the choice of "right" over "wrong" solutions. . . .

Soviet theory . . . assigned the media a role as collective agitator, propagandist and educator in the building of communism. . . . The main principle was subordination of the media to the Communist Party—the only legitimate voice and agent of the working class. Not surprisingly, the theory did not favor free expression, but it did propose a positive role for the media in society and in the world, with a strong emphasis on culture and information and on the task of economic and social development. . . .

Social responsibility theory involved the view that media ownership and operation are a form of public trust or stewardship, rather than an unlimited private franchise. For the privately owned media, social responsibility theory has been expressed and applied mainly in the form of codes of professional journalistic standards, ethics and conduct or in various kinds of council or tribunal for dealing with individual complaints against the press, or by way of public commissions of inquiry into particular media. Most such councils have been organized by the press themselves, a key feature of the theory being its emphasis on self-regulation. . . .

Development media theory . . . was intended to recognize the fact that societies undergoing a transition from underdevelopment and colonialism to independence and better material conditions often lack the infrastructure, the money, the traditions, the professional skills and even the audiences. . . . it emphasizes the following goals: the primacy of the national development task (economic, social, cultural and political); the pursuit of cultural and informational autonomy; support for democracy; and solidarity with other developing countries. Because of the priority given to these ends, limited resources available for media can legitimately be allocated by government, and journalistic freedom can also be restricted. . . .

Democratic-participant media theory . . . supports the right to relevant local information, the right to answer back and the right to use the new means of communication for interaction and social action in small-scale settings of community, interest group or subculture. Both theory and technology have challenged the necessity for and desirability of uniform, centralized, highcost, commercialized, professionalized or statecontrolled media. In their place should be encouraged multiple, small-scale, local, noninstitutional committed media which link senders to receivers and also favour horizontal patterns of interaction. . . . Both freedom and selfregulation are seen to have failed.

SOURCE: Excerpted from *Mass Communication Theory: An Introduction* (3rd ed.), by D. McQuail, 1994, Thousand Oaks, CA: Sage. Reprinted with permission.

between media systems ruled by state regulation and censorship, and media systems ruled by capitalist moneymaking priorities. By *social responsibility*, the authors effectively meant a different order of reality again: namely, media operating within a capitalist dynamic but simultaneously committed to serving the public's needs. These needs were for a watchdog on government and business malpractice and for a steady flow of reliable information to help the citizens of a democracy make up their minds on matters of public concern.

A strong underlying .assumption in all four models was that news and information were the primary roles of media, a view that rather heavily downplayed their entertainment function and ignored the significant informative and thought-provoking dimensions that entertainment also carries. Indeed, despite the title *Four Theories of the Press,* the book even effectively sidelined many types of print media (comics, trade magazines, fashion magazines, sports publications, and so on). Effectively, its obsession was with the democratic functions of serious, "quality" newspapers and weekly newsmagazines, with their contribution to rational public debate and policy making. The model the authors endorsed as the best was the social responsibility model.

These theories—of which we shall review two later ones in a moment—were what is called *deontic,* or normative. That is to say, they did not seek simply to explain or contrast comparative media systems but to define how those systems ought to operate according to certain guiding principles. In particular, by touting the social responsibility model as superior, the authors effectively directed attention to what they saw as the highest duties of media in a democracy. They did not, however, explain why media should follow that model other than as a result of the high ethical principles of their owners and executives. Whether media owners actually worked by such codes, and what might stimulate them to do so, was left unexplained. The social responsibility model was simply a series of ethically inspired decisions by owners and editors for the public good.

The two later categories/models (cf. McQuail, 1994, pp. 131–132) added still further variety. One was the development model; the other, the participatory/democratic model. The *development* model meant media that addressed issues of poverty, health care, literacy, and education, particularly in Third World settings. Media were defined as being vitally responsible for informing the public—for example, about more efficient agricultural methods or about health hazards and how to combat them. Radio campaigns against the spread of HIV and AIDS would be a typical example. Development media were also held to an important role in fostering a sense of nationhood in countries with highly disparate groups in the population, territories often artificially created by European colonialists as recently as the late 19th century.

Participatory media, the sixth category/model, typically designated local, small-scale, and more democratically organized media, such as community radio stations or public access video, with their staff and producers having considerable input into editorial decisions. This alone sharply distinguished them from mainstream media of all kinds. In addition, participatory media were defined as closely involved with the ongoing life of the communities they served so that their readers or listeners could also have considerable influence over editorial policies. Sometimes these media shared the same development goals as the previous model cited but not on any kind of authoritative top-down basis or as agents of government development policies. Public participation and a democratic process were central to their operation.

These six models did indeed cover a great variety of media structures internationally. Whether they did so satisfactorily is another matter. Let us look briefly at some of their shortcomings. Aside from their typical failure to engage with entertainment, as already mentioned, their distinction among Soviet, authoritarian, and development models was very blurred in practice.

For instance, the mechanisms of Soviet and authoritarian media control were often very similar, and many Third World regimes hid behind "development priorities" and "national unity" to justify their iron control over any media critique of their behavior. The liberal model of free capitalist competition spoke to a bygone age, already vanishing by the time the original *Four Theories* book was published, an age when many small newspapers and radio stations competed with each other. In the current era of global media transnational corporations—giants valued in tens, twenties, or even hundreds of billions of U.S. dollars—it is quaintly archaic to be imagining still a free media market where all media are on a level playing field.

But perhaps the chief problem with the four (or six) theories approach goes back to the deontic, or normative, dimension of the theories. The two terms used previously—*categories* and *models*—illustrate this problem, for though they can be synonyms, *model* implies something that ought to be followed. While media, like any cultural organization, clearly do follow certain guiding principles and do not reinvent their priorities day by day, what media executives claim those principles are and how the same media executives behave in actuality may often be light-years apart. Let us look at some examples.

Communist media in the former Soviet bloc claimed their purpose was to serve the general public, the industrial workers, and the farmers who made up the vast majority of the population. Yet when the opportunity arose in those countries in the late 1980s, public criticism of the cover-ups and distortions of Communist media became a tidal wave.

In the social responsibility model, objectivity is trumpeted as the journalists' core principle, the driving force of their daily investigation and writing. Yet as media researchers in a number of countries have demonstrated, journalists readily place patriotism above objectivity and define objectivity in practice as the middle point between two opposing views, often those of rival political parties, not troubling to question whether truth may lie somewhere else. In the 1990s and into the next decade, the pathetic U.S. news media coverage of battles over how to reconstruct the ever more problematic U.S. health care system offered a sadly accurate confirmation of the failure of objectivity once it was defined as the midpoint between the Republican and Democratic parties (Blendon, 1995; Fallows, 1996, pp. 204–234).

Development media, as noted, were often steered away from sensitive topics by arrogant, autocratic regimes in the name of national unity and the need to focus on bettering economic production. Even media activists working for peanuts in participatory media sometimes claimed a dedication to "the cause" that masked their own obsession with wielding petty power in their community.

In other words, media researchers need to penetrate well below the surface of media professionals' assertions that they are driven by distinguished values, such as development or social responsibility or the public good, and to examine the full range of forces actually at work in media. Not to do so is hopelessly naive and blots out the prime force in media all across the planet at the beginning of this century: the ferocious elimination, as a result of the worship of market forces, of any ethical values in media save naked profitability.

A DIFFERENT APPROACH I: COMPARING
AND CONTRASTING MEDIA

In this section, we will examine some lessons that can be drawn from the now-extinct Soviet Russian media system in order to understand media internationally, rather than basing our examination on a single nation. The system lasted, in different forms, from the revolution late in 1917 to December 25, 1991, when the last Soviet president, Mikhail Gorbachev, formally signed a document dissolving the Soviet Union. Many people would agree that some of the USSR's principal features persisted well after that date, with new private banks supplanting the old Communist Party as media bosses. However, although the Soviet media system is extinct in its original form, its history has a lot to contribute to our understanding of media elsewhere in the world.

First, as noted, Soviet media had a strong overlap with media under other dictatorships and with so-called development media. As an illustration, in the first 40 years of Taiwan's existence as an entity separate from mainland China, following the end of Japanese colonial rule in 1945, the media system of Taiwan was that of a dictatorial one-party state (whose leader, Chiang Kai-shek, had been schooled in Soviet Russia). Chiang Kai-shek was fiercely opposed to Communism but that certainly did not mean he gave his own media any freedom. Another example is India, which was not a dictatorship like Taiwan but a country where, until the beginning of the 1990s, broadcast media were government-owned in the name of national development and unity, and where the Soviet model of the state as the basic agency of economic development had held sway ever since independence from British rule in 1947. Thus, the study of Soviet Russian media throws light on a variety of the world's media systems, even though privatizing and liberalizing media are increasingly visible globally as time goes by. (Privatizing and liberalizing are *not* the same thing, as we will see in the next section.)

Second, those of us who live in economically advanced and politically stable countries are in a poor position to understand how media work on much of the rest of the planet. Most, if not all, of what we read is about research based on the United States or Britain, two nations with a considerable shared culture and the same majority language. We have little information even about media in Canada, France, Germany, Italy, or Japan—the other members of the elite Group of Eight (G8) countries—and least of all about Russia, the odd-man-out number eight that is, as I will argue, much more like the world at large.

In the world at large, issues of extreme poverty, economic crisis, political instability even to the point of civil war, turbulent insurgent movements, military or other authoritarian regimes, and violent repression of political dissent are the central context of media. To pretend that we can generalize about what all media are by just studying U.S. or British media, or even just media in the G8 countries minus

Russia, is wildly silly. Seemingly obvious claims such as "broadcasting is . . ." or "the Internet is . . ." or "the press is . . ." are inaccurate, however authoritative they may look at first glance—not because "every country is a bit different" but because of the major factors named at the beginning of this paragraph.

To be sure, some countries not in G8 are politically stable and economically affluent (Denmark and New Zealand, for example); even some crisis-torn nations have many positive dimensions that offset their acute problems (the Congo and Indonesia, for example). The media of affluent countries spend so little time on the constructive dimensions of other nations that the average media user in those countries can be forgiven up to a point for being unaware that there are any. But to return to the basic point here: Russia, the outsider in the G8 group, is a valuable entry point for understanding media in the world at large and thus for avoiding being imprisoned in superficial assumptions about what media are. I have argued this case elsewhere in much more detail than can be offered here (Downing, 1996), but let us see why this is, at least in outline.

At least four important issues must be considered—namely, how we understand the relation of mainstream media to (1) political power, (2) economic crisis, (3) dramatic social transitions, and (4) small-scale alternative media (such as *samizdat,* a term explained later in this chapter). Each of the following Russian examples offers a contrast case to the usual U.S./U.K. profile of media and provokes a basic question about media in capitalist democracies.

Political Power

The relationship between political power and Communist media always seemed a "no-brainer." Communist media were seen as simple mirror-opposites of media in the West. Communism equaled repression and censorship, in the name of a forlorn ideal of justice, but capitalist democracy (the West) won out in the end, and over the years 1989–1991 the entire Communist system foundered, never to return. Soviet media were the favorite counterexample for proving what was right with Western media.

Now, it is indeed true that state control over media was extremely detailed in Soviet Russia, even more so than in some other dictatorships. The Communist Party's Propaganda Committee established ideological priorities. Its cell groups in every newspaper, magazine, publishing house, and broadcast channel kept a close watch over any subversive tendencies. Media executives were chosen from a list of party members who had proven their loyalty. And the KGB (the political police) would quickly intervene if any trouble seemed evident or imminent. With all this, the official censorship body, known as Glavlit, had relatively little to do. Typewriters were licensed by the state, and a copy of the characters produced on paper by their keys—which were always slightly out of sync and therefore could be used to identify where a subversive document had originated—was on file with the local KGB. When photocopy machines came into use, access to them was governed in microscopic detail. Bugging technology was one of the most advanced aspects of Soviet industry.

This outrageous and unnerving machinery of control over communication did not, in the end, win. Many factors served to subvert it, including *samizdat* media (explained later in the chapter). But one factor perhaps was the least controllable of all—namely, the extreme difficulty of producing media that were credible or interesting inside this straitjacket. Communist Party members read *Pravda* (The Truth) daily because they knew they were expected to, not because they were convinced it was factually informative. People in general expected authentic news to arrive by conversational rumor, and honest opinion by *samizdat*. Only if that rumor confirmed what Soviet media announced did many people take the latter as reliable (and then only on the given topic).

Thus, in the later decades of the Soviet system in Russia a dual-level public realm developed: official truths that the media blared out, that everyone mouthed, and that few believed; and an unofficial realism that was the stuff of everyday private conversation, or *samizdat*. When Gorbachev came to power in 1985, intent on reform, he gradually introduced a new degree of frankness and directness in media (the famous glasnost policy), intended to reduce the gap between these two levels.

This media credibility dilemma is a significant one in any dictatorship. And perhaps the longer the dictatorship lasts, the worse the dilemma.

Question for Stable, Affluent Nations.   The fascinating contrast is with the relatively ready trust in mainstream media, the bulk of which are owned by very large and unaccountable capitalist firms. Were Soviet media so bluntly and clumsily controlled that skepticism was a self-evident response? Are Western media sufficiently subtle, flexible, and savvy so that their message is much more attractive and their plausibility much tougher to question?

Economic Crisis

Economic crisis was a daily experience for the majority of Russians, especially from the time of the Soviet bloc's collapse up to the time of writing this essay, but it had been gathering momentum from the early 1980s onward. It continues to be a daily experience of citizens in many of the world's nations, including the impoverished sectors within the other G8 countries. The "Structural Adjustment Policies" of the International Monetary Fund (IMF), as the IMF so abstractly termed them over the 1980s and 1990s, blighted the lives of untold hundreds of millions in the countries to which the fund applied its ruthless capitalist logic. The health, housing, and education prospects of children, women, the aged, peasant farmers, and slum dwellers have been sacrificed to the dictates of debt repayment to international banks, to the point that great chunks of national income go back to the banks in interest payments instead of to the public (cf. Barratt Brown, 1997; Stein, 1995).

"It's their governments' fault," cry the public relations specialists of the banks and the IMF, holding up their holy hands in pious denial. Their denial blots out the banks' full knowledge of what kind of governments they were dealing with at the time they contracted the loans in question: kleptocracies, or thief regimes, that spend a good chunk of the loan on themselves and another chunk on buying weapons from the West's arms factories to put down civil unrest directed against their rule—or to manufacture wars with their neighbors in order to divert attention from their own abuses.

The Soviet and post-Soviet Russian experience of economic crisis has been profound, except during the 1970s and early 1980s, when oil revenues shot up on the world market. But during the 1990s, Russian life expectancy actually fell, which in turn meant that infant mortality increased, for the death rate among children under one year old is the prime factor in average life expectancy. Once again, among the G8 countries, Russia is the exception that stands in for much of the rest of the planet. Russian media, until the last few years of the old Soviet Union, were silent about this decline in living standards and stagnation in productivity, and asserted that the capitalist countries were suffering from acute and irremediable economic problems. In the post-Soviet period, Russian media have often found it easier to point the finger at the IMF—not, it must be said, without reason—than to take aim at the Russian kleptocracy.

How do media in general deal with these economic crises? Do they explore them or avoid them? Do they blame them on distant scapegoats? On the IMF if theirs is the country affected? Or on Third World governments if they are in an affluent nation? Or on domestic scapegoats—immigrants, Gypsies, Chinese, Jews, refugees, Muslims?

Question for Stable, Affluent Nations. How thoroughly do media really explain economic crisis? How well do they explain strategies to deal with it that do not hit the poor and poorest much harder than the wealthy? Although global indices indicated that living standards in the United States in the 1990s were remarkably high and crisis was remote, wages had fallen well below what they were in real terms during the 1960s. Typically, both parents had to work full-time to retain a stable income level, and single-parent households, a sizable proportion of the total number of households, mostly struggled to get by. The U.S. media at the turn of the millennium suggested universal prosperity, but the facts suggested a slow-burning invisible crisis, one in which the public, despite working many hours, was mostly one or two paychecks away from "welfare," a racially defined form of public humiliation that few embraced if they could avoid it. When did you last see a TV program, watch an ad, or read a newspaper that got into these realities in a way that struck you?

Dramatic Social Transitions

The third issue is the relation of media to dramatic social transitions. Russia went through many transitions in the 20th century, beginning with the disastrous World War I, which opened the way to the 1917 revolution and the three-year civil war that followed the revolution. Next came the tyrannical and savage uprooting of Russian and Ukrainian farmers in 1928–1933 and Stalin's ongoing terror and vast prison camp population. Then came the loss of 20 to 25 million lives in the war against Hitler in 1941–1945, the severe economic disruptions of Gorbachev's attempt to reform the system in the late 1980s, and the economic chaos of the 1990s. This is a dimension that, with the exception of the two world wars, has not characterized the affluent nations' experience, but once again Russian experience in this regard has been much more characteristic of the world's. Colonial rule, invasion, war, vast social movements, civil war, entrenched ethnic conflicts, wrenching changes of government, and dictatorships were common experiences across the planet. Media in Russia also went through many transitions during the 20th century. Let us briefly note them.

Before the revolution, there was an active newspaper, magazine, and book industry, but it was restricted to people who could read, perhaps a quarter of the population at most, and they were nearly all concentrated in towns. Furthermore, the imperial censorship made it risky indeed for anyone to print anything directly critical of the czars. Jail or exile in frozen Siberia were standard penalties for challenging the status quo, which included, during the war against Germany in 1914–1917, any criticism of the slaughter into which many Russian generals forced their troops. Come the revolution, the Bolshevik leadership sought peace with Germany, and criticism of the old status quo was everywhere. Literacy campaigns began, in part to enable the new revolutionary regime to get its message across. This was the first media transition.

At the time of the revolution, the arts in Russia were in ferment and had been for more than a decade. Some of the most inventive and spectacular artistic work in Europe was being done by a new generation of Russian artists. For the first 10 years or so of the revolutionary era, these artists were actively encouraged by the new regime to express their talents in theater, advertising, public campaigns, cinema, photography, and music, along with painting and sculpture. Russian media were on the cutting edge, especially in the then-newer technologies of cinema and photography. However, with the rise of Stalin to power as Soviet dictator, this innovative work was shoved aside in the name of "Soviet progress." Those who did not bend to the new orthodoxy suffered at least disgrace and, at worst, prison camps or even death. This was the second media transition.

Next, for a period of about 25 years until Stalin's death in 1953, Russian media marched to the dictator's tread, looking neither right nor left. Not only did they follow the official line unwaveringly but their language was also wooden, saturated with political jargon, endlessly grinding out the messages given them from above. Whenever the official line changed—when Stalin suddenly signed a pact in 1939 with the Nazi regime; when the Nazis invaded in 1941; when the United States supported the USSR in the Lend-Lease program; when, in the aftermath of the Nazis' defeat, Stalin annexed three Baltic and five east-central European countries, along with a chunk of eastern Germany; when Stalin began a comprehensive anti-Semitic campaign in the years just before he died—each time the media instantly changed their tune to support the switch. George Orwell's famous novel *1984* conveys some taste of the way that media during the Cold War massaged such 180-degree reversals, including the World War II portrayal of Stalin in U.S. media as "friendly Uncle Joe" and the redefinition of him as a monster after the war.

In the decade that followed Stalin's death, some Russian media professionals made cautious attempts to open up the media, with intermittent encouragement from Khrushchev, Stalin's successor. A famous short novel, Aleksandr Solzhenitsyn's *One Day in the Life of Ivan Denisovich,* was the first publication of anything about the vast prison camp system Stalin had brought into being. It was in some ways the high point of the attempt to open up the media system, even just a little, but in 1964 Khrushchev was thrown out of office and the lid was jammed back on Russian media. Some other brave dissidents who tried to publish works critical of the regime were sentenced to long terms of hard labor in highly publicized trials meant to scare off any would-be imitators—another media transition.

Only in the mid-1980s, as the Russian economic system began to grind to a halt, was there a push in favor of media reform, the glasnost era, led by the USSR's last leader, Mikhail Gorbachev. This ultimately led to an avalanche of media, which challenged the long-established status quo, even to the point, eventually, of attacking the original revolution in 1917 and thus the very foundations of the Soviet system—a further media transition.

Finally, after the collapse of the USSR in 1991, yet another media transition emerged: a print media sector mostly allowed to follow its own path and commercial dictates; a TV sector under heavy government surveillance and control; and a radio sector somewhere in-between. Independent media existed to a greater extent than under the Soviet regime, but Russians were still largely deprived of anything approaching a genuinely democratic media system.

This postage-stamp account of Russian media in the 20th century has shown the significant transitions through which they passed. Again, in much of the world, such wrenching changes in media have been an everyday experience. Many specifics might vary, but the Russian experience is not unique. In the stable nations of the West, with the exception of the Nazi era in Europe, this kind of experience of media was foreign. But we cannot take that minority experience as typical. If we are to think intelligently about media, the Russian experience is much more the norm. To assume that a particular media system is permanent or normal, that transition is not inherent in media, flies in the face of the media experience of most of humankind in the 20th century.

Question for Stable, Affluent Nations.   Media seem so familiar, so much part of the landscape, so central in the way we entertain ourselves, that even rapidly changing delivery technologies—fiber optic cables, compression technologies, digitization, satellites—seem to promise only sexy new options. Yet what does the bewilderingly rapid concentration of media ownership into the hands of giant transnational corporations mean for our media future (Bagdikian, 2000; McChesney, 1999)? Is citizen influence over media, despite being an obvious necessity for a true democracy, fated to dwindle slowly and imperceptibly away to nothing? Post-9/11, in the name of defending American national security, the U.S. Patriot Act and other new laws and regulations have stiffened many forms of control over our freedom to communicate. We are in the midst of our own media transition in the United States, and we had better find out what those changes are. And watch out!

A DIFFERENT APPROACH II: GLOBALIZATION
AND MEDIA

Comparing and contrasting media is then one way to get a clearer focus on what it is that media actually do in our world. A second, complementary approach is to focus on the current trends toward the globalization of media and of other cultural processes.

The term *globalization* is often used widely and loosely. Sometimes it signifies structural economic changes. Examples include the global rise of government policies on "liberalization" that push for firms to compete for business in previously state-monopoly sectors such as broadcasting, telecommunications, and water or air travel; and the wave of "privatizations," selling off state-owned companies to private investors (although sometimes these may simply substitute a privately held monopoly for a state monopoly). The IMF's Structural Adjustment Policies referred to in the previous section included global policies of this nature.

Sometimes, however, globalization is applied as well to, or even instead of, cultural and media processes. The earliest concept of this kind was "cultural imperialism," itself sometimes reformulated more specifically as "media imperialism." The basic idea here was that hand in hand with the economic, military and political expansion of European colonization from 1492 onwards into the Americas, Africa, and Asia went the attempted imposition of European culture via religious conversions, efforts to ban traditional religious beliefs, missionary schooling, intensive commercialization, and various forms of media dominated by the colonial powers. In the latter 20th century, some began to speak derisively of "coca-colonization," using the invented word as a condensed image of the spread of specifically U.S. daily culture and everyday products throughout the world. Certainly if you travel through the planet today, it is easy to see billboards everywhere advertising typical U.S. or other everyday Western firms and their products, such as Coca Cola, KFC, Exxon, Ford, and Sony. It is also common for Hollywood movies to be screened in theaters in Canada, France, Japan, Russia, and many other countries, rather than nationally produced films, and both U.S. and British television are widely marketed overseas, although today Indian "Bollywood" movies, Japanese *anime* (animated movies), and Chinese martial arts movies are making their presence felt globally too.

So for some writers, globalization more or less means Americanization, though many Latin Americans think even this word evidences the problem, because why, they ask, should a single country's cultural and media dominance in the whole hemisphere of the Americas be termed Americanization rather than, perhaps, "U.S.-ization"? No one expects this actually to happen, but the point is a real one.

For others such as the late Herbert Schiller (1991), an earlier U.S. dominance in global culture and media in the decades after World War II began in the latter 20th century to give way to a more multiple form of dominance by transnational corporations, rather than just U.S.-based ones. Japan's Sony, South Korea's

Samsung, Germany's Bertelsmann, Spain's Telefónica, and Brazil's Globo television company, would be examples, although Schiller's argument went further than that. He argued that transnational corporations today do not necessarily reflect the priorities of their home governments but rather their varying challenges in the global market. That is why they are truly transnational. Against this, most such companies find the U.S. government very supportive by and large, and prefer to keep their home base in the United States.

Other analysts have sharply criticized the "imperialism" school, arguing that it falsely assumes global media audiences are moldable plastic in the hands of global media firms and pointing to research that shows how differently varying audiences around the world react to U.S. media. These writers are highly skeptical of the notion that global media corporations are able to act like cultural steamrollers, effortlessly flattening out people's cultural values and priorities and turning them into little peas in an Americanized or Westernized cultural pod.

Some from this school claim that people's cultural resistance is proof against cultural invasion, but more commonly, writers of this approach use the terms *hybridization* and *hybridity* to try to capture what they see happening (Pieterse, 2004). In other words, they point to neither flat-out resistance nor pathetic defeat but a merging of different perspectives and values to form a new blended culture. Thus, Indian Bollywood films began to include in the 1990s scenes shot in the West in order to appeal to the 25 million or so people of Indian origin in the world who live outside India itself, but they retained the dance and song sequences characteristic of Indian movies. Thus too, younger Brazilian musicians often deserted the samba and other traditional styles for hip-hop and rap, but they continued to sing in Portuguese and to address Brazilian realities in their lyrics. Are Spanglish (Spanish/English) or Hinglish (Hindi/English) resistance to the global dominance of the English language, or its transformation?

A problem with the *hybridity* approach is that it can become rather woolly and vague, content just to say that what is happening is a blend but not to probe further into what kind of blend it is, or why it is that kind of blend, or how rooted or unstable is that blend. Hybridity can become just a quick label to pin on quite subtle and complicated cultural and media processes that need to be understood more deeply. An interesting study by Koichi Iwabuchi (2002) of *regional* cultural dominance, in this case Japan's cultural and media exports to Taiwan, Hong Kong, and mainland China, takes us very productively into some of the real complexities of hybridization, stressing how the much more cosmopolitan feel of Hong Kong and Taiwan makes young Japanese, Taiwanese, and Hong Kong consumers' mutual cultural relation very lively, much more so at the time of his writing than with mainland China. He adds to this equation a historical dimension, namely the contrasting experience of Taiwan under Japanese colonial rule (1895–1945), relatively milder than the barbaric ferocity of Japan's invasion of mainland China (1931–1945), which as a result produced very different everyday responses to Japanese cultural products in the two terrains.

The final theoretical approach to understanding media issues under the heading of globalization is that of Chicago-based scholar Arjun Appadurai (1996). His argument is much larger and more detailed than this, but a key component is his twinning of two factors, media and migration, in analyzing the global media process. In his perspective, the huge process of transnational labor migration that characterized the second half of the 20th century and now this one generated tremendous cultural dislocation *and* expansion of cultural horizons among the migrant communities, the communities they left behind, and the communities they diversified following their arrival. At the same time, he suggests, the expansion of media images and coverage of the rest of the planet opened up many people's eyes to realities wider than their immediate and local experience. It is Appadurai's fusion of the mass movement of actual human beings and the global dissemination of images of the rest of the planet that, by concentrating especially on these two facets, opens up our thinking and prompts us to take very seriously the numerous forms of "diasporic" media that are with us today, whether radio programs of overseas music, foreign language newspapers, magazines, satellite and cable channels, or websites. (*Diaspora* began as a term to describe the 2,000-year migratory settlement of Jewish peoples, sometimes forced, but is now used more generally to refer to mass migratory settlement.) This foreign media sector is not at all new in principle and was rife in immigrant neighbor-hoods of U.S. cities from the 1880s onward, but the contemporary range of these media, especially when combined with more affordable air travel to people's countries of origin, marks a distinctive new step in our media and more general cultural environment (Cunningham & Sinclair, 2001; Karim, 2003).

However, whatever uses we make of these varying theoretical approaches, we need never to lose sight of the further reality that global media and cultural flows are also most often big business, similar to but also at points different from the big business of aerospace, shoes, cars, agriculture, and all other industries. This dynamic takes a variety of forms but is never absent entirely. More often than not, indeed, it is this dynamic that dominates. And it has no compulsion to be people friendly.

A DIFFERENT APPROACH III: SMALL-SCALE ALTERNATIVE MEDIA

I made several references to the term *samizdat media* in the section on Soviet Russia. The term refers to the hand-circulated pamphlets, poems, essays, plays, short stories, novels, and, at a later stage, audio- and videocassettes *(magnitizdat)* that began to emerge in Soviet Russia and later in other Soviet bloc countries from the 1960s onward. They contained material that was banned by the Soviet regimes. Writing, distributing, or possessing these materials carried sentences in hard-labor camps. *Samizdat* contained widely varied messages—some religious, some nationalist, some ecological, some reformist, some revising the myths of official Soviet history, some attacking Soviet policies, some defending citizens victimized by arbitrary arrest and imprisonment. The term *samizdat* literally means "self-published," in contradistinction to "state-published," that is, approved by the Soviet regime as "safe." These micromedia took a long time to make a dent in the Soviet system—more than a generation. But their impact was extraordinary, for up until the last year of the USSR, even when the east-central European regimes had already shaken off Soviet rule, the Soviet Union appeared to be one of those fact-of-life institutions that few observers imagined could collapse. Those Russians, Ukrainians, Poles, and others who labored over those decades to create *samizdat,* and often paid a heavy price in jail for their pains, showed amazing spirit, determination, and foresight. They were aided by the foreign shortwave radio stations that broadcast in the region's languages into Soviet bloc territory: the BBC World Service, Radio Liberty, Radio Free Europe, Deutsche Welle, and Voice of America. These stations would read *samizdat* texts over the air as part of their programming and thus amplified their message outside the major urban centers, which were normally the only places where *samizdat* was circulated. Sometimes the Soviet bloc governments jammed their broadcasts but not always.

Historically and comparatively, small-scale radical media of this kind have been common (Downing, 2001). They have been used in the United States from the time of the War of Independence through the abolitionist and suffragist movements to the civil rights and the anti-Vietnam War movements, right up to global movements in Europe, Canada, Australia, and elsewhere opposing the U.S. war on Iraq. Yet their significant role in slowly rotting away at Soviet power flags their importance in developing our own definition of media. All too often, we mistake size and speed for significance, as if they were the only way that media can wield power. In relation to the dizzying speed with which transnational corporations are merging media ownership, it is all too easy to slip into a fatalistic acceptance that these colossuses are too much for us to take on. Yet the *samizdat* story and its parallels in many other parts of the world suggest a diametrically different conclusion, one that begins to put media power in our hands instead of governmental, corporate, or religious leaders' hands.

Question for Stable, Affluent Nations.   The Internet greatly expanded citizens' communication options in economically advanced nations during the 1990s. Can it (1) be extended to many ordinary citizens outside those nations and (2) be preserved from virtually total corporate control? Corporate control can take various forms—for example, charging long-distance phone tariffs to Internet users, putting ever-higher prices on access to informational websites, and reserving high bandwidth access for corporate users or wealthy clients. Can this trend be fought off successfully?

CONCLUSIONS

I set out in this essay to challenge the easy assumption that by studying media in just the United States or Britain, the currently dominant nations in media research publication, we can succeed in "drawing a bead" on media. In a deliberate paradox, I selected what seems to be a closed chapter in 20th-century history—namely, the story of Soviet media—to illustrate some heavy-duty media issues that conventional theories fail to get in their sights. But, as I argued, those media issues are common in most of the contemporary world. I also argued that, in certain ways, they direct our attention back to pivotal media issues even in stable, affluent nations. Global comparisons, globalization, small-scale alternative media—all need to be central to media research.

For more information on the topics that appear in this chapter, use the password that came free with this book to access InfoTrac College Edition. Use the following words as keyterms and subject searches: mass communication theories, normative theories, participatory media, Communist media, social transitions, alternative media, globalization, cultural imperialism, hybridity.

QUESTIONS FOR DISCUSSION

1. What are the chief problems with deontic, or normative, theories of media?

2. Why does a study of Russian media, whether during or since the 1917–1991 Soviet era, help us understand our own media system more clearly?

3. How do our own news media present economic crises, either at home or in other parts of the planet?

4. What changes in communication rights and surveillance issues do some people argue have taken place for the worse in the United States since the attacks of 9/11?

5. What roles may diasporic, alternative, or underground media play in energizing active democracy and social movements?

REFERENCES

Appadurai, A. (1996). *Modernity at large: Cultural dimensions of globalization.* Minneapolis: University of Minnesota Press.

Bagdikian, B. (2000). *The media monopoly* (6th ed.). Boston: Beacon Press.

Barratt Brown, M. (1997). *Africa's choices: After thirty years of the World Bank.* Boulder, CO: Westview.

Blendon, R. J. (1995). Health care reform: The press failed to inform the public of alternative strategies. *Nieman Reports, 49*(3), 17–19.

Cunningham, S., & Sinclair, J. (Eds.). (2001). *Floating lives: The media and Asian diasporas.* Lanham, MD: Rowman & Littlefield.

Downing, J. (1996). *Internationalizing media theory: Transition, power, culture: Reflections on media in Russia, Poland, and Hungary, 1980–95.* London: Sage.

Downing, J. (2001). *Radical media: Rebellious communication and social movements.* Thousand Oaks, CA: Sage.

Fallows, J. (1996). *Breaking the news: How the media undermine American democracy.* New York: Pantheon.

Iwabuchi, K. (2002). *Recentering globalization: Popular culture and Japanese transnationalism.* New York: Routledge.

Karim, K.H. (Ed.). (2003). *The media of diaspora.* New York: Routledge.

McChesney, R. (1999). *Rich media, poor democracy.* Urbana: University of Illinois Press.

McQuail, D. (1994). *Mass communication theory: An introduction* (3rd ed.). London: Sage.

Pieterse, J. N. (2004). *Globalization and culture: Global mélange.* Lanham, MD: Rowman & Littlefield.

Siebert, F., Peterson, T., & Schramm, W. (1956). *Four theories of the press.* Urbana: University of Illinois Press.

Schiller, H. (1991). Not yet the post-imperialist era. *Critical Studies in Mass Communication, 8,* 13–28.

Stein, H. (Ed.). (1995). *Asian industrialization and Africa: Studies in policy alternatives to structural adjustment.* New York: St. Martin's Press.

3

Global Economy
and International
Telecommunications
Networks

HARMEET SAWHNEY

Harmeet Sawhney (PhD, University of Texas at Austin) is an associate
professor in the Department of Telecommunications, Indiana
University, Bloomington. He works on issues related
to telecommunications infrastructure planning and policy. His research
has been published in a variety of academic journals, including *Journal
of Broadcasting and Electronic Media; Media, Culture, and Society;*
and *Telecommunications Policy*. He is currently serving as Editor-in-Chief
of *The Information Society Journal*.

W e often hear the term *global economy* in news accounts of distant events such
as Asian financial crises, International Monetary Fund loans, and free trade
agreements. However, the global economy is not an abstraction. It affects our lives
in personal ways. If we look at just the things that clothe our body at any point in
time, we are likely to encounter products from all over the world. In my case, at
the time I first wrote these words, I was wearing a shirt from Sri Lanka, pants from

For additional online resources, access the Global Media Monitor website
that accompanies this book on the Wadsworth Communication Cafe website
at http://communication.wadsworth.com.

the United States, sandals from Mexico, a watch from Korea, and glasses from France. If we look beyond our personal possessions, we will see that the influence of the global economy percolates down to the most mundane of our everyday activities. The price of gas is determined by global oil markets, the ups and downs of interest rates are prompted by global money flows, and the availability of jobs is greatly affected by activities of global corporations.

The global economy is also closely related to global communication, the focus of this book. They are inseparably intertwined, for the global economy requires global communication to control and coordinate global division of labor. To fully comprehend the relationship between the two, we will first look at the world before the advent of the Industrial Revolution. That will help us understand how global division of labor has transformed the world and in the process given birth to both the global economy and global communications.

PREMODERN WORLD

In the 13th century, the world was very different from the world of today. Among other things, the personal possessions of our predecessors were all made locally—not in a town 100 miles away but in the town or village in which one actually lived. Foreign products were rare. The only people who had access to them were kings, queens, and the rich. Even then, foreign products were basically exotic items—such as gems, silks, and spices—that were easy to transport because of their light weight and yet were of high value. Everyday goods were made by local shoemakers, tailors, blacksmiths, wheelwrights, goldsmiths, and other such artisans and craftsmen who worked more or less independently. For example, a shoemaker working in a workshop next to his cottage would process the leather, cut it, create the sole and the upper, stitch the different pieces together, make a lace, and insert it into the eyelets to make a complete shoe. The shoe thus created would be custom made and hence tailored to each customer's feet. However, since he had to do everything by himself from beginning to end, he would be able to make only a limited number of shoes per day.

DIVISION OF LABOR

One of the things that distinguished the modern world from the premodern world was the extent to which division of labor was used in the production process. With division of labor, the shoemakers in a town no longer work independently at their own workshops. They instead work together as a group in a factory. Shoemaker A processes the leather, shoemaker B creates the sole, shoemaker C crafts the uppers, shoemaker D stitches the shoe together, and shoemaker E makes the lace and puts it into the eyelets. The overall number of shoes produced in the town will grow exponentially as division of labor creates specialization that in turn increases efficiency. Because shoemaker A only processes the leather day in and day out, he becomes an expert in leather processing and thereby is able to greatly enhance his output per day. Similarly with specialization, the expertise of shoemakers B, C, D, and E increases, and correspondingly, so does the overall output of shoes.

The flip side to division of labor is that it creates interdependencies. Whereas in the old system shoemaker A could wake up whenever he wanted and start working whenever it suited his mood, the new system based on division of labor requires coordination. All five shoemakers have to work in sync with each other.

Even if just one of them performs suboptimally, the entire production process will slow down. Just imagine a situation where shoemaker B develops a tendency to be slow in the morning and fast in the afternoon. This skewed pattern will create a serious problem if shoemakers A, C, D, and E continue to work steadily throughout the day. Therefore, the interdependencies created by the division of labor require coordination and control to keep the production going smoothly.

In many ways, division of labor is a devil's bargain. It increases productivity via specialization, which in turn creates problems of coordination and control. In the early stages of the Industrial Revolution, division of labor was first employed on a small scale in small factories. The problems created by division of labor were taken care of by managers who coordinated and controlled the activities of individual workers performing specialized tasks. In the shoe factory just mentioned, the manager would walk around the factory floor, keep track of the performance of each worker, and give instructions to them to make sure they all worked in sync with each other. Within the confined space of a factory, coordination and control problems can be handled on a face-to-face level, but these problems become more severe when division of labor occurs across geographical space as companies seek to capitalize on the locational advantage of each place.

Henry Ford's automobile factory in Dearborn, Michigan, was a huge establishment employing more than 10,000 workers. It was said that iron, rubber, and sand went in one end and the finished car came out the other end. In other words, Ford made almost all the components of his car in the same factory.

However, when business owners started realizing that some components could be made more cheaply in other parts of the country, they moved away from centralized production—for example, horns were made in Indiana, steering wheels in Ohio, and brakes in Illinois. The reasons for lower costs could vary, from easier access to raw materials to availability of skilled labor to lower real estate costs. These days, division of labor has even spilled over beyond national boundaries. In a modern car company, one component may be made in Korea, another in India, yet another in Brazil, and so on, and the final car assembled in the United States. This would not be possible without the whole array of modern communication technologies, ranging from fiber optics to satellites. Thus, we see that the global division of labor is intricately tied to modern communication technologies. While telecommunications technologies allow for global coordination and control, transportation technologies move raw materials and products from one corner of the world to another. Whereas global trade in the past was limited to lightweight items, today tons of steels, oil, grain, and other commodities are routinely moved across the world. These movements affect not only the consumption of luxuries by the wealthy, as in the past, but also the consumption of everyday items by the common people.

This discussion explains the changes brought about by global economy, global division of labor, and global communication in a purely conceptual way, as if they were abstract phenomena. These transformations, however, actually took place in the real world of international politics. In order to comprehend their impact on our own lives, we need to understand the historical context within which they occurred. The next section provides an overview of how the world changed with the rise of the industrial powers.

IMPERIALISM

In the 13th century, the world was multipolar. Multiple centers of power—China, Egypt, India, Italy, Iraq, and others—dominated decentralized trading circuits. Figure 3.1 captures the overall structure of the world system. Although most of the trading took place within each of the trading circuits, they were not isolated from one another. For example, considerable evidence suggests that India and Italy traded with one another via Egypt and Iraq. The world was interconnected but in a loosely coupled way.

The picture changed dramatically with the emergence of Portuguese, Spanish, Dutch, French, and British empires in the 14th and 15th centuries. The Western powers transformed the multipolar world into a monopolar one (Figure 3.2). The development of science in western European countries gave them technologically superior weaponry, such as guns, that simply overwhelmed the indigenous people of Africa, America, Asia, and Australia, who were still fighting with bows and arrows. Therefore, the relatively small western European countries could subjugate other nations with much larger populations. Their empires were vast as they spanned the globe. It was said that the sun never set on the British Empire; that is, its empire was so extensive and far-flung that the sun was always shining on some part of its holdings. Britain alone controlled about a quarter of the world's landmass. In addition, the French, Spaniards, Portuguese, Dutch, and others had their own empires. This was the era of imperialism.

These new empires were not like earlier ones in history. First, they were far-flung and disjointed, unlike the old empires, which were created through the conquest of neighboring countries. For example, when Genghis Khan stirred the spirit of the Mongols in the 13th century, they went on to conquer China, central Asia, and Iraq, and swept into Europe as far as Hungary. Because these empires were contiguous, the cultural differences between the conquerors and the conquered were relatively small, though significant. Although the Iraqis may not have liked the Mongols, they at least knew who they were. On the other hand, in the 16th century, the Aztecs knew hardly anything about their conquerors, the Spaniards. To the Aztecs, they might as well have been aliens from another planet.

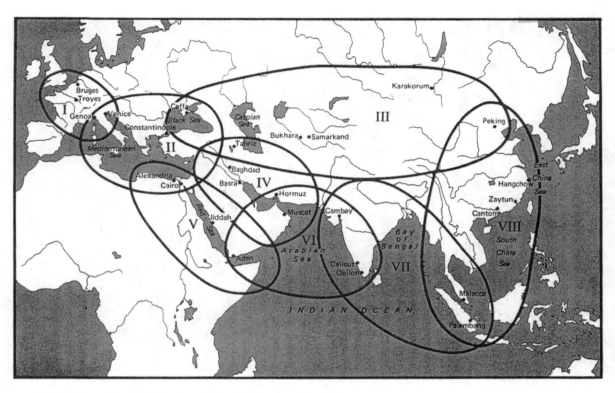

FIGURE 3.1 The Eight Circuits of the 13th-Century World System.

SOURCE: *Before European Hegemony* by Janet L. Abu-Lughod. Copyright © 1989 by Oxford University Press, Inc. Used by permission of Oxford University Press, Inc.

Second, the economic relationship between the imperial powers and the subject territories changed in the age of imperialism. Although this relationship has always been an exploitative one, the nature of exploitation was different now. In the past, exploitation consisted of plunder and tribute. The conquerors simply smashed the palaces and temples and took away gold, jewels, and other precious materials. In addition, they extracted tribute in the form of gifts, grain, or taxes every year. Although this form of exploitation still existed in the new empires, it was minor relative to what took place through commercial means.

One of the main reasons the imperial powers were interested in acquiring colonies was to gain access to raw materials for their growing industries. These industries needed cotton, rubber, tin, jute, indigo, and a whole range of other raw materials. After conquering new territory, the imperial powers soon set up plantations, mines, and the means for transporting the raw materials to the factories in the mother country, especially railroads after they were invented. Once the raw materials were processed into finished goods, the empires used the colonies as captive markets for selling their factories' outputs. The colonies

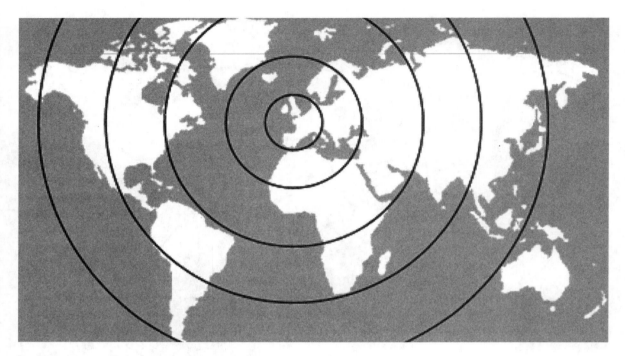

F I G U R E 3.2   Euro-centered Monopolar World

were thereby squeezed both ways as suppliers of cheap raw materials and captive markets for finished products.

How did the imperial powers maintain their control over their colonial possessions? It is important to ponder this question before we start discussing contemporary global communications issues because the past provides a good backdrop for understanding the present. Quite obviously, brute military power played a critical role in the creation and maintenance of empires. At the same time, a number of more subtle strategies were employed. One of them was to co-opt the native elite into the colonial administrative apparatus by educating them in Western ways and then giving them positions of privilege in the administrative hierarchy. This co-opted class of people spoke the language of the colonial masters, attended schools modeled on European schools, went to the mother country for higher education, and in many other ways acquired European habits of the mind. At times, the effort to impose European culture on colonial subjects went beyond the native elites to the masses. The logic behind this strategy was quite simple: People who are culturally closer to the mother country than their own native traditions are less likely to revolt.

The imperial administrations also hampered collaboration among native groups to forestall the emergence of united opposition to colonial rule. On the one hand, they would often use the divide-and-conquer strategy and

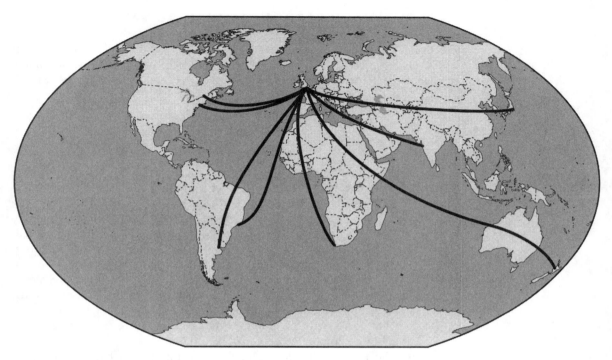

FIGURE 3.3 London-centric Telegraph Network

manipulate historical animosities among native groups to weaken potential opposition. On the other hand, administrators would create structural barriers among native groups with shared affinities to prevent any joint action by them. With this dynamic in mind, it is instructive to note certain characteristics of the global telegraph network that the British used to manage their vast empire (see Figure 3.3). First, the network was totally London-centric, as telegraph lines from all over the empire converged onto the imperial capital. Second, lateral lines were rare. If people at any two points in the empire wanted to communicate with each other, they had to do so through London even if they were geographically adjacent to each other. This configuration is a classic structural characteristic of relationships between the power center and subjugated periphery. Typically, in a center-periphery relation, the center encourages centralized relationships and discourages lateral ones.

This sets the stage for us to examine the complexities of global communications. Today, in the eyes of many scholars, we have moved from an era of imperialism to one of electronic imperialism. Although this analogy suggests a degree of similarity between the past and the present, the word *electronic* suggests some differences. In the following section, we will study what they are.

ELECTRONIC IMPERIALISM

Electronic imperialism is a broad concept that can encompass a wide range of issues. Here we will focus on two major issues—global media flows and international trade in services—so that we can attain a certain depth in our discussions.

Global Media Flows

After World War II, the age of imperialism came to an end as the colonies won independence one by one. The center of the world also moved across the Atlantic to the United States. The world was for the most part still monocentric (see Figure 3.4). However, the way the center projected power over the periphery was qualitatively different.

The main source of U.S. power was its economic rather than its military strength, even though the importance of the latter should not be discounted. Although the United States did not formally have an empire, in many quarters, the present world order dominated by the United States is believed to be no different. The only difference is that today the center—the United States— projects its power not brazenly, as imperial powers did in the days of gunboat diplomacy, but subtly through economic and, more lately, cultural means. Even if one does not agree with this point of view, one needs to be cognizant of it because it colors all discussions on global communication.

Many scholars argue that although the formal empires have been dissolved, the global political structures created during the age of imperialism remain in place.

These structures create a relationship of dependency between the rich and the poor countries (Galtung, 1971; McPhail, 1981; Schiller, 1969). For example, in Africa even today, a telephone call to a neighboring country is often made via London or Paris or some other former imperial capital. This pattern of global communications is similar to the British telegraph network—monocentric with few lateral connections. The African telephone networks are a legacy of colonial times. Today the United States is the center, and we see a similar pattern with modern communication flows— films, TV programs, and other such cultural products.

The United States overwhelmingly dominates the cinema and television screens all over the world. No other country even comes near the U.S. presence on the world's electronic entertainment stage. Hollywood is correspondingly one of the top-three export industries of the United States, generating more than $8 billion of trade surplus in theatrical films alone. The United States therefore tends to look at its media exports in purely business terms and argues that they are no different from other products.

Other countries, however, do not view films as simply a product or Hollywood as simply as an industry. They are more concerned about the cultural influence of films, fearing that imported films will shape people's attitudes and perceptions in accordance with alien ideas and values. In the developing countries, these fears are deeply rooted in their colonial experience, when their colonial masters imposed their language and culture on them. Developing nations consider the import of U.S. films to be a new kind of invasion—cultural invasion—that is more subtle and

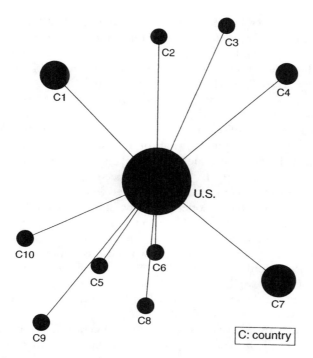

FIGURE 3.4 U.S.-centered World System

insidious. One can debate whether or not these fears and perceptions have any merit, depending on one's overall political position. Yet, one cannot ignore the fact that rich countries such as Canada and France share the concerns of developing countries about U.S. cultural dominance. Their stance on "electronic imperialism" gives the concerns of the developing nations some credence and suggests that those concerns do not stem from pure paranoia.

In fact, when we look at global communication flows, we can easily see that they are disproportionately from the United States (the center) to the rest of the world (the periphery). The flow in the other direction and lateral flow between periphery countries is small. Critics have dubbed this pattern of communication *one-way flow.* In the 1970s, a major debate began about this imbalance in global information flows. Many nations called for a new world information order (NWIO) that would change this asymmetrical pattern and make it more balanced. This idea sounds quite attractive as an abstraction but creates serious problems when implementation is attempted. First, it encourages regulation of information flows by governments, often undemocratic, which might attempt to control the national media for their own domestic political purposes. The NWIO would give them another excuse for their nefarious designs. Second, even if that is acceptable, regulating electronic communication flows is becoming increasingly difficult as the technology becomes ever more elusive to control.

The United States has been dead set against the NWIO because it goes against the First Amendment to the U.S. Constitution, which guarantees freedom of the press. The United States not only opposes the NWIO but also pleads helplessness because the First Amendment makes it impossible for the government to legally do anything about it. However, some scholars have offered some thoughtful criticism of the First Amendment. They point out that it was written more than two centuries ago, when ordinary citizens could enter the newspaper business because the cost of setting up a printing press was low. In effect, ordinary citizens had a voice in the public forum or at least access to a mouthpiece. The newspapers and the electronic media have gradually become concentrated into large conglomerates as the media business has become exceedingly capital intensive. Ordinary citizens no longer have easy access to media, and now essentially a top-down communication, or one-way flow, situation exists even within the United States. In many ways, the U.S. hinterlands have been colonized by Los Angeles and New York. In these current circumstances, the First Amendment basically protects the corporations that own the media rather than free speech itself (Carey, 1989; Innis, 1951; Schiller, 1974). What good is free speech when only a few people own loudspeakers? When we look at the current global situation, we can ask the same question: What good is a free flow of information when only a few countries have loudspeakers?

We see here a tussle between the First Amendment and its critics. The debate takes place within the backdrop of past colonial experience that has colored the responses of developing countries, which see a new threat to their sovereignty in the free flow of information.

Transborder Data Flow

Although the tensions are overt in the case of global flow of cultural products, similar, less obvious problems exist in other realms of international trade. With the improvement in transportation technologies, international trade progressively moved beyond lightweight, high-value items to heavier and bulkier commodities. However, services such as accounting, insurance, and advertising remained local for the most part.

One of the main reasons that services changed little was that they required an intense amount of interaction between the service provider and the consumer. They were not like a product one could pick off a store shelf without ever knowing the manufacturer personally. The accountant could provide help only if the client shared the relevant information. Furthermore, this sharing of information took place over multiple interactions because the accountant had to query the client often for additional information and clarification. Because this interaction previously took place mainly in person, the production and consumption of services were restricted to a small area. Modern communication and information technologies have radically changed all this. First, a computer software package such as Microsoft Quicken^{TM} can often perform functions that only a trained human being could previously do in person. Second, modern telecommunications networks can support a level of interaction between the service provider and the client that could be achieved only face-to-face in the past. The service

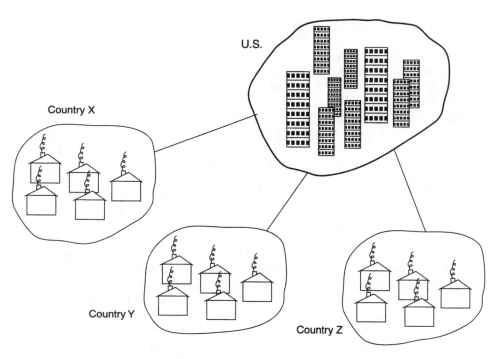

FIGURE 3.5 The United States as a World Headquarters

provider and the client need no longer be in the same place. Even though they are at great distance from each other, even halfway around the world, they can do business via email, fax, and other communication technologies. These technological developments finally made even services tradable.

The trade in services assumes a great importance in the global economy. As the global division of labor has progressed, manufacturing jobs have moved overseas from the United States to developing countries, where labor costs are much cheaper. This movement of industry across the globe in search of locational advantage is in many ways an extension of what happened in the United States. Earlier, auto parts suppliers moved out of Detroit to other locations that offered a comparative advantage in either labor or raw materials costs. Today the same process is happening across national boundaries. The transportation and communications technologies, which made this dispersal possible within a country, are now making it possible across the world. In this new world of international division of labor, the United States is increasingly emerging as a world headquarters of sorts (see Figure 3.5). While corporations are moving manufacturing facilities overseas, they are investing more and more in research and development, corporate services, management, and other coordination and control activities in the United States. The United States has thereby become the command-and-control node for global business activities.

The perspectives and interests of the United States and the developing countries are quite different on issues related to the global economy. The United States favors both free trade and free flow of information. It promotes free trade because free trade leads to ever-increasing global division of labor as businesses keep seeking locations with cost advantages, which in turn increases overall productivity. At the same time, because the increasing division of labor leads to increasing interdependency, the United States also favors free flow of information, mostly over computer networks, to ensure coordination and control among the specialized units located in different parts of the world. For example, a large corporation like Proctor and Gamble needs unimpeded communication between its computers in its Cincinnati headquarters and those in its plants all over the world in order to operate a global enterprise successfully. This computer-to-computer communication across national boundaries is known as transborder data flow (TDF). From a purely business point of view, it is essential for global corporations that this information flow take place in an unhindered manner.

Developing countries, on the other hand, have a different point of view. They are suspicious of both free trade and free flow of communication. They are suspicious of free trade because free trade among unequals more often than not leads to the exploitation of the weaker countries, which get relegated to being the source of cheap raw materials and labor for low value-added manufacturing activities.

Furthermore, the structural relationships that develop leave them in a position of almost permanent dependency. If one were to use the brain–brawn analogy, the industrialized countries remain the brains of the world system and the developing countries, the brawn. Finally, although the greater division of labor facilitated by free trade leads to greater productivity, there is no guarantee that the additional wealth thus generated will be shared equitably among the countries. In the case of the factory, which can be considered the cradle of division of labor, history has shown that the owners will appropriate a disproportionate share of the additional wealth produced by specialization and leave the ordinary workers poorly compensated for their labor. A similar process is seen on the global scale. The industrialized countries take a disproportionate share of wealth generated by global division of labor, leaving the developing countries poorly rewarded for their contributions. Often, this exploitation does not take place in an overt manner but in many subtle ways. Among other things, all the high value-added activities like consultancy, advertising, research and development, and others take place in industrialized countries, and thereby a disproportionate part of the wealth created stays there.

This suspicion of free trade spills over onto issues related to the free flow of information. Although the United States and industrialized countries view free flow of information as a normal commercial activity essential for coordination and control of business processes, developing countries see it as a vehicle for foreign influence that undermines local centers of authority. In their perspective, free flow of information blurs national boundaries and thereby threatens national sovereignty. Consequently, transborder data flow has become a matter of heated debate. It can be argued that these concerns are ill founded. However, there is no denying that they are deeply rooted in historical experience. Among other things, as discussed earlier, the telegraph was used a means of maintaining imperial power. Therefore, alien communication networks and the contents that flow over them are often viewed with suspicion.

The current imbalance in world trade further aggravates the problem. If one walks around a mall in the United States and looks at the labels of different products in the stores, one will come across products made in China, Korea, Malaysia, Brazil, Jamaica, Mexico, and many other countries but few made in the United States. This phenomenon is a reflection of the fact that most U.S. manufacturing has moved overseas, and most of the products needed in the United States have to be imported. Many of the manufacturing countries, particularly China, have huge a balance of payments in their favor. On the other hand, what the United States exports is intangible products, such as computer software, insurance, banking services, and films. So when the United States tries to close the balance of trade by exporting information products, in which it has a comparative advantage, it resents the opposition from other countries. The other countries, however, do not see these products as purely commercial products with no political or cultural implications. Their concern is that the unchecked inflow of these products will undermine their sovereignty.

So who is right? Perhaps both sides. The perceptions on both sides are shaped by their respective interests.[1] In the case of developing countries, their perceptions continue to be influenced by the colonial experience. The echoes of the past can be heard even today.

Our discussion of global media flows and trade in services shows one major similarity and one major difference between imperialism and electronic imperialism. The similarity is that they both exhibit a strong center–periphery relationship with few lateral connections among the periphery; in effect, the center almost totally dominates the periphery. The difference is that today the center employs more subtle means to dominate the periphery than the brute force used in the past. Overall, we see significant continuity between imperialism and electronic imperialism. Will newer technologies like the Internet, which are said to have decentralizing tendencies, change the established center–periphery relationship? In the next section, we will explore the impact of emerging network structures on global communication.

---

1. In 1942, Kent Cooper, president of the Associated Press, bitterly complained,

> So Reuters decided what news was to be sent from America. It told the world about Indians on the war path in the West, lynchings in the South and bizarre crimes in the North. The charge for decades was that nothing creditable to America ever was sent. American business criticized The Associated Press for permitting Reuters to belittle America abroad. (Cooper, 1942, p. 12)

Cooper's ire was directed against the British, who through their news agency Reuters were portraying America in a negative light. At that time, Britain was the center, and the United States was part of the semiperiphery. Today the tables have turned. Now that the United States is the center, the Americans find it difficult to understand the complaints of periphery countries about how they are covered by the U.S. media.

EMERGING NETWORK STRUCTURES

Older technologies such as TV were amenable to centralized control. The high costs of program production and transmission make television a top-down mode of communication where the sources are few and the receivers are many. However, newer technologies do not seem to follow the same logic, at least on the surface. The cost of production equipment has dropped sharply. Similarly, transmission costs have declined as bandwidths have significantly increased with the deployment of fiber optic and other broadband technologies. We have also seen the emergence of new transmission systems, such as the Internet, that follow an entirely different logic in terms of organization. These days, an ordinary citizen can shoot video with a camcorder and make it accessible via the Internet to anyone interested. Now the question arises, will supposedly decentralizing technologies like the Internet strengthen or loosen U.S. control over world communications?

On the surface, the Internet looks like a democratic medium because nobody seems to control it. However, a closer examination reveals deeply embedded structural inequities. Rich countries, with only 16 percent of the world's population, have 97 percent of all Internet hosts. This inequity is even more striking when one considers that the 100 poorest countries have 20 times fewer Internet hosts than Iceland, a country with a population of only 250,000 (Petrazzini & Kibati, 1999). Furthermore, the global Internet exhibits a center–periphery relationship similar to that of the British imperial telegraph network and African telephone networks. An email from Stockholm to London goes via the United States, even though the direct physical distance between them is shorter (Cohen, 1999).

The U.S.-centric nature of the global Internet is also evident in the financial arrangements for international circuits. Unlike the telephone system, in which the cost of the international circuit connecting two countries is evenly split between them, Internet service providers (ISPs) in other countries pay the entire cost of the circuit connecting them to the United States. The U.S. carriers are able to get away with this because of their leverage with overseas ISPs. The ISPs are willing to pay for the entire circuit because they need access to U.S. websites and exchange points that can connect them to other countries. This free ride by U.S. ISPs is particularly galling for developing countries because the traffic flows over the international circuits are quite skewed. Typically, traffic from the United States to other countries is greater than the other way around. For example, the traffic from the United States to Ghana is twice that of the traffic from Ghana to the United States (Petrazzini & Kibati, 1999).

Network investment patterns suggest that in the future we will see the emergence of regional networks in Europe and Asia (Cohen, 1999; Townsend, 2001; Zook, 2001). However, the change in the overall structure of the global Internet is unlikely in the near future. Even if the overseas ISPs try to create lateral connections among them, the economics of the entrenched infrastructure work heavily against them. So many high-capacity, U.S.-bound international circuits have already been deployed that lateral connections between overseas ISPs, if created, will find it extremely difficult to survive the price competition with them. Thus, it seems that the U.S.-centered structure of the global Internet is here to stay, at least for the time being (Petrazzini & Kibati, 1999). The Internet, with all its lateral communication potentialities, is at present like the British imperial telegraph network and is likely to remain like that for the foreseeable future.

TOWARD A NEW WORLD SYSTEM?

Throughout history there have been centers and peripheries. However, the specific places (cities, countries, regions) that have played the roles of center and periphery have varied over time. During the colonial era, Western Europe (England, France, Spain, and a few other countries) was the center, and the rest of the world was the periphery. After World War II, the center moved across the Atlantic to the United States, and the rest of the world became the periphery. However, the nature of the center–periphery relationship has changed significantly. For one thing, we have a global division of labor on an unprecedented scale and enormous interdependencies that come with it. For another, the center—the United States—projects its power over the periphery in subtle ways instead of using the brute force seen in the empires of the past. One of these subtle ways includes international communication systems, the focus of this book. The existing systems that include the global Internet reflect the center–periphery relationship, and any major change in the structure of international communications systems is unlikely in the near future. However, as history provides ample evidence, the center–periphery relationship is bound to change over the long run because nothing lasts forever. The question is, once the U.S. power declines, will the center merely pass from the United States to another country? Or will there be an emergence of a multipolar world like that of the 13th century?

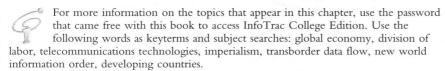 For more information on the topics that appear in this chapter, use the password that came free with this book to access InfoTrac College Edition. Use the following words as keyterms and subject searches: global economy, division of labor, telecommunications technologies, imperialism, transborder data flow, new world information order, developing countries.

QUESTIONS FOR DISCUSSION

1. Explain what is meant by division of labor. How does division of labor increase productivity? What problems does it create? How do communications technologies help us manage these problems? What does division of labor have to do with the global economy?

2. Describe the structure of the British imperial telegraph network. Discuss why this configuration is a classic structural characteristic of relationships between the power center and subjugated periphery.

3. Explain what the term *transborder data flow* (TDF) means. Why has TDF become important over the last few decades? Why do industrialized countries want unrestricted TDF? Why are developing countries apprehensive about TDF?

4. Explain the economic forces that have shaped the structure of the global Internet. Is the U.S.-centric nature of the Internet a transitory phase in the Internet's growth curve, or will it harden into a long-term structure similar to that of the British imperial telegraph network?

5. In this chapter, we saw how the multicentered world of the 13th century was transformed into a single-centered world system during the colonial era. Later the center moved across the Atlantic to the United States. How do you think new communications technologies will affect the configuration of the world system? Will it remain single-centered or become multicentered? Why? Why not?

REFERENCES

Carey, J. (1989). *Communication as culture*. Boston: Unwin Hyman.

Cohen, R. B. (1999). Moving toward a non-U.S.-centric international Internet. *Communications of the ACM, 42*(6), 37–40.

Cooper, K. (1942). *Barriers down*. New York: Farrar & Rinehart.

Galtung, J. (1971). A structural theory of imperialism. *Journal of Peace Research, 2,* 81–117.

Innis, H. A. (1951). *The bias of communication*. Toronto: University of Toronto Press.

McPhail, T. L. (1981). *Electronic colonialism*. Beverly Hills, CA: Sage.

Petrazzini, B., & Kibati, M. (1999). The Internet in developing countries. *Communications of the ACM, 42*(6), 31–36.

Schiller, H. I. (1969). *Mass communications and American empire*. New York: A. M. Kelley.

Schiller, H. I. (1974). Freedom from the "free flow." *Journal of Communication, 24*(1), 110–117.

Townsend, A. M. (2001). Network cities and the global structure of the Internet. *American Behavioral Scientist, 44*(10), 1697–1716.

Zook, M. A. (2001). Old hierarchies or new networks of centrality? The global geography of the Internet content market. *American Behavioral Scientist, 44*(10), 1679–1696.

The Transnational Media Corporation and the Economics of Global Competition

RICHARD A. GERSHON

Richard A. Gershon (PhD, Ohio University) is a professor and cofounder of the Telecommunications & Information Management program at Western Michigan University where he teaches courses in Telecommunications Management, and Communication Law & Policy. He is the author of *The Transnational Media Corporation: Global Messages and Free Market Competition,* winner of the 1998 Book of the Year selected by the National Cable Television Center. Dr. Gershon has twice been selected for teaching honors, including the Steven H. Coltrin Professor of the Year Award (2000) by the International Radio & Television Society (IRTS) and the Barry Sherman Award for Teaching Excellence (2001) by the Management and Economics division of the Association for Education in Journalism and Mass Communication (AEJMC). He is a cofounder of the International Telecommunications Education & Research Association (ITERA) and served as the organization's first president.

The transnational corporation (TNC), as a system of organization, represents a natural evolution beyond the multinational corporation of the 1960s and 1970s. One distinctive feature of the TNC is that strategic decision making and

For additional online resources, access the Global Media Monitor website that accompanies this book on the Wadsworth Communication Cafe website at http://communication.wadsworth.com.

the allocation of resources are predicated upon economic goals and efficiencies with little regard to national boundaries. What distinguishes the transnational media corporation (TNMC) from other types of TNCs is that the principal commodity being sold is information and entertainment. It has become a salient feature of today's global economic landscape (Albarran & Chan-Olmsted, 1998; Demers, 1999; Gershon, 1997; Herman & McChesney, 1997).

The TNMC is the most powerful economic force for global media activity in the world today. As Herman and McChesney (1997) point out, transnational media are a necessary component of global capitalism. They provide the informational and ideological environment that enables international free market trade to occur. Through a process of foreign direct investment, the TNMC actively promotes the use of advanced media and information technology on a worldwide basis. This chapter considers the underlying economic principles that help to explain the causes and consequences of transnational media ownership.

THE TRANSNATIONAL MEDIA CORPORATION

During the past two decades, scholars and media critics alike have become increasingly suspicious of the better-known, high-profile media mergers. Such suspicions have given way to a number of myths concerning the intentions of TNMCs and the people who run them. The first myth is that such companies operate in most or all markets of the world. Although today's TNMCs are highly global in their approach to business, few companies operate in all markets of the world. Instead, the TNMC tends to operate in preferred markets with an obvious preference (and familiarity) toward its home market (Gershon, 1997, 2000). Thus, a company like Bertelsmann AG describes its strategic planning philosophy as follows:

> Many years ago, Bertelsmann set as a strategic goal the establishment of an even balance among its businesses in Germany, other European countries and the United States. We have succeeded in this area as well; each of these regions accounts for just under a third of overall revenues. A smaller portion of our business is being generated in Asia. That's why we truly consider ourselves a European American media company with German roots. (Bertelsmann, 1998, p. 3)

A second prevalent myth concerning TNMCs is that such companies are monolithic in their approach to business. In fact, just the opposite is true. The business strategies and corporate culture of a company are often a direct reflection of the person (or people) who were responsible for developing the organization and its business mission (Bennis,1986; Gershon, 1997, 2000; Morley & Shockley-Zalabak,1991). The Sony Corporation, for example, is a company that was largely shaped and developed by its founders, Masaru Ibuka and Akio Morita. Together they formed a unique partnership that left an indelible imprint on Sony's worldwide business operations (Nathan, 1999). For many years, all of Sony's top officials were Japanese and strategic decision making occurred at the company's Tokyo headquarters. There was a sense of family and missionary zeal that was uniquely Japanese in approach. In the book, *Made in Japan* (1986), Akio Morita once wrote: "The most important mission for a Japanese manager is to develop a healthy relationship with his employees, to create a family-like feeling with the corporation, a feeling that employees and managers share the same fate" (p. 130). Today, Sony is a very different company than at the time of Morita's writing. The family-like feel has dramatically changed in light of worldwide economic pressures. In March 2005, Sony announced for the first time in its corporate history the promotion of Welsh-born Howard Stringer—President of Sony Corporation of America—to the position of Chairman and CEO ("Shakeup at Sony," 2005).

In contrast, Bertelsmann is a TNMC that reflects the business philosophy and media interests of its founder, Reinhard Mohn, who believed in the importance of decentralization. Bertelsmann's success can be attributed to long-range strategic planning and decentralization, a legacy that Mohn instilled in the company before his retirement in 1981. That philosophy is captured in the company charter, which stresses:

- Entrepreneurial leadership and decentralization of operations
- Creativity and innovation at every level of the corporation
- Commitment to being a valued corporate citizen of the communities in which Bertelsmann companies operate (Bertelsmann, 1993, p. 7)

THE PURPOSE OF A GLOBAL MEDIA STRATEGY

Most companies do not set out with an established plan for becoming a major international company. Rather, as a company's exports steadily increase, it establishes a foreign office to handle the sales and services of its products. In the beginning stages, the foreign office tends to be flexible and highly independent. As the firm gains experience, it may get involved in other facets of international business, such as licensing and manufacturing abroad. Later, as pressures arise from various international operations, the company begins to recognize the need for a more comprehensive global strategy (Gershon 1993, 1997; Robock & Simmonds, 1989). Historically, the TNMC begins as a company that is especially strong in one or two areas. At the start of the 1980s, for example, the Walt Disney Company was principally in the business of children's animated films and theme parks, whereas News Corporation Limited (parent company to Fox Broadcasting) was principally a newspaper publisher. Today both companies are transnational in scope, with a highly diverse set of products and services. In sum, most major corporations become foreign direct investors through a process of gradual evolution rather than by deliberate choice.

THE GLOBALIZATION OF MARKETS

The globalization of markets involves the full integration of transnational business, nation-states, and technologies operating at high speed. Globalization is being driven by a broad and powerful set of forces including worldwide deregulation and privatization trends, advancements in new technology, market integration (such as the European Community, NAFTA, Mercosur, etc.), and the fall of communism. The basic requirements for all would-be players are free trade and a willingness to compete internationally. As Friedman (1999) points out, "Globalization has its own set of economic rules—rules that revolve around opening, deregulating and privatizing your company" (p. 8).

The Rules of Free Market Trade

Today, there is only one economic system operating in the world. And that system is called *free market capitalism*. Whereas communism provided a safety net for inefficient business practices, free market capitalism rewards only those who create new and innovative products and services. It is admittedly a fast-paced and uncertain world. According to German political theorist Carl Schmitt, "The Cold War was a world of friends and enemies. The globalization world, by contrast, tends to turn all friends and enemies into competitors" (Friedman, 1999, p. 11).

A basic tenet of free market trade is that the private sector is the primary engine of growth. It presupposes that the nation-state can maintain a low rate of inflation and keep prices stable. It further attempts to keep the size of government small and to achieve a balanced budget, if not a surplus. The rules of free market trade adhere to the principles of deregulation and privatization of business. At the domestic level, free market trade attempts to promote as much domestic competition as possible ("The New Economy," 2000). Free market trade opens up banking and telecommunication systems to private ownership and competition, and provides a nation and its citizens with access to a wide variety of choices.

The rules of free market trade extend internationally as well. Free market trade presupposes a willingness to open up one's domestic market to foreign direct investment. It further attempts to eliminate, or at least reduce, tariffs and quotas on imported goods. Not all countries adhere to the rules of free market trade in the same way. Some countries tailor the rules to protect certain industries and/or certain facets of domestic culture. As an example, Japan is highly protective of its banking industry ("Rebuilding the Banks," 1999), whereas France is highly protective of its culture. Even Russia and China have embraced capitalism, albeit in different ways. What they share in common is a rejection of the command economies of the past and the perceived inefficiency of centralized planning and government-protected monopolies. In sum, free market trade in its varying forms provides the basic architecture for today's global economy.

Foreign Direct Investment

Foreign direct investment (FDI) refers to the ownership of a company in a foreign country. This includes the control of assets. As part of its commitment, the investing company will transfer some of its managerial, financial, and technical expertise to the foreign-owned company. In a transnational economy, media decision making and FDI are largely based on economic efficiencies, with little regard for national boundaries (Gershon, 1993, 1997). The decision to engage in FDI is based upon the profitability of the market and future growth potential (Grosse & Kujawa, 1988). Let us consider five reasons why a company engages in FDI.

Proprietary and Physical Assets. Some TNCs invest abroad for the purpose of obtaining specific proprietary assets and natural resources. The ownership of talent or specialized expertise can be considered a type of proprietary asset. Sony Corporation's purchase of CBS records in 1988 and Columbia Pictures in 1989 enabled the company to become a formidable player in the field of music and entertainment. Rather than trying to create an altogether new company, Sony purchased proprietary assets in the form of an exclusive film library as well as contracts with some of the world's leading musicians and entertainers. In 2004, Sony applied the same strategy by acquiring Metro Goldwyn Mayer (MGM) Studios for $5.8 billion. Today, Sony holds the exclusive copyright to various films that once belonged to Columbia Pictures and MGM Studios.

Foreign Market Penetration. Some TNCs invest abroad for the purpose of entering a foreign market and serving it from that location. The market may exist or may have to be developed. The ability to buy an existing media property is the easiest and most direct method for market entry. This was the strategy employed by Bertelsmann AG when it entered the United States in 1986 and purchased Doubleday Publishing ($475 million) and RCA Records ($330 million). One year later, Bertelsmann consolidated its U.S. recording labels by forming the Bertelsmann Music Group, which is headquartered in New York City. Today, the U.S. division is responsible for 24.4 percent of the company's worldwide revenues.

Production and Distribution Efficiencies. The costs of production and labor are important factors in the selection of foreign locations. Some countries offer significant advantages such as lower labor costs, tax relief, and technology infrastructure. Depending upon the country and/or technical facility, products and services can be produced for less cost with greater efficiency. This is one reason for shooting on location (i.e., Canada and Ireland) where production costs are less expensive when compared to Hollywood and New York. To use a different example, Ireland serves an important communications center for many high-tech companies. Thus, Dell Computer centralizes all of its billing, inventory management, and distribution for its European operations by having the various functions flow through a single call center in Ireland. By centralizing these functions, the company is able to achieve significant cost savings.

Overcoming Regulatory Barriers to Entry. Some TNCs invest abroad for the purpose of entering into a market that is heavily tariffed. It is not uncommon for nations to engage in various protectionist policies designed to protect local industry. Such protectionist policies usually take the form of tariffs or import quotas. On October 3, 1989, the European Community (EC), in a meeting of the 12 nations' foreign ministers, adopted by a 10 to 2 vote the "Television Without Frontiers" directive. Specifically, EC Directive 89/552 was intended to promote European television and film production. The plan called for imposing restrictions on the import of U.S. television programming and films (Cate, 1990; Kevin, 2003). For the TNMC (and other television and film distributors), the EC directive was initially viewed as a form of trade protectionism. One way to offset the potential effects of program quotas is to form international partnerships and/or engage in coproduction ventures. By becoming a European company (or having a European affiliate), the TNMC is able to circumvent perceived regulatory barriers and is able to exercise greater control over international television/film trade matters (Litman, 1998).

Empire Building. Writers like Bennis (1986) contend that the CEO is the person most responsible for shaping the beliefs, motivations, and expectations for the organization as a whole. The importance of the CEO is particularly evident when it comes to the formation of business strategy. For CEOs like Rupert Murdoch (News Corp.), Sumner Redstone (Viacom), and John Malone (Liberty Media), there is a certain amount of personal competitiveness and business gamesmanship that goes along with managing a major company. Success is measured in ways that go beyond straight profitability. A high premium is placed on successful deal making and new project ventures. Today's generation of transnational media owners and CEOs are risk takers at the highest level, willing and able to spend billions of dollars in order to advance the cause of a new project venture. Viacom's Sumner Redstone, for example, is known for his aggressive leadership style and his tenacity as a negotiator. He is a fierce competitor. Redstone's competitive style can be seen in a comment he made in *Fortune* magazine:

> There are two or three of us who started with nothing. Ted Turner started with a half-bankrupt billboard company. Rupert Murdoch started with a little newspaper someplace in Australia. I was born in a tenement, my father became reasonably successful, and I started with two drive-in theaters before people knew what a drive-in theater was. . . . So I do share that sort of background with Rupert. People say I want to emulate him [Murdoch]. I don't want to emulate him. I'd like to beat him. ("There's No Business," 1998, p. 104)

The Risks Associated with FDI

The decision to invest in a foreign country can pose serious risks to the company operating abroad. The TNC is subject to the laws and regulations of the host country. It is also vulnerable to the host country's politics and business policies. What are the kinds of risks associated with FDI? There are the problems associated with political instability, including wars, revolutions, and coups. Less dramatic, but equally important, are changes stemming from the election of socialist or nationalist governments that may prove hostile to private business and particularly to foreign-owned business (Ball & McCulloch, 1996). Changes in labor conditions and wage requirements are also relevant factors in terms of a company's ability to do business abroad. Foreign governments may impose laws concerning taxes, currency convertibility, and/or technology transfer. Dymsza (1984) writes that FDI can occur only if the host country is perceived to be politically stable, provides sufficient economic investment opportunities, and has business regulations that are considered reasonable. In light of such issues, the TNC will carefully consider the potential risks by doing what is called a *country risk assessment* before committing capital and resources (Gershon, 2000).

TRANSNATIONAL MEDIA OWNERSHIP

The decades of the 1990s and early 21st century witnessed an unprecedented number of international mergers and acquisitions that have brought about a major realignment of business players. Concerns for antitrust violations seem overshadowed by a general acceptance that such changes are inevitable in a global economy. The result has been a consolidation of players in all aspects of business, including banking, pharmaceuticals, aviation, media, and telecommunications. Table 4.1 identifies several of the world's leading transnational media corporations and includes information pertaining to their principal business operations.

Mergers, Acquisitions, and Strategic Alliances

Today's TNMCs are taking advantage of deregulatory and privatization trends to make ever-larger combinations. Starting in 1995, the field of media and telecommunications has undergone a new round of corporate consolidation, as evidenced by Viacom's purchase of CBS for $37 billion (1999); America Online's purchase of Time Warner for $163 billion (2001), and Comcast's $54 billion purchase of AT&T Broadband (2002), to name only a few (Compaine & Gomery, 2000). Mergers, acquisitions, and strategic alliances represent different ways that companies can join (or partner together) to achieve increased market share, to diversify product line, and/or to create greater efficiency of operation. The goal, simply put, is to possess the size and resources necessary in order to compete on a global playing field.

Mergers. In a *merger* transaction, two companies are combined into one company. The newly formed company assumes the assets and liabilities of both companies (Ozanich & Wirth, 1998). A clear example was the joining of Time Inc. and Warner Communications in March 1989 to form Time Warner Inc. Under the terms of the agreement, there would be no cash purchase but rather an exchange of stock with an agreed-upon exchange ratio. The newly proposed

T A B L E 4.1 **The Transnational Media Corporation**

Companies	World Hdq.	Principal Business Operations
Bertelsmann AG	Germany	Book & record clubs, book publishing, magazines, music and film entertainment
Comcast	USA	Cable television systems operation, acquired AT&T Broadband, cable television programming
NBC Universal	USA	Television and film entertainment, cable programming, theme parks
News Corp. Ltd.	Australia/ USA	Newspapers, magazines, television and film entertainment, direct broadcast satellite
Sony	Japan	Consumer electronics, videogame consoles, and software, music and film entertainment
Time-Warner	USA	Cable, magazines, publishing, music and film entertainment, Internet service provision
Viacom	USA	Television and film entertainment, cable programming, broadcast television, publishing, videocassette and DVD rental & sale
Walt Disney	USA	Theme parks, film entertainment, broadcasting, cable programming, consumer merchandise

SOURCE: Company 10 K reports.

Time Warner Board of Directors would consist of 24 members with equal representation from both sides. Although technically Time was acquiring Warner Communication, attorney Arthur Liman wrote at the time:

> The merger is a true combination of two great companies. For either company to be looked upon as anything but an equal partner in this transaction would sap that company of its vitality and destroy the very benefits and synergy that the combination is intended to achieve. (Clurman, 1992: 189)

Acquisitions. By contrast, an *acquisition* involves the purchase of one company by another company for the purpose of adding (or enhancing) the acquiring firm's productive capacity. During an acquisition, one company acquires the operating assets of another company in exchange for cash, securities, or a combination of both. A clear example of an acquisition was Viacom's 1999 decision to purchase CBS for $37 billion. For Viacom, the purchase of CBS represented an opportunity to obtain a well-established television network as well as a company that owns Infinity Broadcasting, representing more than 1,600 U.S. radio stations. For its part, Viacom is home to several well-established cable network services, including MTV, Nickelodeon, and Showtime. The purchase of CBS was expected to provide a steady distribution outlet for Viacom programs and to offer numerous cross-licensing and marketing opportunities ("CBS," 1999).

TABLE 4.2   Mergers and Acquisitions: Media and Telecommunication Companies (2000–2005)

Mergers & Acquisitions	Description	Price	Time
Verizon and MCI	Verizon purchase long distance carrier MCI and expand both its local and long-distance telephone service.	$6.7 Bil.	2005
SBC and AT&T	SBC purchase long-distance carrier AT&T and expand both its local and long-distance telephone service.	$16.7 Bil.	2005
NewsCorp and DirecTV	NewsCorp paid Hughes Communication $6.1 billion in order to obtain the DirecTV satellite network.	$6.1 Bil.	2004
NBC and Universal	NBC acquired Universal Studios from Vivendi Inc. for $3.8 billion.	$3.8 Bil.	2004
Comcast and AT&T	Comcast acquired AT&T Broadband (cable) for $54 billion. The combined company is now the largest cable television operator in the United States.	$54 Bil.	2002
Vivendi S.A. and Seagrams (Universal and Polygram)	French media group Vivendi S.A. purchased Seagrams, which owns Universal Studios and Polygram Records, for $43.3 billion.	$43.3 Bil.	2001
America On-line and Time Warner	AOL acquired Time Warner Inc for $163 billion. This was the first combination of a major ISP with a traditional media company.	$163 Bil.	2001
Verizon Bell Atlantic and GTE	Bell Atlantic purchased independent telephone Company GTE for $52.8 billion. The combined company was later renamed Verizon.	$52.8 Bil.	2000
Viacom and CBS	Viacom purchased CBS Inc. for $37 billion. Viacom has major investments in cable programming and film production.	$37 Bil.	2000

SOURCES: R. Gershon; company reports.

Strategic Alliance.   A *strategic alliance* is a business relationship in which two or more companies work to achieve a collective advantage. The strategic alliance can vary in its approach and design, ranging from a simple licensing agreement to the actual combining of physical resources (Chan-Olmsted, 1998). A good example of a strategic alliance can be seen in the form of the Walt Disney Company's licensing agreement with Tokyo Disneyland in Japan, which is privately owned by the Oriental Land Company. The Walt Disney Company licenses the operation, provides marketing support, and collects royalties.

In sum, mergers, acquisitions and strategic alliances are the most direct ways for a company to expand and diversify into new product lines without having to undergo the problems associated with a new startup. Table 4.2 identifies the major mergers and acquisitions of media and telecommunication companies in the United States (both pending and complete) for the years 2000–2005.

When Mergers and Acquisitions Fail

Not all mergers and acquisitions are successful. As companies feel the pressures of increased competition, they embrace a somewhat faulty assumption that increased size makes for a better company. Yet, upon closer examination, it becomes clear that this is not always the case. Often, the combining of two major firms creates problems that no one could foresee. A failed merger or acquisition can be highly disruptive to both organizations in terms of lost revenue, capital debt, and a decrease in job performance. The inevitable result is the elimination of staff and operations, as well as the potential for bankruptcy. In addition, the effects on the support, or host, communities can be quite destructive (Wasserstein, 1998).

There are four reasons that help to explain why mergers and acquisitions can sometimes fail. They include the lack of a compelling strategic rationale, failure to perform due diligence, post-merger planning and integration failures, and financing and the problems of excessive debt.

The Lack of a Compelling Strategic Rationale. The decision to merge is sometimes not supported by a compelling strategic rationale. In the desire to be globally competitive, both companies go into the proposed merger with unrealistic expectations of complementary strengths and presumed synergies. More often than not, the very problems that prompted a merger consideration in the first place become further exacerbated once the deal is complete.

Failure to Perform Due Diligence. In the highly charged atmosphere of intense negotiations, the merging parties fail to perform due diligence prior to the merger agreement. The acquiring company only later discovers that the intended acquisition may not accomplish the desired objectives ("The Case against Mergers," 1995). Often the lack of due diligence results in the acquiring company paying too much for the acquisition.

Post–Merger Planning and Integration Failures. One of the most important reasons that mergers fail is bad post-merger planning and integration. If the proposed merger does not include an effective plan for combining divisions with similar products, the duplication can be a source of friction rather than synergy. Turf wars erupt, and reporting functions among managers become divisive. The problem becomes further complicated when there are significant differences in corporate culture.

Financing and the Problem of Excessive Debt. In order to finance the merger or acquisition, some companies will assume major amounts of debt through short-term loans. If or when performance does not meet expectations, such companies may be unable to meet their loan obligations. The said companies may be forced to sell off entire divisions in order to raise capital or, worse still, may default on their payment altogether. In the end, excessive debt can be highly destabilizing to the newly formed company.

MEDIA AND GLOBAL FINANCE

The business of media and telecommunications is an industry characterized by high startup costs and high risk. The decision to launch a direct broadcast satellite service or produce a new film is a high-risk venture with few guarantees. In order to obtain the necessary financing, today's media and telecommunication companies will either use their own money or seek the assistance of a financial lending institution. Researchers Ozanich and Wirth (1992) identify the importance of size and reputation of a TNC as the basis for being able to raise capital in a foreign market. The globalization of capital markets enables such companies to issue securities and obtain loans.

The Role of Global Capital Markets

What is a global capital market? What is its purpose? A global capital market brings together those companies and individuals who want to invest money and those who want to borrow it. For investors, the global capital market offers a much wider range of investment opportunities than can be found in purely domestic capital markets. For borrowers, the principal advantage of a global capital market is that it increases the supply of funds available for borrowing and decreases the cost of capital. If a company borrows strictly from a domestic capital market, the pool of investment sources is limited to one country. Moreover, the cost of borrowing money in a domestic market is often higher than in the international market.

Financial service groups serve as intermediaries between investors and borrowers. Such financial service groups include commercial banks (such as U.S. Bank, J.P. Morgan Chase, and Fleet Boston) and investment companies (such as Goldman Sachs, Credit Suisse Group, and Merrill Lynch). Commercial banks take the cash deposits from corporations and individual depositors and pay them a rate of interest in return. The banks, in turn, lend that money to borrowers at a higher rate of interest. The commercial banks make a profit based on the difference between the said interest rates. This difference is referred to as the interest rate spread. Investment companies bring investors and borrowers together and charge commissions for doing so. Investment companies are also portfolio managers, managing billions of dollars on behalf of mutual fund investors, pension funds, and insurance companies (Hill, 2000).

Capital Market Loans

Capital market loans are either equity loans or debt loans. An equity loan is made when a corporation sells stock to investors. A stock offering enables individual investors to purchase shares. A share of stock gives its holder a claim to a firm's profit stream. Investors purchase stock in anticipation of gains in the price of stock as well as possible dividends issued by the company. The money the corporation raises in return for its stock issuance can be used to purchase plants and equipment. Alternatively, debt financing requires the corporation to repay a predetermined portion of the loan amount (that is, principal + interest) at regular intervals for a specified period of time. Debt loans can be obtained from either cash loans made from a bank or funds raised through the sale of corporate bonds. In the latter case, the bondholder purchases the right to receive a specified number of payments over a set number of years until the bond maturity date.

Debt Financing

The TNMC, like any other company, needs to be able to invest in new product development as well as engage in potential mergers and acquisitions if and when it is deemed appropriate. To accomplish this, a company may finance the project venture by means of a debt loan, that is, borrowing money from various financial institutions. Banks, investment firms, and other financial institutions will loan money, using the borrowing firm's assets to secure the loan. If the firm's assets are not used as collateral, the lender may provide an unsecured loan at a higher interest rate. The length of the loan determines whether it is short-term, intermediate, or long-term debt. Short-term loans are used to meet immediate cash requirements, whereas long-term loans (5–10 years) are used to underwrite the cost of business operations and expansion.

The problem is that too much debt load can be highly destabilizing to an organization. The debt-driven deal can sometimes impose suffocating interest charges and repayment schedules on companies that were once financially stable. The borrower, in turn, is unable to withstand financial downturns in the marketplace, thus causing the value of their stock to decline significantly. In the worst-case scenario, excessive debt may force a company to default on its loans and seek Chapter 11 bankruptcy protection (Wasserstein, 1998).

Profiling News Corp. Ltd. Rupert Murdoch, CEO of News Corp. Ltd., was unique in his ability to structure debt and to obtain global financing. The Murdoch formula was to carefully build cash flow while borrowing aggressively. Throughout the early 1980s, Murdoch's excellent credit rating proved to be the essential ingredient to this formula. Each major purchase was expected to generate positive cash flow and thereby pay off what had been borrowed. Each successive purchase was expected to be bigger than the one before, thereby ensuring greater cash flow. In his desire to maintain control over his operations, Murdoch developed a special ability to manage debt at a higher level than most companies and organizations do (Gershon, 1997).

Throughout the 1980s, Murdoch's borrow-and-buy formula was bolstered by the fact that the market values of his media properties were growing faster than their underlying cash flows. The problem with News Corp.'s debt financing reached crisis proportions in 1991 when the company was carrying an estimated debt of $8.3 billion. The problem was compounded by the significant cash drains from the company's Fox Television and BSkyB DBS business operations (Shawcross, 1992). All this came at a time when the media industries (in general) were experiencing a worldwide economic recession. Murdoch was finally able to restructure the company's debt after several long and difficult meetings with some 146 investors. He was able to obtain the necessary financing but not before the divestment of some important assets and an agreement to significantly pare down the company's debt load. In summarizing Murdoch's business activities throughout the 1980s, *The Economist* (1990) wrote, "Nobody exploited the booming media industry in the late 1980's better than Mr. Rupert Murdoch's News Corporation—and few borrowed more money to do it" ("Murdoch's Kingdom," 1990, p. 62).

BUSINESS AND PLANNING STRATEGIES

As today's media and telecommunications companies continue to grow and expand, the challenges of staying globally competitive become increasingly more difficult. The main role of strategy is to plan for the future as well as to react to changes in the marketplace.

Strategic planning is the set of managerial decisions and actions that determine the long-term performance of a company or organization. Strategic planning presupposes the use of environmental scanning whose purpose is to monitor, evaluate, and disseminate information from both the internal and the external business environments to the key decision makers within the organization. Environmental scanning requires assessing the internal strengths and weaknesses of the organization as well as the external opportunities and threats to the organization. Researchers like Wheelen and Hunger (1998) suggest that the need for strategic planning is sometimes caused by triggering events. A triggering event can be caused by changes in the competitive marketplace, changes in the management structure of an organization, or changes associated with internal performance and operations.

Understanding Core Competency

The principle of core competency suggests that a highly successful company is one that possesses a specialized production process, brand recognition, or ownership of talent that enables it to achieve higher revenues and market dominance relative to its competitors. A good example of core competency can be seen with Cisco Systems, which specializes in the design and installation of Internet routers. Today, more than 80 percent of the world's Internet routers are made by Cisco Systems (Mr. Internet, 1999, p. 129). Core competency can be measured in many ways, including brand identity (Disney, ESPN, CNN), technological leadership (Cisco, Intel, Microsoft), superior research and development (Sony, Philips), and customer service (Dell, Gateway, Amazon.com). In sum, a company's core competency is something the organization does especially well in comparison with its competitors (Daft, 1997, p. 249).

Vertical Integration (and Cross Media Ownership)

A major corporation can strategically plan for its future in several ways. One common growth strategy is vertical integration, whereby, a company will control most or all of its operational phases. In principle, the TNMC can control an idea from its appearance in a book or magazine to its debut in domestic and foreign movie theaters as well as later distribution via cable, satellite, or DVD. The rationale is that vertical integration will allow a large-sized company to be more efficient and creative by promoting combined synergies among its various operating divisions.

To that end, many of today's TNMCs engage in cross-media ownership, that is, owning a combination of news, entertainment, and enhanced information services. Cross-media ownership allows for a variety of efficiencies:

1. Cross licensing and marketing opportunities between company-owned media properties.

2. Sharing of newsgathering, printing, and distribution facilities among company-owned media properties.

3. Negotiating licensing and sales agreements across different media platforms.

4. Offering clients package discounts in advertising that cut across different media platforms. TNMCs like Time Warner, Viacom, and News Corp. routinely offer clients package discounts.

Profiling Time Warner, Inc.   The company once known as Time Inc. has been a party to three major business combinations since 1989. In July of that year, Time Inc. and Warner Communications completed a corporate merger that made it the largest media company in the world. The Time–Warner merger was conceived as a global strategy that would enable the company to compete head-to-head with the world's leading media companies. At the time, company strategists believed that by the year 2000 there would be an international oligopoly of six or seven transnational media corporations (Saporito, 1989).

Both companies were highly complementary in their assets. Time Inc. brought to the merger agreement such notable magazines as *Time, Life, People, Fortune, Money,* and *Sports Illustrated.* In 1988, the magazine group was the largest magazine publisher in the United States. In addition, Time Inc. was America's leading pay-television programmer, with Home Box Office (HBO) and Cinemax. The company also owned America's second-largest cable multiple system operator (MSO), Time Warner Cable.

Warner Communications brought to the merger agreement a major presence in television/film studio production, including Warner Brothers Studios (one of Hollywood's top three studios) and Lorimar Television Entertainment (a leading producer of television programs). In addition, Warner Brothers Studios was a key supplier of programming to the cable industry, including Time's very own HBO and Cinemax cable services. In the area of music entertainment, Warner Communications had a strong presence as well, including Warner Brothers Records, Atlantic Records, and Electra Entertainment (Clurman, 1992).

For several years, Time Inc. had wanted to acquire CNN. The opportunity presented itself in September 1995 when the newly created Time Warner Inc. acquired Turner Broadcasting Systems in a stock swap valued at $8 billion ("It's TBS Time," 1995). The rationale behind the purchase of Turner Broadcasting was to combine the news and programming assets of Turner Broadcasting with the highly complementary assets of Time Warner. According to Time Warner president and CEO Jerry Levin, "The complementary nature of the two organizations will allow us to maximize the value of our assets and distribution

T A B L E 4.3 Time Warner Inc. Media & Telecommunication Products
and Services

ENTERTAINMENT

Time Warner	**Turner Broadcasting**
Warner Brothers (film, television, music)	TBS Turner Network Television (TNT)
Home Box Office (Cinemax, HBO international services)	Castle Rock Entertainment Cartoon Network
Time Warner Cable (cable operating system)	New Line Cinema Hanna-Barbera Cartoons Atlanta Braves Baseball Atlanta Hawks Basketball

NEWS AND INFORMATION

Magazines (*Time, People, Sports Illustrated, Fortune,* 30+ magazines)	Cable News Network (CNN *Headline News,* international services)

INTERNET

America Online (Internet service provision)

SOURCE: From Time Warner Inc.

systems and position us as the leading media company in an increasingly competitive global marketplace" (Time Warner, 1995).

In January 2000, America Online (AOL), the largest Internet service provider in the United States, announced that it would purchase Time Warner Inc. for an estimated $163 billion. The deal was unique, given that AOL, with one fifth of the revenue and 15 percent of the workforce of Time Warner, was planning to purchase the largest TNMC in the world. Such was the nature of Internet economics, which allowed Wall Street to assign a monetary value to AOL well in excess of its actual value. AOL was valued higher than such companies as Walt Disney and even Time Warner itself.

At the time of the original announcement, however, AOL president Steve Case recognized that his company was ultimately in a vulnerable position. It was only a matter of time before Wall Street would come to realize that AOL was an overvalued company. AOL did not have any recognizable brand content to speak of, nor did the company have any major deals with cable companies for delivery. Instead, it was dependent on local telephone lines and satellite delivery. Time Warner represented an opportunity to partner with some of the most highly recognized media brands in the world. It was promoted as the marriage between old media and new media. The combination of AOL and Time Warner Inc. would take the philosophy of cross-media ownership to a whole new level in terms of strategic planning and operations (see Table 4.3).

The Federal Communications Commission gave its approval for AOL to acquire Time Warner Inc. in January 2001. In the end, the combining of

AOL and Time Warner may well be remembered as one of the worst mergers in U.S. corporate history. The first signs of trouble occurred in the aftermath of the so-called "dotcom crash," beginning in March 2000. AOL, like most other Internet stocks, took an immediate hit. AOL's ad sales experienced a free fall and subscriber rates flattened out. By 2002, AOL Time Warner stock was down 70 percent ("AOL, You've Got Misery," 2002). In the weeks and months that followed, the economic downturn and subsequent loss of advertising had a strong negative impact on AOL's core business. The once-hoped-for synergies did not materialize, leaving the company with an unwieldy structure and bitter corporate infighting.

The AOL Time Warner merger suffered from a faulty strategic rationale as well as post-merger integration failures. In January 2003, AOL Time Warner reported a $99 billion loss from the previous year, making it the highest recorded loss in U.S. corporate history. Perhaps the most symbolic aspect of AOL Time Warner as a failed business strategy was the decision in September 2003 by the company's board of directors to change the name AOL Time Warner back to its original form, Time Warner Inc.

Broadband Communication

The clear lines and historic boundaries that once separated media and telecommunications are becoming less distinct. The result is a convergence of modes whereby technologies and services are becoming more fully integrated. The main driving force behind convergence is the digitalization of media and information technology. It increases the potential for the manipulation and transformation of data. The term *broadband communication* is used to describe the ability to distribute multichannel information and entertainment services to the home. Broadband also connotes high-speed Internet access.

A second important strategy for the future is the ability to own both software content and the means of distribution to the home. The goal for both cable operators and local exchange carriers is to offer consumers a whole host of software products via an electronic supermarket to the home. Both the cable and telephone industries are capable of delivering broadband services, albeit in different ways. The cable industry understands the business of delivering video communication and high-speed Internet access using coaxial cable and a cable modem. In contrast, the telephone industry understands the business of switching and routing voice traffic and high speed Internet using a blend of fiber optic delivery, traditional telephone lines, and DSL.

Several of the major telephone companies, most notably Verizon and SBC, have committed themselves to rolling out fiber optic cable that would greatly increase speed and throughput to the home. Increasingly, more and more companies will rely on Voice-Over Internet Protocol (VOIP), or Internet telephony, as the basis for the switching and routing of voice and video communication. The future of tomorrow's so-called "smart homes" will allow for the full integration of voice, data, and video service, and give new meaning to the term "programming."

TRANSNATIONAL MEDIA AND
THE MARKETPLACE OF IDEAS

The combination of deregulation and privatization has transformed the conduct of international business. The TNMC of the 21st century is looking to position itself as a full-service provider of media and telecommunications products and services. Through a process of FDI, the TNMC actively promotes the use of traditional and advanced media technology. Such efforts have ignited the transborder flow of media products worldwide. The resulting globalization of media activity has forced governments and policy makers alike to consider the long-term implications. The concluding section of this chapter considers the issue of economic concentration and the marketplace of ideas.

Transnational Media and Economic Consolidation

In all areas of media and telecommunications, there has been a clear movement toward economic concentration. The increase in group and cross-media ownership is the direct result of TNMCs looking for ways to increase market share and promote greater internal efficiencies. The term *economic concentration* is used to describe the number of sellers within a given market. A market is said to be highly concentrated if it is dominated by a limited number of firms (Albarran & Miszerjewksi, 2004). The fewer the number of product manufacturers or service providers, the higher the degree of concentration within a given market. This, in turn, can affect the degree of rivalry between competing firms in terms of product quality, diversity, and cost. Moreover, highly concentrated markets exhibit strong barriers to entry for new competitors.

As Albarran and Miszerjewksi (2004) point out, there are two ways to examine the problem of media concentration. The first way is to look at media concentration in terms of single-industry concentration. How much does a single company dominate a specific area of media and telecommunications? Two examples of this can be seen with respect to desktop business software and direct broadcast satellites. Microsoft dominates the field of computer software and is responsible for over 80 percent of the world's PC desktop software. Similarly, News Corporation Ltd. is highly dominant in the area of direct broadcast satellites (British Sky Broadcasting, Star TV, Direct TV, etc.). The company controls over 70 percent of the world's market share in satellite-to-home delivery.

The second way to look at economic concentration is in terms of cross-media ownership. How much does a single company control (or influence) multiple areas of media products and telecommunication services? A TNMC like Viacom Inc. is a highly diverse media company that exhibits a strong market presence in a wide variety of areas, including broadcast television (CBS and UPN), cable television programming (MTV, Nickelodeon, BET, etc.), film production (Paramount), and radio (Infinity Broadcasting).

The Deregulation Paradox

In principle, deregulation is supposed to foster competition and thereby open markets to new service providers. The problem, however, is that complete and unfettered deregulation can sometimes create the very problem it was meant to solve—namely, a lack of competition. Instead of fostering an open marketplace of new players and competitors, too much consolidation leads to fewer players and hence less competition (Demers, 1999; Gershon, 1997; Mosco, 1990). Researchers like Mosco (1990) call it the "mythology of telecommunications deregulation." Other writers, such as Demers (1999), refer to it as the "great paradox of capitalism." I simply call it the deregulation paradox. As Demers (2000) points out,

> The history of most industries in so-called free market economies is the history of the growth of oligopolies, where a few large companies eventually come to dominate. The first examples occurred during the late 1800s in the oil, steel and railroad industries ... Antitrust laws eventually were used to break up many of these companies but oligopolistic tendencies continue in these and other industries. (p. 1)

The communications industry is no exception. One clear example can be seen in the field of radio communication in the United States. Since the passage of the Telecommunications Act of 1996, Clear Channel Communication owns in excess of 1,100 radio stations in the United States, representing some 60 percent of all U.S. radio stations.

Do all such companies exhibit the classic forms of anticompetitive behavior? Do they contribute to a decline in the marketplace of ideas? Not exactly. It would be more accurate to say that most of today's better-known media and telecommunication companies are market leaders in select areas of communication and information technology with a strong tendency toward oligopolies. This can be seen in Table 4.4, which examines the top U.S. cable television programmers and film production companies for the year 2004.

The Marketplace of Ideas

Numerous writers, including Bagdikian (1990), McChesney (1997, 2004), and Schiller (1990) argue that a small set of dominant media corporations exercises a disproportionate effect over the marketplace of ideas. According to author Ben Bagdikian, in his seminal work, the *Media Monopoly* (1990), the major issue is one of influence.

> Market dominant corporations in the mass media have dominant influence over the public's news, information, public ideas, popular culture, and political attitudes. The same corporations exert considerable influence within government precisely because they influence their audiences' perceptions of public life, including perceptions of politics and politicians as they appear—or do not appear—in the media. (pp. 4–5)

TABLE 4.4 A Comparison of Transnational Media Ownership in Cable and Film Production—2004

Top 15 Cable Network Services (by Subscribers)	Top 7 Film Production Companies (by Revenue)
■ Time Warner Inc. (TBS)	■ News Corp. Ltd. (20th Century Fox)
■ Walt Disney Co. (ESPN)	■ Viacom Inc. (Paramount Pictures)
■ (C-SPAN)	■ Sony Corporation (Columbia TriStar)
■ (Discovery Channel)	■ Walt Disney Co. (Walt Disney Pictures)
■ (USA Network)	■ Sony Corporation (MGM)
■ Time Warner Inc. (CNN)	■ NBC Universal (Universal Studios)
■ Time Warner Inc. (TNT)	■ Time Warner Inc. (Warner Brothers)
■ Walt Disney Co. (Lifetime Television)	
■ Viacom Inc. (Nickelodeon)	
■ Walt Disney Co. (A&E Network)	
■ Time Warner Inc. (Spike TV)	
■ (The Weather Channel)	
■ Viacom Inc. (MTV)	
■ QVC	
■ Walt Disney Co. (ABC Family)	

SOURCES: NCTA, MPAA.

Implicit in such arguments is that the TNMC should be treated differently from other TNCs because of its unique ability to influence public opinion. Corporate size is presumed to limit the diversity and availability of new media products and ideas, in favor of promoting some kind of corporate agenda. As McChesney (1997) argues,

> A specter now haunts the world; a global commercial media system dominated by a small number of super-powerful, mostly U.S. based transnational media corporations. It is a system that works to advance the cause of the global market and promote commercial values, while denigrating journalism and culture not conducive to the immediate bottom line or long run corporate interests. (p. 11)

Various writers reject many of the traditional arguments associated with economic concentration (de Sola Poole, 1983; Compaine, 1985; Friedman, 1999; Compaine & Gomery, 2000). Compaine and Gomery (2000) argue that media diversity does not necessarily translate into higher quality of content.

If the proliferation of television, books, and websites reveals anything, it is that greater diversity means just that: more low-brow shows, trash journalism, and pandering politics to go along with opportunities for finding more thoughtful and quality outlets for analysis, entertainment, and information. Diversity cuts all ways (p. 578).

Many of the same writers would further argue that advancements in new media technologies (including converging media formats and multiple distribution channels) preclude the possibility of a few dominant media companies controlling the marketplace of ideas.

Global Competition and the Diffusion of Authority

What are the real problems that face the TNMC in the years ahead? The answer to this question is not unique to the TNMC. Rather, the problems have to do with all companies that operate in an increasingly deregulated and privatized world of business. Global competition has engendered a new competitive spirit that cuts across nationalities and borders. A new form of economic Darwinism abounds, characterized by a belief that size and complementary strengths are crucial to business survival. The relentless pursuit of profits (and the fear of failure) has made companies around the world ferocious in their attempts to right-size, reorganize, and reengineer their business operations. No company, large or small, remains unaffected by the intense drive to increase profits and decrease costs. The challenges and difficulties faced by today's media and telecommunications companies call into question some basic assumptions regarding deregulation and the principle of self-regulation. Deregulated markets do many things well. But they are not effective at policing themselves.

In the aftermath of the Enron and WorldCom debacles, researchers, policy analysts, and government officials are recognizing the need to take a new activism in monitoring the actions of wayward corporations. At issue are the excesses of senior level executives who pursue personal enrichment schemes and cash out millions in stock options while employees lose their jobs and life savings. A second problem has to do with what Cohan (2002) describes as a "diffusion of authority" situation, where neither company nor person is fully aware of or takes responsibility for the actions of senior management.

The real issue is not the size or number of today's TNMCs. Rather, it has to do with business priorities where the pursuit of profits can sometimes promote egregious forms of media violence and lower the standards of quality journalism. In the area of journalism, the issue plays out in the crossing of the line between serious journalism and entertainment. Former CBS news anchor Walter Cronkite (1996) states the problem unequivocally:

> Will the journalism center hold in the changed economic environment of the future? In the last decade the networks have cut back news budgets while supporting the emergence of tabloid news shows, travesties of genuine news presentations. They bear the same relationship to the network news broadcasts as the *Enquirer* does to the *New York Times*. (p. 375)

What distinguishes the TNMC from other TNCs is that the principle commodity being sold is information and entertainment. It is a business mission that requires a greater degree of responsibility, given the media's unique power to inform, persuade, and entertain. What is clear, however, is that the pursuit of profits and organizational efficiency can sometimes blind senior management from exercising critical judgment when it comes to message content. A TNMC without a core business ethic is simply an organizational machine producing highly efficient products without considering its potential effect on domestic and international audiences.

TNMCs and Nation–States

The problems cited become all the more complex at the international level. The TNMC possesses a level of power and influence that is second only to nation–states. Through a process of FDI, the TNMC actively promotes the use of advanced media and information technology. As a result, the geopolitical and cultural walls that once separated the nations of the earth are no longer sustainable. The globalization of media activity continues to pose a unique dilemma for many of today's host nations. On the one hand are the clear benefits of international free trade and the specific advantages that a TNMC offers, including jobs, investment capital, technology resources, and tax revenue. On the other hand are the problems associated with media imports, including cultural trespass, challenges to political sovereignty, and privacy invasion.

In the end, the goals of profitability and political sovereignty should not be considered mutually exclusive, but they do require a level of mutual cooperation and respect between the TNMC and the host nation. Host nations have a right and a responsibility to exercise appropriate controls when corporate behavior (or product quality) is deemed harmful or hazardous. Such rules, however, should be consistent and uniformly applied to all commercial traders. The decision to impose regulatory barriers to entry cannot be justified due to a company's size or scale of operation. Both the host nation and the TNMC have a shared responsibility to create a system of globalization that is both desirable and sustainable.

For more information on the topics that appear in this chapter, use the password that came free with this book to access InfoTrac College Edition. Use the following words as keyterms and subject searches: transnational media, media mergers, media acquisitions, media corporations, media ownership, telecommunication, media synergy, cross-media ownership, media industry, old media, new media, global capital market, media economy.

QUESTIONS FOR DISCUSSION

1. Why does a company engage in foreign direct investment? What are some of the risks associated with FDI, for the company as well as for the host nation?

2. Why do media and telecommunications companies engage in a mergers or acquisitions strategy? What are some of the reasons and more notable examples for doing so? Why does a mergers or acquisitions strategy sometimes fail?

3. As today's media and telecommunications companies continue to grow and expand, the challenges of staying globally competitive become increasingly

more difficult. What does strategic planning mean? What are some of the more common strategies employed by today's TNMCs?

4. Do today's TNMCs control the marketplace of ideas? Consider the arguments from both a social and an economic standpoint.

5. In looking to the future, what are some of the responsibilities and obligations of today's TNMC in dealing with the general public and host nations?

REFERENCES

Albarran, A., & Chan-Olmsted, S. (Eds.). (1998). *Global media economics*. Ames: Iowa State University Press.

Albarran, A., & Miszerjewksi, B. (2004, May 12). Media concentration in the U.S. and European Union: A comparative analysis. Paper presented at the 6th World Media Economics Conference, Montreal, Canada.

AOL, you've got misery. (2002, April 8). *Business Week*, pp. 58–59.

Bagdikian, B. (1990). *The media monopoly* (3rd ed.). Boston: Beacon Press.

Ball, D., & McCulloch, W. H. (1996). *International business: The challenge of global competition* (6th ed.). Chicago: Irwin.

Bennis, W. (1986). Leaders and visions: Orchestrating the corporate culture. New York: Conference Board.

Bertelsmann AG. (1993). *Bertelsmann: A world of experience* (press release). New York.

Bertelsmann AG. (1998). Annual report, 1998. Retrieved April 10, 2002, from http://www.bertelsmann.de/english/geschber98/woessnerhtml

The case against mergers. (1995, October 30). *Business Week,* pp. 122–126.

Cate, F. (1990). The European broadcasting directive. *Communications Committee Monograph Series*. Washington, DC: American Bar Association.

CBS. (1999, April 5). *Business Week,* pp. 75–82.

Chan-Olmsted, S. (1998). The strategic alliances of broadcasting, cable television, and telephone services. *Journal of Media Economics, 11*(3), 33–46.

Cohan, J. (2002). I didn't know and I was only doing my job: Has corporate governance careened out of control? A Case study of Enron's information myopia. *Journal of Business Ethics, 40,* 275–299.

Clurman, R. (1992). *To the end of time*. New York: Simon & Schuster.

Compaine, B. (1985). The expanding base of media competition. *Journal of Communication. 35*(3).

Compaine, B., & Gomery, D. (2000). *Who owns the media?* (3rd ed.). Mahwah, NJ: Lawrence Erlbaum Associates.

Cronkite, W. (1996). *A reporter's life*. New York: Alfred A. Knopf.

Daft, R. (1997). *Management* (4th ed.). New York: Harcourt Brace.

Demers, D. (1999). *Global media: Menace or messiah?* Cresskill, NJ: Hampton Press.

Demers, D. (2000, Winter). Global media news. *GMN Newsletter, 2*(1), 1.

Dymsza, W. (1984, Winter). Trends in multinational business and global environments: A perspective. *Journal of International Business Studies*, pp. 25–45.

Friedman, T. (1999). *The Lexus and the olive tree.* New York: Farrar, Straus & Giroux.

Gershon, R. A. (1993). International deregulation and the rise of transnational media corporations. *Journal of Media Economics, 6*(2), 3–22.

Gershon, R. A. (1997). *The transnational media corporation: Global messages and free market competition.* Mahwah, NJ: Lawrence Erlbaum Associates.

Gershon, R. A. (2000). The transnational media corporation: Environmental scanning and strategy formulation. *Journal of Media Economics, 13*(2), 81–101.

Grosse, R., & Kujawa, D. (1988). *International business: Theory and application.* Homewood, IL: Irwin.

Herman, E., & McChesney, R. (1997). *The global media: The new missionaries of corporate capitalism.* London: Cassell.

Hill, C. W. (2000). *International business: Competing in the global marketplace* (3rd ed.). New York: McGraw-Hill.

It's TBS time. (1995, September 25). *Broadcasting and Cable,* pp. 8–10.

Kevin, D. (2003). *Europe in the media.* Mahwah, NJ: Lawrence Erlbaum Associates.

Litman, B. (1998). *The motion picture industry.* Boston: Allyn and Bacon.

McChesney, R. (1997, November/December). The global media giants: The nine firms that dominate the world. *Extra, 10*(6).

McChesney, R. W. (2004). *The problem of the media: US communication politics in the 21st century.* New York: Monthly Review.

Mr. Internet. (1999, September 13). *Business Week,* p. 129.

Morley, D., & Shockley-Zalabak, P. (1991). Setting the rules: An examination of the influence of organizational founders' values. *Management Communication Quarterly, 4,* 422–449.

Morita, A., Shimomura, M., & Reingold, E. (1986). *Made in Japan.* New York: E. P. Dutton.

Mosco, V. (1990, Winter). The mythology of telecommunications deregulation. *Journal of Communication, 40*(1), 36–49.

Murdoch's kingdom. (1990, August 18). *The Economist,* p. 62.

Nathan, J. (1999). *Sony: The private life.* Boston: Houghton Mifflin.

The new economy. (2000, January 31). *Business Week,* pp. 74–92.

Ozanich, G., & Wirth, M. (1992, April 12). *Trends in globalization: Direct foreign investments in media companies 1985–1991.* Paper presented at the 37th Annual Broadcast Education Association Conference, Las Vegas, NV.

Ozanich, G., & Wirth, M. (1998). Mergers and acquisitions: A communications industry overview. In A. Alexander, R. Carveth, & J. Owers (Eds.), *Media economics* (2nd ed.). Mahwah, NJ: Lawrence Erlbaum Associates.

Poole, I. S. (1983). *Technologies of freedom.* Cambridge, MA: Belknap Press.

Rebuilding the banks. (1999, September 6). *Business Week,* pp. 48–49.

Robock, S., & Simmonds, K. (1989). *International business and multinational enterprises* (4th ed.). Homewood, IL: Irwin.

Saporito, B. (1989, November 20). The inside story of Time Warner. *Fortune,* pp. 170–183.

Schiller, H. (1990). The global commercialization of culture. *Directions PCDS, 4,* 1–4.

Shakeup at Sony puts westerner in leader's role. (2005, March 7). Retrieved March 7, 2005, from http://www.nytimes.com/2005/03/07/business/worldbusiness/07sony.html?pagewanted=2&th

Shawcross, W. (1992). *Murdoch*. New York: Simon & Schuster.

There's no business like show business. (1998, June 22). *Fortune*, pp. 92–104.

Time Warner Inc. (1995). *Time Warner Inc. and Turner Broadcasting System Inc. agree to merge* (press release). New York.

Wasserstein, B. (1998). *Big deal: The battle for control of America's leading corporations*. New York: Warner Books.

Wheelen, T., & Hunger, D. (1998). *Strategic management and business policy*. Reading, MA: Addison Wesley Longman.

5

Global Communication Law

JOHN L. HUFFMAN, DENISE M. TRAUTH, AND JAN H. SAMORISKI

John L. Huffman (PhD, University of Iowa) is Professor Emeritus of Communication Studies at the University of North Carolina at Charlotte and Professor Emeritus of Mass Communication at Bowling Green State University. He is one of the founders of the Communication Law and Policy Division of the International Communication Association.

Denise M. Trauth (PhD, University of Iowa) is the president of Texas State University in San Marcos, Texas. She is the former provost and vice chancellor for academic affairs at the University of North Carolina at Charlotte. She also served as dean of the graduate school and Professor of Communication Studies at UNC Charlotte.

Jan H. Samoriski (PhD, Bowling Green State University) is Associate Professor of Communications at The University of Michigan–Dearborn and former Director of the Communications Program. He is author of a text on cyberspace law, *Issues in Cyberspace: Communication, Technology, Law and Society on the Internet Frontier.* Samoriski's research interests include the Internet, new media technology, and telecommunications law and policy.

The study of communication law and policy has, in large measure, traditionally been nation-specific except in those areas where particular technologies or common goals mandated a degree of international cooperation. Thus, freedom of speech and freedom of the press, prior restraint and censorship, libel and

For additional online resources, access the Global Media Monitor website that accompanies this book on the Wadsworth Communication Cafe website at http://communication.wadsworth.com.

slander, the right to privacy, free press–fair trial conflicts, freedom of information, obscenity, and advertising regulation were studied in the context of a particular nation. A global approach to the implementation of international law and policy administered by an agency such as the International Telecommunication Union (ITU) was reserved for areas such as broadcasting. Radio and television signals, freely crossing international boundaries, had the potential to interfere with one another and destroy any utility the medium might have; they also had the potential to carry political and social messages that affected countries might object to. A global approach has also been embraced when mutual cooperation furthered social goals such as the protection of intellectual property rights—patents, trademarks, and copyrights—under the Berne Convention, the Universal Copyright Convention (UCC), the General Agreement on Tariffs and Trade (GATT), and World Intellectual Property Organization (WIPO).

However, Marshall McLuhan's global village is inexorably, if somewhat belatedly, becoming more of a reality, and the unforeseen catalytic medium is the computer tied to the Internet. Suddenly, all of the aforementioned nation-specific areas of communication law and policy are going to have global dimensions as the Internet continues at breakneck speed to interconnect the planet and make gratuitous the physical boundaries formerly used by nation–states to control communication.

This chapter will address the following issues:

- The traditional role of freedom of expression in Western democracies
- International and national limitations on freedom of expression
- Censorship and national security
- Censorship for moral and religious reasons
- Existing international regulatory and policymaking bodies and their roles
- The Internet and its impact on global communication law

THE TRADITIONAL ROLE OF FREEDOM OF EXPRESSION

Conditions Accompanying Freedom

The term *freedom of expression* was made coherent and given substance by Yale law professor Thomas I. Emerson in his seminal work, *The System of Freedom of Expression,* published in 1970. Emerson saw freedom of expression in a modern democratic society as a set of rights. Among these were the right of citizens to think and believe whatever they wanted and the right to communicate those thoughts and beliefs in any medium. Also residing in freedom of expression was a right to remain silent, a right to hear others and enjoy access to information, and a right to assemble with others for purposes of joint expression. More recent legal commentators embrace the same litany of rights constituting freedom of expression.

According to Rodney A. Smolla (1992), a nation committed to an open culture will defend human expression and conscience in all its wonderful variety, protecting freedom of speech, freedom of the press, freedom of religion, freedom of association, freedom of assembly, and freedom of peaceful mass protest. These freedoms will be extended not only to political discourse but also to the infinite range of artistic, scientific, religious, and philosophical inquiries that capture and cajole the human imagination. Freedom of expression is assigned a primacy among social values in a modern democratic society. It is considered a foundational value, a core underpinning in such a society. Its importance stems from four resultant conditions that are essential to a true democracy and that are present in a society only when freedom of expression is present.

The first of these four resultant conditions is human dignity and self-fulfillment. U.S. Supreme Court Justice Thurgood Marshall spoke of the human spirit as "a spirit that demands self-expression" (*Procunier v. Martinez,* 1974, p. 427). Freedom to express one's self without externally imposed restraints leads to self-realization and self-identity, to growth and development as a human being. Without that freedom, individual evolution is stunted. It would be "an insult to the humanity of a mature adult that others (particularly the state) should presume to determine for him what expressions he will hear or see in forming his own conception of what is worthy in his life" (Murphy, 1997, p. 557). Self-fulfillment through free expression is, in a Lockean sense, a natural, intrinsic, and inalienable right that we are endowed with at birth.

The second of the four conditions that emanate from freedom of expression and are vital to a democratic society is a progression toward truth through an unfettered "marketplace of ideas." U.S. Supreme Court Justice Oliver Wendell Holmes argued that "the best test of truth is the power of the thought to get itself accepted in the competition of the market" (*Abrams v. United States,* 1919, p. 630).

Rational human beings, given time, will reject that which is false and embrace that which is true. They can do so, however, only if truth is present in the marketplace; censorship poses the grave risk of removing truth as an alternative in the marketplace.

An oft-quoted passage that English author John Milton wrote in 1644, in an essay entitled "Areopagitica," captures well the essential need for a marketplace of ideas:

> And though all the windes of doctrine were let loose to play upon the earth, so Truth be in the field, we do injuriously by licencing and prohibiting to misdoubt her strength. Let her and Falshood grapple; who ever knew truth put to the worse in a free and open encounter. (pp. 681–682)

The third of the four conditions that accompany freedom of expression and are essential to the operation of a modern democracy is the provision of the instrument, or means, of democratic decision making. In a democracy, the majority is charged with making the state's political decisions. Citizens must gather and analyze information and ideas in order to arrive at and render a reasoned judgment. The vehicle for this process is, obviously, their freedom of expression. "Freedom to think as you will and to speak as you think are means indispensable to the discovery and spread of political truth" (*Whitney v. California*, 1927, p. 375).

Likewise, decisions that are made outside of the political realm in a democratic society—decisions about art, culture, music, science, and all conceivable areas of human endeavor—are enabled by freedom of expression. Without this freedom, democratic decision making is an oxymoron.

The fourth condition that is produced by freedom of expression is one in which conflict can take place without any necessary recourse to violence. As Emerson (1970) points out, suppression of expression denies the opportunity for rational discussion and reasoned judgment, and leaves violence as a plausible alternative for those who passionately wish to change circumstances or develop new ideas. Expression can act, then, as a safety valve in a modern democracy. U.S. Supreme Court Justice Louis Brandeis saw this function of freedom of expression as one that motivated the framers of the U.S. Constitution:

> [They] knew that order cannot be secured merely through fear of punishment for its infraction; that it is hazardous to discourage thought, hope and imagination; that fear breeds repression; that repression breeds hate; that hate menaces stable government; that the path of safety lies in the opportunity to discuss freely supposed grievances and proposed remedies; and that the fitting remedy for evil counsels is good ones. (*Whitney v. California*, 1927, p. 375)

These four resultant conditions springing from freedom of expression thus provide the rationale underlying the paramount position of this freedom in a democratic society. Not all democratic societies value the conditions in the same manner or assign the same priorities to them as justifications for freedom of expression.

In the United States, the U.S. Supreme Court has relied most heavily on the "marketplace of ideas" function in its 20th-century decisions supporting freedom of expression (Hall, 1992). Uyttendaele and Dumortier (1998) note that the Council of Europe, on the other hand, has explicitly recognized the function of democratic decision making as the primary rationale underlying freedom of expression, and they argue that Europe has generally rejected both the marketplace of ideas rationale and the natural rights rationale. Regardless of the relative valuing of the four rationales by Western democracies, it should be apparent that, taken together, they represent a cogent argument for the presence of freedom of expression as a primary prerequisite for the existence of a truly democratic state.

INTERNATIONAL AND NATIONAL LIMITATIONS
ON FREEDOM OF EXPRESSION

The United States

Although freedom of expression is a foundational value in a modern democracy, other societal values *at specific times and in specific circumstances* are equally important or of greater importance to democratic nation–states. National security is a societal value that is embraced by all nation–states. Likewise, protection of citizens' physical well-being and protection of property are universally important societal values. Even those democracies that most strongly champion freedom of expression will draw the line at expression that clearly puts the nation–state at risk or imminently endangers the life of its citizens or puts their private or commonly held property at jeopardy. Absolute freedom of expression is nonexistent; no nation–state is willing to allow highly classified national security materials to be passed without penalty to an enemy, nor to allow a conspiracy to murder a group of innocent citizens, nor to allow a leader at a demonstration to urge the burning of nearby buildings. Instead, lines are drawn by democratic governments: A citizen's speech is protected up to a particular point, but after that point, the citizen's speech can be suppressed or punished if it does occur.

Modern democracies differ as to both the critical societal values that must be balanced against freedom of expression and the formulas that are to be used in the balancing process. In the United States, where polls show that the citizens believe they have too much freedom of expression ("Survey Finds," 1999), the modern Supreme Court has fashioned legal principles that balance the scales strongly in favor of freedom of expression in its conflicts with numerous social values. Thus, offensive, vulgar, uncivil, and indecent expression is protected. Even so-called hate speech and hate symbols such as swastikas and Ku Klux Klan robes are protected.

As a general rule, expression in the United States can be penalized only when it causes the following: (1) real injuries to individuals or property; (2) real injuries to social relationships that have traditionally been defined as important to society, such as the destruction of one's reputation [libel or slander]; (3) real injuries to business operations or business relationships, such as fraud or false advertising; (4) real injuries to confidentiality, both personal (invasion of one's privacy) or national (release of vital security information); and (5) real injuries to private and corporate ownership of intellectual property (copyright, trademark, appropriation).

An exception to this general rule in the United States is the area of obscenity, which, while arguably causing no tangible or assessable harm, is nonetheless subject to legal sanctions by both the federal government and the individual states.

Punishment for expression that causes these real injuries usually occurs in the United States *after* the expression has taken place; prior restraint or classic censorship of expression has been constitutionally disfavored by the U.S. Supreme Court, which has said, "Any system of prior restraints of expression comes to this Court bearing a heavy presumption against its constitutional validity" (*Bantam Books, Inc. v. Sullivan*, 1963, p. 70). In order to justify any blocking of expression before it takes place, the government must usually prove that the projected injury done by the expression will be direct, immediate, and substantial, which is, at least in the majority of cases, an impossible task. Finally, expression in the United States can usually be penalized only when the definition of injurious speech is specific and understandable so that speakers are forewarned.

Thus, the United States allows much expression that is punished or banned in some modern democracies. Emotional or intellectual responses to expression by either the majority of society or minorities within society provide no legal grounds for punishment of that expression. Expression that engenders emotional distress or disgust; expression that causes embarrassment; expression that might be perceived as insulting, blasphemous, sexist, racist, vulgar, or indecent—all are protected and tolerated as free speech in American society.

International Covenants

"The right of free speech stands as a general norm of customary international law," according to legal scholar Thomas David Jones (1998, p. 37). Indeed, provisions in all of the major international human rights instruments list freedom of expression as a fundamental human right. This is true of the Universal Declaration of Human Rights (1948), the European Convention for the Protection of Human Rights and Fundamental Freedoms (1953), the International Convention on the Elimination of All Forms of Racial Discrimination (1969), the International Covenant on Civil and Political Rights (1976), the American Convention on Human Rights (1978), and the Banjul Charter of Human and Peoples' Rights (1982).

All of these instruments defend freedom of expression in language similar to that used in the Universal Declaration of Human Rights: "Everyone has the right to freedom of opinion and expression; this right includes freedom to hold opinions without interference and to seek, receive, and impart information and ideas through any media and regardless of frontiers" (p. 71). At the same time, these same instruments make patently clear that the freedom of expression they trumpet is not an absolute freedom but instead may be limited by the signatories to the instruments. Under international law such limitations must be legitimate, legal, and a democratic necessity (Turk & Joinet, 1992), but these terms intentionally allow a wide latitude of restriction by the signatories. Most human rights treaties signed by democratic countries overtly permit restrictions on speech to promote respect for the rights of others, national security, public order or safety, and public health and morals. Covertly, most of these treaties allow additional restrictions by means of provisions like that contained in the European Convention (1953) that "the exercise of these freedoms . . . may be subject to such formalities, conditions, restrictions or penalties as are prescribed by law" (p. 230). What happens, of course, is that these statements of formal law are filtered through disparate cultures and traditions and unique social structures as they are translated into nation–states' laws. The result is that while all democratic nation–states champion freedom of expression, the contours of that freedom vary in major ways from country to country.

National Limitations

Democratic nation–states diverge in significant ways in their respective limitations on freedom of expression. As noted, in the United States expressions of racial hatred and group defamation are protected speech. Groups and individuals who openly engage in speech disparaging people of particular races, creeds, or colors can do so freely. They can even go so far as to advocate genocide as the ultimate solution to the problems they perceive as associated with the group they choose to hate. Such speech can be curtailed only if it is on the brink of resulting in direct physical harm to those who are being attacked. The laissez-faire attitude of the United States in the area of hate expression can be contrasted with that of Great Britain, Canada, India, and Nigeria, for example. These countries all regulate group defamation through restrictive legislation (Jones, 1998), as does Sweden (Swedish Penal Code, 1986). Germany, a nation–state that formed much of its present legal system in large part as a reaction to its own historical experience with racial hatred, permits wide restrictions on extremist political speech, even to the point of prohibiting any writing or broadcast that incites racial hatred or "describes cruel or otherwise inhuman acts of violence against humans in a manner which glorifies or minimizes such acts" (Stein, 1986, p. 131).

Similar divergences by democratic nation–states in assigning the parameters of freedom of expression are readily apparent in areas such as prior restraint and censorship for national security purposes, the definition and treatment of libel and slander, a right to privacy, free press–fair trial conflicts, freedom of governmental information, and obscenity. One good example of such a divergence is the Mitterrand–Dr. Gubler affair, which occurred in France in 1996. Aspects of prior restraint, libel, a right to privacy, and a free press were all intertwined in this case. At the request of President François Mitterrand's widow and three children, a series of French judges upheld the censorship of a book and the punishment of its authors and publisher for divulging a "professional secret," a criminal offense in France. The book, entitled *The Great Secret,* disclosed that Mitterrand had contracted a fatal cancer in 1981 and that by 1994, though still in office, was in reality no longer capable of carrying out his duties. When the widow and children went to court in an attempt to preserve Mitterrand's reputation, a judge initially issued a preliminary injunction that halted all future sales of the book, even though the book had gone on sale the day before and sold 40,000 copies throughout France. A court of appeals affirmed this injunction; a subsequent criminal court convicted Dr. Gubler, his coauthor, and his publisher of violating the criminal code; and a trial court made the injunction permanent and awarded damages to the Mitterrand family (Sokol, 1999, p. 5).

In the United States, it is impossible to conceive of any of this happening. Judges conversant with First Amendment law would have been unwilling to issue the original preliminary injunction; if a judge could be found to issue the order, an appeals court would quickly stay it. There could have been no criminal conviction, because no parallel criminal privacy law exists in the United States. There could have been no damage award, because any civil privacy concerns would have been outweighed by the fact that the matter was of public concern.

Such revelations are routinely published in the United States without even a hint of possible censorship or subsequent punishment.

When particular forms of expression strike at the most cherished values in a particular society, it is quite often the case that the society will opt for restrictions rather than open expression. Although it is impossible to deal with all areas of divergence adequately in a single chapter, the areas of censorship for national security purposes and censorship for moral and religious reasons are especially worthy of further examination.

CENSORSHIP AND NATIONAL SECURITY

The U.S. Situation

As mentioned previously, the general concept of censorship—that is, the concept of the government's taking overt action to prevent its people from having access to particular facts, ideals, and opinions—is constitutionally repugnant in the United States. This is true even when national security is advanced as the compelling reason that censorship must be enforced. In fact, the modern constitutional definition of what freedom of expression means in the United States had its genesis in a series of U.S. Supreme Court cases early in the 20th century that dealt explicitly with national security issues.

In cases such as *Abrams v. U.S.* (1919), *Gitlow v. New York* (1925), and *Whitney v. California* (1927), Justice Holmes and Justice Brandeis wrote decisions that crafted the country's modern-day approach to freedom of expression. These decisions, mainly in the form of dissents written against the majority reasoning of the Supreme Court and the dominant mood of the country as a whole, argued against a wide-ranging power on the part of the government to stifle protest and unpopular ideas in times of perceived national threat. They argued that socialists, anarchists, radicals, and revolutionaries should enjoy freedom of expression up to the point where the national security was truly threatened. The line that they drew is known as the "clear and present danger" doctrine. Justice Brandeis defined the boundaries of the doctrine in a famous opinion written in *Whitney v. California* (1927):

> [N]o danger flowing from speech can be deemed clear and present, unless the incidence of the evil apprehended is so imminent that it may befall before there is opportunity for discussion. If there be time to expose through discussion the falsehood and fallacies, to avert the evil by the processes of education, the remedy to be applied is more speech, not enforced silence. Only an emergency can justify repression. (p. 377)

Thus, expression that condemns the United States, expression that attempts to thwart the aims of the United States, even expression that advocates the overthrow of the United States government by force or violence, is protected up to the point where the expression poses a large, imminent danger to the well-being of the United States.

In the United States, most recent charges of governmental censorship in the national security arena have centered on the treatment of the press during military operations. It is important to note that most of the charges have been leveled not on the basis of any denial of freedom to speak or freedom to publish but on the denial of access to information. The Supreme Court of the United States has been reluctant to grant the press any special First Amendment right of access to any information except in the limited context of criminal proceedings (*Richmond Newspapers v. Virginia,* 1980). The First Amendment, then, protects speaking and publishing but has not been generally interpreted as guaranteeing that the press has a coextensive constitutional recourse to government information and materials. Complaints about limited access were made by the press when the government militarily intervened in Grenada, Panama, the Persian Gulf, Afghanistan, and Iraq.

A 1997 agreement between representatives of the press and the government was mutually accepted as balancing national security needs with the duty of the press to inform American citizens (Terry, 1997). The agreed-upon principles include open and independent coverage by the press, use of "pool" coverage when conditions mandate it, credentialing of journalists, access to all major military units, noninterference with reporting by public affairs officers, the provision of transport and communication facilities for journalists, and an "agreement to disagree" on the issue of security review of stories produced by the journalists, which is, of course, a problem area (Terry, 1997). The deletion of certain stories and facts might well result from such a security review by the armed forces, and this would constitute prior restraint or censorship, which, as noted, would traditionally be upheld by the courts only when the information at issue posed a clear and present danger to the armed forces. However, the conservative judicial philosophy of the present federal court system has resulted in an "extreme deference accorded the government and the military" (Jazayerli, 1997, p. 161) that might well work in favor of any governmental assertion of a threat to national security. One indication that the agreement between the press and government has worked to some degree can be found in the fact that relatively few charges of censorship were made by the press over U.S. military actions in Bosnia and Kosovo.

During the war in Iraq, however, U.S. and British forces placed restrictive regulations on the media through an interim media counsel. The regulations, aimed primarily at Arab satellite broadcasts of Al-Jazeera and Arabia, warned that foreign news operations could be closed down if they advocated the return of the Baath party. The Baghdad offices of Al-Jazeera were temporarily closed down after the organization was accused of inciting violence. The closure drew widespread criticism ("Iraq Ban on Al-Jazeera," 2004).

Despite some restrictions in the early months of the war, the media later enjoyed considerable latitude in reporting on events in Iraq. This included allowing journalists unique access to the battlefield by integrating them with operational military units. A report by the Paris-based organization, Reporters Sans Frontiers (RSF), characterized Iraq's media as a "prolific written press in full bloom" in the post–Saddam Hussein era. After Saddam's removal from office, once-banned cybercafes reopened and stores selling satellite TV dishes reappeared ("Iraq: RSF Report on Press Freedom," 2003).

In the absence of a constitutional right, the general notion of a right of the American people to have access to governmental information has been embedded in the federal Freedom of Information Act (FOIA, 1994 & Suppl. 1996) and in similar state statutes in almost every state. These laws affirmatively grant a right of access and affirmatively impose a duty for government agencies to make available and publish particular kinds of information. Although Congress and the courts are not covered by the laws, and the federal law and state laws do contain exceptions (such as, notably, national security information, internal agency rules, commercial secrets, and so on), freedom of information laws have proven to be an effective way of opening government operations to citizen scrutiny in the United States.

The culture of a "right to information" has permeated American society since the original adoption of the FOIA in 1966. So, even without the umbrella protection of the First Amendment, American citizens are privy to much of the innermost workings of their government, and the court system stands by as arbiter and potential ally when the government does attempt to block the flow of information.

The World Situation

Censorship in the name of national security is prevalent throughout modern democracies. Great Britain provides a good example of a country that does not hesitate to curtail expression for what it claims are national security reasons. Britain does not have a written constitution that sets forth the respective responsibilities and rights of the government and the people. Rather than constitutional law, British law has developed in parliamentary statutes, common law, judicial decisions, and custom and tradition. Without a "First Amendment" to serve as a foundational guardian of free expression and without a judiciary committed to such constitutionally mandated freedom as the supreme law of the land, Britain has evolved into what some commentators have described as "one of the most secretive democracies in the world today" (Silverman, 1997, p. 471).

In 2000, Britain incorporated the European Convention on Human Rights into its own domestic law, providing Britons with at least the opportunity to have a right of freedom of expression that can be enforced in the British courts. Under Britain's Official Secrets Act (1911), it is a criminal offense to disclose official information without authority, and it is likewise a criminal offense to receive such information. All government information is presumed official and thereby not subject to disclosure. Local governments have adopted the national model and are perhaps even more secretive than the national government (*United Kingdom Parliamentary Debates,* 1985). The British government has, in numerous instances in recent times, blocked publication of information it posited as a threat to national security, even going so far as to censor information in Britain that had already been published in other countries (Silverman, 1997). In the area of freedom of information, Britain has made progress in recent years. Britain's obsession with official secrecy was relaxed in 2005 when a Freedom of Information Act went into effect.

The Act, which took over two decades to become law, allows anyone to request information held by public authorities and to expect an answer within 20 days. Like other freedom of information statutes in western democracies, there are exemptions for national security, personal data and information that may compromise the conduct of governmental affairs. Under Britain's freedom of information law, an independent information commissioner has the power make exemptions subject to a public interest test. Britain's information commissioner, Richard Thomas, has indicated that he will be inclined to err on the side of the public's right to know ("Out of the Darkness," 2005).

Germany provides another example of a democratic society that does not hesitate to censor in the name of national security. The German constitutional system, or Basic Law, establishes numerous individual rights, including the right to free speech. However, basic rights must give way if they are perceived to be a threat to the fundamental constitutional structure of the country. Laws are allowed to limit individual liberties if the "purpose of the law has a higher rank of importance than the individual liberty itself" (McGuire, 1999, p. 765). Some forms of political speech are viewed as dangerous expression that potentially could do great harm to the internal security of the nation. Thus, German laws exist banning Nazi propaganda, the Hitler salute, and even radical political parties as national security threats.

And Britain and Germany certainly do not stand alone among modern Western democracies. The Japanese Supreme Court, which has a textual mandate to protect freedom of expression through judicial review, "has never struck down a local, prefectural, or national ordinance or law on free speech grounds" (Krotoszynski, 1998, p. 905) even though numerous Japanese laws that are justified by a national security claim would appear as censorship to American eyes. The Irish Constitution specifies that free expression by both individuals and the press is qualified and that "seditious" speech and speech undermining "public order" are subject to punishment and control, and the government employs official censors (O'Callaghan, 1998, p. 53). France has been described as a nation where "patterns of thought remain firmly rooted in a monarchical tradition, because the French establishment is fearful of an open society, and because in France much is hidden and confidentiality esteemed," a nation where "censorship prevailed because the press is weak, the broadcasting media fearful of a government which has historically owned and subsidized it," and a nation "where the judiciary is timid and impoverished" (Sokol, 1999, p. 41).

Although this appraisal seems somewhat harsh, nonetheless France has openly and almost disdainfully exercised censorship in the name of security. In October 1995, when France set off underground nuclear tests in the Pacific Ocean that resulted in anti-French demonstrations around the world, 25 Danish high school students visiting Paris were deported for the threat they posed to French security. The threat was that they were wearing T-shirts decorated with the saying "Chirac Non" (Whitney, 1995).

Britain, Germany, Japan, Ireland, and France represent relatively long-established democracies. If similar scrutiny were applied to more recently emerged democracies in various parts of the world, the tendency of nations to censor for perceived national security reasons would become even more apparent.

When freedom of expression comes into conflict with nation-specific values that are identified as crucial to that nation's continued existence, freedom of expression may well be curtailed. And that continued existence need not necessarily be the nation's actual physical existence; a great deal of censorship in the modern world is engaged in by governments intent on preserving a particular moral or religious existence.

CENSORSHIP FOR MORAL AND RELIGIOUS REASONS

American Censorship

As indicated before in this chapter, the American position with regard to obscenity is somewhat at odds with its general posture as the world's leading defender of freedom of expression. In 1896, the U.S. Supreme Court confronted the challenge of deciding an obscenity case for the first time. Rather than legally defining *obscenity,* the Court chose to dwell on what it was not. The Court's ruling was that vulgar and coarse language was not obscene, and that obscenity, whatever its definition might be, was a concept dealing with a message "of immorality which has relation to sexual impurity" (*Swearingen v. U.S.,* 1896, p. 446). The Court next mentioned the subject of obscenity in *Near v. Minnesota* in 1931. It did so in an almost offhanded way, noting that obscenity was one of the few areas of expression that could be censored without raising any kind of constitutional problem.

Chief Justice Hughes offered no legal explanation why this was true, nor did he offer any further definition of the term *obscenity.* In *Chaplinsky v. New Hampshire* in 1942, the Court felt comfortable in citing the *Near* position on obscenity and declaring that it fell into that class of expressions "of such slight value as a step to truth that any benefit that may be derived from them is clearly outweighed by the social interest in order and morality" (p. 572), still without clarifying the term *obscenity.*

Finally, in 1957 the Supreme Court took on the task of legally defining obscenity and spent the next 16 years finding that it could not do so. Justice Brennan, writing in the 1957 case *Roth v. U.S.,* accepted the Near–Chaplinsky position that obscenity was valueless speech that had no constitutional protection and made an initial attempt to define it: "Whether to the average person, applying contemporary community standards, the dominant theme of the material taken as a whole appeals to prurient interest" (p. 476). The problem with this definition became quickly apparent to Court members as they attempted to apply it to material charged as obscene in subsequent cases. What was "a contemporary community standard"? How does "prurient interest" manifest itself? In case after case throughout the 1960s, the Court wrestled with the problem of making what was "obscene" clear and understandable to the judiciary and the American people.

What resulted was dissension, frustration, and confusion among both Court members and the American public, illustrated in the now-famous disgruntled observation of Justice Potter Stewart that he could not define obscenity but "I know it when I see it" (*Jacobellis v. Ohio,* 1964, p. 184).

No definition of obscenity could command a majority of the Court during the 1960s and early 1970s. When a new, more-conservative Court led by Chief Justice Burger faced the issue in 1973, they reached a solution that was more practical than elegant: Give the states some general guidelines and turn the vexing problem over to them. The definition of *obscenity* did not have to be uniform from state to state and community to community. Individual juries could make the determination. This solution by the Court forms the core of obscenity regulation in the United States today. Citizens in the United States must confront the legal fact that a videotape that is legal entertainment in Oregon (which provides state constitutional protection for obscenity) could well be a felony crime in North Carolina.

The general guidelines provided by the Burger Court for juries and judges in 1973 were as follows: "(a) whether the 'average person, applying contemporary community standards' would find that the work, taken as a whole, appeals to the prurient interest; (b) whether the work depicts or describes, in a patently offensive way, sexual conduct specifically defined by the applicable state law; and (c) whether the work, taken as a whole, lacks serious literary, artistic, political, or scientific value" (*Miller v. California,* 1973, p. 24). The Court also offered some examples of sexual representations that states might find obscene, including "patently offensive representations or descriptions of ultimate sexual acts real or perverted, actual or simulated," and "patently offensive representations or descriptions of masturbation, excretory functions, and lewd exhibition of the genitals" (p. 25).

What the Court did in *Miller* was to provide somewhat hazy boundaries for what might be termed hard-core pornography and then allow the states, if they wished, to define the material within these boundaries as potentially obscene, subject to a final finding of obscenity by the local community. Some communities have almost become obscenity refuges, safe from any obscenity convictions. The last successful obscenity prosecution in Manhattan, for example, occurred in 1973 (*People v. Heller,* 1973).

At the federal level, under political pressure after almost a decade of little enforcement activity the Justice Department began an aggressive program of obscenity prosecutions (Blum, 2004). Observers said the rapid growth of the Internet during the 1990s led to "an explosion of illegal pornographic material that can no longer be ignored" (p. 3). Previously, prosecutors focused only on cases where children were involved. Under the new crackdown, federal agents began targeting adult obscenity. FBI investigations increased over 300 percent during the first year and a half of the program. While prosecutions are traditionally left to local law enforcement, government officials say the nature of the modern Internet now requires that federal prosecutors play a key role. How this will play out under the community standards approach to obscenity enforcement remains to be seen.

A much different position is taken in the United States with regard to censorship for religious reasons, such as heresy, blasphemy, or sacrilege, and dissenting views concerning private morality. In these areas, the United States steps back into its role of defender of free expression. Censorship in these areas is never allowed; such speech is fully protected under the First Amendment, and even though such speech is often verbally attacked by those serving in government positions, no laws banning or punishing such speech have been upheld in modern constitutional history.

Moral-Religious Censorship around the World

The American predilection to single out obscenity as an area of expression bereft of protection is not necessarily shared around the globe. "Such 'puritanism' in the United States stands in contrast to many European countries' views of the subject" (McGuire, 1999, p. 756). In Germany, for example, obscenity is not "as central a policy concern" (p. 756). Likewise, England takes a more permissive legal stance on obscenity than the United States, defining obscenity according to the type of person who may obtain the material. The U.K. Obscene Publications Act of 1959 states that if a viewer is likely to be depraved and corrupted by the material, then the material meets the standards for obscenity. Thus, the law is primarily aimed at the protection of children, and graphic sexual materials that are restricted to the adult population are not necessarily considered obscene (Edick, 1998).

Sweden and Holland have virtually no laws restricting obscenity, and both of these countries have large pornography industries (Friel, 1997). The same is true in Denmark, where the use of pornography by adults is completely unhindered (Ditthavong, 1996). In Italy, a generally liberal legal position prevails for pornography. Obscenity laws are vague. Material featuring juveniles is a crime, as it now is in many European countries, but otherwise it is up to a local Italian judge to decide what can go on sale ("Controlling Pornography," 1998).

However, some countries engage in even more intense censorship of obscenity than the United States does. In Ireland, for example, "banning a book or periodical is alarmingly simple" (O'Callaghan, 1998, p. 57). The Irish Constitution explicitly allows censorship, and censorship boards can and do operate to protect traditional Catholic ideas of morality. Ireland also employs government censors for videos and film.

A global look at the reaction of nation–states to pornographic and obscene materials thus reveals the same divergences in policy and law that affect all other areas of expression. In some parts of the world, extremely strict laws banning obscene materials are combined with equally strict laws dealing with religious heresy or blasphemy. An example of this occurs in the Muslim countries of Iran and Saudi Arabia, and the Muslim population of Iraq, all of which assert that Islam justifies and mandates a special approach to human rights, including freedom of expression, and that the traditional Western democratic approaches are not suitable in their societies (Mayer, 1994). These countries argue that concepts like individualism, liberty, democracy, free markets, and the separation of church and state are out of place in an Islamic civilization.

In Islam, the claim to a unique and valid alternative position on human rights based on religion has led to censorship. The 1990 Cairo Declaration on Human Rights in Islam, which was issued in Iran, enumerates rights and freedoms on which Islamic qualifications have been imposed. No freedom of religion is afforded in the Cairo Declaration. "The Declaration assumed that Islam is the true faith and that adherence to Islam is natural, with the consequence that it effectively bans other faiths from proselytizing" (Mayer, 1994, p. 334). The declaration does not provide for freedom of the press; in fact, Islamic criteria are used to limit freedom of speech. Opinions must be expressed in a manner not contrary to Islamic law, and people can advocate only what is "right" and "good," as specified in Islamic tenets. The declaration "bars the exploitation of misuse of information 'in such a way as may violate sanctities and the dignity of Prophets, undermine moral and ethical values or disintegrate, corrupt or harm society or weaken its faith' " (Mayer, 1994, p. 334).

In a manner similar to the declaration emanating from Iran, the Basic Law of Saudi Arabia denies any right to freedom of expression that might counter Islamic tenets. No guarantee of freedom of expression is included in the Basic Law. The media and the people are called upon to adhere to all state regulations while supporting the unity of the country, contributing to Islamic education, and using courteous language, and they are forbidden to publish or disseminate ideas that could lead to strife or degrade man's dignity. The law endorses "the existing censorship standards, which are extensive and stringently enforced by the government" (Mayer, 1994, p. 361).

A rejection of the Western concept of human rights as some form of cultural imperialism, and an acceptance of Islam as the source of human rights, can give rise to censorship activities that seem quite foreign from a Western democratic perspective. Such was the now-famous case of Salman Rushdie, an Indian-born, internationally acclaimed British writer who won the prestigious Booker Prize for literature in 1981 and was a candidate in 1999 for the Nobel Prize in literature.

The year after Rushdie published his novel *The Satanic Verses* in 1988, Iranian Ayatollah Khomeini issued a "fatwa," or law, that read as follows:

> To God we belong and to Him we shall return. I inform all zealous
> Muslims of the world that the author of *The Satanic Verses*—which has
> been compiled, printed, and published in opposition to Islam, the Prophet,
> and the Qur'an—and all those involved in its publication who were aware
> of its content are sentenced to death. I call on all zealous Muslims to
> execute them quickly, wherever they may be found. (Chase, 1996, p. 375)

The novel was perceived to be an obscene and mocking insult that attempted to undermine the authority of Islam's founder and its founding text. And, in the context of Islam, Rushdie had committed sacrilege, blasphemy, and heresy so great that death was a suitable punishment, to be carried out by believers regardless of where Rushdie might be. Western countries reacted to the original death sentence with horror and shock, and many countries severed formal relationships with Iran.

After years of living under protection and in constant fear of death, Rushdie finally received a reprieve of sorts in 1998 when the government and religious leaders of Iran chose to distance themselves from the death sentence.

What is obvious from the foregoing example is that some nation–states deny the universality of the Western democratic conception of human rights and the subsequent importance of freedom of expression. Arguing from a perspective of religious purity, ethnic purity, cultural purity, monarchical fiat, or dictatorial necessity, these nation–states reject external norms as irrelevant or antithetical to their societies and embrace censorship as a means to a greater end.

In Iraq, early indications were that the country was leaning toward an Islamic constitution, much like Iran's (Cambanis, 2005). With elections over and the constitutional process underway, it appeared that much of the debate was likely to take place between hard-core Islamics, who want a constitution based on Koranic law, and more moderate Islamists, who favor a milder form of religious law. One of the key issues in Iraq's future is whether democracy, where the majority rules, is compatible with Islam, where the law is based on religion. A two-thirds vote of Iraq's Transitional National Assembly is required to approve a constitution.

On a global scale of freedom of expression ranging from total censorship to absolute freedom, nation–states can be found that occupy almost all available positions. However, it is worthy to note that as the world advances in the direction of the "global village," the direction of movement on the scale seems conclusively toward the freedom end.

EXISTING INTERNATIONAL REGULATORY BODIES

As mentioned in the introduction of this chapter, numerous international regulatory and policymaking bodies govern aspects of the global trade in information and ideas. For the most part, the scope of these agencies is limited to areas such as broadcasting, where radio and television signals spanning international boundaries have the capability of interfering with one another (as well as the potential to carry political and social messages that are at odds with national standards). This "traffic cop" role is perhaps the primary role of such agencies. International agencies have also been formed when mutual cooperation forwarded social goals such as the protection of intellectual property rights—patents, trademarks, and copyrights—under treaties and conventions. The roles of the major international agencies will now be examined.

International Telecommunication Union

The International Telecommunication Union (ITU) was formed in 1932, growing out of the International Telegraph Union, which was itself formed in 1865. In 1947, the ITU became a specialized agency of the United Nations, with its headquarters in Geneva. In various forms, it has played a dominant role in international cooperation and standard setting throughout the history of telecommunications, presiding over the first radiotelegraph convention, the first provisions for international telephone service, the first trials of broadcasting, the first world space radiocommunication conference, and the first world telecommunications standardization conference. It has played an active role in the implementation of virtually all communication technologies through standardization, technical coordination, and regulation oversight. It now functions as the ultimate manager of the world's telecommunications resources, allocating radio frequencies and communication satellite orbital positions to its member nation–states (Allison, 1993). It does so at periodic meetings of the World Administrative Radio Conference (WARC).

The ITU has its own convention, constitution, and operating regulations, all of which have the status of international treaties. Its membership is made up exclusively of nation–states and includes most of the members of the United Nations, but nonstate entities, such as private telecommunications companies, can become members of the individual sectors. It is governed by a full Plenipotentiary Conference meeting every four years, at which a 43-member council that meets annually is elected. A general secretariat exists for administrative and management functions, and there is a secretariat for each of the ITU's three sectors: the radiocommunications sector, the telecommunications sector, and the telecommunications development sector (two-thirds of ITU's membership consists of developing countries).

Two major criticisms currently threaten the continued dominance of the ITU in its role as global overseer of telecommunications (Cook, 1999). The first deals with voting power. Every member state has one vote, as in the General Assembly of the United Nations. The second concerns financial contributions, "which can vary by as much as a factor of 640 between the lowest level of contribution and the highest" (Cook, 1999, p. 672). A small minority of its members contributes the great majority of the ITU budget, yet the great majority of the voting power resides in those countries that contribute "less than ten percent of its finances" (Cook, 1999, p. 672).

Yet another problem facing the ITU is the growing importance of nonstate actors, primarily large commercial telecommunications firms, on the world telecommunications scene. They are currently without full membership privileges in the ITU but obviously are major players in the telecommunications area. Some people fear that these firms might together form a new organization that would lessen the role and impact of the ITU.

Intelsat

The International Telecommunications Satellite Organization (Intelsat) was established by the United States and various European countries in 1964. Initially, like the ITU, Intelsat was primarily an organization directed by its member nation–states, although state-designated telecommunications entities also were part of a multilevel governance scheme. Operated much as a commercial cooperative, Intelsat is a wholesaler of satellite communications and links the world's telecommunications networks together.

After nearly 40 years as a treaty-based organization, Intelsat went private in 2001 (Taveria, 2001). The company operates under a private international holding company. Rather than answering to 145 member governments and 200 investors, the management of Intelsat now reports to a 17-member shareholder elected board with its headquarters in Washington DC. The move to privatize was driven by the need to be competitive in a global communications environment. As a private entity, Intelsat expects to be more flexible in pricing and in the way it markets its services. Intelsat's fleet of 20 satellites serves 214 countries.

The Communications Satellite Organization (COMSAT), the U.S. signatory representing U.S. interests to Intelsat, also went private. COMSAT provides satellite communications in and out of the United States for 700 international customers, including telephony providers (AT&T, MCI WorldCom, and Sprint), broadcasters, other corporations, and the U.S. government; it also operates an integrated group of telecommunications companies. In 2000, Lockheed Martin received permission from the Justice Department and the Federal Communications Commission to acquire 49 percent of COMSAT's stock.

World Trade Organization

The World Trade Organization (WTO) is a Geneva-based international organization of nearly 150 nation–states dealing with the global rules of trade between nations. It presently has an impact on telecommunications policy and intellectual property rights and may have a greater impact in the future as telecommunications, satellite technology, and computer technology converge. The WTO came into being in 1995 as a successor to the General Agreement on Tariffs and Trade (GATT) that was established after World War II, and now it administers all GATT provisions.

Decisions in the WTO are typically made by consensus arrived at through negotiations, or "rounds," at ministerial conferences held every two years in various countries and then are ratified by the members' parliaments. The WTO has a dispute settlement process established to interpret agreements and commitments and to make sure that members' trade policies conform to them. In February 1997, 69 WTO member governments, including the United States and its major trading partners, agreed to wide-ranging liberalization measures in the area of telecommunications services. Essentially, these members have agreed not to engage in anticompetitive behaviors and to open their telecommunications systems up to foreign investment and control. Members made commitments toward increasing international competition in voice telephony, data transmission, facsimile services, fixed and mobile satellite services, paging, and personal communication services.

Compliance with the WTO telecommunications agreement has been controversial and the liberalization of global telecom markets slow ("U.S. Trade Body," 2004). U.S. telecommunications companies have complained that anticompetitive practices in 13 countries, including Japan, India, China, South Africa,

France, and Germany, have hurt global competition. Among the complaints are charges of excessive prices for leased lines and unreasonable fees for licenses to operate overseas.

World Intellectual Property Organization

The World Intellectual Property Organization (WIPO) is an intergovernmental organization headquartered in Geneva, Switzerland. It is one of the 16 specialized agencies of the United Nations system of organizations. WIPO is responsible for the promotion of the protection of intellectual property throughout the world through cooperation among nation–states. The organization also administers various multilateral treaties dealing with the legal and administrative aspects of intellectual property.

The intellectual property concerns of WIPO fall into two categories: industrial property, chiefly in inventions, trademarks, industrial designs, and appellations of origin; and copyright, chiefly in literary, musical, artistic, photographic, and audiovisual works. A substantial part of the activities and the resources of WIPO is devoted to development cooperation with developing countries. The number of nation–states that are members of WIPO was 182 as of March 2005.

Industrial property deals principally with the protection of inventions by patents, marks (registered trademarks and service marks) and industrial designs, and the repression of unfair competition. The laws of a nation–state relating to industrial property are generally concerned only with acts accomplished or committed in the nation–state itself. Consequently, a patent, the registration of a mark, or the registration of an industrial design is effective only where the government office granted them. It is not effective in other nation–states. In 1883, in order to guarantee protection in foreign countries, 11 countries established the International Union for the Protection of Industrial Property by signing the Paris Convention for the Protection of Industrial Property. Since that time, all but a few members of WIPO have signed the agreements. The convention has been revised several times.

The Paris Union and WIPO—which furnishes the secretariat of the union—pursue the aim of strengthening cooperation among sovereign nations in the field of industrial property. The aim is to ensure that such protection be adequate, easy to obtain, and, once obtained, effectively respected.

In copyright, as in industrial property, the laws of a nation–state are generally concerned only with acts accomplished or committed in the nation–state. In order to guarantee protection in foreign countries for their own citizens, 10 countries established the International Union for the Protection of Literary and Artistic Works in 1886 by signing the Berne Convention for the Protection of Literary and Artistic Works. By 2005, more than 150 countries had signed the Berne Convention, which requires member states to recognize the moral rights of integrity and attribution. A member country must already have copyright protection within its own legal system that provides protection without a requirement for copyright registration and without a requirement for a notice of copyright to appear on the work. The author's work may not be exploited. The Berne Convention explicitly grants economic rights—the author has exclusive right to translate, reproduce, perform, or adapt protected works and may bring suit in any member country for actual damages and other remedies.

In 1996, WIPO, recognizing the dangers posed by the new global information system, passed two new treaties. The first, the Copyright Treaty, was intended to strengthen the Berne Convention by including protection for cyberspace commerce.

The provisions of the WIPO Copyright Treaty included protection for computer programs and mandated that nation–states develop legal remedies to preserve the integrity of "rights management information" (Andrepont, 1999, p. 402). The second WIPO treaty, the Performances and Phonograms Treaty, dealt with protection for sound recordings in a digital environment.

The two WIPO treaties update the existing Berne Convention protections for creators of intellectual property and make clear the illegality of encryption violations and the circumvention of copyright protections. They also increase the protection provided to online works such as music, software, movies, and literary works. The treaties specify the limits of liability for information service providers and the telephone companies that serve as carriers for the protected works. The treaties also deal with the limits of the fair use exception to copyright violation for educational institutions and libraries.

By 2005, enough countries had ratified the treaties for them to achieve full force in the international community.

The Internet and Its Impact on Global Communication Law

The increasingly widespread use of the Internet, a borderless technology with no international boundaries, has called into question traditional approaches to communication law and regulation in Western democracies. The traditional approaches are to some measure, as has been pointed out in this chapter, idiosyncratic and nation-specific, tailored to the perceived needs of different societies and different cultural heritages.

As might be expected, the United States is endorsing the principle of self-regulation for the Internet. Grounded in a constitutional system that has produced broad principles of freedom of speech, the United States has proposed that the content of the Internet be subjected to the same minimal controls that are applied to traditional media, such as newspapers and magazines, in the United States (Clinton & Gore, 1998) and that the Internet be allowed to respond to free market demands.

In the wake of *Reno v. ACLU* in 1997, in which the U.S. Supreme Court struck down as unconstitutional the Communications Decency Act passed by the U.S. Congress, the Administration appeared to relax attempts to police pornography on the Internet, instead supporting software filters as a way to protect children from indecent Internet content (Clinton & Gore, 1998). Another law that Congress passed and President Clinton signed in 1999 to try to cure the defects of the Communications Decency Act—the Child Online Protection Act (COPA, 1999)—was also found unconstitutional. Suppliers and distributors of pornographic materials that reach the level of illegal obscenity under *Miller v. California* can, of course, still be punished (if they reside in the United States) in those communities that are able to successfully try and convict them, in the same manner that suppliers and distributors can be punished for obscene materials in traditional media such as magazines and videotapes (*United States v. Thomas,* 1996). Likewise, existing laws aimed at child pornography can be enforced against U.S. violators who use the Internet as a medium. However, half of the sexually explicit material available over the Internet originates outside of the country and is thus exempt from the laws of the United States (Merchant, 1998).

Existing libel and slander laws can be applied, as can privacy provisions, advertising regulations, and all other aspects of existing U.S. communication regulation, as long as all parties to all disputes reside within the United States. Because the current system of communication in the United States is the freest in the world, the U.S. vision of Internet control endorses a largely unfettered medium.

Other nations are not so sanguine about a relatively uncontrolled and unrestricted Internet that passes through national boundaries and exposes citizens to ideas and images that their cultures reject. Germany compelled CompuServe Inc., an Internet service provider, to completely block 200 discussion groups to German websites in reaction to pro-Nazi messages (Knoll, 1996).

A number of European countries have made it illegal to purchase Third Reich memorabilia. In France, a judge ordered Yahoo to filter U.S. websites that offer Nazi memorabilia and literature, something considered technically impossible (Elvin, 2002). Yielding to pressure from overseas, both Yahoo and eBay put policies into effect that prohibit the sale of Nazi items online. France has prosecuted a website owner for uploading a book bearing secrets about a former French president. Singapore punishes both Internet users and providers who download and upload politically and morally objectionable material and imposes proxy servers, or "censoring computers," that keep its people from accessing outside web pages that are currently banned by the government. China, in an attempt to protect its people from Western influences, built an Intranet that blocks Chinese people from the Internet, substituting for it a Chinese version, and plans to use proxy servers like those employed in Singapore when it does allow its citizens to access the worldwide Internet. Malaysia has condemned the Internet because of its Western ideas that are alien to Malaysian society and culture (Hanley, 1998).

Despite the best attempts of various countries to regulate the Internet, no country's method has been globally effective. Nation–states can to some extent seek out and punish violators of communication laws within their own national boundaries, but absent some kind of agreement that is binding in all parts of the world, they are powerless to control totally and effectively messages and images that emanate from other nation–states. To compound the problem, senders of messages increasingly have the power to encrypt the transmission so that the receiver of the message has no capability of knowing who sent it. Screening and filtering software is imprecise and at the same time overwhelmed by the vast amount of information traveling across the Internet and the time required to properly classify and filter all information. Network providers have neither the jurisdiction in most countries nor the physical capacity to actively and adequately censor the entire Internet. Proxy servers, as described, could be employed to limit a nation's citizens to carefully selected Internet sites, but this solution obviates the major benefit of the Internet—worldwide communication—and isolates the censoring country from the rest of the world.

The only apparent regulatory solution for the Internet is international agreement on censorship of intolerable speech. This censorship does not now exist and probably never will, except perhaps in the area of protection of children. International satellite and telephone agreements exist, but they are aimed at resolving technical problems, not on achieving a desirable level of censorship among countries with vastly different cultures and mores.

So, in the absence of a satisfactory method of global Internet control, nation–states have two major alternatives: They can either embrace the direction in which the United States is heading—that is, endorse self-regulation for the Internet and then for the most part leave it alone—or they can opt out of the free flow of information and ideas that is the Internet and substitute a heavily censored, governmentally approved version that is expensive and difficult to maintain and only partially effective.

The "borderless" nature of the Internet may end up having profound effects on traditional communication law and policy enforced within a nation–state's borders. For instance, with material that could be judged obscene in the United States available to a U.S. citizen on the Internet from hundreds of sites around the world, does it still make logical sense to prosecute similar material that is generated in the United States? If a libelous statement about a British citizen can be published with impunity on the Internet because the statement originates outside the borders of England, should a similar statement be subjected to civil penalty just because it originates in England? Communication law and policy that are unenforceable on one medium—the Internet—are tainted with unfairness when they are applied to another medium—books, newspapers, movies, and the like—simply because that medium is more susceptible to control.

Long range, it may well be that what the Internet will cause is the erosion and eventual disappearance of communication law and policy aimed at any kind of content control in those countries that embrace a free Internet. And if projections hold true and many or most of the traditional media, such as telephone, broadcasting, and newspapers, converge and fold into the Internet, and if the Internet does become the backbone of international commerce in the 21st century, it may also well be that nation after nation will have to drop Internet censorship if they are to function on an equal basis with the other nations of the world, and thus they also will have to face the problems of an ungovernable medium. Is it possible that the birth of the Internet may indeed have signaled the death of all censorship throughout the world? Well, we shall see.

For more information on the topics that appear in this chapter, use the password that came free with this book to access InfoTrac College Edition. Use the following words as keyterms and subject searches: global communication law, freedom of expression, international covenants, media censorship, Freedom of Information Act, media regulations, human rights, regulatory agencies, trade organizations.

QUESTIONS FOR DISCUSSION

1. Is it a worthwhile goal to work for a common approach to freedom of expression throughout the world?

2. What is the best course for nations to take when national security seems threatened by free speech?

3. What position should nations take with regard to religious and moral censorship attempts by other nations on their own populations?

4. Should the roles of existing international communication regulatory/ policymaking bodies be expanded? How?

5. What are various impacts the Internet might have on global communication law?

REFERENCES

Abrams v. U.S., 250 U.S. 616 (1919).

Allison, A. (1993). Meeting the challenges of change: The reform of the International Telecommunication Union. *Federal Communications Law Journal, 45,* 491–514.

American Convention on Human Rights, 1144 U.N.T.S. 143 (1978).

Andrepont, C. (1999). Legislative update: Digital Millennium Copyright Act: Copyright protections for the digital age. *Journal of Art and Entertainment Law, 9,* 397–413.

Banjul Charter of Human and Peoples' Rights, 21 I.L.M. 58 (1982).

Bantam Books, Inc. v. Sullivan, 372 U.S. 58 (1963).

Blum, V. (2004, March 11). DOJ returns attention to policing the porn industry. *The Recorder, 128*(48), 3.

Cambanis, T. (2005, February 2). Top Shi'ite clerics begin to press for an Islamic Constitution. *The Boston Globe,* p. A10.

Chaplinsky v. New Hampshire, 315 U.S. 568 (1942).

Chase, A. (1996). Legal guardians: Islamic law, international law, human rights law, and the Salman Rushdie affair. *American University Journal of International Law and Policy, 11,* 375–435.

Child Online Protection Act, 47 U.S.C.S. § 231, Title 4 (1999).

Clinton, W. J., & Gore, A. (1998). *A framework for global electronic commerce.* Retrieved November 11, 1999, from http://www.iitf.nist.gov/eleccomm/execsu.htm

Controlling pornography: Law/how Britain compares with other countries in dealing with the problem of obscenity. (1998, August 13). *The Guardian* (London), p. 4.

Cook, K. V. (1999). The discovery of lunar water: An opportunity to develop a workable moon theory. *Georgetown International Environmental Law Review, 11,* 647–706.

Ditthavong, K. (1996). Paving the way for women on the information superhighway: Curbing sexism not freedoms. *American University Journal of Gender and the Law, 4,* 455–509.

Edick, D. (1998). Regulation of pornography on the Internet in the United States and the United Kingdom. *Boston College International and Comparative Law Review, 21,* 437–460.

Elvin, J. (2002, October 1). War relics of World War II GIs resurface as the Reich stuff. *Insight on the News,* p. 34.

Emerson, T. I. (1970). *The system of freedom of expression.* New York: Random House.

European Convention for the Protection of Human Rights and Fundamental Freedoms, 213 U.N.T.S. 221 (1953).

Freedom of Information Act, 5 U.S.C. § 552 (1994) and Suppl. (1996).

Friel, S. (1997). Porn by any other name? A constitutional alternative to regulating "victimless" computer-generated child pornography. *Valparaiso University Law Review, 32,* 207–267.

Gitlow v. New York, 268 U.S. 652 (1925).

Hall, K. L. (Ed.). (1992). *The Oxford companion to the Supreme Court.* New York: Oxford University Press.

Hanley, S. M. (1998). International Internet regulation: A multinational approach. *John Marshall Journal of Computer and Information Law, 16,* 997–1024.

International Convention on the Elimination of All Forms of Racial Discrimination, 660 U.N.T.S. 195 (1969).

International Covenant on Civil and Political Rights, 999 U.N.T.S. 171 (1976).

Iraq ban on Al-Jazeera is "serious blow" to press freedom: RSF. (2004, August 8). *Agence France Presse* (English).

Iraq: RSF report on press freedom three months after the war. (2003, July 24). *BBC Monitoring World Media.*

Jacobellis v. Ohio, 378 U.S. 184 (1964).

Jazayerli, R. (1997). War and the First Amendment: A call for legislation to protect a press' right of access to military operations. *Columbia Journal of Transnational Law, 35,* 131–173.

Jones, T. D. (1998). *Human rights: Group defamation, freedom of expression, and the law of nations.* Boston: Martinus Nijhoff.

Knoll, A. (1996). Any which way but loose: Nations regulate the Internet. *Tulane Journal of International and Comparative Law, 4,* 288–301.

Krotoszynski, R. (1998). The chrysanthemum, the sword, and the First Amendment: Disentangling culture, community, and freedom of expression. *Wisconsin Law Review, 1998,* 905–922.

Mayer, A. E. (1994). Universal versus Islamic human rights: A clash of cultures or a clash with a construct. *Michigan Journal of International Law, 15,* 307–403.

McGuire, J. F. (1999). Note: When speech is heard around the world: Internet content regulation in the United States and Germany. *New York University Law Review, 74,* 750–792.

Merchant, M. J. (1998). Establishing the boundaries of First Amendment protection for speech in the cyberspace frontier: Reno v. ACLU. *Villanova Sports and Entertainment Law Forum, 5,* 429.

Miller v. California, 413 U.S. 15 (1973).

Milton, J. (Orig. 1644/1950). Areopagitica. In *Complete poetry and works of John Milton.* New York: Modern Library.

Murphy, J. G. (1997). Freedom of expression and the arts. *Arizona State Law Journal, 29,* 549.

Near v. Minnesota, 283 U.S. 697 (1931).

O'Callaghan, J. (1998). Censorship of indecency in Ireland: A view from abroad. *Cardozo Arts and Entertainment Law Journal, 16,* 53–80.

Official Secrets Act (OSA), 1911 (England).

Out of the darkness: Freedom of information. (2005, January 1). *The Economist* (U.S. Edition).

People v. Heller, 33 N.Y.2d 314 (1973).

Procunier v. Martinez, 416 U.S. 396 (1974).

Reno v. ACLU, 521 U.S. 844 (1997).

Richmond Newspapers v. Virginia, 448 U.S. 555 (1980).

Roth v. U.S., 354 U.S. 476 (1957).

Silverman, D. L. (1997). Freedom of information: Will Blair be able to break the walls of secrecy in Britain? *American University International Law Review, 13,* 471.

Smolla, R. A. (1992). *Free speech in an open society.* New York: Alfred A. Knopf.

Sokol, R. P. (1999). Freedom of expression in France: The Mitterrand–Dr. Gubler affair. *Tulane Journal of International and Comparative Law, 7,* 5–42.

Stein, E. (1986). History against free speech: The new German law against the Auschwitz:—and other—"lies." *Michigan Law Review, 85,* 277–324.

Survey finds lukewarm support for free speech. (1999, July 28). *EPIC Alert, 6*(12), 6. Retrieved January 5, 2006, from http://www.epic.orig

Swearingen v. U.S., 161 U.S. 446 (1896).

Swedish Penal Code, ch. 16, § 8 (1986).

Taveria, K. L. (2001, July 30). Private time—Intelsat, looking to stay nimble, sheds bureaucratic weight. *Tele.Com.* p. 17.

Terry, J. P. (1997). Press access to combatant operations in the post-peacekeeping era. *Military Law Review, 154,* 1–26.

Turk, D., & Joinet, L. (1992). *The right to freedom of opinion and expression: Final report* (U.N. Doc. E/CN.4/Sub.2/1992/9). New York: United Nations Commission on Human Rights.

U.S. trade body denounces WTO telecoms violations. (2004, December 22). *Total Telecom.*

United Kingdom Parliamentary Debates. (1985). Commons, 6th ser., vol. 72, col. 547.

United States v. Thomas, 74 F. 3d 701 (6th Cir., 1996).

Universal Declaration of Human Rights, G.A. Res. 217 (III), U.N. Doc. A/810 (1948).

Uyttendaele, C., & Dumortier, J. (1998). Free speech on the information superhighway: European perspectives. *John Marshall Journal of Computer and Information Law, 16,* 905–936.

Whitney v. California, 274 U.S. 357 (1927).

Whitney, C. R. (1995, October 17). Anti-nuke shirts get under Paris's skin. *International Herald Tribune,* p. 10.

6

Global News
and Information Flow
in the Internet Age

KULDIP R. RAMPAL

Kuldip R. Rampal (PhD, University of Missouri—Columbia) is
Professor of Mass Communication at Central Missouri State
University in Warrensburg. A widely published author, Rampal
received the 1993 International Communication Award from the
Republic of China on Taiwan for his writings on press and political
liberalization in Taiwan. He has coauthored a reference book,
International Afro Mass Media: A Reference Guide (Greenwood Press,
1996), and co-edited *Media, Sex, Violence and Drugs in the
Global Village* (Rowman & Littlefield, 2001). He is coeditor (with
Y. R. Kamalipour) of the State University of New York Press series
in Global Media Studies.

At the beginning of the 21st century, global news and information flow is at a
crossroads. The International Telecommunications Union reported in early
December 2004 that by the middle of that year the number of Internet users
worldwide had grown to nearly 700 million from around 360 million in 2000.
The Internet is universally characterized as a revolutionary medium because it has
opened up an altogether new world of information and communication. Apart

For additional online resources, access the Global Media Monitor website
that accompanies this book on the Wadsworth Communication Cafe website at
http://communication.wadsworth.com.

from using the Internet as a speedy means of communication for personal and professional reasons, users are turning to this multimedia, interactive medium to specify and obtain the news, information, and entertainment they need from across the world. This need-based information consumption pattern facilitated by the Internet is radically different from the centuries-old model in which the consumer is at the receiving end of news and information selected and purveyed by traditional media gatekeepers.

Internet reach, however, has a long way to go before it becomes a medium of choice for most people around the world. Only 12.7 percent of the world population was using the Internet by September 2004 ("Internet World Stats," 2004). Although thousands of new users are logging on every day, only about 1.5 billion people out of the estimated 6.8 billion people on the planet in 2010 are projected to be using the Internet by then. The number of users, however, has more to do with the logistics of hooking into the Internet than with the appeal of this remarkable medium. Three-quarters of the world's population at the beginning of this century did not own a telephone, much less a computer and a modem. Those who are not faced with these barriers, however, are adopting the Internet at a rate unmatched by many other innovations in history. In addition, the coming together of the Internet and mobile communications will provide a major future driver for growth. Mobile phone subscribers around the globe, whose number is growing faster than fixed-line telephone subscribers, totaled nearly 1.5 billion by mid-2004, just under one-quarter of the world's population (Reuters, 2004b). As the convergence of mobile and Internet technologies comes to a fruition in the next few years, news and information consumption patterns of Internet users are bound to show ever more reliance on this digital medium as opposed to the traditional media, which are already grappling with decreasing circulations in nearly Internet-saturated societies like the United States.

Purveyors of news and information worldwide, therefore, are faced with difficult choices. The interactive attribute of the Internet naturally makes the online consumer of news and information use this medium to meet specific needs. To remain relevant to this new class of information consumers, producers of mass media have to find new ways to fulfill their specialized and varied needs. Yet for at least another decade, traditional media will remain the primary sources of news and information for those of the world's population who lack access to the Internet. Thus, a critical question faces mass media producers in this age of information revolution: Do you just glue on to the Internet the paper-and-ink version of the traditional newspaper or magazine, or do you go beyond that in view of the versatility of this revolutionary medium and the unique information needs of the online consumer?

This chapter will first discuss the traditional news operations of international print and broadcast news agencies and news organizations, and then review new directions in the packaging of news for online consumers. The chapter will also explore issues of quality and quantity in the flow of news between the developed and developing countries.

ORIGIN AND EARLY HISTORY
OF NEWS AGENCIES

News and mercantile information needs of the mass market press that emerged in the first half of the 1800s on both sides of the Atlantic provided the incentive for the creation of at least three of the major Western news agencies—the Associated Press (AP), Reuters, and Agence France-Presse (AFP). The mass market press, generally known as the penny press, had emerged as advertising became a significant source of revenue in industrially expanding societies, and readership increased because of the rising literacy and economic levels.

Sociologist Michael Schudson (1978) attributed the mass market for news in 1830s America to the emergence of a "democratic market society." More Americans were interested in business and politics than ever before. In business, this movement was expressed in the growth of a capitalistic middle class; in politics, it was known as Jacksonian, or "mass," democracy. The French saw their own versions of the so-called cheap press in 1836 as a vehicle for the restive middle class to push for more democracy—only 200,000 people could vote under the limited monarchy of Louis Philippe. In Britain, decreased newspaper production costs due to the removal of the newspaper stamp tax enabled the penny press to emerge in the 1850s to cater to a large, urban middle class.

Because no newspaper at the time had the financial and technical resources to gather and transmit news from far-flung areas to satisfy readers' growing demand for news, the stage was set for the establishment of news agencies. By selling their product to many newspapers, news agencies could supply a large amount of news at less expense than a newspaper would incur if it were to gather the same amount of news on its own. News agencies also had greater financial resources than the average newspaper to invest in technical facilities, such as the telegraph, to transmit the news as quickly as possible.

Agence France-Presse

The oldest of what were to eventually become the four major Western international news agencies, the Agence France-Presse (AFP) was created by Frenchman Charles-Louis Havas in 1835. Known as the Havas Agency at that time, the Paris-based news agency grew out of a news distribution service, used mostly by merchants and government officials, that Havas had started 10 years earlier. With the demand for news substantially up because of the emergence of the "cheap press" in France, Havas expanded his operations by hiring more correspondents and using the newly invented telegraph for faster delivery of news. By 1860 his agency was reporting news from all over Europe, and newspapers in most parts of the continent were subscribing to his agency.

Faced with Nazi aggression, the French government purchased the agency's news branch in 1940 to set up a propaganda office. The victorious Germans took over the agency and turned it into a part of the official Nazi news agency, DNB. In 1944, following liberation from occupying Nazi forces, the Havas Agency was given its present name, Agence France-Presse. In 1957, the French parliament passed legislation guaranteeing independence to the AFP.

Associated Press

The Associated Press (AP) grew out of the Harbor News Association, formed by 10 men representing six New York City newspapers in 1848 to pool efforts for collecting international news and to offset the prohibitive cost of transmitting news by telegraph. The newspapers at that time competed by sending reporters out in rowboats to meet the ships as they arrived in New York harbor. Competition had grown so fierce and expensive that it was decided to form a news cooperative. Cooperation among newspapers continues to be the operational policy of today's AP. In 1849, the Harbor News Association opened its first overseas bureau in Halifax, Nova Scotia, to meet ships arriving from Europe. This step enabled the association to telegraph stories to newspapers before ships docked in New York. Nine years later, news from Europe was arriving directly by transoceanic cable.

Following its merger with another news agency, the Harbor News Association became the New York Associated Press in 1857. To cut telegraphic costs, the New York AP formed news exchange agreements with regional newspaper groups in other parts of the country, including Western Associated Press, Southern Associated Press, and Philadelphia Associated Press. The New York AP distributed the most important news to them, including news from Washington DC and overseas. To this, each group added regional coverage. The Western Associated Press withdrew from the cooperative in 1885 and went on to form the Associated Press (AP), incorporated in Illinois, in 1892. The New York AP, which had fought this reorganization, went out of business that year. The AP expanded rapidly, with 700 newspapers subscribing to its service by the mid-1890s. In 1900, the AP was reorganized and incorporated in New York, where its headquarters have been ever since.

Two major changes have taken place in AP organization since 1945. In a historic decision, the U.S. Supreme Court held illegal a clause in AP bylaws under which members could block the effort of a competitor in the same city to obtain AP news service by requiring election to membership. As a result of the court ruling, AP membership was opened to all qualified U.S. newspapers. In 1946, radio stations, for the first time, were granted associate membership in AP, which allowed them to subscribe to its regular service. Previously, radio stations could subscribe only to a subsidiary service designed exclusively for them.

Reuters

Paul Julius Reuter, a German-born immigrant who took British citizenship in March 1857, opened a London office in October 1851, which transmitted stock market quotations between London and Paris using the first undersea cable. Two years earlier he had started using pigeons to fly stock prices between Aachen and Brussels. By 1859, Reuter had extended his service to the entire British press as well as to other European countries, expanding its content to include general and economic news. Read (1999) says that Reuter rightly regarded his general news service as running in tandem with his commercial services. "[Reuter] was well aware that reports of battles lost and won, of political crises, or even of bad weather could affect markets, and that, conversely, news of market crises often had political effects" (p. 28). Branch offices sprang up throughout Europe and beyond as the international telegraph network developed. By 1861, Reuter reporters were located in Asia, South Africa, and Australia. By 1874, Reuter had established a presence in the Far East and South America.

A family concern until 1915, the agency became a private company later that year with its current name, Reuters Limited. The Press Association, the U.K. press agency, took a majority holding in Reuters in 1925, and in 1939 the company moved its corporate headquarters to its present location at 85 Fleet Street in London. In 1941, following acquisition of a substantial amount of Reuters stock by British press associations, the agency became cooperative property of the British press. A Reuter Trust was also formed that year to safeguard the neutrality and independence of Reuters. Reuters was floated as a public company in 1984 on the London Stock Exchange and on NASDAQ in the United States. Reuters share ownership is now spread around the world, with the most significant holdings in Britain and the United States.

United Press International

The United Press International (UPI) was established on July 21, 1907, as the United Press Associations because its founder, E. W. Scripps, believed there should be no restrictions on who could buy news from a news service. Scripps was opposed to the restrictive membership rules of the AP, as they existed then, because member publishers could deny AP's service to new publishers.

His determination to fight this restriction caused him to organize the Scripps–McRae Press Association in the Midwest and the Scripps News Association on the Pacific Coast in the early 1900s. In 1906, he purchased control of the Publishers Press, a small news service in the East, and merged the three services the following year to form the United Press Associations. The news agency's name was changed to United Press International on May 16, 1958, when its facilities were joined with those of William Randolph Hearst's International News Service and International News Photos.

A significant highlight in UPI's history is that it was instrumental in freeing up news collection and dissemination worldwide by rejecting a cartel arrangement established by the other major Western news agencies in 1869. The AP, Reuters, AFP, and the German news agency Wolff had agreed to collect and distribute news exclusively in certain regions of the world and to exchange it among themselves for subsequent distribution to their subscribers. Soon after its creation in 1907, UPI challenged the cartel by selling its service abroad, first to Britain and then to Japan and South America. Not wanting to be left behind, the AP signed agreements with Havas in 1918 and Reuters in 1926 to sell its service in their exclusive zones. The closure of Wolff in 1933 and operational disagreements among the remaining three members led to the formal breakup of the cartel in 1934.

UPI, the world's largest privately owned news agency, eventually could not keep up with competing services and has gone through two bankruptcy reorganizations and five owners since being sold by the Scripps family in 1982. Under the control of a group of Saudi Arabian investors since 1992 ("UPI Sold," 1992), UPI was sold in mid-May 2000 to News World Communications, a global media company founded by the Rev. Sun Myung Moon of South Korea. This company publishes *The Washington Times,* and other newspapers and magazines in more than 20 countries. Arnaud de Borchgrave, who was UPI's president and CEO and has been its editor-at-large since 2003, told its staff members that although some top officials of News World Communications are members of the Unification Church, led by the Rev. Sun Myung Moon, the church has no formal ties to News World Communications ("Moonies Acquire UPI," 2000).

ITAR-TASS

Another of the world's largest news agencies is the Information Telegraph Agency of Russia (ITAR-TASS), the successor to the Soviet TASS news agency, whose origins date back to 1904. Concerned that false reports were being circulated abroad about Russia's economic state, Emperor Nikolai II gave the go-ahead on July 21, 1904, to establish the St. Petersburg Telegraph Agency (SPTA) "to make internal business developments widely known" (ITAR-TASS, 2004a). The agency began work on September 1, 1904.

SPTA became a comprehensive news agency in 1909, and its name was changed to Petrograd Telegraph Agency (PTA) in 1914. After the Bolshevik revolution of 1917, PTA was merged with Press Bureau, another government agency, and became Russian Telegraph Agency (ROSTA). ROSTA was created to distribute official communiqués and news items, as well as to send out propaganda material to the press in areas under Bolshevik control. The Telegraph Agency of the Soviet Union (TASS), with its headquarters in Moscow, replaced ROSTA on July 10, 1925. Under the Soviet media structure, TASS provided federal, state, and foreign news to national media and to each Soviet state's local news agency.

After the breakup of the Soviet Union in late 1991, Russia adopted the "Law of the Press," which abolished censorship for the first time in Russian history. A number of media organizations, however, were classified as "official," to be financed by the state budget. TASS was identified as one such official organization, although its director-general expected it to operate in an objective and professional manner (Ignatenko, 1993). In February 1992, the agency's name was changed to ITAR-TASS, following TASS's merger with the Information Telegraph Agency of Russia. It has retained its status as the state central information agency.

INTERNATIONAL NEWS AGENCIES TODAY

News dissemination by international news agencies has come a long way from Teletype delivery at 60 words per minute in the early 1950s. Today, news agencies using state-of-the-art telecommunications facilities—telephone, radio, cable, satellite phones, photo uplinks with mobile antennas, laptop computers with wireless satellite uplinks, and the Internet—can transmit up to 10,000 words per minute between any two points on the globe. On a typical day, the Associated Press, for example, is said to deliver millions of words and hundreds of photos and graphics. Let us turn to the contemporary operations of international print and broadcast news agencies.

Associated Press

The AP's stated mission is to provide factual coverage of news to all parts of the globe for use by the media around the world. "News bearing the AP logotype can be counted on to be accurate, balanced and informed" (AP, 2005). The AP subscribes to the code of ethics written by the Associated Press Managing Editors Association. As a not-for-profit cooperative, AP is owned by its 1,500 U.S. daily newspaper members. They elect a board of directors that directs the cooperative. The AP serves 1,700 U.S. daily, weekly, non-English, and college newspapers; 5,000 radio and television stations in the United States; and 8,500 newspaper, radio, and television subscribers in 121 countries. It has 3,700 employees, including 500 staff members abroad and 150 in Washington DC. The agency maintains 242 bureaus, with 120 of them abroad.

The AP says it sends more than 20 million words and about 1,000 photos each day to its subscribers worldwide. It serves as a source of news, photos, graphics, audio, and video for more than 1 billion people every day. As a cooperative, the AP also reserves the right to distribute stories done by its member newspapers to all its subscribers. The AP news services are delivered in the form of state, national, and international wires. A story that runs on a state wire will be seen only by newspaper and broadcast members in that state. A story that also "moves" nationally can be used by AP's U.S. newspaper members. A story that appears on AP's international wire reaches all of its international subscribers. In addition to its English-language service, AP's international wire is available in four foreign languages: French, Spanish, German, and Dutch (AP, 2005). The AP has also offered a separate sports wire since 1946.

In the early days of the Internet, AP began to offer its services via the Web through the Information Services division created in 1990. This division offered AP content to corporations and government agencies, and licensed it to distributors that provide news to the corporate market. Recognizing that online services had a huge business potential, the Associated Press announced the formation of a new unit called AP Digital on March 28, 2000, to concentrate on commercial sales of national, international, and other nonlocal categories of news and information to tap the large and growing Internet market. AP Information Services was integrated into AP Digital. To meet the specialized and varied information needs of the Web-based clientele, Thomas E. Slaughter, an AP Digital vice president, said, "We'll dramatically enhance content in several areas, including technology, business, entertainment and celebrities and health" (AP, 2000). By the end of 2000, AP had added staff to do niche-oriented news in the areas of business, technology, sports, entertainment, health, and science as a result of surveys on information needs and preferences of online consumers (Cunningham, 2000).

AP Digital offers news services with text, photos, audio, graphics, and video on a wide variety of topics to the Web and wireless markets. This division's Web-based services include news and information in the categories of U.S. and world, global perspectives, sports, business, technology, entertainment, politics and government, elections, health and wellness, and weather. Financial tools, another service by this division, offers stock quotes and content publishing tools from Stockgroup, a financial media and technology company, to AP's interactive customers. All of these services are supplemented with content from AP's Audio Services, which streams a live, 24-hour news and information radio format feed; and Video Services, which delivers the top international and U.S. stories from Associated Press Television News (APTN) 24 hours a day. For wireless Internet devices, AP Wireless Services offers news headlines, Short Message Service (SMS) news, financial market data, sports news in both headlines and streaming audio, and world news video.

AP Special News Packages, one of the services offered by AP Digital, delivers news and features with a combination of text, photos, audio, and video around a topic or theme. According to the AP Digital (2005) website, this service "engages your audience with a news presentation around a topic or theme in an easy-to-use and interactive pop-up window." It delivers top international and U.S. news by explaining complex issues with simplicity. State and local stories are not offered on this service so that the AP does not compete directly with its core customers—U.S. daily newspapers that cooperatively own AP. This service also offers news and features in the areas of sports, entertainment, business, and special events, and includes access to photo galleries of the day and week, and from the world of sports.

United Press International

Stating that "the world does not need another traditional wire service," then-UPI president Arnaud de Borchgrave announced in August 1999, that UPI would be transformed into a leading supplier of knowledge-based products to the Internet, "the fastest growing segment of the global news and information services market." According to de Borchgrave, who has been UPI's editor at large since 2003, this new line of products would be available under the company's new Knowledge@Work umbrella, "designed to meet the appetite of today's Internet clients for on-demand news, analysis, expert advisories and guidance, investigative pieces, and practical intelligence" (de Borchgrave, 1999).

Upon its launch, UPI's Knowledge@Work products included Global Impact Net, WebLine, and SpecializedWeb Newsletters. They offered in-depth news, investigative pieces, and news analysis through Global Impact Net; brief, real-time, breaking news through WebLine; and a host of specialized news and information services for professionals and businesses through SpecializedWeb Newsletters. The company has renamed its Web-based services as UPI News-Track, UPI Perspectives, UPI Science Desk, and UPI Newspictures.

According to the company's website, UPI NewsTrack provides up-to-date information for readers who are looking for news in a short, concise format of 100 to 200 words. NewsTrack stories are tailored to meet the needs of websites that need frequently changing news items, publications looking for short stories, and broadcasters in need of current news. Headlines can be extracted from each story as a hypertext link. UPI NewsTrack follows and updates the day's top stories in the areas of national and international news, science, business, entertainment, sports, and "quirks" in the news.

UPI Perspectives provides readers with issue-focused reports required to make informed business or policy decisions. Covering a cross-section of economic, financial, policy, scientific, geopolitical, and sociological topics, UPI Perspectives covers the day's current issues from multiple angles while looking ahead at the major issues of tomorrow. Reports are issued in the form of analysis, commentary, feature stories and special reports, and people in the news.

UPI Science Report provides daily updates on a host of topics of concern to the business of science, technology, and health. The UPI Science Report package consists of 30 to 50 features and news stories per business day.

UPI Newspictures makes available pictures for purchase in the areas of news, entertainment, sports, Washington, and lifestyle and culture. The Washington photo file focuses on the president and Congress, including meetings with world leaders, speeches, state dinners, and daily politics.

A pioneer in radio news wire, UPI got out of the broadcast news business in 1999 as part of its plan to devote attention exclusively to products for and delivered via the Internet. The Associated Press acquired the UPI broadcast wire service and radio division and its 400 subscribers in August 1999.

UPI has a total of 157 employees, including 107 in the United States, 28 in London, 16 in Latin America, and 6 in Asia. Its reports are disseminated through contracts with about 150 "redistributors" throughout the world, such as the Kyodo News agency of Japan. In addition to its English report, UPI provides news coverage coming out of the Middle East in Arabic and a Spanish-language news report from its correspondents in Latin America. Clients include print publications, websites, multimedia companies, corporations, governments, and academic and policy institutions. At the time of this writing in February 2005, no information was available from UPI on its revenue or the number of subscribers to its new line of services.

Reuters

Reuters dedicates the bulk of its resources to providing financial information to the global financial markets, although it is also heavily involved in supplying news services to media subscribers worldwide. Its information and news products include real-time financial data; collective investment data; numerical, textual, historical, and graphical databases; plus news services for print and broadcast media, websites, and consumers.

Reuters claims to be the world's largest international multimedia news agency, although more than 90 percent of its revenue is derived from its financial services business. Some 327,000 financial market professionals working in the equities, fixed income, foreign exchange, money, commodities, and energy markets around the world use Reuters products. Data are provided for more than 940,000 shares, bonds, and other financial instruments, as well as for 40,000 companies. Financial information is obtained from 258 exchanges and over-the-counter markets, contributed by 5008 clients. Reuters provides real-time data on 5.5 million financial records, typically updating financial data 8,000 times per second. At peak times, the data are updated 23,000 times per second (Reuters, 2004a).

News organizations in 157 countries subscribe to the agency's news services either directly or through their national news agencies, which translate the Reuters copy into their own languages for distribution. Reuters news wires are available in English, Spanish, and Portuguese. Reuters, which has a total of 14,700 staff members, employs 2,300 editorial staff, journalists, photographers, and camera operators in 197 bureaus in 130 countries. News is gathered and edited for both business and media clients, with over 8 million words published daily in 19 languages. Reuters says its services are delivered to clients over the world's most extensive private satellite, cable communications, and Internet network. The company's profit soared to $666 million in 2004 from $95 million in 2003 (*The New York Times, 2005*).

Reuters is also using the Internet extensively for wider distribution of information and news and claims to be among the most-read news sources on the Internet, reaching millions in their offices, in their homes, or on PDAs. In addition to the traditional print and TV media, Reuters provides online services to more than 1,000 Internet sites globally, reaching an estimated 50 million users each month, according to the Reuters Media website. Reuters provides its online services in seven categories: Online Reports, Financial Products, Target News, News Wires for Online, Online Video, Pictures, and News Graphics.

Online Reports provides continually updated news reports delivered in a prioritized, "Top-Ten" story package that automatically posts the latest breaking news summaries around the clock. Financial Products provides real-time updates on company and market news, financial data, and commodities and energy. According to Reuters, a key objective of this service is to serve the needs of businesses at all levels because the Internet is ideally suited to the needs of smaller and geographically dispersed markets throughout the world. For example, potential customers for commodities and energy products include farmers, agricultural cooperatives, food processors, traders, utilities, and other participants in the electricity and gas markets.

Target News, another of the agency's online services, offers continually updated news reports on preselected topics—such as "Legal," "Cancer," or "Employment" Target News—delivered every five minutes in 10 languages. News Wires for Online offers comprehensive news feeds that allow websites to support in-house news operations and site-specific presentations of the day's most important news developments. Online Video offers video reports of up to 40 stories daily featuring general news, financial, health, and entertainment video news updates. The Pictures online service provides news images and archival pictures. This service also provides access to the Reuters Entertainment Pictures Service. News Graphics provides informative graphic elements that explain concepts behind the news.

Reuters believes that its premier position as a global news and information group is based on a reputation for speed, accuracy, integrity, and impartiality, as well as continuous technological innovation.

Agence France-Presse

Agence France-Presse is the third-largest global wire service after the Associated Press and Reuters. Like Reuters and AP, AFP continues to provide a variety of services for the traditional media but has also developed a new line of services for the online sector. With its headquarters in central Paris, AFP provides general, economic, and sports news services in English, French, German, Spanish, Portuguese, and Arabic, delivering 2 million words a day.

The flagship general news wire carries about 400,000 to 600,000 words a day on politics, diplomacy, economics, society, sports, science, medicine, culture, people, and human interest. Subscribers include the new and traditional media, businesses, universities, embassies, institutions, and public offices. In 1995, AFP ended its agreement with the Associated Press on its provision of American news and set up an autonomous newsgathering network in the United States. The AFP Sports Service provides an average of 10,000 words of sports news daily in six languages and is the only international agency to distribute in Arabic. Volume can double on weekends and quadruple during multisport events such as the Olympics.

AFP has developed a niche among news agencies for its photo service, which is recognized in the industry for its unique angle on general, international, and sports news. The photo service carries about 1,000 news, sports, business, entertainment, and feature photos and 50 news graphics each day, as well as feature packages (AFP, 2005b). AFP's archives contain more than 7 million photos, dating as far back as 1930. AFP says it has set up a state-of-the-art photo server called ImageForum, which allows subscribers to download images directly or through the Internet. The digital photo service is supplemented with about 80 maps, charts, and other graphics daily.

AFP's subscribers include 650 newspapers and periodicals; 400 radio and television stations; 1,500 businesses, banks, and public and private organizations; and about 100 national news agencies around the world. In addition to its editorial staff, AFP employs 1,200 reporters, 200 photographers, and 2,000 stringers in 165 countries. It also supplies radio features and reports, computer graphics, and multimedia services on the Internet and Intranet (AFP, 2005a).

AFX News is the economic wire, a wholly owned subsidiary of Agence France-Presse, with its headquarters in London. With a focus on European coverage, its real-time business and financial news services are designed to meet the requirements of the international banking and investor community in English, French, German, Italian, Spanish, and Dutch. Over 6,000 financial news items each workday are written by the international network of AFX News and its partners and journalists working from bureaus in all major financial centers around the world with a strong focus on equities and economic commentary. AFX News products are available over all common open news platforms, including Internet, satellite, and terrestrial links.

Through agreements in early 2000 with France's Alcatel telecommunications company and Finland's Nokia Corporation, AFP began to distribute information services through any fixed or mobile Internet device, including mobile phones, screen phones, and set-top boxes for televisions. General, economic, and sports news stories are automatically formatted for the appropriate user device, regardless of screen size or operating system. AFP says the new service will enable telecommunications carriers to provide their users with access to personalized information services anywhere, anytime, and on any device. They will have access to extensive personalization and filtering tools that focus on the individual user's profile and interests (AFP, 2000). The online services have been available in English, German, French, Spanish, Portuguese, and Arabic.

In early 2005, AFP was offering a variety of online services, including AFP News Online, AFP Direct, AFP a la carte, Lifestyle Europe, Formula 1, European Football Championships, and Magazine Forum. AFP News Online supplies websites with a specially crafted, real-time news service covering the latest international news and sports with pictures. AFP Direct offers AFP news wires to individual subscribers directly. Stories can be selected by subject, degree of urgency, and geographical origin. AFP Pocket is a lighter version of this service designed for mobile phones. AFP a la Carte is a customized subscription service. Clients select the type of information they wish to receive by predefining key words and other profiling criteria. Updates are delivered live via email, ftp, or other Internet delivery methods. Lifestyle Europe service offers what AFP calls "the inside track on modern European living," with a focus on news, travel, celebrities, home life, food and wine, art, fashion, and music. Formula 1 service provides complete coverage of the Grand Prix racing season in 15 languages, whereas European Football Championships service provides coverage of seven of the most popular championships in Europe. Finally, the Magazine Forum service offers ready-to-use articles in the areas of culture, lifestyle, sports, science, and leisure.

ITAR-TASS and Interfax

In existence since 1992, ITAR-TASS is the state-owned successor to the Soviet-era TASS news agency. Whereas TASS was a propaganda arm of the Soviet communist system, often providing its news service practically free to countries that were potential candidates for communism, ITAR-TASS has been struggling to become a credible, mainstream international news agency. That objective will be difficult to accomplish as long as ITAR-TASS remains the state news agency. By its own admission, ITAR-TASS's transition to an independent, objective, and reliable agency is still far from complete. Vitali Ignatenko, current director general of ITAR-TASS, told the International Press Institute several years ago that, despite the abolition of censorship and other official restraints over the media in Russia, the political desire to make use of the media remained

(Ignatenko, 1993). The International Press Institute, in its annual report for 2003 on the Russian media, said that under Vladimir Putin's presidency, the government has secured greater control over the state-owned media. "In consequence, the media and government are very closely related and reporting a contrary view can lead to substantial financial and legal obstacles" (IPI, 2005).

In order to improve the quality of service to its clients, ITAR-TASS says it has developed a new set of priorities designed to streamline and improve key aspects of its operation, including how topics are selected, expansion of news coverage, and timely delivery of news. It has 130 bureaus and offices, with about 200 reporters, in Russia and abroad. It has cooperative relationships with more than 80 foreign news agencies. In addition to Russian, the agency's news service is available in English, French, German, Spanish, and Arabic. The agency describes its daily volume of transmitted information at "about 200 newspaper pages" (ITAR-TASS, 2004b). With an output ranging from 50 to 100 photos daily, ITAR-TASS also distributes pictures of current developments in Russia, the CIS, and world. The video news service of the agency, called TASS-TV, maintains television bureaus in major capitals of the world. The agency's news service is available on the Internet on a subscription basis. It also offers specialized reports on Russian political and economic life in English on a subscription basis by fax or email.

ITAR-TASS is facing stiff competition from another Russian news agency called Interfax, which offers general and financial news services. Interfax was set up by several officials of Radio Moscow, Soviet Union's international broadcasting station, as the first independent news agency at a time when the decline of the Soviet era was imminent. Interfax established its credibility while covering the 1991 coup attempt in Russia, when, unlike TASS, it became a major source of accurate and reliable information. Interfax claims that its current credibility is reinforced by the kind of customers it draws, including "the most distinguished corporations, investment funds, brokerage houses, banks, institutions, federal agencies and government structures worldwide" (Interfax, 2003). It has subscribers in more than 100 countries. The agency has about 1,000 staff members in more than 70 bureaus. It produces more than 1,500 stories a day.

SUPPLEMENTAL NEWS AGENCIES

Whereas traditional news agencies, such as the AP and Reuters, are excellent in providing spot coverage, newspapers needing more specialized fare—such as hard news exclusives, investigative reporting, political commentary, and concentrated business coverage—turn to supplemental wire services. David Shaw, media writer for the *Los Angeles Times,* says that reporters who like to write investigative stories or stories that challenge the establishment find little opportunity to do so with traditional wire services such as the AP or Reuters because they are in the business of mass marketing the news (Shaw, 1988).

The major supplemental services in the United States are the New York Times News Service, the Los Angeles Times–Washington Post News Service, and Dow Jones Newswires. Founded in 1917, the New York Times News Service is the world's largest supplemental news service, distributing op-ed essays by the *Times'* columnists and about 300 news articles gathered by the *Times* and its 11 partner news organizations to 650 clients in more than 50 countries each day. In addition, the New York Times Syndicate distributes more than 70 columns, special features, and news services from the *Times* and other sources to 2,000 clients worldwide. The service is available in English and Spanish (New York Times News Service/Syndicate, 2004).

Subscribing to the Los Angeles Times-Washington Post News Service gives organizations access to the reports of 10 contributing publications. The service provides national and international news, analysis, and features, averaging 110 stories a day and more than 100 weekly columns. This service, also available on the Internet, has 600 clients worldwide (Los Angeles Times–Washington Post News Service, 2005).

Dow Jones & Company's rebranded news service, Dow Jones Newswires, provides economic, financial, and market-moving political news from around the world. It is also a leading real-time financial news provider, delivering up to 10,000 news items a day to more than 323,000 financial professionals in 66 countries in 11 languages. It has 700 real-time editors and reporters. This news service is part of Dow Jones & Company's global news network of nearly 1,600 news staff. Dow Jones Newswires also draws on the resources of several of its media partners, including the Associated Press and Nikkei. Dow Jones Newswires content is also accessible through various corporate Internet sites, electronic exchanges, corporate intranets, and business information services ("Dow Jones Press Release," 2004).

BROADCAST NEWS SERVICES

Reuters and Associated Press Television News (APTN) are the two dominant video news agencies in the world today, after taking over the operations of Visnews and WTN, respectively. Reuters has long claimed to have the world's largest television news service, twice the size of CNN's international news-gathering operations (Wood, 1998). Reuters' World News Service is the prime delivery vehicle for its breaking news feeds in the categories of international news, business, and sports. Reuters' correspondents directly transmit raw news footage to the London newsroom, where stories are edited, scripted, and packaged for distribution via Reuters satellite network. Live video is flashed to supplement the regular schedule, bringing breaking stories direct to broadcasters as they happen. Every video story on World News Service is accompanied by detailed shot-lists, scripts, and background to provide broadcasters the context to tell the whole story.

Reuters Reports, a specialized service of the agency, provides the top 15 news stories of the moment in ready-to-air format, with a total of 60 international news, sports, and business stories daily. An English-language voiceover on one audio channel is supplemented by natural sound on the other. A transcript of each voiceover is also provided to enable translation. Updated every six hours, Reuters Reports are available for primetime news, online offerings, wireless applications, or in-flight news.

Reuters News Video Online, another service, includes up to 15 stories of the moment throughout the day, ready for online or wireless publication with virtually no additional processing. An English-language voiceover is provided, and a transcript of each voiceover is also available to allow translation, if required. The Reuters network of 80 television bureaus worldwide forms the backbone of the video agency's newsgathering activities. Some 310 subscribers plus their networks and affiliates in 93 countries use Reuters' television news coverage (Reuters, 2005).

APTN has been the international television arm of the Associated Press since 1998 and the successor to APTV, a video news service launched in 1994. APTN provides video of the day's top news, sports, and entertainment stories by satellite to major news organizations worldwide from 80 bureaus worldwide. A total of 330 international broadcasters receive AP's global video news service, APTN; and SNTV, a sports joint-venture video service. AP Broadcast, another division of the Associated Press, provides coverage of news, sports, weather, entertainment, business, and politics to over 5,000 television and radio stations in the United States (APTN, 2005). The AP launched the AP Radio Network in 1974 to provide hourly newscasts, sportscasts, and business programs. In early 2005, the service was received by nearly 1,000 AP broadcast members. In August 1999, AP acquired United Press International's broadcast news division and its 400 subscribers.

AP Digital is a division of the Associated Press that provides video news, sports, and entertainment content to over 500 broadcast newsrooms, portals, Web, broadband, and mobile customers worldwide. AP Digital creates interactive products using AP text, photos, graphics, audio and video, and selected information from content partners. This division also provides targeted industry-specific news packages and custom content categories for specific audiences. Services are offered in English, Spanish, French, Dutch, and German. News videos produced by APTN are also available through an online feed or hosted platform for websites and interactive services. Clips cover U.S. and international news, politics, entertainment, business, and human-interest stories, plus daily one-minute world news and financial markets summaries. AP Financial News provides coverage of companies and financial markets around the world (AP Digital Services, 2005).

Among other major broadcast services, The Wall Street Journal Report offers financial and business newscasts for both television and radio in the form of 2-minute reports every hour, Monday through Friday. This network also offers the Dow Jones Money Report, which provides 1-minute news briefs on money news and consumer trends from 5 A.M. to 9 P.M. Eastern Time. These services air on more than 230 broadcast stations in the United States. CNN operates a national and international radio network known as CNN Radio Network. Beginning every hour, the network offers a 5-minute newscast, with the latest information on news in the United States and around the world. Stations have a choice of running 2 minute, 3.5 minute, or the full 5-minute newscast. The network also offers a 2-minute newscast at half past every hour. Affiliate stations are alerted ahead of time when this broadcast will be breaking news. CNN's other radio divisions provide sports and business news.

GLOBAL NEWSPAPERS, MAGAZINES, AND BROADCASTERS

Several international newspapers, magazines, and broadcasting organizations also play a significant role as purveyors of news globally. Three newspapers that are especially valued by opinion leaders around the world are *The New York Times, The Times* of London, and *The Guardian,* also from Britain. In 2004, the *New York Times* had a weekday circulation of just over 1.1 million and Sunday circulation of 1.7 million. The *New York Times* online had almost 14 million registered users as of January 2005, with approximately 30 percent from abroad. Almost 74 percent of the users had a graduate or post-graduate level of university education (nytimes.com, 2005). The London *Times,* which became a tabloid in November 2004, had a daily circulation of 682,109, and *The Guardian* sold 377,292 copies daily in late 2004 (LexisNexis, 2004). Both British newspapers are available on the Internet as well. A truly global newspaper, although not as influential among global opinion makers as the preceding three, is *The International Herald Tribune,* which has been owned by *The New York Times* since January 2003 and is based in Paris. It is printed simultaneously via satellite at 28 locations worldwide and distributed globally. In early 2005, it had a daily circulation of 240,000, with a total readership of more than 600,000 in 180 countries. Much of its copy comes from *The New York Times.*

The Wall Street Journal, the flagship publication of Dow Jones & Company, is a global business daily. With *The Wall Street Journal Europe,* published in Brussels, and *The Asian Wall Street Journal,* published in Hong Kong, it had a worldwide circulation of 2.6 million in early 2005, including 167,159 subscribers in the United States. Its online edition had 712,000 subscribers. Another prestigious global business newspaper is *The Financial Times* of London, which also publishes a North American edition via satellite. In early 2005, it had a global circulation of 426,826, including about 60,000 copies sold in the United States (Media Life, 2005).

Among newsmagazines, three stand out for their global reach—*Time, Newsweek,* and Britain's *Economist. TIME,* with its early 2005 circulation of 4.2 million in the United States alone, sold an additional million-plus copies to readers overseas. It publishes editions for Canada, Europe, the Middle East, Asia, Africa, and Latin America. *Newsweek's* U.S. circulation in early 2005 was 3.1 million; in addition, the magazine sold about 1 million copies internationally through its editions for Europe, Japan, Latin America, the Pacific, and Southeast Asia. *The Economist,* with a strong reputation for its comprehensive coverage of global issues and good writing, had a worldwide circulation surpassing 1 million in early 2005, turning it into one of the world's fastest-growing weekly newsmagazines (Goldfarb, 2005).

In international television news broadcasting, CNN International (CNNI) is a global, 24-hour news network, offering comprehensive news coverage from the CNN News Group's 37 worldwide bureaus in early 2005. Programmed specifically for a global audience, CNNI transmits five separate feeds that broadcast to Europe/Middle East/Africa, South Asia, Asia Pacific, Latin America, and North America. CNNI can be seen in more than 176 million television households in more than 200 countries and territories worldwide. In addition, CNN/US has 86 million subscribers in the United States. The CNN News Group has a news-gathering network of 4,000 staff and 900 global television affiliates (CNN, 2005).

CNN International's biggest competitor today is BBC World, the British Broadcasting Corporation's international news and information television channel, broadcasting 24 hours a day around the world from its headquarters in London. In operation since 1991, BBC World can be seen in 258 million homes in more than 200 countries and territories. BBC World provides news, business, sports, and weather 24 hours a day, plus the best of the BBC's current affairs, documentary, and lifestyle programming. BBC claims that it is the world's largest and most trusted news organization. BBC News, which supplies news programming for BBC World, has 58 bureaus worldwide, with more than 250 news correspondents and a staff of more than 2,000. BBC World is a commercial channel funded by advertising and subscription (BBC World, 2005b).

In the United States, BBC's U.S.-specific channel, BBC America, is received in nearly 35 million homes. This channel, which primarily shows U.K.-focused arts and entertainment programming, carries BBC World's half-hour news bulletins during morning and evening hours. Since a 1998 agreement with U.S. public television, BBC World News bulletins reached over 80 percent of homes on PBS stations in early 2005. BBC World provides dedicated local programming for the channel's substantial audiences in Europe and India, plus 70 hours per week of Japanese translation. Partly for that reason, BBC World's reach in India as of late 2004, for example, was double that of CNN International's. BBC World became available on the Internet in 1999, when it dedicated the world's first all-digital 24-hour newsroom in London (BBC World, 2005a).

Another significant player in international television news broadcasting is Deutsche Welle TV, the German public broadcaster's international satellite television channel. DW-TV broadcasts news and public affairs programming in German, English, and Spanish in rotating 2-hour time slots. Canada's Newsworld International, another 24-hour news channel, has been available in the United States for several years by direct-to-home satellite television. This channel also rebroadcasts news programming from some countries.

As more countries take advantage of satellite communication technology, additional sources of television news are becoming available for international audiences. Among the countries operating 24-hour international channels that carry some news programming in English are Japan (NHK), India (DD World), China (CCTV), Egypt (Nile News), and South Korea (Arirang TV World).

A particularly noteworthy new contender in international news broadcasting is the Qatar-based Al Jazeera. Founded in 1996, it is the fastest-growing news network among Arab communities and Arabic-speaking people around the world, with a global audience approaching 50 million in December 2004. Criticism from various governments in the Middle East because of its candid and aggressive coverage of the region has helped the channel increase its credibility with an audience that is used to censorship and biased coverage from official government outlets. Because of its credibility and wide viewership, Al Jazeera has also been a source of concern to some Western governments for its independent and Arab perspective on international issues.

France is also getting ready to enter the global broadcast news competition. French Prime Minister Jean-Pierre Raffarin announced in late 2004 that his country will launch a global French-language satellite TV news channel in early 2006. President Jacques Chirac floated the idea of a French global TV channel in 2002 to raise the profile of his country's diplomacy, as France led international opposition to U.S. plans to invade Iraq. France has long wanted to counter what it sees as the dominance of Anglo-American coverage of world events, spearheaded by CNN and the BBC. Analysts in Paris said the French government's objective is to use the new broadcaster as a platform to counter the prevailing U.S. view of world affairs, particularly in Africa and the Middle East, where France has mostly good relations (BBC News, 2004).

India, the world's largest democracy and an emerging economic power, is also eyeing the international news market. Prime Minister Manmohan Singh told the country's broadcasters in February 2005 that they should seriously consider going global to compete with the "BBCs and CNNs." Considering that India's press has a tradition of objective reporting and the country is set to emerge as the largest English-speaking nation in the world (Crystal, 2004), India stands a good chance of becoming an important player in the international news and information market.

The flow of news internationally through radio has been a reality for several decades, although it has generally been viewed as propaganda because international radio broadcasting has been performed primarily by government-run stations. Two government-sponsored stations, however, have established their credibility as reliable sources of news to listeners worldwide. They are the BBC World Service and the Voice of America. The BBC World Service, which went on the air in 1932, broadcast in June 2004 in English and 42 other languages to an international radio audience of 146 million, including 4.7 million regular listeners in the United States (BBC Press Office, 2004). The service is also available on the Internet. Studies have shown that, in several countries, BBC World Service news is regarded as more credible than the native radio newscasts (Rampal & Adams, 1990).

The Voice of America (VOA), established as the international broadcasting service of U.S. government in 1942, reached some 100 million listeners worldwide as of early 2005. VOA puts out more than 1,000 hours per week of broadcasts in English and 43 other languages through radio, satellite television, and the Internet. It has more than 30 correspondents at 22 news bureaus in the

United States and many other countries, along with several hundred stringers around the world (VOA, 2005). Other major international broadcasters include Radio Moscow, Radio Beijing, Deutsche Welle Radio, Radio France International, Radio Nederland, All India Radio, and Radio Cairo.

NEWS FLOW PATTERNS: OFFLINE AND ONLINE

Before turning to the implications of the Internet for global news flow, let us review the problems and patterns in the flow of news associated with the traditional media system. Developing countries have been long concerned because the four major Western news agencies control the bulk of the world's news flow, with an output of about 30 million words daily; the next five leading news agencies accounted for only 1.09 million words daily in early 1990s (Frederick, 1993).

Developing countries have also raised specific concerns since the 1970s regarding the pattern of news flow emerging from the dominance of Western news agencies. First, people in developing countries are forced to see each other, and even themselves, through the medium of these agencies because they are major suppliers of news to the developing world. Second, Western information dominance confines judgments and decisions on what should be known, and how it should be made known, into the hands of a few, resulting in an inadequate, negative, and stereotypical portrayal of developing countries. Third, the flow of news is heavily imbalanced, with information moving predominantly from advanced Western countries to developing countries. The fourth area of concern is that the West exercises a kind of "soft power" by virtue of the strong appeal of its cultural fare—films, television, music, books, and magazines—in the developing world, to the detriment of local cultural traditions.

Some recent studies lend support to these concerns. A 1996 study on the Associated Press, the largest news agency, found that "the distribution of AP bureaus and correspondents seems to reflect American corporate and government priorities among core regions and glacial disinterest in peripheral Third World regions" (Schiff, 1996, p. 12). The "core regions" for the AP constituted Western Europe and Japan, the sources of much of the AP output outside the United States. The study also found that the republics and satellites of the former Soviet Union, central and south Asia, Central America, and Africa are undercovered by the AP. A content analysis study of *The New York Times* found that the foreign news hole was shrinking and that international news was increasingly being reported within the context of U.S. interests. Additionally, reports on Western industrial nations dominated, and coverage of developing nations had decreased (Riffe, 1996).

The imbalance of news flow is not just a developed/developing countries phenomenon, however. A content analysis study of *The New York Times, The Washington Post,* the three major newsmagazines, and the commercial network news found that Scandinavian coverage was mostly crisis oriented, "enough so as to conclude that the Third World has no exclusive right to complaints that the U.S. media largely overlook developmental stories in favor of spot crisis–oriented news" (Fridriksson, 1993). The study also found that, were it not for the reporting of various isolated crises, overall coverage of Scandinavia in the American media would be so scant as to be practically nonexistent.

In a 1998 article, Herbert Schiller notes that "the American state of ignorance of the rest of the world has been extended since the end of the Cold War" (p. 189). Schiller cites a television news study to prove his point:

> [T]he number and length of foreign topics in the evening news have declined far below Cold War levels. As a percentage of all topics between 1970 and 1995, the share of foreign stories fell from 35 percent to 23 percent, and the average length of these stories dropped from 1.7 minutes to 1.2 minutes. Worse, while the networks devoted on average more than 40 percent of total news time to foreign items in the 1970s, that share had been cut to 13.5 percent of news time by 1995. (p. 189)

Support for developing countries' concern over "soft power" comes from a 1998 article in the *Washington Post,* which reports that international sales of American popular culture products totaled $60.2 billion in 1996. The article quotes sociologist Todd Gitlin, who calls American popular culture "the latest in a long succession of bidders for global unification." Gitlin continues, "It succeeds the Latin imposed by the Roman Empire and the Catholic Church, and Marxist Leninism imposed by Communist government" (Farhi & Rosenfeld, 1998, p. A1).

These studies and articles also support some earlier theories on international news flow. Hester (1973) posits that nations of the world have designated places in an international pecking order. Perceptions of positions in that order partially determine the flow, direction, and volume of news. Hester also argues that strong economic relations or cultural affinities will increase the flow of news among nations, as will the perception of threat between any two nations. Galtung (1971) says that there is a "center-periphery" pattern in the flow of international news. News, he notes, flows mostly from the "center," or dominant countries, to the "periphery," or dependent areas. Kariel and Rosenvall (1984) find that the "eliteness" of a nation as a news source is the most important criterion for news selection.

Developing countries have tried various ways to address their concerns regarding international news flow. Beginning in the mid-1970s, they pushed for a new world information order (NWIO) through UNESCO. Among a variety of actions proposed to address problems associated with international news flow, one proposal called for regulating collection, processing, and transmission of news and data across national frontiers. Western countries strongly rejected such a move, with the United States and Britain eventually pulling out of UNESCO when the NWIO debate was seen to be taking political overtones. Then, upon UNESCO's recommendation, developing countries moved to establish or expand their own regional and global newsgathering operations. As a result, the developing world saw a variety of regional news agencies, including the Non-Aligned News Agencies Pool, Latin America's Inter Press Service,

Manila-based DEPTH, the Pan African News Agency, and the Caribbean News Agency. With the possible exception of Inter Press Service, none of these agencies has posed a serious challenge to the major Western news agencies or acquired significant credibility for its own news service. The Internet offers the best hope to developing countries seeking a low-cost vehicle for news distribution and a more balanced flow of news globally. For example, Gopal Raju, publisher of the New York–based newspaper for the Indian community, *India Abroad,* started India Abroad News Service in 1987, which later was renamed Indo-Asian News Service (IANS).

From serving a single subscriber free in 1987, IANS today is India's first multinational and multilingual wire service, having carved a niche in reporting on India, South Asia, and events of interest to this region around the world. IANS dispatches find a place in national and regional newspapers throughout India, publications and websites serving the global Indian diaspora, and newspapers looking at India and South Asia in other parts of the world, particularly in the Gulf region, where there is a large expatriate South Asian population. Based in New Delhi and accredited with the Indian government as an Indian news agency, IANS has subscribers in the United Arab Emirates, South Africa, Bangladesh, Sri Lanka, Australia, and Canada (IANS, 2005). An IANS spokesman in New York said that such an operation would not have been possible without the Internet, which greatly reduces the cost of news distribution to subscribers. According to a news release from the agency, "For the first time, news about India or of interest to India from different countries is being reported by IANS with an Indian perspective and not seen through the prism of the State Department or Whitehall or through the tinted eye glasses of a Western reporter" (IANS, 2000).

The Internet, however, is not a panacea for tackling the various concerns that the developing world has raised about global news flow. Although the distribution of news by a news agency to its clients via the Internet is much cheaper than via the traditional telecommunications system, a budding news agency must meet other costs and challenges before it acquires the necessary credibility as a global news service. For an emerging news agency to offer a comprehensive and quality news service, it must have an adequate number of professionally educated and trained reporters around the world. The financing required to hire the necessary staff and maintain news bureaus around the world is beyond the reach of most developing countries. And then there is the issue of quality of information. In the glut of information available on the Internet, credibility will be a key source of power and influence. Keohane and Nye (1998) say that news organizations in the United States, Britain, and France have capabilities for collecting intelligent information that dwarf those of other nations, adding that "information power flows to those who can edit and credibly validate information to sort out what is both correct and important . . . Brand names and the ability to bestow an international seal of approval will become more important" (pp. 88–89). Emerging news agencies will have a lot of catching up to do before they can compete with the established Western news agencies, and that will not be an easy task. As Keohane and Nye say, "In some commercial situations, a fast follower can do better than a first mover, but in terms of power among states, it is usually better to be first" (p. 88).

The Internet has greater promise in serving as an equalizer in the skewed flow of news and information globally, another of the concerns raised by the developing world. The typical 8 percent of the news and editorial space devoted to international news by an average U.S. metro daily—or about 14 percent (just over 3 minutes) of news time for such news programmed by television networks in the United States—does not offer much of a window on the world. Now, at the click of a mouse, an Internet subscriber can be reading newspapers from across the world while at the same time taking in the audiovisual news services of an increasing number of Web-based international broadcasters, such as BBC World. For example, *The Washington Post* ombudsman noted with embarrassment that it took until November 12, 1999, for the *Post* to carry a comprehensive story from its Delhi-based correspondent about a cyclone that hit the East Indian state of Orissa at the end of October.

The *Post* story on the cyclone, which had claimed 10,000 lives and affected 15 million people, was not on the front page; it ran, instead, on page A27. One reader, having found the news about the cyclone in a number of English-language Indian newspapers and other news outlets on the Web, wondered in a letter to the editor whether the *Post* was ignoring the story because "Orissa is not Europe and does not have oil underground" (*The Washington Post,* 1999, p. B6).

Another component of the information age, international satellite television, is providing more international news and information than ever before. Dozens of countries are transmitting daily television programs around the clock from Europe, the Middle East, Asia, and Latin America to niche and ethnic markets in the United States and elsewhere in the world. The huge supply of digital channels is also bringing crystal-clear radio programming from scores of countries via both communication satellites and the Internet.

A significant dimension of news flow on the Internet is that people in nondemocratic states are beginning to have access to uncensored news, analysis, and discussions about political developments in their own countries, even though regimes in such countries are jittery about the free flow of information. For example, the *New York Times* reported on March 18, 1999, that in the Middle East every government has jammed radio broadcasts, intercepted publications, scuttled fax transmissions, barred mobile telephones, or prohibited satellite television at one time or another (Jehl, 1999). The *Times* story adds that with the arrival of the Internet in the mid-1990s, many countries, including Egypt, Jordan, and Lebanon, have quietly conceded the fight, concluding that the benefits of the new technology far outweigh the cost. Other countries, such as Saudi Arabia, Iran, China, Malaysia, and Singapore ("Singapore Unveils," 1996), have been in the news in recent years for taking action to keep politically objectionable material out of the reach of their Internet subscribers, even as they embrace this technology for economic development and other uses. With new websites emerging every day, however, it is practically impossible to keep Internet users in authoritarian and totalitarian regimes from gaining access to freewheeling news and political discussions. Nye and Owens (1996) see a great opportunity in the

Internet for the United States to "engage the people, keeping them informed on world events and helping them prepare to build democratic market societies when the opportunity arises" (p. 30).

With all the promise that the Web holds for addressing some of the asymmetries in the global news and information flow, there is a major problem. As mentioned at the beginning of this chapter, less than one-fourth of humanity will be on the Internet by 2010. Most people will not have access to the Internet because of the underdevelopment of telecommunications infrastructure necessary for getting online. That only about 550 million people outside North America were using the Internet in late 2004, however, indicates that, even when there are no infrastructure problems, millions of people are not able to get online. In a move to narrow the "digital divide" between countries with access to information technology and those without, the World Bank and a Japanese Internet investment group, Softbank, set up a fund in February 2000 to help developing nations expand Internet projects. James Wolfensohn, president of the World Bank, said that the $520 million fund will be used to help set up indigenous companies to promote the Internet in 140 developing countries (BBC World Service, 2000).

THE OUTLOOK

The expansion of political and civil liberties, including press freedom, in several parts of the world bodes well for the collection and free flow of news. The emergence of democracy, albeit in varying degrees, in Eastern Europe, Russia, Latin America, and a number of African countries, as well as the expansion of democracy in Asia, has considerably lessened, if not eliminated, the obstacles that news agencies and foreign correspondents encounter in covering news. The New York–based Freedom House, which annually publishes a report on the status of civil liberties and press freedom around the world, said in its 2002 report that 89 of the world's 192 countries (46 percent) were rated as "free," meaning that they maintain a high degree of such freedoms. Although this is the largest number of free countries on record, the remaining 54 percent still pose a major challenge to unhindered collection and flow of news. Totalitarian holdovers and authoritarian governments in many countries continue to create several obstacles in the coverage of news, including restricted access, explicit or implicit censorship, and pressure against correspondents, extending as far as expulsion. Two publications, *International Press Institute Report* and *Index on Censorship,* regularly chronicle the pressures and dangers that local and international journalists face in carrying out their duties.

As international news agencies like the AP note in their annual reports, restricted access results in incomplete and unreliable information because information must be obtained from visitors and from radio broadcasts, which are mostly produced by state-run radio. Explicit censorship results in deletions or refusal to transmit correspondents' copy. Implicit censorship is less obvious but nearly as inhibiting to balanced news coverage. Often the most difficult official sources for the foreign correspondent to reach are those who can best explain the story of their countries to the world. Also, when the local press is restricted to publishing only government-approved news, foreign correspondents' access to balanced local information suffers. This makes more difficult the foreign correspondents' efforts to understand and explain the country to readers in distant places.

Direct action against foreign correspondents is the most extreme and dangerous obstacle to free news coverage. Wire service correspondents are often expelled because the government objects to the reporting of specific news. With the expansion of democracy, the trend against such restrictions will continue to grow.

Economic growth and the opportunities provided by the Internet should make it easier for many developing countries to expand their newsgathering and news dissemination operations. The Indo-Asian News Service is a good example of such possibilities, as is Bernama, the Malaysian news agency, which has expanded its reach into the member countries of the Association of Southeast Asian Nations.

Several developing nations—including India, China, Indonesia, Brazil, Mexico, and countries in the Arab League—have their own communication satellites, providing them added abilities to collect and disseminate news globally. Developing countries are also increasingly stationing their own correspondents in major news capitals of the world. These factors should facilitate the newsgathering abilities of a number of developing countries and help reduce their dependence on Western news agencies. But developing countries need more than the newsgathering and transmission infrastructure before they can be seen as credible purveyors of news at home or globally. They need to appreciate and have their news agency staff employ sound journalistic practices within the framework of democratic political systems, human rights, and press freedoms. Fifty-four percent of the world's nations do not operate under such a framework, which will make it difficult for them to have their own viable and credible news agencies.

As for global news flow, various technologies of the information age will alter the patterns of news and information flow as well as the packaging of media products. For the online consumer and the person willing to spend money to receive international television, patterns of news and information flow have already changed radically since the mid-1990s. Online consumers can go straight to the Web editions of newspapers and magazines and, increasingly, to radio and television news broadcasts from many countries to satisfy their information needs when they feel that the indigenous media are not meeting those needs. At the same time, viewers using free-to-home satellite receivers hooked to a small dish can select from a host of international channels from around the world, usually without any subscription fee. Marshall McLuhan's "global village" is indeed upon us.

News and information packaging for the Internet generation is also changing. As noted in this chapter, every major news organization is putting its services online and looking for new ways to better serve the consumer using this interactive medium. UPI's decision to offer only Web-based specialized information services is a clear indication of the media industry's recognition that the

Internet will become the primary source of information for people and that they will use it to fulfill specialized information needs. No wonder then that media organizations going online are constantly improving both the packaging and the diversity of their Web services. Online newspapers are updating the news frequently between editions and offering links, both text and broadcast, to related items or sites. They are also adding new special sections to serve the varied needs of consumers. Broadcast services on the Web, such as CNN's, are equally expanding the scope of their offerings, allowing consumers to have access to a news item from a geographical area of their choice. Media organizations are also offering news, information, and entertainment services adapted to the subscriber's interest profile, either through email or through a web page created for the subscriber.

The media consumer fragmentation that accompanied the high-tech American economy starting in the 1970s is reaching altogether new levels in the age of the Internet. Media owners worldwide are learning their lessons and are reshaping the nature, quantity, and quality of their output. Clearly, at the dawn of the new millennium, the Internet is creating new opportunities in and putting altogether new demands on the collection and dissemination of news and information globally. The consumer of news, information, and entertainment is emerging as the winner from the new dynamics unleashed by the information age.

For more information on the topics that appear in this chapter, use the password that came free with this book to access InfoTrac College Edition. Use the following words as keyterms and subject searches: global news, global news agencies, international news, international broadcast services, Cold War, the Internet, press freedom, international satellite television, world news, information flow.

QUESTIONS FOR DISCUSSION

1. How will the traditional news agencies adapt their services to the Internet? Is UPI's decision to offer primarily Internet-delivered and subscriber-specific services the direction that all news agencies will have to take, making traditional newspapers and broadcast news services increasingly irrelevant? Why or why not?

2. Are online newspapers becoming more competitive with broadcast news by offering regular news updates? What new directions will broadcast news have to take to maintain its uniqueness and competitiveness in the new media environment?

3. Does the audience appeal, and therefore competitive success, of international television news networks, such as CNN and BBC World, depend on offering dedicated local programming in large countries like India? Why or why not?

4. Will the Internet make it more feasible for news agencies in developing countries to successfully compete worldwide with established Western news agencies? Why or why not?

5. Will the Internet facilitate an equitable flow of news between developed and developing countries? Why or why not? What direction will news flow take in the future?

REFERENCES

AFP. (2000, February 2). *Alcatel and AFP team up on mobile Internet content*. Retrieved July 13, 2000, from http://www.afp.com/english/afp/?cat_new&page_index&release_alcatel

AFP. (2005a, February 10). *AFP: A world news agency*. Information supplied by AFP.

AFP. (2005b, March 2). *In brief*. Retrieved March 2, 2005, from http://www.afp.com/english/afp/?pid=about

AP. (2000, March 28). *Associated Press launches new unit called AP Digital*. Retrieved June 6, 2000, from http://www.apdigitalnews.com/PressRelease/launch.html

AP. (2004, February 10). *Facts about AP*. Retrieved February 17, 2005, from http://www.ap.org/pages/about/about.html

AP Digital Services. (2005). Retrieved February 17, 2005, from http://www.ap.org/pages/product/apdigitalservices.html

APTN. (2005). *About AP*. Retrieved February 17, 2005, from http://www.ap.org/pages/about/about.html

BBC News. (2004, December 10). *France to launch global TV news*. Retrieved January 9, 2005, from http://news.bbc.co.uk/2/hi/europe/4085369.stm

BBC Press Office. (2004, June 21). BBC World Service remains world's leading international radio broadcaster. Retrieved January 10, 2005, from http://www.bbc.co.uk/pressoffice/pressreleases/stories/2004/06_june/21/ws_figures.shtml

BBC World. (2005a). *About the BBC*. Retrieved January 10, 2005, from http://www.bbc.co.uk/info/channels/

BBC World. (2005b). *Key facts*. Retrieved January 10, 2005, from http://www.bbcworld.com/content/template_clickpage.asp?pageid=141

BBC World Service. (2000, February 14). *World business report*. Retrieved January 11, 2005, from http://www.bbc.co.uk/worldservice/worldbusinessreport/

CNN. (2005). *CNN News Group*. Retrieved January 27, 2005, from http://www.cnnasiapacific.com/en/groups/corporate/index.asp

Crystal, D. (2004, November 19–25). Subcontinent raises its voice. *Manchester Guardian Weekly, 171*(22), 1.

Cunningham, B. (2000, November–December). The AP now. *Columbia Journalism Review*. Retrieved February 17, 2005, from http://www.cjr.org/archives.asp?url=/00/4/ap.asp

de Borchgrave, A. (1999, August 6). *Largescale expansion to Internet services announced by UPI*. Retrieved December 12, 1999, from http://www.upi.com/corp/press/990806.shtml

Dow Jones press release. (2004, February 5). Retrieved January 12, 2005, from http://www.dowjones.com/Pressroom/PressReleases/Other/Europe/2004/0205_Europe_DowJonesNewswires_6801.htm

Farhi, P., & Rosenfeld, M. (1998, October 25). American pop penetrates worldwide. *Washington Post,* p. A1.

Frederick, H. H. (1993). *Global communication and international relations.* Belmont, CA: Wadsworth.

Fridriksson, L. (1993). *Coverage of Scandinavia in U.S. news media.* Paper presented at the Association for Education in Journalism and Mass Communication annual conference, Kansas City, Missouri.

Galtung, J. (1971). A structural theory of imperialism. *Journal of Peace Research, 8*(2), 81–117.

Goldfarb, J. (2005, February 18). *Two UK weeklies break circulation record.* Retrieved March 1, 2005, from http://www.jang-group.com/thenews/feb2005-daily/18-02-2005/world/w15.htm

Hester, A. (1973). Theoretical considerations in predicting volume and direction of information flow. *Gazette, 19,* 238–247.

IANS. (2000, February 18). *The global rise of India Abroad News Service.* Retrieved March 28, 2000, from http://www.indiaabroad.com/ians/ians.html

IANS. (2005) *About us.* Retrieved February 10, 2005, from http://www.eians.com/aboutus.shtml

Ignatenko, V. (1993, June/July). *IPI Report, 42.*

Interfax. (2003). *About Interfax.* Retrieved February 16, 2005, from http://www.interfax-news.com/AboutInterfax/about.html

Internet world stats. (2004). Retrieved January 27, 2005, from http://www.internetworldstats.com/stats.htm

IPI. (2005, March 4). *2003 World Press freedom review.* Retrieved March 4, 2005, from http://www.freemedia.at/wpfr/Europe/russia.htm

ITAR-TASS. (2004a). *ITAR-TASS history.* Retrieved February 15, 2005, from http://corp.itar-tass.com/eng/about/history.html

ITAR-TASS. (2004b). *News.* Retrieved February 15, 2005, from http://corp.itar-tass.com/eng/products/news/index.html

Jehl, D. (1999, March 18). Riyadh journal: The Internet's "open sesame" is answered warily. *New York Times* [electronic version]. Retrieved March 19, 1999, from http://www.nytimes.com/

Kariel, H. G., & Rosenvall, L. A. (1984, Autumn). Factors influencing international news flow. *Journalism Quarterly, 61,* 509–516.

Keohane, R. O., & Nye, J. S., Jr. (1998, September/October). Power and interdependence in the information age. *Foreign Affairs, 77*(5), 81–94.

LexisNexis. (2004, December 12). *Media: Why compacts haven't won yet.* Retrieved February 7, 2005, from http://web.lexis-nexis.com/universe/printdoc

Los Angeles Times–Washington Post News Service. (2005). Retrieved February 19, 2005, from http://www.newsservice.com/

Media Life. (2005, March 7). *IHT's ambition.* Retrieved March 7, 2005, from http://69.20.6.242/News2005/feb05/feb28/2_tues/news4tuesday.html

Moonies acquire UPI. (2000, May 15). Retrieved June 20, 2000, from http://www.auburn.edu/_lowrygr/moon.html

The New York Times [electronic version]. (2005, February 16). Reuters profit jumps in 2004 on cost cuts. Retrieved February 17, 2005, from http://www.nytimes.com/aponline/business/AP-Britain-Earns-Reuters.html?pagewanted=print&position=

New York Times News Service/Syndicate. (2004). Retrieved February 13, 2005, from http://www.nytsyn.com/nytsyn.html

Nye, J. S., Jr., & Owens, W. A. (1996, March/April). America's information edge. *Foreign Affairs, 75*(2), 20–36.

nytimes.com. (2005, January). Audience profile. Retrieved March 2, 2005, from http://www.nytimes.com/marketing/adinfo/audience/audienceprofile.html

Rampal, K., & Adams, W. C. (1990). Credibility of the Asian news broadcasts of the Voice of America and the British Broadcasting Corporation. *Gazette, 46,* 93–111.

Read, D. (1999). *The power of news: The history of Reuters.* Oxford: Oxford University Press.

Reuters. (2004a, March). *Key facts.* Retrieved February 17, 2005, from http://about.reuters.com/aboutus/overview/facts/index.asp

Reuters. (2004b, December 9). *Mobile phone users double since 2000.* Retrieved January 19, 2005, from http://www.reuters.com/newsArticle.jhtml?type=technologyNews&storyID=7040640&src=rss/technologyNews

Reuters. (2005). *Television and video.* Retrieved February 7, 2005, from http://about.reuters.com/tv/support/location.htm

Riffe, D. (1996, Spring). Linking international news to U.S. interests: A content analysis. *International Communication Bulletin, 31*(1–2), 14–18.

Schiff, F. (1996, Spring). The Associated Press: Its worldwide bureaus and American interests. *International Communication Bulletin, 31*(1–2), 7–13.

Schiller, H. (1998, April). Living in the number one society. *Gazette, 60*(2), 181–196.

Schudson, M. (1978). *Discovering the news: A social history of American newspapers.* New York: Basic Books.

Shaw, D. (1988, April 3). The AP: It's everywhere and powerful. *LA Times Monograph.* Reprinted from the *Los Angeles Times.* pp. 1–11.

Singapore unveils sweeping measures to control words, images on Internet. (1996, March 6). *The Wall Street Journal,* p. B8.

UPI sold to Arab firm. (1992, June 27). *Editor and Publisher, 125*(26), 9.

VOA. (2005). *Fast facts.* Retrieved February 20, 2005, from http://www.voanews.com/english/About/FastFacts.cfm

The Washington Post. (1999, November 28). Where in the world? p. B6.

Wood, M. (1998, March 19). Interview with Deutsche Welle TV for a DW program on the history of Reuters.

7

International Broadcasting

JOSEPH D. STRAUBHAAR
AND DOUGLAS A. BOYD

Joseph D. Straubhaar (PhD, Tufts University) is the Amon G. Carter
Professor of Communication, Radio-TV-Film Department, at the
University of Texas at Austin. He previously taught at Brigham
Young University and Michigan State University. He also worked
as a Foreign Service officer in Brazil and Washington. Straubhaar
coauthored *Communication Media in the Information Society,* is
coauthor of *Video Cassette Recorders in the Third World,* and has
published extensively on international media studies. Straubhaar
has received awards and grants from the Fulbright Commission,
U.S. Department of Education, and Department of Agriculture.
He serves on the editorial board of the *Journal of Broadcasting and
Electronic Media.*

Douglas A. Boyd (PhD, University of Minnesota) is Professor of
Communication and Journalism and Telecommunications, and Chief
of Staff, Office of the President, University of Kentucky, Lexington.
He is a former dean of the College of Communications and Information
Studies, University of Kentucky. Boyd has received several significant
awards (including from the Ford Foundation, Japan's Hoso-Bunka
Foundation, UNESCO). He authored *Broadcasting in the Arab World*
and is coauthor of *Video Cassette Recorders in the Third World.*
He serves on the editorial board of the *Journal of Broadcasting
and Electronic Media.*

For additional online resources, access the Global Media Monitor website that
accompanies this book on the Wadsworth Communication Cafe website at
http://communication.wadsworth.com.

Countries and cultures have long been in communication across borders; however, in the 20th century, first radio, then television and the Internet accelerated that process dramatically. National leaders are often unnerved when broadcasts or other information comes straight across borders, without any chance to stop, control, or mediate it. In the 1930s and 1940s, around World War II and the Cold War, radio seemed menacingly effective in propaganda across borders. Radio competitions and clashes, even some miniature Cold Wars of their own, erupted among a number of countries, companies, and churches in Europe, the Middle East, Asia, North America, and Latin America. By contrast, broadcast television seemed comfortingly short range as it took preeminence from the late 1940s on.

Satellite television was the next big technological development in international broadcasting. As early as the 1960s, the United Nations debated controlling direct broadcast satellite (DBS) transmission of television signals across borders because many countries feared that DBS, or direct-to-home (DTH), broadcasts would be used for propaganda or unwanted cultural influence. The global spread of satellite and cable TV channels in the 1990s has seemed to increase the outflow of American and European television programming and films to other countries.

The Internet has become the latest major technology to deliver radio, television, music downloads, video downloads, films, news stories, newspapers, and new forms of content, like weblogs (or blogs), across national and cultural borders. The growth of the Internet in the late 1990s and 2000s has also threatened the ability of national governments to control cross-border flow of information and entertainment. China, for example, has put a great deal of policy force into controlling satellite television but is currently much more focused on trying to control what people bring into China over the Internet. The Internet continues to bring a great deal of content from the United States and other dominant countries into other parts of the world. However, it is also much cheaper to produce either information or entertainment for the statement, so many governments, cultures, religions, and ideologies now produce for and distribute over the Internet.

Governments dominated activity in international radio, despite early developments and precedents from commercial international shortwave broadcasting prior to World War II. However, it seems private actors instead of governments now dominate global television news and entertainment. Is the shift due to cost restraints or to a lack of consensus on need or desirability? What are the implications of a shift from government international radio broadcasting to private international satellite television? What of the further shift on the Internet to supplement the dominance of major commercial media with a widening array for voices by religious groups, nongovernmental groups, cultural minority groups, and tens of millions of individuals? What are the relations between public diplomacy and private media actors, as well as concerns by receiving countries about the propriety of direct or even indirect satellite broadcasting that evades government controls? What of the ability of small groups like Al-Qaeda to use the internet to spread their messages globally at very low cost, instantly?

FROM LOCAL TO GLOBAL

A variety of forms of international broadcasting take place, from accidental cross-border spillover to highly globalized systems that reach almost worldwide in various languages. The most local are the almost inevitable cross-border reaches of local radio on AM and FM and of local television on VHF and UHF. In fact, the rules of the International Telecommunications Union (ITU), which allocates radio frequencies to nations, officially reserve both AM and FM for purely domestic broadcasting and forbid using either to cross borders deliberately, although various stations on the U.S. border with Canada, such as Wolfman Jack's Tijuana station that covered much of the western United States in the 1960s, and stations like Radio Luxembourg in Europe have long ignored those rules, deliberately seeking audiences across borders for their advertisers. In another example, the United States, Britain, and France broadcast to the Middle East from AM (medium wave) transmitters on Cyprus.

Such commercial incursions across borders assume that a receptive audience, with similar language skills and cultural dispositions, waits on the other side. That is true in relatively few places, interestingly enough. Most radio audiences tend to be quite localized, given a choice, particularly with the spread of higher-fidelity stereo FM broadcasts, which deliver the best available radio sound quality but seldom cover more than a limited metropolitan area. Radio stations may carry a great deal of foreign music, but they do tend to broadcast from within national and even local boundaries. From allocations given them by the ITU, national governments distribute specific licenses to use certain frequencies, which gives governments a powerful tool to keep national control over broadcasting.

Successful cross-border commercial operations tend to flourish only when local commercial competitors are few, as when Radio Luxembourg was one of the few commercial rock music–oriented stations on the AM band in Europe in the 1960s and early 1970s. Similar cross-cultural spillover took place from expatriate operations like the U.S. Armed Forces Radio–Television Service (AFRTS) in South Korea or the Arab–American Oil Company (ARAMCO) television service for its North American employees in Saudi Arabia. Most governments try to protect their commercial radio and television markets for their own stations and advertisers, which has led to clashes between the Canadian and U.S. governments when the former denied legal approval for tax deductions for advertising placed on U.S. stations targeted at Canadian listeners.

Both AM and shortwave have been used for deliberate international broadcasts since the 1930s, mostly by governments and religious organizations. Radio Moscow, the Voice of America, Radio Havana, and other stations, mostly on shortwave, have become famous as vehicles of government propaganda. Their motives and operations are discussed later in this chapter. Governments began to try to use direct broadcast satellite television for similar purposes, but private companies have come to dominate DBS. Similarly, a number of governments now put out their radio and television broadcasts over the Internet. Some, like Radio Netherlands, which had been extensively involved with early short-wave broadcasting, have moved some programming to the Internet. Others, particularly smaller governments, revolutionary movements like Al Qaeda, nongovernmental organizations like Alternative Media Centers, and religious movements like the Mormon Church as well as various Islamic groups all broadcast various forms of audio and video on the Internet.

MOTIVATIONS FOR BROADCASTING INTERNATIONALLY

Boyd (1986) identified four major reasons that both state-run and private organizations transmit directly across borders: to enhance national (or organizational) prestige; to promote national (or organizational) interests; to attempt religious, ideological, or political indoctrination; and to foster cultural ties.

When governments are the primary actors, the goal is often summed up as public diplomacy.[1] That is the deliberate effort by governments to affect foreign public opinion in a manner that is positive to their goals. According to the U.K. government Diplomacy Strategy Board (2005), "Public Diplomacy can be defined as: Work which aims at influencing in a positive way, including through the creation of relationships and partnerships, the perceptions of individuals and organisations overseas about the UK and their engagement with the UK, in support of HMG's overseas objectives."

In the age of satellite-delivered television programming, Straubhaar and Boyd (2002) added a fifth reason, to sell advertising for multicountry products; and a sixth, to sell access to pay-TV broadcasts, either directly from satellite (DTH) or by satellite-fed cable TV. The age of the Internet adds a host of personal and group motivations, since any website or email exchange is potentially a site of international communication. However, one could argue that the chief motivations of the Internet groups with most visibility seem to be e-commerce (selling culture and information across borders); downloading music and video for free (a.k.a music and video piracy); viewing or listening to a wide variety of streaming video and music entertainment; personal/group expression

---

1. The term was first coined in the mid-1960s by Dean Edmund A. Gullion of the Fletcher School of Law and Diplomacy. Explaining the origin of the term, Gullion (1967) wrote:

> Even beyond the organ of the Government set up to handle information about the United States and to explain our policies, what is important today is the interaction of groups, peoples, and cultures beyond national borders, influencing the way groups and peoples in other countries think about foreign affairs, react to our policies, and affect the policies of their respective governments.

> To connote this activity, we at the Fletcher School tried to find a name. I would have liked to call it "propaganda." It seemed like the nearest thing in the pure interpretation of the word to what we were doing. But "propaganda" has always a pejorative connotation in this country. To describe the whole range of communications, information, and propaganda, we hit upon "public diplomacy." (http://www.publicdiplomacy.org/)

of identity, ideology, and religion; and both distributing and accessing traditional media such as *The New York Times* or the BBC.

Some of the main precedents for current cross-border satellite television and Internet broadcasts come from international radio. Browne (1982) discusses international radio broadcasting within the context of purposes: as an instrument of foreign policy, as a mirror of society, as a symbolic presence, as a converter and sustainer, as a coercer and intimidator, as an educator, as an entertainer, and as a seller of goods and services. Almost all international broadcasting intends some variety of influence over the audience, for few government or other major groups broadcast internationally solely to entertain without intent to sell, influence, or persuade.

Evidence of the importance that governments attach to international communication can be found in their total transmission hours; the major radio broadcasters have been either single-party states or large Western democracies. Of course, no international broadcaster organizes programming for reception outside the originating country for only one purpose, yet every broadcaster probably has at least one of the previously listed motivations in mind as a major reason for transmitting. Similarly, as the Internet now permits a greater variety of players to broadcast, many more have entered to pursue similar goals.

WHY AUDIENCES LISTEN OR VIEW
ACROSS BORDERS

Until the 20th century, few people had been exposed on a frequent basis to direct contact with foreign sources of information. International flows of news and culture existed but were slower, less extensive, and more mediated by a series of personal sources and interpreters. However, the mass media, and now the Internet, have widened and sped up this process of contact and influence, creating the possibility for direct efforts to influence the thoughts and opinions of people within and across nations, or what has come to be considered public opinion. Cross-border efforts to influence public opinion are accordingly referred to as public diplomacy.

According to the categories of listening motivations listed by Boyd (1986), audiences tune in to hear news and information, to be entertained, to learn, to hear religious or political broadcasts, to enhance their status, to protest, or to pursue a hobby. The U.S. Information Agency (USIA)/Voice of America (VOA), and the British Broadcasting Company (BBC) conduct extensive audience surveys in many countries, but the results are rarely published. Mytton (1993) does give some audience data as well as interesting overviews. Some audience data can also be found in the annual reports of the VOA, the BBC, and Radio Free Europe/Radio Liberty (RFE/RL), particularly about the size of the listening audience. Recent discussions on the effectiveness of U.S. public diplomacy in the Middle East have included some data about the size of audiences of U.S.–operated stations there, which indicate limited audiences.

In most cases, one would have to conclude that, as with questions of media effects, the available studies show the effects of international radio to have been relatively limited. Nevertheless, there are at least some historical cases in which international radio as part of public diplomacy had considerable impact. Radio Free Europe clearly had a role in fomenting the Hungarian uprising of 1956. The United States conducted what Frederick (1986) called radio wars against Cuba and Nicaragua, fomenting refugee flight if nothing else. And the U.S. government's public diplomacy media, as well as exposure to Western European commercial media across borders, all seem to have helped push Eastern Europeans toward demanding the opening that began in Poland and continued with the fall of the Berlin Wall. These incidents indicate that governments whose publics are the target of official radio public diplomacy are concerned enough about radio efforts to jam the broadcasts (as the Soviet Union did to international shortwave broadcasts), to pursue ideological indoctrination, or even to offer counterinformation against foreign radio efforts. This creates a strong aversion to the potential for similar public diplomacy on direct cross-border television, which is generally seen as an even more powerful medium. Cross-border television from West to East Germany (Boyd, 1983) and radio from west to east before the fall of the Berlin Wall in 1989 are credited with communicating an image of Western lifestyles that led to invidious comparisons with the Socialist East.

Concerns about Public Diplomacy and Propaganda

The need to influence public opinion as part of diplomacy is relatively new and still controversial. The New World Information and Communication Order (NWICO) debate in UNESCO and other United Nations bodies looked at imbalances in the flow of media from large Western countries, like the United States, to other countries. The debate also looked at the power that the United States and a few other countries exerted over others through international media.

Within that debate, both Eastern European and some developing countries complained about direct attempts to influence publics in other nations via international radio broadcasts (mostly but not entirely on shortwave), advertising, and the like. They saw them as harmful propaganda and an infringement on national sovereignty (McPhail, 1987; Whitton, 1979). This debate has touched official public diplomacy by governments as well as private information flow in the media. In fact, it is clear from what is most prominent in the NWICO debate that developing nations consider private media flow to be a much greater issue than official public diplomacy, although that has also been criticized. The developing countries' concern has focused primarily on commercially oriented media sales (film, news, music, television programs) that have flowed predominantly from the First World to the developing nations.

Beginning in the 1970s, the unequal nature of these radio broadcasts and flow of news, music, television programs, and films began to strike many researchers as an example of media imperialism (MacBride Commission, 1980; Nordenstreng & Varis, 1974; Schiller, 1971). While some research showed that flows of television and music were becoming less dominated by the United States in the 1980s and 1990s, film and news flows continued to be quite dominated by the United States. The onset of direct transborder satellite broadcasting in the 1980s also revived fears of unequal television flow, even in parts of the world like East Asia and Latin America where nations had either begun to produce most of their own television programming or to import it from neighboring countries rather than from the United States (Varis, 1984). The Soviet and Eastern European governments' complaints focused more often on official government cross-border radio broadcasts because U.S. and Western European official broadcasts were targeted at Eastern Europe and the USSR. Also, audiences for foreign radio broadcasts in Eastern Europe were much larger than foreign radio audiences elsewhere, according to research by VOA, RFE/RL, and BBC.

THE HISTORY OF INTERNATIONAL BROADCASTING

Propaganda Radio and the World Wars

Most colonial powers started services in the 1920s to communicate with their nationals or citizens overseas. The Netherlands started in 1927, Germany in 1929, France in 1931, and Britain in 1932 (Head, 1985). Effectively beginning with the efforts by various nations during World War I to influence publics in other nations—notably the Allied efforts to influence U.S. opinion toward entering the war—the idea of propaganda on radio gathered currency. British and German World War I propaganda on posters and other preradio media was seen as highly effective by early writers like Lippman (1965). Adolf Hitler seemed preoccupied with propaganda in *Mein Kampf,* his 1933 book that announced his plans for the takeover and governance of Germany. Propaganda continued to be directly associated with war or open conflict through World War II.

Pre-World War II Commercial International Radio Efforts

With the exception of Radio Luxembourg's commercial broadcasts to other European countries, pre–World War II international radio in Europe did not develop along commercial lines. Rather, it evolved as a state activity (as in Germany and Italy), as a public corporation (like the BBC), or as a representative of other nongovernmental international interests (like Radio Vatican). In all these cases, the interests were noncommercial, educational, informative, and cultural, as the BBC intended to be. They became more openly persuasive, even propagandistic, in the case of wartime radio in Germany, Italy, Japan, and, to some degree, Great Britain.

However, in the United States and Latin America, radio was predominantly commercial, so things were different. Until World War II induced the United States to create the government-operated Voice of America, international radio was a commercial activity based on a perception that profit could be made in international radio broadcasting. As the number of shortwave receivers increased in Europe and Latin America, the U.S. radio networks saw the possibility of an enormous foreign audience for American programming. To help foster international commercial broadcasting, the Federal Communications Commission (FCC) (1936) reworked the original classification of shortwave stations and ruled that they could provide an international service.

In 1938, the National Broadcasting Company (NBC) started an international division with 38 employees to transmit in five foreign languages plus English ("Hearings," 1938). The Columbia Broadcasting Corporation (CBS) also saw the commercial possibilities of shortwave programming, and in 1939 it established an international division that had 9 employees organizing programs for Europe and Latin America. Although primarily interested in the technical aspects of shortwave, General Electric by 1938 had a 10-person international staff at Schenectady, New York ("Hearings," 1938).

In retrospect, Fejes (1983), Schwoch (1990) and others believe that both private and public U.S. international radio broadcasting had considerable effects, particularly in Latin America. U.S. broadcasting, together with other private-sector public diplomacy, such as advertising, film exports, news wire service coverage, and book and magazine exports, seems to have reinforced both the official U.S. diplomatic agenda during World War II and the broader public and private agenda of drawing Latin America into close trade and investment ties favorable to the United States. They also reinforced the development of a commercialized system of broadcasting compatible with U.S. commercial interests.

World War II

The Soviet Union's Radio Moscow started a regular external service in 1929 "to explain their revolution to both sympathizers and opponents in the West" (Head, 1985, p. 37). In 1935, Italy began broadcasting a shortwave service in Arabic to the Middle East. Great Britain countered with its own service in 1938 (Browne, 1982). The United States took over several existing private shortwave broadcasters aimed at international audiences and pulled them into the Voice of America in 1942. All of these broadcasters tried to influence third parties; examples include the German and American competition for influence in Latin America and the British–Italian radio war in the Middle East. Many of them also directly targeted each other, such as in the Soviet–Nazi radio war, or each other's troops—for example, the way Tokyo Rose broadcast music and propaganda to American troops in the Pacific.

It was the declarations of war against both Germany and Japan that prompted the U.S. government to create the official Voice of America. U.S. broadcasters in the 1930s feared that a government-operated international station would create competition that would later have domestic broadcasting implications, but that did not develop. However, the VOA did subsequently dominate international radio broadcasting. For years after World War II, the government permitted only WRUL, later renamed WNYW, to operate, but eventually other stations received licenses. Most U.S. shortwave stations are now owned by religious organizations.

Cold War Radio

After World War II, as a less open but still intense ideological struggle between the United States and the Soviet Union began, U.S. policy makers began to talk about public diplomacy as a new but necessary addition to traditional diplomacy. Ideological struggle required a more explicit effort to reach and influence public opinion in other countries, those that were effectively being "fought" over.

For a time after World War II, governments, or public corporations sanctioned by the government (such as the BBC), had a monopoly on international broadcasting. Reasons for this situation involve both economics and technology: Commercial radio broadcasters concentrated on the profitable domestic market rather than the uncertain international market. International radio was seen as the domain of propaganda and public diplomacy.

At the peak of international radio propaganda, more than 80 countries had official international services aimed at other countries (Head, 1985). In one of the peak years, 1982, the largest operations were the Soviet Union, which broadcast more than 2,000 hours a week; the United States, which broadcast almost 2,000 hours; China, 1,300 hours; West Germany, almost 800 hours; and the United Kingdom, more than 700 hours (BBC Annual Report, 1983).

The primary U.S. international radio service has been the Voice of America, which has broadcast in dozens of languages to almost all parts of the world. The addition and deletion of language services over the years has reflected the list of countries with which the United States was politically preoccupied, dropping Brazilian Portuguese and adding hours to Arabic (targeting the West Bank and Gaza) in 2001, for example.

After 9/11, new services were added targeting the Middle East. Operated by the U.S. Broadcasting Board of Governors rather than the VOA, the most prominent of these is Radio Sawa ("togetherness" in Arabic) that replaced the old VOA Arabic service. It broadcasts from Washington DC in Arabic, featuring essentially a news and popular music format that alternates U.S. popular songs with those in Arabic. Radio Sawa transmits on both medium wave and FM throughout the Arab world 24 hours per day via six programs that target specific geographic areas, including Iraq. Unfortunately, there is no FM Radio Sawa rebroadcasting in two of the Arab world's most important countries—Egypt and Saudi Arabia (Radio Sawa).

The VOA has tended to concentrate on international news and on U.S. news, music, and culture. In contrast, the United States has also spent about half its broadcast time on several operations, sometimes called surrogate stations, which focus on providing some target country with news about itself (Head, 1985). Those stations have included Radio Free Europe (aimed at Eastern Europe), Radio Liberty (aimed at the former USSR), Radio (and TV) Martí (aimed at Cuba), Radio Free Asia (aimed largely at China), and, post-9/11, AlHurra television and the previously noted Radio Sawa.

These surrogate local stations have been more controversial than those that simply broadcast the views of the home country. However, the stations targeting the former Soviet Bloc have been complimented by post–Soviet era politicians, such as former President Vaclav Havel of the Czech Republic, for bringing into those countries news that was unavailable under the previous regimes.

By the end of World War II, the BBC had evolved a quite different model from that of the VOA. Although the BBC had clearly served British government interests during the war and continued to do so during the Cold War, it was structured in a somewhat more independent manner than the VOA, which has always been under direct U.S. government policy control. BBC International is the overseas arm of the domestic BBC, which is carefully structured as an independent public corporation funded by license fees, whereas the VOA is directly funded by the U.S. Congress. Although the British Foreign Office funds the external service and sets its policies, like which languages to broadcast in, the BBC has retained considerable editorial independence, which has increased its credibility to listeners abroad. USIA audience studies during the 1982 Falklands/Malvinas Islands war between the United Kingdom and Argentina found that even Argentine listeners turned to the BBC for accounts of the war (Head, 1985; U.S. Information Agency, 1982).

Radio Moscow began regular service in 1929, with the explicit mission of explaining and promoting the Soviet Revolution abroad. It expanded during World War II to focus on supporting the Soviet government in that conflict and continued to expand after the war, extending the languages and hours of broadcast into Eastern Europe and China and gradually into other developing countries, such as Cuba (after 1959) and elsewhere. Radio Moscow at its peak broadcast in more than 80 languages, including relatively minor ones like Quechua (Head, 1985).

Government radio changed with the decline of the Cold War in 1989–1991 as Eastern European countries and the Soviet Union moved away from communist governments. Much of the ideological rationale for international radio propaganda seemed to slip away, and the major broadcasters began to decrease the number of hours and languages they broadcast (Boyd, 1999).

The VOA used listener data as a basis for reducing language services that had small audiences or relatively low political priority, such as Portuguese and Turkish broadcasts. Cutting language services saved $4.2 million dollars, which was reallocated toward more current political priorities, such as Radio Sawa. The VOA had decreased the number of languages in which it broadcast to just over 30 in 2001 (Voice of America, 2001). Likewise, the Voice of Russia (formerly Radio Moscow) broadcast in 32 languages in 2001 (Voice of Russia, 2001). The BBC maintained 43 language services in 2005 (BBC, 2005).

However, a number of internal studies and outside panels after 9/11 examined the decline of U.S. public diplomacy capabilities. International official U.S. radio and television capabilities began to grow again, first targeted at Afghanistan, then Iraq and the Middle East in general. President Bush finally put his own trusted personal public relations counselor, Karen Hughes, in charge of public diplomacy in 2005, indicating a reprioritization of the field (Hoagland, 2005).

The structure of the broadcasting services was changed along with this shift in emphasis. The VOA was put together with the former surrogate services—Radio Marti, RFE/RL, Radio Free Iraq, and Radio Free Asia—as the International Board of Broadcasters, itself under the supervision of the Board of Broadcast Governors. The official U.S. international broadcasters are now independent of the rest of the former USIA, which became the Educational and Cultural Bureau of the Department of State in 1998. The BBC international radio structure remains largely unchanged, although as we shall see, the international BBC television operation has become increasingly privatized.

The use of radio in international broadcasting is changing decisively. Most of the international radio services are moving away from transmitting on shortwave radio and moving toward rebroadcasting or retransmitting on leased local FM facilities in the Arab world, Africa, Asia, and parts of Latin America. The BBC World Service annual review in 1998–1999 indicated that placement of BBC materials on FM stations around the world had become a top priority (BBC, 2005), a trend that has continued.

Another major trend is for international broadcasters to put their signals out as streaming audio feeds on the Internet. This is a particularly significant move for small international broadcasters who have tracked their audiences' movement toward the Internet as a new convenient information source. For example, Jonathan Marks, formerly of Radio Netherlands, says that its priority is now Internet audio streaming (personal communication, April 2000). However, large broadcasters like the VOA and the BBC are also moving a number of their services onto the Internet. The BBC also highlights the need for a Web presence and audio and video streaming services to supplement its traditional shortwave and medium wave broadcasting, as well as its new continued emphasis on local FM placement.

Cold War Propaganda: From Radio to Satellite

Except for cross-border transmissions such as those from the United States to Mexico and Canada, and Luxembourg's popular pan-European services, presatellite broadcasting technology did not permit direct international television communication without an investment that would have been impossible to recover. Satellites, however, have made the distribution of international television news and programming economically feasible and sometimes even profitable, especially from the mid-1990s with direct-to-home satellite transmissions in Europe, Asia, and the Middle East.

For international television operations, perspectives are quite different from shortwave radio precedents. Television news by satellite is similar to shortwave in that it can be directly received anywhere in the satellite footprint by an appropriate receiver. However, access and control are issues. Access to DTH channels is severely limited in many countries by price. DTH access is limited in a number of other countries by national government prohibitions. China, Iran, Malaysia, Saudi Arabia, and others officially prohibit or discourage satellite television reception dishes (Boyd, 1999; Chan, 1994).

Both types of limits on access are eased in some countries by offering satellite channels through cable TV systems. Cable is often cheaper than DTH service, and some governments allow cable but not DTH, because cable retransmission is more easily controlled. Most of the television news services are delivered for cable or broadcast retransmission, not for DTH.

In fact, the predominance of cable retransmission systems over DTH might remove some of the most glaring questions about national sovereignty and control in many countries because some level of control over retransmission will or could exist on the ground in the receiving country. Still, some of the concerns about uncontrolled cross-border news influence are germane because several of the current services, such as Cable News Network International (CNNI), are being retransmitted on cable television in the Caribbean, Western Europe, Central America, and Japan without any editing or local control over content. Some of the services, again most notably CNNI, are also being directly received from satellites by homes and hotels with satellite dishes. Several of the current operations are intended for DTH news delivery, such as Britain's Sky Television; the British Broadcasting Corporation's World; CNN International; Asian Business News (Singapore); and the Dubai-based, Arabic-language Middle East Broadcasting Centre (MBC). The most notable of these new entrants has been Al-Jazeera, an Arabic-language news channel subsidized by and operated out of Qatar (El-Nawawy & Iskandar, 2003).

The DBS Debate

The realization of direct international television broadcasting remained a distant possibility even after satellites were introduced to relay programs from one continent to another. Several factors—such as improved high-power satellite technology and abundant satellite transponders made possible by digital compression—resulted in inexpensive transmission time that increased the use of Intelsat and other existing international satellite systems for transmission of programs from one country or system to another. This led first to increased use of satellites for transmission of television news events, sports, and news footage. Next came transmission of entire newscasts on a regular basis, then cable system–oriented news channels, such as CNN. It was not until the 1990s that DTH became a real possibility.

The technological possibilities of television news transmission via satellite created several policy issues. Long before satellite distribution of programs from one country or broadcasting/cable institution to another, and even longer before direct satellite broadcasting to small home dishes became a physical reality, the implications of international satellite television news for political propaganda were anticipated in debates among UNESCO, COPUOS (United Nations Committee on the Peaceful Use of Outer Space), and the International Telecommunications Union (ITU) on DTH in the 1960s and 1970s.

Laskin and Chayes (1975) noted that most countries other than the United States feared not only political propaganda but also cultural influence and commercial consumer influence from advertising if DTH-type services were to flourish unrestricted by international law. Still, it was primarily the prospect of video versions of shortwave radio information and public diplomacy operations like VOA that worried many nations that did not like the idea of the direct flow of news and information. The Soviet Union and others had conducted extensive jamming of certain radio signals, such as those of Radio Liberty and Radio Free Europe, and they indicated in these debates that unrestricted DTH would be unacceptable (McPhail, 1987).

Despite U.S. protestations that restrictions would violate the principle of free flow of information, the United Nations General Assembly, based on a COPUOS working-group recommendation, voted 100 to 1 (the United States) in 1972 to establish restrictions. The essential condition was eventually established that before a country or company based in it could broadcast to another country, the receiving country had to give its prior consent (McPhail, 1987). The key point of the whole debate, emphasized by its taking place so long before the actual debut of DTH, is that policy makers in almost all countries other than the United States were concerned about the potential impact of both news and entertainment-oriented propaganda from cross-border television broadcasting. At least until recently, they have been unwilling to let a party beyond their borders make decisions about what might be telecast into the country.

However, despite all the attention given in the 1970s to creating international policies requiring prior consent by receiving nations for international satellite TV, relatively few nations, such as China, Saudi Arabia, and Malaysia (Boyd, 1999; Chan, 1994), as well as Iran and pre-Saddam Iraq, officially restricted access to cross-border DBS. This principle of prior consent has been honored only when pressed for by rigorous national policy, as in China. However, China's effective pressure on Murdoch's Star TV to discontinue showing the BBC World television service has shown that determined leaders of a large country can force a major international satellite television operator to make major changes in hopes of thereby gaining approval for reception of their channels.

Government Satellite TV

Despite the cautionary debates and research that have been conducted on previous forms of international television news flow, relatively little attention has been focused on government or official international television news services. Those services are made possible technically by satellites and are coming closer to realization for both commercial and political motives.

For example, two international television news services have been offered, one by the U.S. Broadcasting Board of Governors (BBG) (AlHurraTV) and the old VOA Worldnet, and the other by the BBC World Service. This again raises the question discussed by receiving nations in the DTH debate about the appropriateness and acceptability of video news programs created by existing international radio broadcasters and government public diplomacy agencies. Both China and Saudi Arabia have forcefully protested the contents of BBC news and have succeeded in forcing the BBC channel off of Star TV and Orbit, respectively (Boyd, 1999; Thomas, 1999).

Ironically, the United States, once feared as the most likely source of international satellite television propaganda, has complained severely since 9/11 about the news coverage of another quasi-state service, Al-Jazeera. U.S. Secretary of Defense Donald Rumsfeld and other officials have complained repeatedly of what they see as bias against U.S. war efforts in Iraq, in terms of too much emphasis on civilian casualties; too much space given to views and statements by Al Qaeda leaders, like Osama bin laden; and "negative" news about U.S. forces in Iraq.

Critics in both the United States and the United Kingdom have raised executive and legislative questions about the appropriateness and feasibility of such "official" international TV news services, viewed from the originating country's point of view. The goals, and the payoffs, would presumably be similar to those described for international radio broadcasting: enhancing prestige, promoting national interests, fostering cultural ties, and, conceivably, attempting political indoctrination (Boyd, 1986). The British government refused to provide startup funds for BBC World because the government did not believe it could justify the expense to the British taxpayers. However, the BBC was successful in raising funds from the private sector through its commercial department. The U.S. government's former WorldNet Television project, after a several-year trial, was found to be too costly and was reduced to a fairly minor service for relaying existing public affairs programs and interactive videoconferences.

USIA's Worldnet.   As a public diplomacy agency, USIA was not new to television. It had been making and placing television news footage—and finished television features, documentaries, and discussion programs—for years. As a satellite television service, Worldnet was preceded and succeeded by a more modest, ad hoc series of USIA videoconferences. These typically featured a one-way video transmission of a speaker from the United States to one or several other countries and usually had two-way audio via international telephone lines so that local journalists or other audiences could ask questions. These conferences have been conducted since the late 1970s and continued under the Worldnet aegis with greatly increased frequency under the Reagan administration. In the 1980s, substantial investment was made in satellite receiving dishes for a number of USIA posts overseas to foster this type of videoconferencing.

USIA's Worldnet was a major innovation of USIA during the Reagan administration. It was an expensive project and was cancelled by the U.S. Congress, primarily for reasons of cost counted against benefit. The teleconferencing component (Worldnet Dialogues) was generally well regarded as cost effective because it tended to generate coverage in local media. The value of the regular news and magazine format transmissions, however, was challenged. In 1988, Congress required USIA to show evidence of effectiveness in the form of an audience of at least 2 million viewers in Western Europe ("Audience Survey," 1987) for funding to continue. A survey commissioned by USIA did not produce the mandated viewing numbers, and the television service was suspended when funding stopped in November 1988. Subsequently, VOA itself became a television service when it started regular satellite television transmissions in Russian and Farsi with the hope of creating a two-way dialogue as viewers with home dishes were encouraged to call in during live telecasts. WorldNet was merged under VOA Radio and TV in 1998.

British Broadcasting Corporation.   BBC World, the BBC's international television news service, is also not new. BBC television news has been seen in other countries for more than three decades. BBC news is available either through the BBC's participation in the satellite news exchange of the European Broadcasting Union (EBU) or via agreement with broadcasters to use some BBC domestic and international television news stories. Viewers in the Irish Republic and in the Netherlands, for example, see British television news either directly from transmission spillover or via retransmissions of over-the-air signals on local cable systems.

The development of an international television news service was one of the BBC World Service's objectives in the 1988–1993 five-year plan (Checkland, n.d.). Using the off-hour production capacity of the BBC London Television Centre and the foreign expertise of the World Service's journalists, the initial concept involved the production of several daily 30-minute news programs in English. Stations taking the service would have the option of using designated "windows"—where international weather or financial news is featured—within the newscast for either commercial announcements or short local news items.

The British government was concerned about (1) an initial project request from World Service Television of between £6 and £10 million to fund the plan; (2) the technology, that is, whether such a service would be delivered only to broadcasters for retransmission or would also be available for satellite home reception; and (3) the blurring of the traditional lines of responsibility between the domestic service (financed by license fees paid by those owning television receivers) and the World Service (funded by an appropriation from the Foreign Office). In March 1988, the British government stated that it would not provide funds to start the service (Robert Wilson, senior international press officer, BBC World Service, personal communication, August 15, 1988); subsequently, in August 1988, BBC announced that it would seek private funding for the international television news venture (Evans, 1988), and private funding was arranged in 1990 for a proposed 1991 start.

This commercial BBC channel has succeeded well in the United States and other English-speaking markets. BBC America, for example, is a 24-hour channel wholly owned by the BBC and distributed by Discovery Networks as part of a global alliance between the BBC and Discovery Channel International. It shows a mixture of documentaries, comedies, dramas, and news (BBC America, 2005). Increasingly, the BBC co-produces dramas and documentaries with international partners, like PBS and Discovery, while still producing its own news.

Commercial Satellite TV

Still other satellite news operations exist that have quite different motives. The U.S.-based Cable News Network (CNN) and the British Independent Television News (ITN) have started internationally oriented news services for sale to European and other markets. Other commercial news operations have also started, including some outside the developed countries. Those include Al-Jazeera (Qatar) and Saudi-owned, Dubai-based Al-Arabia.

These operations make a profit by selling advertising time on their services. At least in the case of Time Warner's CNNI, there seem to have been motives beyond simply making money that might make CNNI a particularly active player in international public diplomacy. Former Time Warner cochairman and CNN founder Ted Turner himself was quoted as saying, "They are watching us in Moscow right now, in Havana, in London.... Within the next three years, virtually every leader in the world will be watching CNN with a satellite dish" (Schrange & Vise, 1986, p. H3). During the Reagan–Gorbachev summit in May 1988, CNNI was rebroadcast in Moscow on a UHF channel ("Rabbit Ears," 1988) and was thus available to those beyond the select few with satellite dishes (Gregg Creevey, special projects manager, CNNI, personal communication, August 15, 1988). Now CNNI can be seen in every part of the world.

CNN. CNN and its international service (CNNI) are commercial news operations based in Atlanta, Georgia, and owned by U.S. media corporation Time Warner. CNN operates primarily in the United States on cable channels, although parts of its two 24-hour services, regular CNN and CNN *Headline News,* are carried by some U.S. television stations. CNN created CNNI and began selling programming to Australia, then increased its overseas expansion to sell its services at about the same time as did other U.S. suppliers of cable television channels and programming who saw sales potential abroad. CNNI has been targeting hotels, cable systems, and airport departure lounges in Western Europe and Asia. CNNI is also retransmitted, often pirated, by some developing-nation cable and television systems, primarily in the Caribbean and Latin America, because it can be picked up there from the same satellite used for distribution in the United States. CNNI is now carried legitimately by pay-satellite and cable operators in Latin America, and it has an agreement with Egypt to have the news service available via a scrambled UHF service in Cairo. CNNI programming reaches the Middle East via the Orbit Television and Radio network, a Dubai-based, Saudi Arabian–owned DTH satellite service

One problem for CNN is that it is often offering to Europe, Asia, the Middle East, and Latin America regular news programming that is primarily designed for the U.S. market. Although CNN has had a distinct European edition via CNNI since 1985 (Dukes, 1985), it is gradually acquiring more non-U.S.-specific content by originating news from its London and Hong Kong studios. It has also created more-localized versions in Spanish and Turkish.

CNNI seems to operate primarily as a straightforward commercial service initiated in those markets, such as Western Europe, Latin America, and Asia, where a profit is projected. Further, the service operates under standard U.S. commercial news practices and editorial values. Those values, however, while familiar to U.S. television viewers, are not what European, Asian, Middle Eastern, or Latin American viewers often get from their own various government, public, and private television news services. Expanded world exposure to such news will probably have an impact on international news knowledge and opinion, and hence on public diplomacy.

When he ran CNN, Turner seems to have kept his hands off CNN and CNNI editorial policy, but projects such as the Goodwill Games and *World Report* (which shows news items created by local or national news services around the world)—and instances where CNN has juxtaposed BBC and Argentine reports on the Falklands War—indicate that he and CNN were somewhat more committed than many to the deliberate airing of other countries' points of view within an essentially U.S. commercial television news framework. This has interesting implications for public diplomacy. The importance of CNN in public diplomacy was further demonstrated in the 1990–1991 Gulf crisis. Saddam Hussein and George Bush were widely considered to be sending messages to each other's publics via CNN, a practice that continued until the 2003 Iraqi war.

Murdoch and Sky News.   A relatively new competitor for the international satellite news audience has appeared: Rupert Murdoch's News Corporation. In 1989, Sky News, one of several Murdoch-owned satellite-to-home–delivered services under British Sky Broadcasting (BSkyB), started operating a 24-hour CNN-type news service from London. Since then, News Corporation has expanded its worldwide television information and entertainment interests with the purchase of Asia's Star TV and ownership of JSkyB (Japan); LatinSkyB; ASkyB (North America); and Fox News, a New York–based 24-hour news channel. Clearly, Murdoch wishes to compete with Time Warner's CNN on an international level for news viewers, but his strategy seems to be one of localizing news as well as entertainment programs for several regions. Increasingly, he works with local or regional partners, such as Zee-TV (India) for South Asia (Thussu, 2000), and TV Globo (Brazil) and Televisa (Mexico) for Latin America (Duarte, 2001). In order to get governmental approval for his channels in China, Murdoch has agreed to produce almost all his satellite TV for China in China and to help get carriage for an English-language Chinese news channel around the world (Jirik, 2002).

Of course, the major international satellite-delivered news services have primarily been in English and thus useful only to the elite or expatriates. An emerging trend is the regional satellite service, targeting those that can speak the majority language in the area. CNNI has decided to move beyond English-language service with a Spanish-language news channel to Latin America, where it must compete with national channels from Brazil (TV Globo) and Mexico (Televisa), which are becoming regional news channels, as well as a Turkish-language satellite news channel for Turkey and Central Asia. CNBC Asia from Singapore has established a presence in the Asian market, where financial news is important.

Orbit in the Middle East.   The Saudi-owned, Dubai-based Orbit Television and Radio Network soon learned that a news service over which it had no editorial control was not good for business. Alexander Zilo, Orbit's CEO, has said that the former eight-hour daily service in Arabic provided by the BBC in London became a problem when it started devoting time to Saudi dissident Mohammed Al-Masari's specific objections to the way the Saudi royal family was running the country and that he had talked to the BBC about the coverage (A. Zilo, CEO Orbit Television and Radio Network, personal communication, January 3, 1995; Boyd, 1999). Coverage of Al-Masari's efforts peaked in late 1995 and early 1996 when he fought a court battle in London to remain there as a political refugee. However, the event that motivated Orbit to cancel its BBC contract was a *Panorama* program on Orbit's BBC Arabic Television News that showed secretly shot film (taken in Saudi Arabia) of the preparations for a double execution by beheading. For a variety of reasons, including distance from its audience and the expense of operating from Italy, Orbit moved to Bahrain in the early 2000s.

The Qatar-based Al Jazeera news channel seems to have picked up where Orbit's BBC Arabic television news stopped; it now offers the region 24-hour daily television news and information programming. While not only a news service, Saudi-owned Middle East Broadcasting Centre, and virtually every other Arab country, offers some of form of regional satellite-delivered news in Arabic (Boyd, 1999).

International Radio, International DBS, and Isolated Audiences

Several decades of research on international radio audiences show that listening to BBC, VOA, and the others is highest among people who have few domestic options, like those in isolated areas. The numbers of such people have been steadily reduced by the increasing advance of domestic AM, and especially FM radio, in most countries. International radio is also sometimes sought by those who do not trust the local or national media readily available to them. That is still the case in a number of countries, but the number has been reduced by the fall of authoritarian regimes that exercised tight control over media contents in the former USSR, Eastern Europe, Asia, Africa, the Middle East, and Latin America.

Likewise, international television channels, whether brought in by DTH or cable TV, have shown certain patterns and limits in the audience research to date. Audiences for cross-border broadcast television, like those for radio, are largest in those areas where domestic television is not readily available. However, the number of such places is declining steadily. The same satellites that bring in international channels also permit the retransmission of national television channels to receiving dishes, cable head-ends, or rebroadcast transmitters. Studies in both urban and rural Brazil by one of the authors found that most owners of dishes, users of the satellite master antenna systems that serve urban apartment buildings, and cable subscribers primarily watched national channels (Straubhaar, 2000). Few (less than 8 percent of television households) subscribed to the pay-TV systems required to see international channels, according to ratings in *TelaViva* and other trade publications.

Again, as with international radio, some television viewers who are not satisfied with national programming or who seek news information to supplement or replace national news do turn to international channels. International political and economic elites are widely known to use CNN for fast-breaking news to supplement local sources. Many young people watch MTV, although MTV is increasingly presented in localized versions aimed at specific countries or regions and featuring local VJs and an increasing amount of local music. MTV also faces a host of local and regional competitors who tend to emphasize local, national, or regional music videos. Viewers dissatisfied with commercial entertainment channels often turn to various language versions of the Discovery Channel or the BBC.

Research by the present authors in Brazil, Saudi Arabia, and other locations has shown audiences of international television channels to be highly segmented. Few international channels have anything resembling a mass audience. Instead, they have specific, small but important audiences segmented by interests in news, music, foreign movies, documentaries, sports, and so on (Duarte & Straubhaar, 2004). These audiences tend to be smaller than the audiences for regular national broadcast television, for several reasons. First, international channels require either a pay-TV DTH service or a cable subscription, whose prices tend to cut out nonaffluent viewers in many countries. In Brazil, where half of the population makes less than $200 a month, pay TV or cable TV tends to cost $20–30 a month. Second, research has shown that mass audiences tend to prefer national or nearby regional material because it is culturally more proximate or relevant to them (Straubhaar, 1991, 2000). Without the knowledge or cultural interest and awareness developed by international travel, second languages, or advanced education, most audience members find that national or nearby regional jokes are funnier, styles more pleasing, facial expressions more comprehensible, and the like (Straubhaar, 2000).

A somewhat-similar situation seems to apply to Internet radio and television across borders. The Internet makes it easier than was ever true with radio or television for new broadcasters to put their material out for international contact. So many new broadcasters can suddenly reach international audiences; they include American neo-Nazis trying to reach young audiences in North America, Australia, and Northern Europe with white supremacy–oriented heavy metal music from several countries. While that is against the law in Germany, it has been hard for the German government to act against such Internet materials— although they tried several times in the 1990s. These new broadcasts also include a variety of Islamic broadcasts in a number of languages, ranging from open sympathizers of Al-Qaeda to those urging that *jihad* be considered only as an internal struggle for righteous behavior.

With such a wide variety of new offerings in many languages aimed at many interests, the traditional international broadcasters may have an even harder time competing. Still, those traditional media with high credibility, such as the BBC, major newspapers, and, in the Arab World, Al-Jazeera, seem to attract audiences in parts of the world that might not otherwise see or hear their broadcasts and stories.

Public Diplomacy, International Communication, or Media Imperialism?

In current usage, most commonly among U.S. officials, public diplomacy is the use of mass communication and contacts with opinion leaders to influence international public opinion (U.S. Advisory Commission on Public Diplomacy, 1998). Official public diplomacy is conducted by governmental information structures—including state-run news agencies, embassy and other press offices, ministries of information, external radio and television broadcasting services, official exchange programs such as the Fulbright Program, and international communication organizations such as the former U.S. Information Agency (whose functions were absorbed by the State Department). Public diplomacy is emerging as a frequent, if still controversial, part of government activities in the international diplomatic arena, as noted. Some would argue that these activities are best considered simply the current phase of the evolution of propaganda, but U.S. practitioners at least have argued that such activities are open and public, an aboveboard adjunct to diplomacy (Hansen, 1984).

A more important reason for separately defining and studying public diplomacy, though, is that, by our definition at least, it intrinsically involves a whole series of public actors other than governments. Commercial mass media, tourism, academic exchanges, labor union contacts, political party ties, and church activities can all be considered "private" transnational involvement in public diplomacy (Keohane & Nye, 1971). All of these entities are involved in trying to influence government policy (and sometimes private and corporate actions) by influencing general public opinion or selected publics who are particularly relevant to the issue at hand. For example, international environmental groups, like the World Wildlife Fund, give money to groups in countries like Brazil to create projects, in part to attract attention in order to place issues on the agenda of local media and to gain coverage so as to influence local opinion.

Put another way, this is diplomacy in the public sphere, involving not only governments but also a variety of other actors who are trying to affect public opinion. In fact, it seems likely that in the shaping of current world opinion, governments are frequently much less important than key private actors. These include the wire services, which furnish much of the world's news; Hollywood films and television programs, which inform much of the world's interpretive framework about other nations; international television news services, which supply most of the current images peoples have about each other and events elsewhere; and most recently, globally oriented television news channels, such as CNN.

However, critical scholars like Schiller (1991) note that governments frequently benefit greatly from the actions of what is public diplomacy in a technically private form. Joseph Nye (2004) has become famous in American policy circles for promoting the idea that the United States can benefit from the "soft power" of its cultural industries, software, and media. However, after 9/11, it became clear that U.S. and other Western nations' soft power can be a two-edged sword. Several Arab commentators have noted that negative reactions to both depictions of Arabs in American media and the values about sexuality, marriage, and so on shown in U.S. films and videos may well have fed into the rage against the United States that fed 9/11 and subsequent terrorism against U.S. interests.

As governments began to depart from traditional diplomacy—that is, direct government contacts—and began attempts to manipulate foreign publics so as to affect their governments' policies, then governments inadvertently opened up an arena that other actors could more easily enter. While it is difficult, although not impossible or unheard of, for individuals or nongovernmental groups to conduct warfare or traditional diplomacy, it is much easier for nongovernmental actors to reach and influence public opinion. This is particularly true via mass media that can focus on whatever they decide is interesting or newsworthy. For example, modern terrorism can be considered "low-level warfare," but it is probably more often now thought of not as a means of achieving military-type objectives but more as a means of garnering media attention, and hence public attention for a cause.

So with the proliferation of publics to address, both new and traditional international electronic media to address them with, and groups with internationally focused causes to publicize, the use of international broadcasting, over both airwaves and Internet, for public diplomacy is likely to continue to proliferate. Equally likely is the continual increase in direct international broadcasting, particularly on satellite television, for less overtly political purposes of entertaining, informing, selling goods, and advertising.

 For more information on the topics that appear in this chapter, use the password that came free with this book to access InfoTrac College Edition. Use the following words as keyterms and subject searches:

QUESTIONS FOR DISCUSSION

1. What are the main reasons why governments have been the main actors in international radio broadcasting?
2. How has international radio changed since the end of the Cold War?
3. Is public diplomacy a legitimate international activity of governments? Is public diplomacy any different from propaganda?
4. Why have commercial television companies instead of governments emerged as the main direct satellite television broadcasters (DBS)?
5. Is current DBS less of a threat to national cultures if it is done by commercial companies instead of governments?
6. What new groups have entered public diplomacy via satellite TV?
7. How will the Internet change public diplomacy? What kinds of groups have entered public diplomacy via the Internet?

REFERENCES

Audience survey of Worldnet program. (1987, December 14). Cong. Rec.\s 209, H11310.

BBC. (1983). BBC Annual Reports. London, BBC.

BBC. (2000). BBC World Service annual review. Retrieved from http://www.bbc.co.uk/worldservice/aboutus/annualreview/chief.html

BBC. (2005). BBC World Service homepage. Retrieved from http://www.bbc.co.uk/worldservice/index.shtml

BBC America. (2005). Homepage. Retrieved May 10, 2005, from http://www.bbca-merica.com/about.html

Boyd, D. A. (1983). Broadcasting between the two Germanies. *Journalism Quarterly, 60*(2), 232–239.

Boyd, D. A. (1986). International radio broadcasting: Technical developments and listening patterns in the developing world. *Space Communication and Broadcasting, 4*(1), 25–32.

Boyd, D.A. (1999). *Broadcasting in the Arab World: A survey of the electronic media in the Middle East.* Ames: Iowa State University Press.

Boyd-Barrett, O. (1980). *The International News Agencies.* Beverly Hills, CA: Sage.

Browne, D. R. (1982). *International radio broadcasting: The limits of the limitless medium.* New York: Praeger.

Chan, J. M. (1994). National responses and accessibility to STAR TV in Asia. *Journal of Communication, 44*(3), 70–88.

Checkland, M. (n.d.). *The next five years: 1988–1993.* London: BBC.

Diplomacy Strategy Board. (2005). Terms of reference. Retrieved from http://www.fco.gov.uk/Files/kfile/PDStrategyBoard_TORef.pdf

Dizard, W. (1976). Television's global networks. In Fischer & Merrill (Eds.), *International and intercultural communication.* New York: Hastings House.

Duarte, L. G. (2001). *Looking south: American television networks enter Latin America.* Unpublished doctoral dissertation, Michigan State University.

Duarte, L., & Straubhaar, J. (2004). Adapting U.S. transnational television channels to a complex world: From cultural imperialism to localization to hybridization. In J. Challaby (ed.), *Transnational television worldwide.* New York: L. B. Taunis.

Dukes, A. (1985, September 30). Turner prepares to launch European edition of CNN. *Multichannel News,* p. 12.

El-Nawawy, M. & Iskandar, A. (2003). *Al-Jazeera: The story of the network that is rattling governments and redefining modern journalism.* Boulder, CO; Westview Press.

Eugster, E. (1983). *Television programming across national boundaries: The EBU and OIRT experience.* Artech House.

Evans, R. (1988, August 11). BBC asks for private funds. *The Times* (London), p. 1.

Federal Communications Commission. (1936). *Second annual report.* Washington, DC: U.S. Government Printing Office.

Fejes, F. (1983). The U.S. in third world communications: Latin America, 1900–1945. *Journalism Monographs,* 48.

Frederick, H. H. (1986). *Electronic penetration in low intensity warfare: The case of Nicaragua.* Paper presented at 14th Annual Telecommunications Policy Conference, Airlie, VA, April 29.

Gerbner, G., Mowlana, H., & Nordenstreng, K. (1993). *The Global Media Debate.* Norwood, NJ: L. E. Earlbaum.

Hansen, A. (1984). *USIA, public diplomacy in the computer age.* New York: Praeger.

Head, S. (1985). *World broadcasting systems: A comparative analysis.* Belmont, CA.: Wadsworth.

Hearings before a subcommittee of the committee on interstate commerce (1938). Senate, on S. 3342. 75th Cong., 3rd Sess. Washington, DC: U.S. Government Printing Office.

Hitler, A. (1933). *Mein kampf, Zwei bande in einem band; ungekurzte ausgabe.* Munchen: F. Eher.

Hoagland, J. (2005, March 20). For Bush, personnel as policy. *Washington Post.*

Jirik, J. (2002). *The state of the emperor's clothes: Chinese news media today.* Unpublished paper, University of Texas, Austin.

Jirik, J. (2003). *The AOL Time Warner CCTV (China) television exchange: Guanxi in globalization theory.* ICA Conference Paper. San Diego, CA.

Keohane, R. O., & Nye, J. S. (1971). *Transnational relations and world politics.* Cambridge, MA: Harvard Press.

Laskin, P., & Chayes, A. (1975). International satellite controversy. *Society, 12*(6), 30–40.

Lippman, W. (1965). *Public Opinion.* New York: Free Press.

MacBride Commission. (1980). *Many voices, one world: Report by the international commission for the study of communication problems.* New York: Unipub/UNESCO.

McPhail, T. C. (1987). *Electronic colonialism: The future of international broadcasting and communication.* Newbury Park, CA: Sage.

Mytton, G. (1993). *Global audiences: Research for worldwide broadcasting.* London: J. Libbey.

NBC news going worldwide with Visnews. (1988, November 21). *Broadcasting,* pp. 22–23.

Nordenstreng, K., & Varis, T. (1974). *Television traffic—A one-way street. Reports and papers on mass communication.* Paris: UNESCO.

Nye, J. (2004). *Soft power: The means to success in world politics.* New York: Public Affairs.

Paterson, C. (1996). *News production at Worldwide Television News (WTN): An analysis of television news agency coverage of developing countries.* Unpublished doctoral dissertation, University of Texas, Austin.

Rabbit ears and CNN's yours. (1988, June 1). *Variety,* p. 82.

Radio Sawa home page. (2005). Retrieved from http://www.radiosawa.com

Schiller, H. (1971). *Mass communication and American empire.* Boston: Beacon.

Schiller. H. J. (1991). Not yet the post-imperialist era. *Critical Studies in Mass Communication. 9,* 13–38.

Schrange, M., & Vise, D. A. (1986, August 31). Murdoch, Turner launch era of global television. *Washington Post,* pp. H1, H3.

Schwoch, J. (1990). *The American radio industry and its Latin American activities, 1930–1990.* Chicago: University of Illinois Press.

Straubhaar, J. D. (1991). Beyond cultural imperialism: Toward asymmetrical interdependence and cultural proximity. *Critical Studies in Mass Communication, 9,* 1–11.

Straubhaar, J. D. (2000). Cultural capital and media choices. In G. Wang, J. Servaes, & A. Goonasekera (Eds.), *The new communications landscape: Demystifying media globalization.* New York: Routledge.

Thomas, A. C. (1999). Regulating access to transnational satellite television: Shifting government policies in Northeast Asia. *Gazette, 61,* 243–254.

Thussu, D. K. (2000). *International communication: Continuity and change.* New York: Arnold/Oxford University Press.

United States Advisory Commission on Public Diplomacy. (1998). *Publics and diplomats in the global communications age.* Washington, DC: U.S. Information Agency.

U.S. Information Agency. (1982). *Argentine international radio audiences during the Falklands War.* Washington, DC: USIA Office of Research.

Varis, T. (1984). The international flow of television. *Journal of Communication. (Winter),* 143–152

Voice of America. (2001). *Spring 2001–Autumn 2001 broadcast schedules.* Retrieved from http://www.voa.gov/allsked.html

Voice of Russia. (2001). The Voice of Russia homepage. Retrieved from http://www.vor.ru

Whitton, J. (1979). Hostile international propaganda and international law. In K. Nordenstreng & H. I. Schiller (Eds.), *National sovereignty and international communication* (pp. 217–232). Norwood, NJ: Ablex.

8

The Global Implications of the Internet: Challenges and Prospects

GEORGE A. BARNETT AND DEVAN ROSEN

George A. Barnett (PhD, Michigan State University) is Professor and Chair of the Department Communication at the State University of New York at Buffalo. He has written extensively on organizational, mass, international and intercultural, and political communication, as well as the diffusion of innovations. His current research focuses on international information flows, in general; and telecommunications flows including the Internet, in specific; and their role in social and economic development and globalization.

Devan Rosen (PhD, Cornell University) is Assistant Professor at the University of Hawai'i at Mānoa in the Department of Speech. His current research interests center around communication networks and self-organizing systems. He applies these central foci to cooperative emergent networks in organizations and small groups, the small world phenomena as applied to bipartite communication networks and knowledge networks, semantic networks generated from online interaction, global communication networks, and uses of computer-mediated communication.

For additional online resources, access the Global Media Monitor website that accompanies this book on the Wadsworth Communication Cafe website at http://communication.wadsworth.com.

Transmitted at the speed of light, all events on this planet are simultaneous. In the electronic environment of information, all events are simultaneous. There is no time or space separating events . . . The absence of space brings to mind the idea of the village. But actually, at the speed of light, the planet is not much bigger than the room we're in. In terms of time and the speed of the events that are programmed, they hit each other so fast that even a village is too big a thing to use for comparison. The acoustic or simultaneous space in which we now live is like a sphere whose center is everywhere and whose margins are nowhere.

MARSHALL McLUHAN,
FROM AN INTERVIEW IN 1974 (FROM BENEDETTI, 1996)

Human civilization, undergoing massive societal changes over the last several hundred years, is still threaded together by people creating systems (or networks) of communicative interaction. What has changed dramatically is the means by which we create and maintain these networks, and the effects they have on our cultural identity. Advances in communication technology, mainly the Internet, have catalyzed an information revolution, which has accelerated the rate of change and pace to human civilization that is by comparison equivalent in magnitude to the Industrial Revolution (Castells, 2000). However, the effects of this transformation on cultural identity are not fully understood.

This chapter offers a world systems explanation of the global implications of the Internet as related to culture, and is organized as follows: First, convergence theory and cultural identity are described, followed by an explanation of the systems and network perspectives. These perspectives are then applied to convergence theory and communication networks. Then, a structural model of intercultural communication is presented, followed by a case study describing the network structure of the international Internet. The case study is then extrapolated to elaborate short- and long-term implications of the structural model of national identity. Finally, future implications of the model on cultural identity are offered.

CONVERGENCE THEORY AND CULTURAL IDENTITY

Communication may be defined as a process of sharing information in which two or more participants reach mutual understanding. Mutual understanding may be achieved by the successive sharing of additional information (feedback). Usually several cycles of information exchange are required to change the initial differences that prevent understanding. The convergence model posits reduced within-group variance to be the primary result of the communication process and a requirement for collective action and the achievement of social goals (Kincaid, Yum, Woelfel, & Barnett, 1983; Rogers & Kincaid, 1981). Convergence theory may be applied to those communication situations in which the participants are social systems, such as ethnic groups or nation–states, each of which possesses a unique culture. Thus, cultural convergence theory suggests that the variance between groups or national cultures would become smaller over time as a result of international communication (Barnett & Kincaid, 1983).

This chapter suggests a two-fold explanation of the global implications of the Internet based on the short- and long-term effects. First, cultural homogenization will be retarded in the near future by the increased use of advanced Internet-based communication technologies (e.g., Instant Messenger, online communities). Further, the use of the Internet will allow people to maintain cultural ties allowing the culture of the social system to reach a temporary steady state. Second, the long-term effect of the increased communication among the peoples of the world via the Internet will be that the differences among national cultures will diminish, resulting in the formation of a single global culture. One outcome of this process of cultural convergence is that separate cultural identities will also disappear, replaced by a single transnational identity (systemic homeostasis), albeit with considerable variation.

SYSTEMS APPROACH AND SOCIAL NETWORKS

Systems

Central to the systems perspective is nonsummativity, or holism, which implies that the interdependence and interrelationships of the parts of the system determine the whole. The whole is more than the sum of its parts. Systems are wholes with irreducible characteristics. One of the key features of the systems perspective is the causal interdependence among multiple systemic forces, all of which act mutually and more or less simultaneously on each other (Kelly & McGrath, 1988). Thus, holism is not simply aggregate wholeness, when the nature of the entity is the sum of its parts (e.g., pile of sand). Holism is better characterized by organizational structure, when an entity consisting of two or more basic parts, or people, in communication with each other in which the outcome is something more or different than the sum of the parts (e.g., culture).

Another critical element of the systems approach is the presence of coordinating interfaces of subsystems and suprasystems. Coordinating systemic interfaces bring together the behavior of their own components and integrate this joint effort with the behavior of other components, or subsystems, within the greater whole, or suprasystem. For example, a nation–state can be seen as a social system, yet a cultural group within that country can also be treated as a system; or in this case, a subsystem. This notion is important when considering the coupling of cultural networks spanning many nation–states.

In open systems, stability is achieved through self-correcting processes using negative feedback, or a deviation correction process that maintains a desired steady state. When the system is able to maximize the corrective action so that dynamic equilibrium is reached, homeostasis is achieved. From this view, some number of systemic forces operates in a concurrent, mutually interdependent fashion, reinforcing the extant steady state (Barnett, 1997; Kelly & McGrath, 1988).

Growth and change within open systems characterize the open nature of these systems, allowing for input and output, and the ability to maintain a changing steady state in response to environmental changes. Positive feedback, or deviation amplifying, allows change in one part of the system to cause a change in another part of the system, and so on, until the environmental influence is integrated or avoided. This represents the evolutionary dimension of systems, where the system has the propensity to preserve the system (morphostasis), such as cultural maintenance; or grow, change, and differentiate (morphogenesis), such as cultural convergence.

Exchange that occurs between the system and the environment, generally across the system boundary and comprised of both inputs and outputs, allows for several crucial observations of the system. First, the determination of system behavior offers identification of the processes that the system engages in over time as well as the properties that these processes imply. Second, an understanding of the system behavior allows for the stipulation of the environment, and thus determination of the systems evolution can be understood. Thus, the essence of defining systems is not in defining individual components but in the coupling of these components, the organization that results from the coupling, and how this interaction allows for regulation and adaptation. This regulation and adaptation occurs over a time frame that allows for the system components to organize.

Fundamental notions of open systems provide a common framework with which to dissect and understand processes in dynamic communicative systems. Combined with information theory (Shannon & Weaver, 1949), dynamic patterns can be conceptualized in terms of information and the reduction of uncertainty (Fisher, 1978; Shannon & Weaver, 1949). Knowledge of an event at time t can reduce uncertainty of an event at time $t + 1$ (VanLear, 1996). Further, integrating stochastic process into systems and information theory approaches avoids the problem of mechanistic causal determinism. Fisher (1978) posits that, choosing from a universe of alternatives; people may only be constrained by past choices and the choices of others, not determined by them. Thus, certain choices may be more probable than others, creating a redundant sequence of behaviors that form a pattern. It is this pattern that reduces uncertainty in interaction, and a stochastic model best represents these interactions (rules, constraints, and information) because behavior is a result of constraints (rules) on choices, not causal forces (laws) (VanLear, 1996).

However, if the patterns just discussed are to be utilized, a means of revealing patterns in social systems must be used to allow for the identification of system components and the determination of system behavior. Social network analysis provides a rich set of procedures and vocabulary for the elaboration and dissection of social systems, and the prediction of their structure in the future.

Social Networks

Social network perspectives focus on the structure of social systems and how the elements of a social system are put together. From the network perspective, the social environment can be expressed as patterns or regularities in relationships among interacting units. These patterns are often called structure.

The form of network that will be utilized herein is a communication network, defined as the patterns of contact that are created by the flow of messages among communicators through time and space (Rogers & Kincaid, 1981). Communication network analysis identifies the communication structure, or information flow. Relational ties (linkages) between actors are channels for the transfer (flow) of either material or nonmaterial resources, or for an association between actors, such as a friendship tie. The ties that exist between the nodes can vary along several elements, including direction, reciprocity, and strength.

Links between actors can be measured as being either directional, or non-directional. Links that are directional indicate the movement from one actor to another, such as the number of phone calls one country makes to another, or the degree of liking one person has for another. Additionally, these links can also be symmetrical or asymmetrical. If the link is directional but there is not the same value of relation (i.e., the link is not bidirectional), then the link is asymmetrical, lacking reciprocity. Nondirectional links simply indicate an association of two actors in a shared partnership, such as two countries having a trade affiliation.

CONVERGENCE THEORY AND COMMUNICATION NETWORKS

Convergence theory envisions the flow of information through a communication network shared by those who participate in the process. This information has profound effects on the members of the network, which are indicated by changes in the belief systems of the members and the structure of their network (the communicative relations among the participants). Local regions of greater communication density share more information and thus will be characterized by movements toward decreasing variance or difference of opinion at a greater rate than regions of less density.

The process of divergence, or movement toward increased within-group variance, occurs in closed social systems where there are no (or limited) information flows among members. In network terms, they are disconnected or isolated. In this situation, over time members of such a system would be expected to become less similar to one another and the system as a whole would reach a state of greater entropy or disorder. However, when communication is unrestricted, the process leads toward reduced within-group variance among its members. The communication network is completely interconnected or dense. In this case, differences between its members are reduced through the iterative process of information exchange. The social system moves toward an equilibrium, where it remains as long as internal information flows are constant.

The laws of thermodynamics predict that all participants (individuals, groups, or nation–states) in a closed system (the world system or global community) will converge over time on the average collective pattern of thought if communication is allowed to continue indefinitely over time. Thus, the convergence model of communication predicts that all participants in the world system will converge over time on the average collective pattern of thought if communication is allowed to continue unrestricted. Unlimited and unrestricted communication between cultures would eventually lead to a reduction in the differences between cultures and toward greater similarity of beliefs and values (homogenization), with the equilibrium value tending toward the average of the collective as expressed in its messages. Cultural convergence can only be delayed or reversed by the introduction of new information and/or the formation of boundaries that restrict the flow of information. Relatively bounded, isolated groups would experience greater convergence toward their own local system rather than the average of the larger global system, even though the net convergence of the entire system would continue to increase (Barnett & Kincaid, 1983; Kincaid et. al., 1983). However, as a system is adapting to the increased connectivity, it will naturally rest in a temporary steady state in an effort to reduce entropy. Applying this notion to the cultural convergence model, people will use available Internet technologies in an attempt to maintain increased connectivity to their home culture, since increased interaction with a new culture can be an entropic entity.

Past discussions of cultural convergence theory have not taken into account differences in the strength of ties among the participants in social networks. Typically, the strength of the links has been operationalized as the number of messages exchanged or the frequency of communication. This issue was not addressed at the time convergence theory developed because network theory was restricted to dichotomous measures (link–no link). Today, more sophisticated methods allow for the consideration of the measured strength of links (Richards & Barnett, 1993).

Also not addressed by the theory was the difference in the directionality, where one participant initiates the interaction a greater proportion amount of time. What are the differential impacts of encoding and decoding information? This issue was not addressed because communication was defined as a sharing of information between equals rather than considering the differences in power among the participants.

Thus, two additional propositions may be added to convergence theory: (1) The stronger the link between individuals (or higher-level systems), the greater their reciprocal influence. Thus, the faster they will converge on a common set of beliefs. (2) The greater the proportion of messages initiated by an individual (or larger system), the more similar the final equilibrium set of beliefs will be to that initial state of beliefs. Alternatively, the smaller the proportion of messages initiated, the greater those beliefs will change to reach the final equilibrium state. These propositions may be generalized from the dyadic case to social networks composed of many individuals or nation–states. Thus, in the long term the global equilibrium culture will be most similar to the nation encoding the greatest proportion of the system's messages.

This chapter describes one communication network, the Internet, which links the members of the international community. Through the examination of the strength of the connections among the nations of the world system, it will be possible to predict its impact on their individual national cultures and to gain insights into the process leading to the formation of a global or universal culture. The next section explicates the structural model of intercultural communication, which may be operationalized using the tools of network analysis. Then the chapter describes the results of network analyzes of the international Internet. Based upon these findings, it draws inferences from cultural convergence theory to make a series of prognoses about the short-term and long-term impacts of the Internet on global culture.

A STRUCTURAL MODEL OF INTERCULTURAL COMMUNICATION

To help understand the impact of the Internet on global culture, one may adopt a structural model of communication (Barnett & Lee, 2002). It is displayed in Figure 8.1. It represents the process of intercultural communication. It shows a sociogram of a communication network composed of two interacting groups, each with its own culture. Individuals or other information sources (the media and other international organizations) are represented as circles and the communication flows as lines. Arrows indicate the direction of information flows. This system is composed of two groups, *A* and *B,* with porous boundaries. Generally, communication *within* the groups is relatively dense compared to communication *between* the groups, which is sparse (Yum, 1988).

Spanning the cultural boundary is a link between individual *a,* who is a member of Group *A;* and *b,* a member of Group *B.* In network analysis terms, *a* and *b* are referred to as group members with *a bridge link* that connects the individual to a member of the other group. These links tend to be weaker and less frequent and deal

STRUCTURAL MODEL OF INTERCULTURAL COMMUNICATION

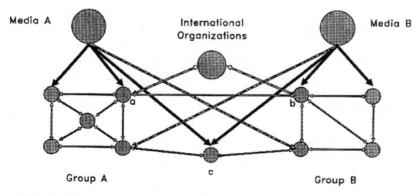

FIGURE 8.1 The Structural Model of Intercultural Communication

with a narrower range of topics than intragroup links (Granovetter, 1973; Yum, 1988). These individuals may be sojourners (Gudykunst & Kim, 1997), individuals who travel to the other country for tourism, educational (Barnett & Wu, 1995; Chen & Barnett, 2000), business (Barnett, Salisbury, Kim, & Langhorne, 1999; Salisbury & Barnett, 1999), military (Kim, 1998), or diplomatic (Kim & Barnett, 2000) reasons. These interactions have been facilitated by innovations in telecommunications (the Internet) and transportation. Members *a* and *b* may also be immigrants, individuals moving relatively permanently to the other country but residing in a location composed primarily of members of their native group (Smith, 1999). Through *a* and *b*, information that reduces the uncertainty about the other group is communicated to the group of which they are a member. In other words, *a* and *b* serve as gatekeepers about information that facilitates the understanding of the other group.

Individual c is a member of neither group. This individual is a *liaison* connecting both groups. As such, *c* is not bound by membership to one particular culture. Generally, *c* is a product of a multicultural marriage and is generally bilingual (Barnett, 1996). Because *c* has the capacity to function in more than one culture effectively, he/she serves as a facilitator for contacts between nations. Individual *c* is what Park (1928) calls a "marginal man" and Adler (1982) labels as a "multicultural man." Intercultural persons develop a "third culture" perspective (Ellingsworth, 1977; Gudykunst, Wiseman, & Hammer, 1977), which enables them to accurately interpret and evaluate intercultural encounters. Through *c*, information about cultures *A* and *B* are passed on to the members of the other nation.

Intercultural communication concerns the linkages between Groups *A* and *B* that involve individuals *a, b,* and *c*. These links also include the mass media and telecommunications, including the Internet (Korzenny, Ting-Toomey & Schiff, 1992; Ware & Dupagne, 1994), because information that facilitates the understanding of Groups *A* and *B* is communicated via the mass media, either print (Kim & Barnett, 1996) or electronic (Varis, 1984). In this model, it is represented as *Media A,* the media expressing the culture of Group *A;* and *Media B,* expressing Group *B's* culture. Typically, they are articulated in the unique language of each group. For example, American media is primarily in English. There may be only a few infrequent paths from *Media A* to Group *B* or from *Media B* to Group *A*. This is the case with non–English language media into the United States, although Western media is widely distributed throughout the world (Nordenstreng & Varis, 1974). *Media A* is more strongly connected to individual *b*. The strength of *Media B's* connections to person *a* is also stronger. Individual *c* receives both media sources. Barnett, Olivieria, and Johnson (1989) report that bilinguals (*a, b,* and *c*) use mass media in both of their languages that may emanate from more than one different group (*A* and *B*).

Also connecting the groups are international organizations that are not part of either group but rather are part of global society transcending any single culture (Boli & Thomas, 1997; Meyer, Boli, Thomas, & Ramirez, 1997). These may be international governmental organizations such as the United Nations or the World Bank whose members are the nations of the world (IGOs), nongovernmental issue-based organizations such as Amnesty International and Greenpeace (INGOs) (Boli & Thomas, 1997; Jacobson, 1979), or transnational corporations (Monge & Fulk,

1999; Walters, 1995). These organizations bring people from different nations together in common forums.

Historically, these linkages among different cultural groups have increased, resulting in globalization—the process of strengthening the worldwide social relations that link distant localities in such a way that local events are shaped by circumstances at remote places in the world (Giddens, 1990). That is, events occurring at one place reduce the uncertainty of the future behavior of groups at other locations. The increase in transborder communication, due in part to innovations in telecommunications and transportation, has led to the rapid global diffusion of values, ideas, opinions, and technologies, that is, the underlying components of culture. Individuals *a* and *b* now have more and stronger ties binding them together. Transborder communication has opened cultural boundaries and begun the process of cultural convergence. It has created a global community with an increasingly homogenous culture, particularly regarding political, economic, educational, and scientific activities, although in the area of religion this process has been much slower (Beyer, 1994; Robertson, 1992).

Globalization stretches the boundaries of social interaction such that the connections among different social contexts or nations become networked across the globe. Thus, the communication between the two groups presented in Figure 8.1 may be generalized to all the nations of the world. The mass media and other communication technologies, especially the Internet, compress time and space, becoming a catalyst for globalization (Giddens, 1990; Robertson, 1990). As a result, McLuhan's notion of the global village is becoming a reality.

Various forms of the Structural Model, also known as the Network Model, have been used to investigate intercultural (Smith, 1999; Weimann, 1989; Yum, 1984, 1988), intergroup (Kim, 1986), and international communication (Barnett, 1999, 2001). Barnett and Lee (2002) recently reviewed this research in depth.

In a recent review of the role of nationality in the process of globalization, Crofts Wiley (2004) suggests that the contextualist approach assumes that the nation "is a porous, perhaps precarious, organization of economic, demographic, and *cultural* flows that must constantly be redefined and reinforced in the midst of a fluid geography." It is "a complex assemblage of flows, materials, bodies, and symbols" (p. 90). This complex of flows may be examined through the structural analysis of social and communication networks as described in this chapter.

THE NETWORK STRUCTURE
OF THE INTERNATIONAL INTERNET

The Internet is one channel that directly connects people of different cultural and national groups from across the globe with one another. Information flows via the Internet may facilitate the convergence of national cultures, leading to a universal set of beliefs that includes a change from national to global identity.

Halavais (2000) examined the role of political borders in cyberspace with a sample of 4,000 websites. He analyzed their external hyperlinks, determining the total percentage of links from the sites to various countries and found that websites were mostly linked to other sites in the same country. When they did link across national borders, most often it was to hosts in the United States.

Barnett, Chon, and Rosen (2001) used data published by the Organization for Economic Cooperation and Development (OECD, 1998) to examine international hyperlink traffic among OECD countries. They found that, the United States was the most central country, the nucleus of Internet traffic. The next most central nations were the United Kingdom, Canada, Germany, and Australia. Most peripheral in the OECD were Iceland and Turkey. The Internet network of the OCED nations formed a single group. Also, the structure of the Internet was significantly related to the structure of the international telecommunications, air traffic, trade, science, and student flow networks at earlier points in time, as well as language and asynchrony, but not cost or physical distance. In combination, only telecommunications, air traffic, science citations, asynchrony, and either trade or student flows were significant, accounting for over 62 percent of the structure of the Internet.

Bharat, Chang, Henzinger, and Ruhl (2001) examined the structure of the World Wide Web using Google and found a much higher number of intranational links than ties to other countries. Typically, only 1 percent of all links were to websites in another country. Further, when the links among the most central countries were removed, geographical, linguistic, and political factors impacted the structure of the web.

Barnett and Park (2005) examined the structure of the international Internet for 47 countries representing approximately 98 percent of Internet traffic with over 350 million hyperlinks, and the Internet infrastructure of the bandwidth capacity between dyads for 63 countries. The analysis of the hyperlink network revealed a dense, completely interconnected system with a single group centered about the United States. Over 15 million web pages connected directly to the United States (not including .com or .net), more than three times that of any other nation. Next most central were Australia, the United Kingdom, China, Japan, Canada, and Germany. Most peripheral in the network were Uruguay, Luxemburg, United Arab Emirates, Thailand, Slovakia, and Romania. The network was also defined by two dimensions: Dimension 1 differentiated Latin America from East Asia; and Dimension 2, United Arab Emirates from Luxemburg. It is represented in Figure 8.2. These results are consistent with our earlier research that found that the Internet formed a dense, completely interconnected network with a single group centered about the United States (Barnett et al., 2001).

The infrastructure (bandwidth) network is fairly sparse. For the countries that compose the hyperlink network, only 18.5 percent of the possible direct links were present. Again, the United States was the most central country, followed by the United Kingdom, Germany, Hong Kong, Singapore, Japan, France, and Italy. Most peripheral in this network were Iceland, Lithuania, Morocco, Croatia, and Guatemala. A cluster analysis resulted in three major

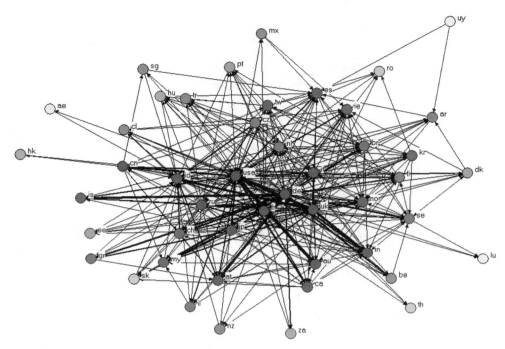

FIGURE 8.2 International Internet Hyperlink Network

Thickness of the line indicates the number of hyperlinks between two countries; 50,000 links is the minimum for the presence of a link. The direction of the hyperlink is indicated by an arrowhead. The luminance of the country indicates its centrality in the network.

groupings: (1) the English-speaking countries (United States, United Kingdom, Canada, Australia, and New Zealand) with Northern Europe and East Asia; (2) Latin America; and (3) Franco-German Europe. It may be represented with two dimensions. The first differentiates the Baltic Republics from North Africa and the second, South America from Eastern Europe. It is presented in Figure 8.3.

Townsend's (2001) examination of the Internet bandwidth resulted in a similar conclusion:

> [E]very region and nearly every country has a direct Internet connection to the United States, direct connections between other countries are less common. Furthermore, direct connections between different major regions such as Asia and Europe are practically nonexistent. . . . This structure dictates that the U.S. Internet infrastructure functions as a massive switching station for traffic that originates and terminates in foreign countries. (p. 1701)

Barnett and Sung (2003, 2005) examined the relationship between the national culture, as operationalized by Hofstede (1991), and the structure

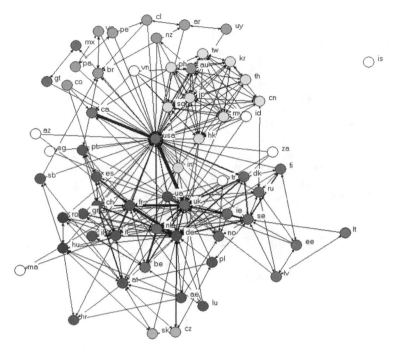

F I G U R E 8.3 International Internet Infrastructure.

Thickness of the line indicates the bandwidth capacity between two countries; 13Mbps is the minimum for the presence of a link. Color indicates membership in a cluster. Shades of a color indicate membership in a subcluster.

of the Internet. They found that national culture is strongly related to a country's position in the Internet network. The more central a country is in the network, the greater its individualism. In societies high in individualism, people look after their own interests and value their independence. Societies low in individualism support group values and beliefs and seek collective interests.

These results suggest that some structural barriers in the infrastructure of the Internet could restrict communication among nations. However, the actual pattern of information flows suggests one completely interconnected system. Thus, the potential for the convergence among the cultures of individual nation–states into a homogenous universal system of beliefs exists. The results also show that the United States encodes significantly more messages on the Internet than any other nation, putting it at the center of these flows. This suggests that if the status quo were to continue, that universal culture is in the process of forming about the culture of the United States. Because it is also very individualistic, as are the United Kingdom, Canada, and Australia, global culture could evolve with little emphasis on the collective, as is typical of East Asia.

IMPLICATIONS OF THE STRUCTURAL MODEL
FOR NATIONAL IDENTITY: CURRENT TRENDS

Our past research indicates that the nations of the world are components in a completely interconnected hyperlink network, unrestricted by cost or physical distance, although others (Bharat et al., 2001; Ciolek, 2001; Halavais, 2000) find that most hyperlinks are directed to other sites within the same country. Also, other barriers restrict the flow of information among nations, including language and political policies implemented in the form of firewalls, and other forms of network surveillance that prevent the access to websites containing particular content perceived as dangerous to individual societies.

Also, the infrastructure (bandwidth) may limit the flow of information among countries. It is sparse, creating barriers to the direct contact among nations. For example, Barnett and Park (2005) report that there are no direct connections between any Islamic countries, as all flows among these nations must be routed by way of the United States, Japan, United Kingdom, France, Germany, Hong Kong, or Singapore. The latter two provide links only between Indonesia and Malaysia. This suggests the capability of the core nations to monitor or restrict the flows within the Islamic world.

Focusing on the countries that are most central in the network finds that Internet flows revolve around the United States and the other English-speaking nations—United Kingdom, Canada, Australia, India, and, to a lesser extent, Japan, Germany, and France. This suggests that global identity will converge about an Anglo-American or, at a minimum, a liberal Western culture.

This position can be further supported by the examination of linguistic data. According to Global Reach (2003), 35.6 percent of the online population speaks English. Other European languages account for an additional 34.9 percent of the users, with 8 percent Spanish, 7 percent German, 3.7 percent French, and 3.3 percent Italian. Asian languages account for only 29.4 percent, with Chinese, 12.2 percent; Japanese, 9.5 percent; and Korean, 4 percent. Arabic accounts for only 1.2 percent of the total number of users.

Further, Barnett and Sung (2003, 2005) found that individualism is significantly related to centrality in the network. Countries high in individualism include the United States, United Kingdom, Canada, and Australia. This suggests that over time, due to these nations' positions in the flow of Internet information, global culture will become more individualistic. People will identify less with their national or ethnic group and provide less support for these groups' values and beliefs and the interests of the collective. They will take on the culture that places great emphasis on the individual. Individual identity will become less closely tied to a nationality and more highly connected to a universal global civilization.

Based on his research on international telecommunication, Barnett (2001) discusses the implications of these patterns for the long-term development of a universal culture:

> Over the last two decades, the frequency of interaction among the
> nations of the world has increased steadily. While there is regionalization

due to physical and cultural (linguistic) barriers, today, the world consists of a single integrated network of nations centered about North America and Western Europe. One potential consequence of globalization is the cultural homogenization or the convergence of the indigenous cultures of the world into a universal culture. (p. 1650)

While cultural convergence is the likely long-term outcome of international communication of which the Internet is only one channel, the globalization–localization dialectic suggests that globalization involves the linking of locals to the wider world, while localization incorporates trends of globalization. As a result in the near future, local cultures could be developing hybrid characteristics. Over time, with unlimited and unrestricted information exchange among people from different cultural groups, the potential consequence of the Internet is cultural homogenization, that is, the convergence of the indigenous cultures of the world into a universal culture. However, in the short term, international communication will more likely first lead to the development of a number of regional civilizations composed of nations who are culturally similar. The reason for this is that international communication includes a number of different channels where barriers of access, physical distance, cost, and language have a greater impact than they do on the Internet. Additionally, different groups may interpret media content differently due to their unique histories. Further, while certain content areas such as music and sports have seemed to globalize, other topics, especially religion, remain idiosyncratic. As a result, Barnett (2001, 2002) found that the current structure of the world's telecommunication system is organized along the lines of regional groupings of nations, generally with related cultures, similar to those suggested by Galtung (1993) and Huntington (1996).

The process of cultural globalization can be considered homogenization and hybridization. Along with absorption of global patterns, culturally localized or hybridized adaptation plays a strong role. Global forms interplay with local, national, and regional patterns, producing a new pattern best characterized as a hybrid (Bhahbam, 1994). Straubhaar (2002) argues that hybridization is the dominant pattern of cultural interaction over time. He asserts that multicountry markets form on a geocultural or cultural-linguistic basis. Thus, in the near future, while individual identity will transcend the local ethnic or national culture, it may stop far short of the global convergence that has been suggested for the long term. It is likely that individuals will develop pan-Islamic, European, Latin American, or North American identities.

Several other factors may contribute to the slowing of the global convergence in the short term. First, computer-mediated communication (CMC) has been found to be sufficient for the maintenance of long-term meaningful relationships; allowing for the preservation of cultural connections at great distances. Second, content-specific online communities allow people to maintain contact with other individuals centered on mutual interests, such as cultural and social ties; providing a conduit for relationships to be formed and maintained. And third, new Internet-based communication technologies allow for an "outeraction" effect, where the communication connections surpass the traditional "interaction" abilities of communication media, offering an increased level of personal connectivity that extends beyond information exchange.

Maintaining meaningful relationships via CMC is a necessary condition for the social system to reach a temporary steady state regarding cultural maintenance. Some research has shown that CMC may act as a catalyst facilitating communicators' propensity to reach that steady state were mutual commonality is the means of reaching the steady state. Walther (1996) found that when electronic partners experienced commonality and were able to conduct long-term associations, they often idealized their partners and reciprocated exaggerated impressions. Communication became more intimate and positive than even in parallel face-to-face settings (Walther, 2002). It is important to note that the idealization and exaggerated impressions will further catalyze the impression that cultural identity is maintaining constancy.

Likewise, McLeod and Liker (1992) studied groups interacting via CMC as compared to face-to-face with both a history as well as anticipation of future interaction. Findings indicated that the electronic groups were more socially oriented than the face-to-face groups. Also, the performance of the computer-supported groups was significantly less variable than the face-to-face groups, indicating the potential of CMC to catalyze a stable social environment. Similarly, Chidambaram, Bostrom, and Wynne (1991), while comparing CMC to face-to-face groups, found that the electronic groups dealt with conflict better and, as a result, became more cohesive. Findings from Chidambaram et al. (1991), Walther (1996, 2002), and McLeod and Liker (1992) indicate that CMC is able to catalyze a systemic steady state, suggesting that in the near-future stable hybrid civilizations will become the predominant cultural form.

Based on the assumption that individuals can maintain meaningful relationships via CMC, online communities will develop that facilitate content specific ties, which suggests that the global Internet network will become more fragmented into culturally unique groups. The use of content-specific ties allows the social system to maintain its culture in a changing environment. Online communities *are* communities, and this concept extrapolates McLuhan's notion of the global village by representing the notion that one's village could span the globe, as opposed to the globe being one village.

Online communities can be conceptualized as actual communities because they meet the six common elements of community (see Wellman & Gulia, 1999): (1) *place*—online communities represent more frequent interaction and network-tie strength than many "real" communities; (2) *interest*—linked together by factors such as culture, virtual groups can be considered communities as they are interest based; (3) *communion*—many online communities provide emotional or social bonding (refugee support communities); (4) *rituals* and *common frames of reference*—communication rituals are not geographically based, and online communities often map onto cultural frames of reference; (5) *boundaries of inclusion and exclusion*—much like "real" communities, online communities sift out members of their communities by requiring members to apply and conform to the aforementioned rituals; and (6) *common acceptance*—nations must exist in the minds of their citizens in order to exist at all; that is, a nation or a community exists because the concept of its existence is shared by each and every member, and this is not geographically defined.

Online communities provide the opportunity for people to access the cultural resources they need to feel as if they are still part of a cultural group, yet time and travel are reduced. Online communities bring people into a densely populated, homogeneous, interest-based population rather than peripheral low-density, geographically based communities (Rosen, Woelfel, Krikorian, & Barnett, 2003; Wellman & Gulia, 1999). These communities represent a shift to communities organized by shared interest (e.g., culture) rather than shared place. Members share much more than information; they provide social support, a sense of belonging, and assistance with difficult and sensitive issues.

Online communities benefit from the unexpected effect that the Internet has fostered an increased trust of strangers, contrary to the popular belief that people can't trust others online (Wellman & Gulia, 1999). When interacting online, individuals are alone at a screen and tend to offer help because it is not known if there is anyone else to offer support. This is in contrast to face-to-face interactions where people tend to be reluctant to intervene or help strangers, especially when a large number of other individuals are around (Latané & Darley, 1970). Further, online assistance is often recognized by all members of the community through visible archives and can allow members to maintain cultural status based on assistance and altruism. Likewise, cues associated with gender, socioeconomic status, and so on are often filtered out in CMC interaction, further encouraging the egalitarian nature of culturally motivated online interaction and online communities.

Considering the ability for relationships formed or maintained online to be meaningful, and the communities formed to foster those relationships being sufficient for community; we can now visit the "outeractional" effects of emerging communication technologies such as Instant Messenger (IM) (Nardi, Whittaker, & Bradner, 2000). IM is a near-synchronous, computer-based, one-to-one, and one-to-many communication technology. Yet, unlike most other communication technologies, IM provides awareness information about the presence of others. Users create a "buddy list" of people to monitor, and a window shows whether buddies are "online" and can even be modified to indicate whether they are away from their desk, can't talk because they are working, or are out of the house. Yet, most importantly, IM supports "outeraction," a set of communicative processes outside of information exchange (interaction), in which people can reach out to others in deliberately social ways. It is in this sense that IM users can actually have feelings of the presence of their friends, family, or colleagues that go beyond simple communicative abilities. They can actually see and know who is sitting at their computer anywhere in the world and engage in an immediate and rapid exchange with multiple people at once.

IM also circumvents the problem of conversational availability, which acts as a barrier to interaction with individuals of one's home culture when geographically separated. IM helps people negotiate availability by allowing conversational initiators to judge whether recipients are online by consulting the buddy list. IM is often used as a preamble for phone conversations and can be monitored while other communications are taking place (difficult with other media).

Finally, IM produces awareness moments, a sense of social connection to others. Nardi et al. (2000) discovered that people found great value in simply knowing who else was around as they consulted their buddy list, without necessarily desiring interaction. Awareness moments allow for a certain feeling in people; a feeling of connection, inclusion; feelings that support the maintenance of cultural connections. Awareness moments represent a far richer notion of communication than current media theories afford. Above direct information transfer, people want to sustain connections with others outside of specific context, a connection that will allow people to overcome the distances that traditionally inhibit feelings of cultural connection.

As presented, Internet technologies provide a mechanism for meaningful relationships to grow and flourish in content-specific online communities. The deeply human connection afforded by these new communication technologies will allow cultural networks to temporarily slow down and fragment the inevitable homogenization that the same Internet technologies will paradoxically facilitate in the long run.

IMPLICATIONS FOR NATIONAL IDENTITY: THE FUTURE

The notion that cultural convergence will lead to the evolution of a universal set of beliefs, heavily based upon the culture of the United States and other liberal western nations, that places great emphasis on individual identity assumes that the current structure of the Internet will remain relatively stable in the foreseeable future. However, Hargittai (1999) has shown that when a nation adopts the Internet is an important determinant of its position in the international Internet network, and Barabási (2002) has demonstrated that the Internet evolves as new nodes (web pages) link to existing sites. Those web pages with the most connections at one point in time generally remain most central at later points in time. Comparing the results from Barnett and Park (2005) with the more limited description of the structure of the Internet from Barnett et al. (2001), one finds that the same nations that composed the core in 1998 were still the most central nodes five years later. This suggests that the Internet's growth tends to reinforce the influence of those countries that are central in the network on the formation of global culture.

The research reviewed here suggests that the cultural identity represented by the converged global culture will be dominated by the United States. Currently, it is the most central country in the international flow of information, controlling the world's channels of communication, including the Internet. This may be a result, in part, of its level of economic and technological development. It may also be due to its geography. It abuts Latin America, and it has a presence on both the Atlantic and Pacific Oceans, facilitating its function as a gateway (or gatekeeper) between Asia and Europe. Its centrality may also be because Americans speak English, the international language of science, education, and business. Or it may simply be due to U.S. demographics. American society is composed of people from all the world's cultures. Today, although the majority of Americans are of European ancestry, 10 percent come from Latin America, 12 percent have African ancestry, and 3 percent are from Asia (U.S. Bureau of the Census, 1996). It is estimated that by 2050, the majority of the American population will be other than European, with nearly 10 percent from Asia, 25 percent from Latin America, and 25 percent with African ancestry. The United States, the source for the plurality of Internet messages, is a product of cultural convergence. Its culture will be changing in the future due to changes in demographics and the dynamic patterns of international information flows resulting from the process of globalization.

The structure of the Internet is dynamic, changing as non-Western countries increasingly come online. Since 2000, the number of Internet hosts in China has grown annually by 48.7 percent, and in India by 55.4 percent (Internet Software Consortium, 2003). The number of people using the Internet in China reached 94 million in 2004, up from less than 10 million in 1999. For the United States, the number of hosts increased by only 2.3 percent, and for the United Kingdom, 10.6 percent. Thus, if we assume that these rates of growth continue over time, both China and India will have an increasing impact on the converged universal culture in the future, and the Western nations will have a proportionately less effect on the global system. Further, if we consider how the growth of Internet use in China will change the pattern of language use on the Internet, then the converged culture of the world system will have increasing Chinese elements, suggesting that global civilization will be some combination of Chinese and Anglo-American culture. In some sense, it will be similar to Hong Kong or Singapore.

It should be pointed out that the Internet is still not available everywhere on the planet, especially in Africa and parts of Asia and Latin America. Worldwide, only 6 percent of people have access. Further, even in the United States, it is primarily an urban medium. In rural areas of peripheral nations, the Internet, like all forms of telecommunication, is nonexistent. Thus, while a converged global culture is a likely outcome of the Internet, it is not on the near horizon. Hundreds of years may be required to reach this homogenous state.

Current research (Barnett & Jun, 2004) examines the antecedent factors that influence the structure of the Internet. The initial results indicate that many factors are significantly related to the structure of the Internet. Generally, these are indicators of the domestic telecommunication and media infrastructure. International Internet flows are not related to the physical distance between nations or a country's political freedom. Among developmental indicators, GDP, international trade, and media variables are significantly related to a nation's position in the network. Literacy and urbanization are not. As for cultural indicators, only individualism is significant. When examined in combination, only international trade and a nation's number of Internet hosts are significant predictors of the structure of international Internet flows, accounting for between 63 and 86 percent of variance in a nation's position, depending on the measure. Culture (individualism) is a significant predictor of only one measure of structure, the number of hyperlinks sent to other nations.

This research suggests what investments will produce greatest growth in Internet usage and output of messages to the Internet. Freund and Weinhold

(2004) found that growth in a nation's web hosts resulted in an increase in exports. Nations should encourage the establishment of websites and thus increase their interdependency through international trade. Also, it should encourage individual achievement if influence on universal culture is considered a national priority. Countries that are putting resources into these activities will have the greatest long-term impact on global culture.

This chapter has argued that according to cultural convergence theory, the increased communication among the peoples of the world via the Internet will, in the long term, lead to the reduction of the differences among national cultures, eventually resulting in the formation of a single global culture. One outcome of this process is that unique national cultures will disappear, replaced by a single transnational identity. This chapter has also proposed that in the short term, communication technologies via the Internet will temporarily slow the cultural homogenization process and allow the cultural social system to reach a steady state.

One caveat is that the Internet represents only one of many modes of communication between nations. Cultural information is still exchanged via interpersonal contacts, through international sojourners—tourism, the military, business, students and migration, trade (artifactual communication), formal organizations (IGOs, INGOs, and transnational corporations), mail, other forms of telecommunications (telephone and facsimile), and the conventional mass media (print, film, and electronic). Each medium may provide a set of different cultural images, and its flows may be structured differently than the Internet. However, over the past decade, there is evidence for media convergence, and past research indicates that these structures are congruent across the media.

In summary, this chapter describes the Internet, which links the members of the international community. Through the examination of the strength of the connections among the nations of the world, it predicts the Internet's impact on individual cultural identity and the process leading to the formation of a global culture. It began by explicating systems and network perspectives, and the structural model of intercultural communication, which may be operationalized using network analysis. It next reviewed the results of network analyses of the international Internet. Based upon these findings, it drew inferences from cultural convergence theory to make a series of prognoses about the short-term and long-term impacts of the Internet on global culture and national identity.

For more information on the topics that appear in this chapter, use the password that came free with this book to access InfoTrac College Edition. Use the following words as keyterms and subject searches: online communities, homogenization, computer networks, international Internet, Social networks, Internet infrastructure, digital media, cultural convergence, global culture, intercultural communication, hyperlink network, digital technologies.

QUESTIONS FOR DISCUSSION

1. Describe the structure of the international Internet based on hyperlink connections and bandwidth connections between nations.

2. According to cultural convergence theory, what are the long-term implications of the structure of the Internet, if we assume that the current patterns of communication remain constant?

3. What are the likely short-term consequences of the international Internet on national culture and individual identity?

4. What factors will impact the structure of the Internet in the short and long runs? What policy implications do these factors suggest for individual nations in the short and long term?

5. What is "outeraction," and why is it important for the formation and effects of online communities?

REFERENCES

Adler, P. S. (1982). Beyond cultural identity: Reflections on cultural and multicultural man. In L. Samovar, & R. Porter (Eds.), *Intercultural communication: A reader* (3rd ed.). Belmont, CA: Wadsworth.

Barabási, A. L. (2002). *Linked: The new science of networks*. Cambridge, MA: Perseus Publishing.

Barnett, G. A. (1996). Multilingualism and transportation/telecommunication. In H. Goebl, P.H. Nelde, Z. Stary, & W. Wolck (Eds.), *Handbook on contact linguistics: An international handbook of contemporary research* (vol. 1, pp. 431–438). Berlin: Walter De Gruyter.

Barnett, G. A. (1997). Organizational communication systems: The traditional perspective. In G.A. Barnett & L. Thayer (Eds.), *Organization—Communication: Emerging perspectives: (The renaissance in systems thinking)* (vol. 5, pp. 1–46). Norwood, NJ: Ablex.

Barnett, G. A. (1999). The social structure of international telecommunications. In H. Sawhney & G. A. Barnett (Eds.), *Progress in communication sciences: Advances in telecommunications* (vol. 15, pp. 151–186). Greenwich, CT: Ablex.

Barnett, G. A. (2001). A longitudinal analysis of the international telecommunications network: 1978–1996. *American Behavioral Scientist, 44,* 1638–1655.

Barnett, G. A. (2002, April). *A longitudinal analysis of the International Telecommunication Network: 1978–1999,* Paper presented to a conference at Beijing Broadcast Institute, National Centre for Radio and Television Studies, Beijing, PRC.

Barnett, G. A., Chon, B. S., & Rosen, D. (2001). The structure of international Internet flows in cyberspace. *NETCOM (Network and Communication Studies), 15*(1–2), 61–80.

Barnett, G. A., & Jun, S. J. (2004, September). *An examination of the determinants of international Internet structure.* Paper presented to the Association of Internet Research, Sussex, UK.

Barnett, G. A., & Kincaid, D. L. (1983). Cultural convergence: A mathematical theory. In W. B. Gudykunst (Ed.), *Intercultural communication theory: Current perspectives* (pp. 171–194). Beverly Hills, CA: Sage.

Barnett, G. A., & Lee, M. (2002). Issues in intercultural communication. In W. B. Gudykunst & B. Mody (Eds.), *Handbook of international and intercultural communication* (pp. 275–290). Thousand Oaks, CA: Sage.

Barnett, G. A., Olivieria, O. S., & Johnson, J. D. (1989). Multilingual language use and television exposure and preferences: The case of Belize. *Communication Quarterly, 37,* 248–261.

Barnett, G. A., & Park, H. W. (2005). The structure of international Internet hyperlinks and bilateral bandwidth. *Annals of Telecommunication,* in press.

Barnett, G. A., Salisbury, J. G. T., Kim, C., & Langhorne, A. (1999). Globalization and international communication networks: An examination of monetary, telecommunications, and trade networks. *The Journal of International Communication, 6*(2), 7–49.

Barnett, G., & Sung, E. J. (2003, May). *Culture and the structure of international communication.* Paper presented to the International Communication Association, San Diego.

Barnett, G. A., & Sung, E. J. (2005). Culture and the structure of the international hyperlink network. *Journal of Computer Mediated Communication,* in press.

Barnett, G. A., & Wu, Y. (1995). The international student exchange network: 1970 and 1989. *Higher Education, 30,* 353–368.

Benedetti, P. (1996). *Forward through the rearview mirror.* Toronto: Prentice Hall.

Beyer, P. (1994). *Religion and globalization.* London: Sage.

Bhahbam, H. (1994). *The location of culture.* New York: Routledge.

Bharat, K., Chang, B. W., Henzinger, M., & Ruhl, M. (2001). Who links to whom: Mining linkage between web sites. *Proceedings 2001 IEEE International Conference on Data Mining (ICDM),* 51–58.

Boli, J., & Thomas, G. M. (1997). World culture in the world polity: A century of international non-governmental organization. *American Sociological Review, 62,* 171–190.

Castells, M. (2000). *The rise of the network society* (2nd ed.). Malden, MA: Blackwell.

Chen, T., & Barnett, G. A. (2000). Research on international student flows from a macro perspective: A network analysis of 1985, 1989 and 1995. *Higher Education, 39,* 435–553.

Chidambaram, L., Bostrom, R. P., & Wynne, B. E. (1991). The impact of GDSS on group development. *Journal of Management Information Systems, 7,* 3–25.

Ciolek, T. M. (2001, September). *Networked information flows in Asia: The research uses of the Alta Vista search engine and "weblinksurvey" software.* Paper presented to Internet Political Economy Forum 2001: Internet and Development in Asia, The National University of Singapore.

Crofts Wiley, S. B. (2004). Rethinking nationality in the context of globalization. *Communication Theory, 14*(1), 78–96.

Ellingsworth, H. (1977). Conceptualizing intercultural communication. In B. Ruben (Ed.), *Communication Yearbook* (pp. 99–106). New Brunswick, NJ: Transaction.

Fisher, B. A. (1978). *Perspectives on human communication.* New York: Macmillan.

Freund, C. L., & Weinhold, D. (2004). The effect of the Internet on international trade. *Journal of International Economics, 62*(1), 171–189.

Galtung, J. (1993). Geopolitical transformations and the 21st-century world economy. In K. Nordenstreng & H. Schiller (Eds.), *Beyond national sovereignty: International communication in the 1990s* (pp. 28–58). Norwood, NJ: Ablex.

Giddens, A. (1990). *The consequences of modernity.* Stanford, CA: Stanford University Press.

Global Reach (2003). *Global Internet statistics (by language)*. Retrieved April 15, 2003, from http://www.glreach.com/globstats/

Granovetter, M. (1973). The strength of weak ties. *American Journal of Sociology, 73,* 1361–1380.

Gudykunst, W. B., & Kim. Y. Y. (1997). *Communicating with strangers: An approach to intercultural communication* (3rd ed.). New York: McGraw-Hill.

Gudykunst, W. B., Wiseman, R., & Hammer, M. (1977). Determinants of a sojourner's attitudinal satisfaction. In B. Ruben (Ed.), *Communication yearbook* (pp. 415–426). New Brunswick, NJ: Transaction.

Halavais, A. (2000). National borders on the World Wide Web. *New Media and Society, 2,* 7–28.

Hargittai, E. (1999). Weaving the Western web: Explaining the differences in Internet connectivity among OECD countries. *Telecommunications Policy, 23,* 701–718.

Hofstede, G. (1991). *Cultures and organizations: Software of the mind.* London: McGraw-Hill.

Huntington, S. P. (1996). *The clash of civilizations: Remaking the world order.* New York: Touchstone.

Internet Software Consortium (2003). *Distribution of top-level domain names.* Retrieved April 15, 2003, from http://www/isc.org/ds/WWW-200201/dist-bynum.html

Jacobson, H. K. (1979). *Networks and interdependence: International organizations and the global political system.* New York: Knopf.

Kelly, J. R., & McGrath, J. E. (1988). *On time and method.* Newbury Park, CA: Sage.

Kim, C. (1998, July). *The changing structures of global arms trade 1987–1994: A network analysis on major conventional weapons trade.* Paper presented to the International Communication Association, Jerusalem, Israel.

Kim, K., & Barnett, G. A. (1996). The determinants of international news flow. *Communication Research, 23,* 323–352.

Kim, K., & Barnett, G. A. (2000). The structure of the international telecommunications regime in transition: A network analysis of international organizations. *International Interactions, 26,* 91–127.

Kim, Y. Y. (1986). Understanding the social content of intergroup communication: A personal network approach. In W. Gudykunst (Ed.), *Intergroup communication* (pp. 86–95). London: Edward Arnold.

Kincaid, D. L., Yum, J. O., Woelfel, J., & Barnett, G. A. (1983). The cultural convergence of Korean immigrants in Hawaii: An empirical test of a mathematical theory. *Quality and Quantity, 18,* 59–78.

Korzenny, F., Ting-Toomey, S., & Schiff, E. (1992). *Mass media effects across cultures.* Newbury Park, CA: Sage.

Latané, B., & Darley, J. (1970). *The unresponsive bystander: Why doesn't he help?* New York: Appleton.

McLeod, P. L., & Liker, J. K. (1992). Electronic meeting systems: Evidence from a low structure environment. *Information Systems Research, 3,* 195–223.

Meyer, J. W., Boli, J., Thomas, G. M., & Ramirez, F. O. (1997). World society and the nation–state. *American Journal of Sociology, 103*(1), 144–181.

Monge, P. R., & Fulk, J. (1999). Communication technology for global network organizations. In G. DeSanctis & J. Fulk (Eds.), *Shaping organizational form: Communication, connection, and community* (pp. 71–100). Thousand Oaks, CA: Sage.

Nardi, B., Whittaker, S., & Bradner, E. (2000). Interaction and outeraction: Instant messaging in action. In *Proceedings of conference on computer-supported cooperative work* (pp. 78–88). New York: ACM Press.

Nordenstreng, K., & Varis, T. (1974). *Television traffic–A one-way street? Reports and papers on mass communication,* No. *70.* Paris: UNESCO.

OECD. (1998). *Working paper on telecommunication and information service policies: Internet infrastructure indicators.* Paris: OECD.

Park, R. E. (1928). Human migration and the marginal man. *American Journal of Sociology, 33,* 881–893.

Richards, W. D., Jr., & Barnett, G. A. (Eds.). (1993). *Progress in communication sciences,* vol. *12.* Norwood, NJ: Ablex.

Robertson, R. (1990). Mapping the global condition: globalization as the central concept. *Theory, Culture & Society, 7,* 15–30.

Robertson, R. (1992). *Globalization: Social theory and global culture.* London: Sage.

Rogers, E. M., & Kincaid, D. L. (1981). *Communication networks: Toward a new paradigm for research.* New York: Free Press.

Rosen, D., Woelfel, J., Krikorian, D., & Barnett, G. A. (2003). Procedures for analyses of online communities. *Journal of Computer Mediated Communication, 8,* 4.

Salisbury, J. G. T., & Barnett, G. A. (1999). A network analysis of international monetary flows. *Information Society, 15,* 1–19.

Shannon, C., & Weaver, W. (1949). *The mathematical theory of communication.* Urbana: University of Illinois Press.

Smith, L. R. (1999). Intercultural network theory: A cross-paradigmatic approach to acculturation. *International Journal of Intercultural Relations, 23,* 629–658.

Straubhaar, J. D. (2002). (Re)asserting national media and national identity against the global, regional and local levels of world television. In J. M. Chan & B. T. McIntyre (Eds.), *In search of boundaries: Communication, nation–states, and cultural identities* (pp. 181–206). Westport, CT: Ablex.

Townsend, A. M. (2001). Network cities and the global structure of the Internet. *American Behavioral Scientist, 44,* 1697–1716.

U.S. Bureau of the Census. (1996). *Population projections of the United States by age, sex, race, and Hispanic origin: 1995 to 2050.* Washington, DC: Government Printing Office.

VanLear, C. A. (1996). Communication process approaches and models: Patterns, cycles, and dynamic coordination. In J. H. Watt & C. A. Van Lear (Eds.), *Dynamic patterns in communication processes* (pp. 35–70). Thousand Oaks: Sage.

Varis, T. (1984). International flow of television programs. *Journal of Communication, 34*(1), 143–152.

Walters, M. (1995). *Globalization.* London and New York: Routledge.

Walther, J. B. (1996). Computer-mediated communication: Impersonal, interpersonal, and hyperpersonal interaction. *Communication Research, 23,* 3–43.

Walther, J. B. (2002). Time effects in computer-mediated groups: Past, present, and future. In P. Hinds & S. Kiesler (Eds.), *Distributed work* (pp. 235–257). Cambridge, MA: MIT Press.

Ware, W., & Dupagne, M. (1994). Effects of U.S. television programs on foreign audiences: A meta-analysis. *Journalism Quarterly, 71,* 947–959.

Weimann, G. (1989). Social networks and communication. In M. K. Asante & W. B. Gudykunst (Eds.), *Handbook of international and intercultural communication* (pp. 186–203). Newbury Park, CA: Sage.

Wellman, B., & Gulia, M. (1999) Net surfers don't ride alone. In M. Smith & P. Kollock (Eds.), *Communities in cyberspace.* New York: Routledge.

Yum, J. O. (1984). Network analysis. In W. B. Gudykunst & Y. Y. Kim (Eds.), *Methods for intercultural communication research* (pp. 95–116). Beverly Hills, CA: Sage.

Yum, J. O. (1988). Network theory in intercultural communication. In Y. Y. Kim & W. B. Gudykunst (Eds.), *Theories in intercultural communication* (pp. 239–258). Newbury Park, CA: Sage.

9

Milestones in Communication and National Development

VIBERT C. CAMBRIDGE

Vibert C. Cambridge (PhD, Ohio University) is Associate Professor in the School of Telecommunications and Chair of the Department of African American Studies at Ohio University, Athens. His current research interests are in entertainment–education and multicultural broadcasting in the United States. His recent book, *Immigration, Diversity, and Broadcasting in the United States, 1990–2001,* was published by Ohio University Press in January 2005. He is currently writing a book on music in Guyana's 20th-century social development. He has completed projects in communication for development in Africa, Asia, the Caribbean, and the United States.

In this chapter, we explore the communication and development field. Several terms are used to describe the deliberate use of a social system's communication resources to promote, support, and sustain planned social change. Among the terms are *communication and national development, development communication, communication and development,* and *communication for development.* In this chapter, the term *communication for development* is used to describe the systematic use of a social system's communication resources to stimulate, promote, and support human development.

Fraser and Restrepo-Estrada (1998) offered a comprehensive definition of *communication for development:*

> Communication for development is the use of communication processes, techniques and media to help people toward a full awareness of their situation and their options for change, to resolve conflicts, to work toward

consensus, to help people plan actions for change and sustainable development, to help people acquire the knowledge and skills they need to improve their condition and that society, and to improve the effectiveness of institutions. (p. 63)

Several strategies in communication for development are being used by community groups, national governments, regional and international organizations, and nongovernmental organizations to address the range of development challenges facing the world. Public awareness and information campaigns, community mobilization, folk media, social marketing, entertainment–education, and advocacy are among the dominant strategies being used to promote, support, and sustain projects aimed at agriculture, education, the environment, family planning and reproductive health, gender equality, nutrition, and public health. The attributes of these strategies are discussed later in this chapter.

Through an exploration of the contemporary origins of communication for development, especially the practices of the international community, we should develop an appreciation of the milestones associated with the field. Theory-based practice in communication for development is reaching vast populations around the world with critically needed information that could prevent HIV/AIDS infection and help women make informed choices about their reproductive health.

Practitioners of communication for development are engaged in projects aimed at improving the economic, political, and cultural conditions of people all over the world. Practices and processes of communication for development are also facilitating community participation in the public discourses that nourish democratic systems of governance.

This deliberate application of a social system's communication resources to facilitate social change is not new. Humans have always used their communication capacity to bring about improvements in the quality of life. We can call this tendency *purposive communication*—the deliberate use of a social system's communication resources to encourage individual and collective movement in a preferred direction.

This tendency is recognition of the power of communication. Purposive communication is necessary for the formulation and implementation of efforts to improve the quality of human life in the 21st century. Purposive communication must operate in accord with ethical principles. The totalitarian experiences of the 20th century demonstrate that a social system's communication resources can be appropriated for purposes that degrade humans.

That humans can speak and have languages influenced their social organization. The communally agreed-upon codes of speech permitted the sharing of information, and in the process, those who spoke a common language developed a collective identity. Through speech and language, they could coordinate efforts to achieve common goals of the group, such as food gathering and security. The invention of writing, printing, and mass communication provided humans with additional communication capacity to bring about change. Historians have described these developments in human communication capacity as having civilizational consequences. Consider the role that writing played in the creation of the ancient Greek, Roman, Turkish, and Asian empires. Consider also the role that printing played in the spread of reformist ideas in Europe during the Renaissance. Today the mass media, especially print, broadcasting, and the Internet, play important roles in the delivery of formal and informal education in many societies. Lifelong education is essential for functioning in contemporary society.

In this chapter, the work of the international development community in the field of communication for development is emphasized. This community is made up of the United Nations system, development assistance agencies such as the U.S. Agency for International Development, global broadcasters such as the British Broadcasting Corporation, nongovernmental organizations such as Population Communication International, and academic institutions such as the Center for Communication Programs in Johns Hopkins University's School of Hygiene and Public Health. Of course, there are other players, but the focus here is on this particular community. The international development community is humanity's response to the human condition. This community works with national governments and regional organizations to improve the human condition. Contemporary development practice has its origins with the end of World War II and the creation of the United Nations in 1945.

POST–WORLD WAR II REALITIES

At the end of World War II, the human condition was bleak. The destruction caused by the war in Europe and the pervasiveness of poverty in Europe's colonies in Africa, Asia, and the Caribbean meant that millions of humans were living without adequate housing, health care, and food. The devastation caused by the war and the consequences of colonialism challenged the international community to do something about the unacceptable state of the human condition. By the late 1940s, humanity had a range of development challenges. The birth rate in Africa, Asia, and Latin America was almost three times higher than the birth rate in Europe.

Infant mortality rates were almost five times higher in these regions than in Europe and the United States. Life expectancy for males and females in Brazil was about 37 years; in the United States, it was 62 years for males and almost 66 years for females (United Nations, 1949).

The euphoria associated with the success of the Marshall Plan in the European reconstruction after World War II suggested that a similar model could be applied to the conditions that existed in Africa, Asia, Latin America, and the Caribbean. The Marshall Plan had demonstrated the effectiveness of management (a specialized communication system) in economic and social reconstruction (Drucker, 1985). In a relatively short time, European industrial infrastructure was rehabilitated, and the quality of life improved rapidly. In retrospect, it was naive to think that the model could be transferred with similar success to other parts of the world. The objective circumstances were different. Development aid became an important item on the international relations agenda, and the development project became the primary vehicle for connecting aid with the individuals who needed it—the beneficiaries. Development projects in the early postwar years emphasized the transfer of technologies and techniques to support industrialization.

Industrialization was generally accepted as the engine driving social progress. Development aid was not altruistic. According to Gerald Meier and Dudley Seers (1984), from the viewpoint of the governments of the major capitalist countries, there was grave danger that former colonies might, if there was little social progress, fall under communist domination; investment opportunities and access to markets and sources of raw materials would then be diminished. The United States made major investments and funded substantial development aid programs in Iran, Turkey, India, Pakistan, and the other countries that bordered the Soviet Union. The aim was the containment of the Soviet Union.

At the end of World War II, the United States and the Soviet Union emerged as the dominant world powers. Each sought to use its economic, military, and cultural (including communication) power to achieve its national interests. Among the primary national interests were national security and the expansion of spheres of influence. The term *spheres of influence* refers to the ability of powerful states to impose their will on other states through economic, cultural, and military means. The United States and its allies promoted and supported the achievement of progress through modernization by capitalism.

Like the field of development economics, the field of communication and development emerged as a "response to the needs of policymakers to advise governments on what should be done to allow their countries to emerge from chronic poverty" (Meier & Seers, 1984, p. 4).

The United Nations (UN) was created as a mechanism to prevent war and to coordinate the international community's response to the global pervasiveness of poverty, want, fear, ignorance, and disease in vast regions of the world. The preamble to the Charter of the United Nations includes a commitment "to employ international machinery for the promotion of the economic and social advancement of all peoples (United Nations, preamble)." The development project was the principal form of response. In the process, the UN has played a major role in the development of the field of communication for development.

WHAT IS DEVELOPMENT?

At the start of the 21st century, development is recognized as a complex, integrated, participatory process, involving stakeholders and beneficiaries and aimed at improving the overall quality of human life through improvements in a range of social sectors in an environmentally responsible manner. Stakeholders include national governments and politicians, international agencies such as the specialized agencies of the UN system, development assistance agencies such as the U.S. Agency for International Development (USAID), the private sector, nongovernmental organizations, and cultural leaders. Stakeholders have the power to help or hinder the development and implementation of development projects. The beneficiaries are the hundreds of millions of humans who need improvement in their quality of life.

At the start of the 21st century, the list of pressing development challenges facing humanity is intimidating. Among the challenges are the reduction and the elimination of poverty, provision of adequate housing, access to health care and lifelong education, food and nutritional sufficiency, adequate and functioning physical infrastructure, public health (including potable water, reliable sewerage, and waste disposal systems), roads, bridges, reliable transportation systems, protection of the environment, respect for human dignity and rights (including opportunities for self-actualization), access to the means of communication, and participation in the democratic governance of the society. These challenges are global in scope. They are no longer simply Third World problems.

Development is a profound form of social change. Everett Rogers, an influential theorist of the field, described development as a widely participatory process of directed social change in a society, intended to bring about both social and material advancement including greater equality, freedom, and other valued qualities for the majority of the people through their gaining greater control over their environment (Rogers, 1962, cited in Singhal & Domatob, 1993, p. 98). Development projects have been conducted around the world and have become synonymous with purposive social change. In the early postwar days, many of these projects were the result of recommendations by external experts. The execution of these projects has had consequences—both intended and unintended.

The huge hydroelectric dams, like the Volta in Ghana and the Aswan in Egypt, that were developed in the 1950s have been able to produce needed energy to power industries and provide electricity for homes—the intended consequences. However, these dams have also increased the spread of bilharziasis, a debilitating waterborne disease also known as snail fever—an unintended consequence.

New varieties of seeds associated with the green revolution of the late 1950s and the 1960s increased the yield of food grain, reduced hunger, and eliminated famine from India and large regions of Asia. However, the new seed varieties required extensive use of chemical fertilizers. An unintended consequence of the increased use of chemical fertilizers has been the pollution of water resources.

Questions of scope and relevance were also raised about many of these early development projects. Concerns were also raised about the inequitable distribution of the benefits of many of these early projects. Urban groups appeared to have benefited more than the rural poor.

Fifty years of engagement in the development arena by a number of players— the international community, national development agencies, and academics— has led to the acceptance that development was complex, multidimensional and dialectic process that had no universal recipe. There is some consensus on what constitutes development—"good change"—according to Robert Chambers (1994). Among the attributes are the following:

- Giving priority to the poor
- Aiming to meet basic needs
- Striving to be endogenous to a society—that is to say, it should originate from the society's values and its perceptions of its own future
- Making optimal use of natural resources, taking into account the potential of the local ecosystem, as well as the present and future limitations imposed by global considerations for the biosphere
- Basing the process on participatory and truly democratic decision-making practices at all levels of society (Fraser & Restrepo-Estrada, 1998)

According to Andrew Moemeka (2000), communication for development has two roles: support of social change that aims for higher quality of life, social justice, and correction of the dysfunctions from early development interventions; and socialization, creating an environment in which established values that support positive social change are maintained and, further, supporting the development of attitudes and behaviors needed to create a social system that benefits all citizens.

COMMUNICATION FOR DEVELOPMENT

Several forces have influenced the evolution of the field of communication for development. Among these are the growth of capitalism, advances in communication technology, and the ideological rivalries between the United States and the Soviet Union during the Cold War (1945–1992). Of central importance was the nature of the development challenges faced by the former European colonies in Africa, Asia, and the Caribbean that gained political independence during the 1950s–1970s and their subsequent involvement in international relations through mechanisms such as the Non-Aligned Movement, which promoted neutrality, solidarity, and self-reliance (Calvocoressi, 1982). This block was able to use the UN system to highlight the development problems of its member nations and recommend actions to alleviate them.

Of equal importance in the evolution of the field of communication for development were the influences of changing development paradigms and advances in communication theory, especially theories of mass media effects, persuasion, and behavior change. Since World War II, communication theory applicable to the field had grown substantially. Starting in 1930, U.S. and European émigré scholars in the United States have formulated a number of highly heuristic communication theories that have influenced communication for development practice.

Among them are theories of persuasion, theories about the process through which ideas and innovations move through a social system (diffusion of innovations), and theories that explain mass media's ability to influence human behavior at individual, group, and societal levels. A chronicle of the development of these theories is provided in Everett Rogers's *A History of Communication Study* (1994).

Communication for development is the embodiment of Kurt Lewin's dictum, "Nothing is as practical as a good theory." Theory in the field of communication for development has been influential in mapping the scope and nature of development challenges, guiding research methods, and supporting transformative practice. These are the goals of practical theory (Barge, 2001, pp. 5–13).

Most of the early theories that guided the practice of communication for development emerged out of the modernization paradigm. A paradigm is defined as an overarching body of thought whose core assumptions are subscribed to by all who work under its rubric. These core assumptions inform and influence research methods, interpretation of data, and intervention strategies. During the Cold War, the modernization paradigm not only guided the generation of communication theory but also influenced the foreign aid decisions of the United States and its allies. Details on the core assumptions of the modernization paradigm are provided here.

A few examples of interventions by communication for development from around the world—the United States, the former Soviet Union, Africa, and the Caribbean—are offered not only to illustrate the scope of contemporary development challenges but also to suggest the factors that influence the choice of strategy.

Southeastern Ohio, USA

Southeastern Ohio is an example of maldevelopment and the process of underdevelopment. First settled as the Northwest Territories after the end of the U.S. War of Independence in the late 18th century, contemporary southeastern Ohio is predominantly rural, with high levels of unemployment, high levels of physical inactivity, and substantial environmental degradation.

A study on physical inactivity in three Appalachian counties in southeastern Ohio in 2001 revealed unemployment rates in excess of 10 percent. More than 30 percent of the population was overweight, and more than 20 percent obese (Cambridge, 2001).

Overweight and obesity lead to early death from cardiovascular disease and some forms of cancer. The epidemic of overweight and obesity in Ohio has substantial consequences for the state's economy. Reducing overweight and obesity through regular physical activity is a public health goal for Ohio and the United States that is embodied in a program called Healthy Ohioans–Healthy Communities 2010. Social marketing was the dominant communication strategy used by the Ohio Department of Health in response to this public health crisis.

In the late 19th and early 20th centuries, coal mining, clay mining, and logging industries fueled economic development in southeastern Ohio. The coal mines supplied coal for the steel industry in Pittsburgh, and the clay mines provided the raw materials for the manufacture of bricks that were used to build the cities of Ohio and other states. The logging industry fed the paper manufacturing plants and the building industries. By the 1960s, most of these industries were closed, leaving in their wake unemployment, polluted watershed areas, and other manifestations of environmental degradation. These economic and environmental realities have stimulated out-migrations to urban areas.

A consequence of the economic and environmental degradation in southeastern Ohio is low levels of individual and collective efficacy among some sectors of the population, especially the poor and those who did not graduate from high school. Efficacy is an individual or community's belief in its capacity to resolve a problem. The recently mentioned physical inactivity crisis can be considered as a manifestation of the low levels of individual and collective efficacy (Bandura, 1995). Community groups, such as Rural Action and the Monday Creek Watershed Improvement Committee, have been working to improve the economy and the environment by facilitating participatory practices and processes aimed at sustainable development. They use a range of communication resources—traditional channels, such as county fairs; interpersonal channels, such as group meetings; and traditional mass media and the Internet—to build a voluntary coalition of citizens that strives to influence the formulation of policies to support sustainable development by local, state, and federal governments.

The concepts *participatory* and *sustainable* are central to contemporary communication for development practices. Participation refers to the involvement of citizens/beneficiaries in defining, designing, implementing, and evaluating development interventions. Participation is not simply a means for the design and implementation of development interventions. Participation is an end in human development.

It is a requirement for the construction of democratic societies and a requirement for sustainable development (Dervin & Huesca, 1997). The term *sustainable development* is used to describe an intervention whose outcomes are environmentally and culturally sound and can be continued by the community after the end of any resources that may have been provided by external agencies.

Turkmenistan

Communication for development interventions is also evident in the transitional societies that have emerged since the breakup of the Soviet Union. In Turkmenistan, the National Puppet Theater, a new state-supported organization, is using a traditional communication channel (puppets), along with the mass media (radio, television, newspapers, and magazines) to create a sense of national identity and to address a number of pressing social problems such as drug abuse. Turkmenistan, formerly a republic in the Soviet Union, became an independent state in 1992.

The government sees the building of national identity and the nurturing of national pride as important elements in the construction of individual and collective efficacy (Cambridge & Sleight-Brennan, 2000).

Eritrea

In Eritrea and other parts of Africa, modern communication technologies (computers and satellites) are being used to create distance education systems aimed at improving access to formal education and the management of the economy (Cambridge & Araya, 1995).

The Caribbean Community

In the English-speaking Caribbean, the Pan American Health Organization (PAHO) is working in collaboration with the Caribbean Community (CARICOM) and regional communication organizations, such as the Caribbean Broadcasting Union (CBU) and the Caribbean News Agency (CANA), to educate citizens on containing and eradicating mosquito-borne diseases such as dengue and malaria.

These diseases induce high morbidity rates that undermine worker productivity and can make the Caribbean less attractive as a tourist destination. Tourism is a major source of income for Caribbean nations.

THE MODERNIZATION MODEL

The literature of communication for development identifies three development paradigms that have exerted substantial influence on the field since the end of World War II. Scholars have referred to them as the dominant paradigm (or modernization model), the dependency paradigm (or dependency critique), and the alternative paradigm (another development, or participatory, model) (Singhal & Sthapitanonda, 1996, pp. 10–25). What follows is a brief general survey of the evolution and application of these paradigms, including some reflection on the core assumptions and the roles played by select individuals and institutions in this evolution. Readers are encouraged to refer to the primary sources identified in this survey.

Modernization through Capitalism

At the end of World War II, two ideas contended for dominance in the discourse on development and human progress: modernization through capitalism, and communism. The modernization perspective held that human society progresses in a linear fashion from traditional societies to modern systems of social organization and that they will continue to do so in an evolutionary manner. Traditional systems are characterized as predominantly rural, providing limited social and geographic mobility, and subscribing to cultural practices that do not support materialism or capital as a form of wealth. Traditional societies, according to modernization theory, tend to be oriented to maintaining a status quo dominated by ascribed status. Fatalism, or lack of self-efficacy, has also been identified as an attribute of traditional societies.

A modern society, on the other hand, is characterized by "materialism, the dominance of capital as a form of wealth, consumerism, rational-legal authority, sub-cultural diversity, and positive evaluation of change" (Weinstein, 1997, pp. 358–359). Modernization theorists argued that the process of becoming a modern society could be accelerated through the introduction of new ideas and practices. Modernization represented progress.

Modernization's core assumptions are also informed by Talcott Parsons' functionalist theory. This formulation holds that "human society is like a biological organism" (1990, p. 20) whose constituent institutions—economy, government, law, religion, family, and education—play key roles in maintaining the social stability required for progress in a society. In the advanced modern societies, progress is maintained through the increased consumption of material goods made possible by high incomes and higher standards of living (So, 1990). Walt Rostow, David McClelland, Daniel Lerner, Wilbur Schramm, and Everett Rogers were also influential modernization theorists.

Walt Rostow and David McClelland subscribed to the idea that the cause of underdevelopment was to be found exclusively in internal factors. They provided economic and psychological models of the modernization process. Walt Rostow (1990) identified four stages he considered necessary for progressing from a traditional to a modern society: the pre-takeoff stage, the takeoff stage, the road to maturity, and the mass-consumption society. A society must experience these stages before it becomes a modern society. David McClelland (1964) emphasized the importance of a motivated populace if a society is to become modernized. His recommendation was to stimulate the individual need for achievement (nach). The ideas of these two men guided influential development aid projects funded by the United States and the UN.

Modernization scholars such as Daniel Lerner, Wilbur Schramm, and Everett Rogers emphasized the importance of broadcasting in the development process. Mass communication, especially broadcasting, was seen as a vehicle that would accelerate the behavioral and structural changes required for modernization. We will examine the contributions of these theorists later in this chapter.

Communism

The Soviet Union and its allies promoted and supported efforts to achieve progress through revolutionary socialism. Revolutionary socialists contended that true progress could occur only in a socialist society. Socialist transformation would replace inequitable economic practices with more egalitarian ones—for example, equitable distribution of wealth and equity in access to education, health, and nutrition.

In the process, the society would progress materially and spiritually, leading ultimately to "withering away of the state." Information and communication had a special role in revolutionary socialist practice. In the 1970s, Soviet intellectuals posited, "Communication among people, social groups, classes, nations and states contribute to the development of a scientific outlook by individuals. They assist them in arriving at their own understanding of the diverse phenomena and processes that are taking place in social life, in increasing their level of culture and their general education, in assimilating and carrying out laws and general principles, and in struggling with bourgeois and revisionist ideologies that are foreign to socialist norms" (Afanasyev, 1978). The tensions between these two approaches—modernization through capitalism and progress through socialism—influenced practices of communication for development within the international development community. This chapter argues that this superpower tension did not undermine the field of communication for development. Instead, it contributed to the sharpening of the theory and practice of communication for development.

The interplay of ideology, theory, practice, and ethics during the 1980s has influenced the contemporary practice of communication for development.

THE 1980S: DEVELOPMENT SUPPORT COMMUNICATION AND PROJECT SUPPORT COMMUNICATION

The work done by United Nations organizations has contributed much to the field of communication for development. Of special importance is the work of the UN Development Program (UNDP) and the UN Children's Fund (UNICEF) in establishing the importance of communication as a necessary ingredient in implementing development projects. UNDP and UNICEF pioneered communication planning for development at the Development Support Communication Service (Asia) in Bangkok, Thailand. This research and application service was established in 1967 and was led by Erskine Childers. The unit's mission was to provide communication strategies and materials to UN-funded projects in Asia. The approach was termed *development support communication,* or *project support communication.*

Communication's role in this formulation was to accelerate the installation of the engines of modernization, especially the industrial infrastructure to facilitate economic growth. In these early days, development emphasized economic development (Fraser & Restrepo-Estrada, 1998).

The development support communication (DSC) approach arose out of dissatisfaction with the ineffectiveness of many of the UN-sponsored development projects in Asia and other parts of the developing world. Many of these projects were defined and designed outside of the developing world and tended not to reflect the needs of the beneficiaries. Further, these modernization-oriented projects also failed to take into account culture and context. As a result, there was waste, dissatisfaction, and underutilization.

For Childers (1973), development support communication meant "the use of communication techniques to elicit the voluntary and active participation of people in development planning and action" (p. 3). By 1980, UNICEF was actively promoting project support communications (PSC) around the developing world. UNICEF staff were actively assisting governments around the world in designing communication plans to support development (Tuluhungwa, 1981). Table 9.1 identifies the scope and nature of a selection of the development support communication programs fostered by UNICEF in 1980.

Development support communication interventions by the Food and Agriculture Organization (FAO) demonstrated the essential role of communication in its projects aimed at improving food security and the empowerment of citizens, especially women and farmers. The green revolution of the 1950s and 1960s increased food security in many nations in Asia, Africa, Latin America, and the Caribbean.

T A B L E 9.1   UNICEF's Development Support Communication Programs, 1980

Country	Nature of Project Support Communication Intervention
Republic of Korea	Developing a health education strategy and plan for primary health care
	Establishing a PSC clearinghouse through the Saemul Undong (New Village Movement)
Nigeria	Developing a PSC plan for establishing a Development Support Communication Unit in the Federal Ministry of Social Development, Sports, Youth, and Culture
Rwanda	Retraining of radio producers by the Ministry of Information and increasing community-based radio programs to support basic services
Zambia	Establishing an interministerial communication committee for facilitating intersectoral communication cooperation at the community level
Indonesia	Establishing provincial communication units
Syria	Establishing a DSC unit in the Ministry of Information to train extension workers
Vietnam	Establishing an audiovisual production center to produce and distribute materials to schools and health facilities
Malawi	Developing a production and distribution system with the Extension Unit of the Ministry of Agriculture

SOURCE: From "Highlights of PSC Activities in 1980," by R. Tuluhungwa, June 2, 1981, *Project Support Communications Newsletter*, 5(2), pp. 1–2.

The World Health Organization (WHO) demonstrated the centrality of purposive communication in its work to eradicate polio and other diseases. Similar effectiveness has been demonstrated by the UN Children's Fund in its work on immunization and diarrheal diseases. In all of these interventions, broadcasting was assigned an important role.

Broadcasting

In the 1930s, radio in the United States and Europe was used to persuade citizens to become more educated and to consume more goods and services. In Nazi Germany, radio and other mass media mobilized citizens for hate. In the 1950s, radio and television were mobilized to support development. Daniel Lerner, Wilbur Schramm, and Everett Rogers were influential modernization theorists who emphasized the importance of broadcasting in the development process.

Daniel Lerner's (1958) theorizing on broadcasting's role in national development emerged out of a research project conducted for the Voice of America in the Middle East and was associated with the United States' Soviet containment strategy. According to Lerner, broadcasting would serve as a psychic mobilizer, facilitating the modernizing process and preventing the adoption of Soviet ideology and practices.

Wilbur Schramm (1964) emphasized the essential role of broadcasting in nation building. For Schramm, broadcasting was key in constructing national identity and national unity, and in mobilizing the society to execute the development goals designed by the political elites who dominated underdeveloped countries.

Everett Rogers (1962) is internationally acclaimed for his work on diffusion theory. This theory describes the process through which new ideas and technologies—innovations—are diffused in a society. Broadcasting played an essential role in diffusion theory, by making the influential early adopters aware of the innovation. These early adopters, through interpersonal channels, set in motion a process that led to the acceptance of the innovation by the remainder of the society. Broadcasting has remained central to the practice of communication for development.

In times of stress (a constant condition in developing countries), people tend to increase their consumption of media for orientation and the clarification of societal ambiguities. This increased dependency creates the conditions that facilitate individual and collective behavioral change (DeFleur & Ball-Rokeach, 1989).

Collectively, these modernization theorists—Rostow, McClelland, Lerner, Schramm, and Rogers—concluded that internal factors needed to be fixed. External models, especially those found in the industrialized West, were the models to be emulated if progress was to be achieved in the newly independent nations of the developing world. Communication, especially broadcasting, played a major role in the process (Lerner & Schramm, 1967).

As indicated earlier, socialists held similar ideas about human progress. They contended, however, that capitalism had deformed and derailed human progress, resulting in human exploitation. Progress should allow individuals to achieve their full potential for the benefit of society—a collective versus an individualistic orientation.

The end state of socialist progress was communism. According to socialists, capitalism-led modernization, with its gradualism, was really a strategy of appeasement, a strategy for maintaining the exploitative status quo. Socialists argued for a radical transformation, a revolution that would destroy all former patterns of exploitative relationships and replace them by a more egalitarian practice. Socialists argued for self-reliance and regional solidarity.

By the 1960s, developing nations that had followed the modernization route had demonstrated marginal improvements in meeting the basic needs of their citizens. In addition, unacceptable levels of waste, corruption, and human rights abuses were associated with the model. Criticisms against the model, especially from Latin America, became shriller.

The Dependency Critique

By the 1960s, the modernization approach was under attack from several fronts—operational and ideological. The critique of modernization emerged from two intellectual sources: "one rooted in neo-Marxism, or structuralism; the other, in the extensive Latin American debate on development associated with the United Nations' Economic Commission for Latin America" (Servaes & Malikhao, 1994, p. 8).

Among the influential theorists were Andre Gunder Frank, Raul Prebisch, and Immanuel Wallerstein (Rhodes, 1970). Dependency theorists demonstrated that the existing pattern of global economic relations, one dominated by the industrialized North, was contributing to the underdevelopment of the developing regions of the world. Dependency theorists contended that the broadcasting and other mass media systems that were put in place in the developing world to support modernization were actually undermining the possibilities of establishing equitable development. These broadcasting systems, they argued, were antidevelopment, as they tended to promote the agenda of political elites and relied on external sources for programming. Further, the broadcasting systems tended to marginalize indigenous modes of expression, thus undermining the development of national culture and identity. In addition, they encouraged demands for lifestyles that could not be provided by the economy.

In this sense, the broadcasting systems were undermining development, a phenomenon that Howard Frederick (1990) has termed *development sabotage communication*. As stated earlier, these national broadcasting systems in many developing countries were excessively dependent on external entertainment programming, especially from the United States. This programming privileged individualism, consumerism, patriarchy, white male dominance, and many other themes that were considered counterproductive by political, religious, and cultural leaders of the developing world.

In the 1970s, concerns with the imbalanced state of international communication flows coincided with concerns about the inequities in the prevailing global economic system. The desires for change were articulated in UN resolutions calling for a new world economic order (United Nations, 1974) and a new world information and communication order (UNESCO, 1980).

By the 1970s, the former colonies of Europe—now sovereign states—and other developing nations in Asia and Latin America had become an influential bloc in the UN system. This bloc is referred to as the Third World. Although the term now generates images of conflict, poverty, and disease, it initially represented resistance to domination by both the United States and the Soviet Union. It was a Third World because it rejected the notion of a world divided into two, a world in which only the United States and the Soviet Union counted and everybody else had to declare for one or the other. It feared the power of the superpowers, exemplified and magnified by nuclear weapons. It distrusted their intentions, envied (particularly in the American case) their superior wealth, and rejected their insistence that, in the one case through democratic capitalism and in the other through communism, they had discovered a way of life that others need do no more than copy (Calvocoressi, 1982). Dependency theorists have been criticized for offering a critique of the modernization model without offering prescriptive measures. However, the critique raised questions that have influenced contemporary practice of communication for development. The dependency critique focused attention on successful grassroots practices in Latin America, while drawing attention to the lack of genuine participation by citizens in the development process. In Latin America, it was demonstrated that a benefit of genuine participation was more sustainable improvements in the quality of human life (Borda, 1988; Freire, 1983).

The dependency critique of modernization sharpened two essential ideas for communication and development practitioners: the importance of the programming of broadcasting in development; and the importance of practices of participation, not only for achieving a development project goal but also as a crucial element in nurturing democratic practices.

ANOTHER DEVELOPMENT

The dependency idea also emerged at a time when it was obvious that our world was interdependent and that development decisions in a nation–state or region had global significance. This recognition led to the "another development" formulation.

This new perspective on development was initially articulated by the Dag Hammarskjöld Foundation in Sweden and has three fundamental pillars: development should strive to eradicate poverty and satisfy basic human needs, priority should be given to "self-reliant and endogenous change processes," and development should be environmentally responsible (Servaes & Malikhao, 1994, p. 10). Further, it was recognized that the need for development did not exist only in the Third World. Substantial regions of the industrialized world and the recently developed world were also in need.

With the winding down of the Cold War in the 1980s, this interdependent orientation took root. The round of world conferences organized by the United Nations during the 1990s reaffirmed the perspective on interdependence and called for increased global cooperation to deal with the global development crisis.

THE WORLD CONFERENCES

During the late 1980s and the throughout the 1990s, the international community organized or reconvened a number of conferences that focused on the development challenges facing an interdependent world. Conferences focused on the environment (Rio de Janeiro, 1992), population and development (Cairo, 1994), social development (Copenhagen, 1995), women (Beijing, 1995), and food (Rome, 1996). These conferences revealed that, despite marginal improvements in some sectors, the human condition continued to be unacceptable. Further, because of the interrelated and interdependent nature of global society, the development problems faced by a society had global consequences. The conferences reaffirmed the role of communication in the development process and called for its increased use.

CONTEMPORARY STRATEGIES
IN COMMUNICATION FOR DEVELOPMENT

Exciting new strategies in communication for development have emerged over the past three decades. Public awareness campaigns, social marketing, entertainment–education, and advocacy have been effective in communication for development projects. These theory-driven strategies all subscribe to systematic planning. Six planning phases are identifiable: formative research, project design, pretesting of materials, implementation, monitoring, and evaluation. These strategies are integrative, incorporating a wide range of theory, demonstrating ethical awareness, applying powerful methodological strategies, and demonstrating commitment to participation (Piotrow, Kincaid, Rimon, & Rinehart, 1997; see also http://www.comminit.com).

Public Awareness Campaigns

Public awareness campaigns systematically draw upon the power of the mass media, especially broadcasting, to create awareness in societies about the development intervention. Awareness is considered the first step in creating behavior change (Piotrow et al., 1997). Public service announcements (PSAs) are among the dominant artifacts used in this process. PSAs played an important role in awareness development and reinforcement in the "designated driver" anti–drunk driving campaign in the United States.

Social Marketing

Social marketing is the application of commercial marketing ideas to promote and to deliver pro-social interventions. Central to the social marketing approach is harmonizing the four essential elements of the social marketing—price, product, promotion, and place. Social marketing strategies have been applied extensively in the areas of family planning and reproductive health, immunization, and childhood diseases (Piotrow et al., 1997). In Ohio, interventions based on social marketing are being developed to increase the levels of physical activity (Cambridge, 2001).

Entertainment–Education

Entertainment–education has been defined as the systematic embedding of pro-social educational messages in popular entertainment formats. In recent years, this strategy has been used to address a wide range of development challenges, including agricultural improvement, adult education, domestic violence prevention, family planning and reproductive health, HIV/AIDS prevention, and peace and reconciliation (Sherry, 1997; Singhal & Rogers, 1999; Singhal & Rogers, 2002; Soul City, 1999). More than 160 entertainment-education projects were developed between 1990 and 2000. Included in this list is *New Life, New Hope,* a radio soap opera broadcast by BBC External Service. This soap opera promoted peace and reconciliation among Afghanis (Bosch & Ogada, 2000).

Advocacy

When stakeholders and beneficiaries in the development process promote the interventions by reporting on their positive experiences and benefits, the credibility of the communication increases. Advocacy for development does just that. An excellent recent example of effective advocacy is the project called Arab Women Speak Out, jointly conducted by Johns Hopkins University; the Center of Arab Women for Training and Research in Tunisia; and Population Initiative for Peace, a London-based nongovernmental organization. The project involved women in Lebanon, Palestine, Egypt, Tunisia, and Yemen who were engaged in agitating for women's rights in reproduction health decisions. These women became influential agents for social change (Piotrow et al., 1997). For details on these and other strategies, visit the website for the Communication Initiative (http://www.comminit.com).

CHALLENGES IN THE 21ST CENTURY

The development challenges of the 21st century are profound. In a report to the Millennium Conference of the United Nations, Secretary-General Kofi Annan (2000) identified some of the challenges facing humanity at the start of the 21st century:

- Reducing the extreme poverty faced by 1.2 billion people who have to live on less than $1 per day
- Improving the lives of 100 million slum dwellers by 2020
- Ensuring that all children complete primary schooling
- Reducing HIV/AIDS infection in young people by 25 percent by 2010
- Improving agricultural productivity in Africa
- Preserving forests, fisheries, and biodiversity
- Reducing the threat of global warming by reducing by 60 percent emissions of carbon and other greenhouse gases
- Confronting the water crisis
- Defending the soil
- Preventing conflict

Windahl, Signitzer, and Olson (1992) have reminded us that the field of communication for development is not only systematic but also creative. This creativity will be stretched in the 21st century.

LESSONS LEARNED

The field of communication for development has grown in importance since World War II and is now accepted as a necessary element in development. To be effective, communication for development interventions require systematic planning and the involvement of stakeholders and beneficiaries in all aspects of the process—problem identification, design, pretesting of materials, implementation, monitoring, and evaluation. New communication technologies provide designers of communication for development with opportunities to support interactivity and knowledge sharing.

The development challenges facing humankind require increased global cooperation as the consequences of these challenges transcend the nation–state. In addition to addressing specific problems, the practice of communication for development can contribute to the creation and maintenance of the structures required for sustainable development and democratic life.

Today, communication for development interventions, especially those that rely on broadcast media, must be aesthetically competitive if they are to be effective in the global communication environment, which is dominated by slick entertainment programming from the United States and other production centers in Europe and Latin America. Entertainment programs account for more than 60 percent of all broadcast schedules globally. Practitioners of communication for development must take this reality into consideration as they work with beneficiaries to plan, design, implement, monitor, and evaluate purposive social change.

 For more information on the topics that appear in this chapter, use the password that came free with this book to access InfoTrac College Edition. Use the following words as keyterms and subject searches: communication and development, U.S. Agency for International Development, the Marshall Plan, dominant paradigm, dependency paradigm, modernization, communism, UN Development Program.

QUESTIONS FOR DISCUSSION

1. Identify and discuss the phases in the development and implementation of a communication for development project.

2. What was the Marshall Plan?

3. What is a paradigm? Isolate and discuss the attributes of the modernization and other development paradigms.

4. Visit the website of the Communication Initiative (http://www.comminit. com) or the Johns Hopkins University Center for Communications Programs (http://www.jhuccp.org/), and select and study a social marketing intervention and an entertainment–education intervention. Prepare a report on the similarities of their design approaches.

5. How has the dependency critique contributed to improvements in the practice of communication for development?

REFERENCES

Afanasyev, V. (1978). *Social information and the regulation of social development.* Moscow: Progress Publishers.

Annan, Kofi A. (2000). *We the peoples: The role of the United Nations in the 21st century.* Report for the United Nations Millennium Summit. Retrieved October 6, 2000, from http://www.un.org/millennium/sg/report/summ.htm

Bandura, A. (1995). Exercise of personal and collective efficacy in changing societies. In A. Bandura (Ed.), *Self-efficacy in changing societies.* Cambridge: Cambridge University Press.

Barge, J. K. (2001). Practical theory as mapping, engaged reflection, and transformative practice. *Communication Theory, 11*(1), 5–13.

Borda, O. (1988). *Knowledge and people's power: Lessons with peasants in Nicaragua, Mexico, and Colombia*. New Delhi: Indian Social Institute.

Bosch, T. E., & Ogada, J. O. (2000). *Entertainment- education around the world (1989–2000): A report to the third international conference on entertainment-education and social change*. Athens: Communication and Development Studies, Ohio University.

Calvocoressi, P. (1982). *World politics since 1945*. London: Longman.

Cambridge, V., & Araya, B. (1997). The rehabilitation of "failed states": Eritrea as a beta-site for distance education technologies. In *Educational technology 2000: A global vision for open and distance learning* (pp. 325–337). Vancouver, British Columbia: The Commonwealth of Learning.

Cambridge, V. C. (2001). *Formative research for social marketing–based interventions to increase physical activity in Ohio: A study in five counties (Adams, Meigs, Scioto, Defiance, and Lorain)*. Report to Ohio Department of Health's Bureau of Health Promotion and Risk Reduction. Athens: Communication and Development Studies, Ohio University.

Cambridge, V. C., & Sleight-Brennan, S. (2000). *Report to UNESCO on workshop on entertainment-education held for Central Asian media professionals held in Ashgabat, Turkmenistan*. Athens: Communication and Development Studies, Ohio University.

Chambers, R. (1994). *Poverty and livelihoods: Whose reality counts?* Overview paper prepared for the Stockholm roundtable on global change, July 22–24, 1994.

Childers, E. (1973, February 20). *Draft guidelines and instructions for development support communication in country programming, project formulation, and implementation and evaluation*. Document circulated for consideration and revision at RBAFE training workshop and regional meeting.

DeFleur, M. L., & Ball-Rokeach, S. (1989). *Theories of mass communication* (5th ed.). New York: Longman.

Dervin, B., & Huesca, R. (1997). Reaching for the communicating in participatory communication: A meta-theoretical analysis. *Journal of International Communication, 4*(2), 46–74.

Drucker, P. (1985). *Management: Tasks, responsibilities, practices*. New York: Harper & Row.

Fraser, C., & Restrepo-Estrada, S. (1998). *Communicating development: Human change for survival*. New York: I. B. Tauris.

Frederick, H. (1990). *Global communication and international relations*. Belmont, CA: Wadsworth.

Freire, P. (1983). *Pedagogy of the oppressed*. New York: Seabury Press.

Lerner, D. (1958). *The passing of traditional society: Modernizing the Middle East*. New York: Free Press.

Lerner, D., & Schramm, W. (1967). *Communication and change in the developing countries*. Honolulu: University Press of Hawaii.

McClelland, D. (1964). Business drive and national achievement. In A. Etzioni & E. Etzioni (Eds.), *Social change* (pp. 165–178). New York: Basic Books.

Meier, G., & Seers, D. (1984). *Pioneers in development*. New York: Oxford University Press for the World Bank.

Moemeka, A. (2000). *Development communication in action: Building understanding and creating participation*. Lanham, MD: University Press of America.

Parsons, T. Quoted in A. So (1990). *Social change and development: Modernization, dependency, and world system theory*. Newbury Park, CA: Sage, p. 20.

Piotrow, P., Kincaid, D. L., Rimon II, J. G., & Rinehart, W. (1997). *Health communication: Lessons from family planning and reproductive health.* Westport, CT: Praeger.

Rhodes, R. (Ed.). (1970). *Imperialism and underdevelopment.* New York: Monthly Review Press.

Rogers, E. (1962). *Diffusion of innovations.* New York: Free Press.

Rogers, E. (1994). *A history of communication study: A biographical approach.* New York: Free Press.

Rostow, W. (1990). *The stages of economic growth: A non-communist manifesto* (3rd ed.). Cambridge: Cambridge University Press.

Schramm, W. (1964). *Mass media and national development: The role of information in developing nations.* Stanford, CA: Stanford University Press.

Servaes, J., & Malikhao, P. (1994). Concepts: The theoretical underpinnings of approaches to development communication. In *Approaches to development communication.* Paris: UNESCO.

Sherry, J. (1997, December). Pro-social soap operas for development: A review of research and theory. *Journal of International Communication, 4*(2), 75–101.

Singhal, A., & Domatob, J. (1993, December). The field of development communication: An appraisal. A conversation with Professor Everett M. Rogers. *Journal of Development Communication, 2*(4), 97–101.

Singhal, A., & Rogers, E. (1999). *Entertainment-education: A communication strategy for social change.* Mahwah, NJ: Lawrence Erlbaum Associates.

Singhal, A. & Rogers, E. (2002). *Combatting AIDS: Communication Strategies in Action.* London: Sage Publications Ltd.

Singhal, A., & Sthapitanonda, P. (1996, June). The role of communication in development: Lessons learned from a critique of the dominant, dependency, and alternative paradigms. *Journal of Development Communication, 1*(7), 10–25.

So, A. (1990). *Social change and development: Modernization, dependency, and worldsystem theory.* Newbury Park, CA: Sage.

Soul City. (1999). *Edutainment: How to make edutainment work for you.* Houghton, South Africa: Soul City.

Tuluhungwa, R. (1981, June 2). Highlights of PSC activities in 1980. *Project Support Communications Newsletter, 5*(2), 1–2.

UNESCO. (1980, June 7). *Resolution on the new international information order of the 4th Meeting of the Inter-governmental Coordinating Council of Non-aligned Countries for Information.* Baghdad.

United Nations. (1949). *Statistical yearbook 1948.* Lake Success, NY: United Nations.

United Nations (1974, May 1). *Declaration on the establishment of a new international economic order.* New York: United Nations.

United Nations, Preamble. http://www.un.org/aboutun/charter

Weinstein, J. (1997). *Social and cultural change: Social science for a dynamic world.* Boston: Allyn and Bacon.

Windahl, S., Signitzer, B., & Olson, J. (1992). *Using communication theory: An introduction to planned communication.* London: Sage.

10

The Politics of Global Communication

CEES J. HAMELINK

Cees J. Hamelink (PhD, University of Amsterdam) is Professor
of International Communication at the University of Amsterdam
and Professor of Media, Religion, and Culture at the Vrije Universiteit,
Amsterdam, The Netherlands. He is the editor in chief
of the *International Journal for Communication Studies: Gazette*. He is also
honorary president of the International Association for Media
and Communication Research and founder of the People's
Communication Charter. Hamelink's major publications include
Cultural Autonomy in Global Communications (1983), *Finance
and Information* (1983), *The Technology Gamble* (1988), *The Politics
of World Communication* (1994), *World Communication* (1995), *The Ethics
of Cyberspace* (2000), and *Human Rights for Communicators* (2004).

THE THREE SUBSTANTIVE DOMAINS

Since the mid-19th century, global communication has developed into an important concern on the agenda of the international community. Over the past
150 years, the players in this field (governments, commercial firms, and professional
practitioners) have designed and adopted rules (by legislation or by self-regulation),
institutions, and practices that provide limits and incentives for their conduct.

 For additional online resources, access the Global Media Monitor website
that accompanies this book on the Wadsworth Communication Cafe website
at http://communication.wadsworth.com.

During all these years, the substantive domains of global communication politics have largely remained the same. They encompass the fields of telecommunication (now including data communication), intellectual property rights, and mass media.

By and large, the core issues of today's communication politics are still to be found in these three domains. Technological developments have obviously added new dimensions to these issues. In the area of telecommunication, the main issues continue to involve accessibility, allocation, and confidentiality. Today, the accessibility issue refers not only to basic telephony but also to advanced computer networks. In addition to frequencies and settlement rates, the allocation issue today involves the new field of domain names for the use of the Internet.

The confidentiality issue has gained increased urgency through the global proliferation of data networks, data collection activities, and new forms of electronic surveillance. The issues in the domain of intellectual property rights have acquired more urgency through the application of new technologies that make large-scale copying of copyrighted materials easy. In the domain of mass media content, the basic controversy is still focused upon the tension between harmful content and free speech. The regulation of content on the Internet is today an urgent new issue on the agenda of global communication politics.

Global communication politics is initiated, amended, debated, and implemented by a variety of multilateral forums, including both governmental and nongovernmental organizations. For specific issues, distinct multilateral institutions have become responsible. Global communication in the 1990s confronted the world political arena with complex and controversial policy concerns that demanded resolution through multilateral bargaining. A major challenge for the 21st century is the inclusion of actors from global civil society in these bargaining processes.

THE BEGINNINGS

The politics of global communication emerged in the mid-19th century in the domains of telecommunication, intellectual property rights, and mass media.

Telecommunication

In 1868, Heinrich von Stephan, a senior official in the postal administration of the North German Confederation, prepared a proposal for an international postal union. Through his government, this plan was submitted to a plenipotentiary conference that was held at the invitation of the Swiss government at Berne on September 15, 1874. The 22 countries present at the conference founded, through the Treaty of Berne, the General Postal Union.[1] The treaty of this

---

1. The countries present at the conference were Austria, Belgium, Denmark, Egypt, France, Germany, Great Britain, Greece, Hungary, Italy, Luxembourg, the Netherlands, Norway, Portugal, Rumania, Russia, Serbia, Spain, Sweden, Switzerland, Turkey, and the United States.

convention entered into force on July 1, 1875. In 1878, the name of the organization was changed to Universal Postal Union. The 1874 Berne conference introduced basic norms and rules that still hold today. Among these were the guaranteed freedom of transit within the territory of the union and the standardization of charges to be collected by each country for letter-post items addressed to any part of the union's territory.

By 1865, the need was felt to substitute a multiplicity of bilateral, trilateral, and quadrilateral arrangements for a multilateral agreement. In that year, France invited the European states to an international conference that became the founding meeting of the International Telegraphy Union (May 17, 1865). With the establishment of this predecessor of today's International Telecommunication Union (ITU), the first treaty to deal with world communication was adopted: the International Telegraphy Convention. The original text of the convention's treaty stated that the signatories desired to secure for their telegraphy traffic the advantages of simple and reduced tariffs, to improve the conditions of international telegraphy, and to establish a permanent cooperation among themselves while retaining their freedom of operation.[2]

The convention adopted the Morse code as the first international telegraph standard. Among the other norms adopted were the protection of the secrecy of correspondence, the right of all nations to use international telegraphy, and the rejection of all liability for international telegraphy services. The contracting parties also reserved the right to stop any transmission considered dangerous for state security or in violation of national laws, public order, or morals.

Intellectual Property Rights

The Berne meeting of the International Literary and Artistic Society adopted the draft for a multilateral treaty entitled *Convention Establishing a General Union for the Protection of the Rights of Authors in Their Literary and Artistic Works*. This draft was sent to "all civilized countries" through the Federal Council of the Swiss Confederation, with the plan for a diplomatic conference in 1884 to adopt a formal treaty. The third diplomatic conference (September 6–9, 1886) adopted the earlier drafts for a convention, an additional article, and a final protocol. These three texts were signed by Belgium, France, Germany, Great Britain, Haiti, Italy, Liberia, Spain, Switzerland, and Tunisia. These founder members created a union that was open to all countries. The Berne treaty provided international recognition for the national treatment principle. As article 2(1) stated,

> Authors who are subjects or citizens of any of the countries
> of the Union, or their lawful representatives, shall enjoy in the other
> countries for their works, whether published in one of those countries

---

2. The following states attended: Austria, Baden, Bavaria, Belgium, Denmark, France, Hamburg, Hanover, Italy, the Netherlands, Norway, Portugal, Prussia, Russia, Saxony, Spain, Sweden, Turkey, and Würtemburg. Great Britain was excluded because its telegraph network was privately owned. The unions also decided in 1858 that French and German were to be the official languages for international telegrams.

or unpublished, the rights which the respective laws do now or may hereafter grant to natives. (Berne, 1886)

In the field of copyright, the Berne convention treaty remained the only multilateral treaty until 1952. Since 1886, it has been revised at diplomatic conference in 1896 (Paris), in 1908 (Berlin), in 1928 (Rome), in 1948 (Brussels), in 1967 (Stockholm), and in 1971 (Paris).

In the development of author rights, the basic principles have been to ensure remuneration for an author by protecting his or her work against reproduction (for 50 years after the author's lifetime); to demand respect for the individual integrity of the creator; to encourage the development of the arts, literature, and science; and to promote a wider dissemination of literary, artistic, and scientific works.

Mass Media

With the proliferation of printed and especially broadcast media (in the late 19th and early 20th centuries), serious concerns about the social impact of the mass media emerged. The positive, constructive contribution of the media to peaceful international relations generated considerable excitement. Such positive expectations were expressed in the 1933 Convention for Facilitating the International Circulation of Films of an Educational Character. This treaty of this convention was signed at Geneva on October 11, 1933. The contracting parties to the convention, which was registered with the secretariat of the League of Nations, considered the international circulation of educational films that contribute "towards the mutual understanding of peoples, in conformity with the aims of the League of Nations and consequently encourage moral disarmament" (League of Nations, 1933) to be highly desirable. To facilitate the circulation of such films, the signatories agreed to exempt their importation, transit, and exportation from all customs duties and accessory charges of any kind.

However, the negative social impact of the mass media was also a serious concern. A moral, educational concern was expressed regarding the spread of obscene publications across borders. This concern resulted in the adoption of the 1910 and 1924 treaties on traffic in obscene publications. The 1924 International Convention for the Suppression of the Circulation of and Traffic in Obscene Publications declared it a punishable offence "to make or produce or have in possession (for trade or public exhibition) obscene writings, drawings, prints, paintings, printed matter, pictures, posters, emblems, photographs, cinematograph films or any other obscene objects" (League of Nations, 1924). Also punishable was the importation or exportation of obscene materials for trade or public exhibition, and persons committing the offence "shall be amenable to the Courts of the Contracting Party in whose territories the offence...was committed." Concern about the negative impact of the mass media also arose from the increasing use of the mass media in the course of the 19th century as instruments of foreign diplomacy. Although this was particularly the case with newspapers, the development of wireless radio widened the potential for this new form of diplomacy.

Increasingly, diplomats shifted from traditional forms of silent diplomacy to a public diplomacy in which the constituencies of other states were directly addressed. In most cases, this behavior amounted to propagandistic abuse of the medium. During World War I, the means of propaganda were used extensively. This psychological warfare continued after the war ended, as international short-wave radio began to proliferate.

In the immediate postwar period, the League of Nations initiated discussions about the contribution of the international press to peace. In 1931, the league asked the Institute for Intellectual Cooperation (the predecessor of UNESCO) to conduct a study on all questions raised by the use of radio for good international relations. In 1933, the study, *Broadcasting and Peace,* was published, and it recommended the drafting of a binding multilateral treaty. Under the war threat emanating from Germany after 1933, the treaty was indeed drafted, and on September 23, 1936, it was signed by 28 states. The fascist states did not participate. The International Convention Concerning the Use of Broadcasting in the Cause of Peace entered into force on April 2, 1938, after ratification or accession by nine countries: Australia, Brazil, Denmark, France, India, Luxembourg, New Zealand, the Union of South Africa, and the United Kingdom. Basic to the provisions of the treaty was the recognition of the need to prevent, through rules established by common agreement, the use of broadcasting in a manner prejudicial to good international understanding. These agreed-upon rules included the prohibition of transmissions that could incite the population of any territory "to acts incompatible with the internal order or security of contracting parties" or that were likely to harm good international understanding by incorrect statements. The contracting parties also agreed to ensure "that any transmission likely to harm good international understanding by incorrect statements shall be rectified at the earliest possible moment" (League of Nations, 1938). In 1999, the treaty was still in force and had been ratified by 26 member states of the United Nations.

The New Multilateral Institutions

After 1945, global communication politics received a new impetus through the establishment of the United Nations. With the creation of the United Nations and its specialized agencies, a crucial group of institutions for multilateral policy evolution and policy coordination entered the international system. The General Assembly of the UN (particularly through the International Law Commission and several subcommissions) and the International Court of Justice became the primary movers in the progressive development of the norms and rules that make up the current system of international law.

The UN General Assembly has contributed to global communication politics through a vast number of resolutions that address such divergent issues as the jamming of broadcasts, the protection of journalists on dangerous missions, direct satellite broadcasting, and human rights aspects of science and technology.

Among the key standard-setting instruments adopted by the General Assembly that are pertinent to world communication are the basic human rights covenants, declarations and conventions against discrimination, and treaties on outer space law. Among the various organs of the UN General Assembly, special attention for communication matters is located in the Third Committee of the General Assembly (responsible for social, humanitarian, and cultural matters) and the Economic and Social Council. The Economic and Social Council was established as the principal organ to coordinate the economic and social work of the UN and its specialized agencies. In the subsidiary bodies of the council, communication issues are addressed, especially in the case of the Commission on Human Rights or the Commission on Transnational Corporations.

Of particular importance was the 1959 establishment by the General Assembly of the Committee on the Peaceful Uses of Outer Space. This body became the focal point for UN standard setting in outer space law, with important references to world communication politics through regulatory instruments addressing satellite broadcasting.

In 1966, the General Assembly established the Commission on International Trade Law (UNCITRAL), with the mandate to facilitate the harmonization of the laws of international trade. With the increasing importance of computer technology in international transactions, the commission has been required to address such problems as legal validity of computer records and liability in electronic funds transfers.

In 1978, the UN General Assembly established the Committee on Information, which received its mandate through a resolution adopted on December 18, 1979. The committee has contributed to a series of resolutions on the new international information order and the public information activities of the UN.

Specialized Agencies

Multilateral policy is also made by the specialized agencies of the United Nations, and several of these became important regulators for the field of communication, especially the ITU; the Universal Postal Union (UPU); the UN Educational, Scientific, and Cultural Organization (UNESCO); and the World Intellectual Property Organization (WIPO). To a far lesser extent, the International Labor Organization (ILO) became involved through employment questions relating to communication professionals; and the World Health Organization (WHO) and Food and Agriculture Organization (FAO), through work in the field of standards for advertising and marketing of health and food products.

Standards affecting world communications are also set in the International Civil Aviation Organization (ICAO), which has adopted rules for aircraft telecommunications systems; and the International Maritime Organization (IMO), which has addressed issues of maritime communications.

In addition to the already-existing multilateral forums that became UN specialized agencies, new regulatory bodies were also established, such as the now defunct Intergovernmental Bureau for Informatics (IBI) and the UN Conference on Trade and Development (UNCTAD), which has adopted standards in such fields as intellectual property and transfer of technology.

An important multilateral organization that does not belong to the United Nations family is the General Agreement on Tariffs and Trade (GATT). Among the other important multilateral bodies with participation of national governments are the organizations that have been established for the operational application of space telecommunications technology. These are primarily Intelsat and Inmarsat, intergovernmental satellite systems established by treaty.

Three other intergovernmental multilateral institutions should be mentioned, although they are not as broadly representative and in fact are more regionally oriented. However, they have made significant contributions to world communication politics. These are the Organization for Economic Cooperation and Development (OECD), the Conference on Security and Cooperation in Europe (CSCE), and the Council of Europe. In such fields as freedom of information and protection of transborder flows, the standard-setting work of these organizations has had important impacts on the world.

The Nongovernmental Organizations

In the post-1945 phase of the evolution of world communication politics, an important contribution was offered by a rapidly growing group of international nongovernmental organizations (INGOs). INGOs are partly international, in terms of membership and activities, and partly nationally based. Obviously they do not have the legal power to issue binding decisions, but they can influence the policymaking processes of the intergovernmental organizations as expert groups or as lobbying agents. They can also define standards for their own conduct that may have a political significance beyond the members of the group they represent. Illustrations are the efforts of the international professional bodies in journalism to arrive at a self-regulatory code of conduct, or the self-regulatory codes that are adopted by the International Public Relations Association and the International Advertising Association.

The United Nations and its specialized agencies have, from their inception, involved nongovernmental organizations in their policymaking processes. In the development of international human rights law, for example, INGOs have played an important role. INGOs such as Amnesty International have contributed to a crucial instrument for the implementation of human rights standards: "the mobilization of shame." Another example is provided by those INGOs that keep the World Health Organization informed of acts by multinational companies that violate the WHO code on the marketing of breast-milk substitutes. In the field of development cooperation, new policy insights have been forced upon public institutions through INGO pressure regarding concerns about women, population, health, and the environment. Various resolutions by the UN General Assembly have accorded special significance to the contributions of organizations representing scientists, employers, and workers' unions in negotiations on a code of conduct for transnational corporations. In UN agencies such as the ITU, WIPO, and UNESCO, INGOs have made significant contributions to the formulation of world communication politics.

Shifts in Global Communication Politics

Over the past decade, the arena of global communication politics has seen major changes. Among the most important ones are the following:

- The international governance system for communication operated during the past 100 years mainly to coordinate national policies that were independently shaped by sovereign governments. Today's global governance system to a large extent determines supranationally the space that national governments have for independent policy making.

- Global communication politics is increasingly defined by trade and market standards and ever less by political considerations, with a noticeable shift from a predominantly political discourse to a largely economic trade discourse. Evidence of this can be found in the growing emphasis on the economic importance of intellectual property and the related priority of protection for investors and corporate producers. In the telecommunications field, the standards of universal public service and cross-subsidization have given way to cost-based tariff structures. In the area of transborder electronic data flows, politics has changed from political arguments about national sovereignty and cultural autonomy to such notions as trade barriers and market access.

- The most powerful private players have become more overtly significant. The invisible hand of the economic interests that have all along guided political decision making became in recent years more and more visible.

- Transnational corporations became prominent players in the arena and played their role explicitly in the foreground. The locus of policy making shifted from governments to associations of private business actors.

The developments in connection with the proposal for a charter on global communication demonstrate the reversal of roles. During the Interactive Conference of the ITU in September 1997, EU commissioner Martin Bangemann proposed the idea of a charter with key principles for the information society. The charter was to be a nonbinding agreement on a framework for global communications in the 21st century. The idea was further elaborated during a Group of Seven (G7) meeting in Brussels in October 1997.

On June 29, 1998, Commissioner Bangemann invited some 50 board chairpersons and corporate presidents from 15 countries to a roundtable discussion on global communications. Among the companies invited were Microsoft, Bertelsmann AG, Reuters, Polygram, IBM, Siemens, Deutsche Telekom, Sony, Toshiba, and VISA. On the agenda were questions such as What are the most urgent obstacles to global communications, and what are the most effective means to remove them? Intellectual property rights, taxation, tariffs, encryption, authentication, data protection, and liability were identified as urgent issues. The business participants proposed that regulation be kept to a minimum because the global nature of the online economy makes it impossible for any single government or body to regulate.

The industry expressed a clear preference for self-regulation. The meeting proposed to set up a Business Steering Committee to ensure that the initiative would be led by business. The industrialists announced that they would begin a new global business dialogue to which governments and international organizations would be invited.

Ironically, the initial Bangemann plan was for a political declaration that would launch a dialogue between governments and companies on the global electronic marketplace, the goal of which would be a market-led approach in which the private sector would actively participate through a consultative process with governments and international organizations to shape global communications policy. This process has now been taken over by the private sector, which will, when it sees fit, invite governments and international organizations to participate in the shaping of a self-regulatory regime.

The World Trade Organization

Global communication policies were traditionally made in such intergovernmental forums as UNESCO, the World Intellectual Property Organization, and the International Telecommunication Union. These organizations were relatively open to the sociocultural dimension of developments in information and communication technologies. Moreover, they offered a platform where the interests of developing nations could also be voiced. In recent years, the position of these international governmental organizations, or intergovernmental organizations (IGOs), was considerably weakened as the major players began to prefer a forum more conducive to their specific interests. This forum is the successor to the General Agreement on Tariffs and Trade: the World Trade Organization (WTO). The WTO was established as one of the outcomes of the GATT Uruguay Round of multilateral trade negotiations, completed in December 1993.

The WTO is generally more favorable to the trading interests of the major industrial countries than are other intergovernmental bodies. Among its main policy principles are the worldwide liberalization of markets and the nondiscrimination principle, which provides for national treatment of foreign competitors in national markets and for treatment as most-favored nations. Actually, it should surprise no one that communication politics has shifted to this trade forum, given the increasing economic value of communication networks and information services.

Today's global communications market generates more than $1.6 trillion annually. Together with the fact that the major communication and information corporations provide the essential support structures for commodity and financial markets, the governance of communication issues is now largely destined to be subject to a global trade regime. This implies that the rules of "free" trade are applied to the three main components of the world communications market: the manufacturing of hardware, the production and distribution of software (computer programs and contents), and the operation of networks and their services.

CURRENT PRACTICES

The Domain of Telecommunication

The prevailing pattern of thought that guides global politics in relation to telecommunication infrastructures is based on the following assumptions:

- Telecommunication infrastructures are essential to development.
- The installation and upgrading of infrastructures is expensive.
- Private funding is needed.
- To attract private funding, countries will have to liberalize their telecommunication markets and adopt pro-competition regulatory measures.

The global management of telecommunication is in fact left to freely operating private entrepreneurs. The basic thought is that a country's telecommunication infrastructure can be managed by private companies and that, whenever parts of the network are unprofitable, the state can provide the public means to secure that no citizen is disenfranchised.

During the 1980s, deregulation became the leading principle for public policy. Its main aim of "less state and more market" has begun to affect more and more social domains and, in many countries, now also reaches out to primary facilities such as the provision of water and energy, thus rendering access and use of these facilities problematic for those with little income.

For national and global telecommunication markets, the new policy implied privatization and liberalization. According to the deregulators, the creation of competitive markets and the shift from public to private ownership would facilitate the universal accessibility of telecommunication and information services. The key policy principles for global telecommunication are "liberalization of the market" and "universal service." Combining these principles suggests that they are complementary and mutually reinforcing. That, however, remains to be demonstrated. Signals from different parts of the world indicate that leaving markets to private commercial and competitive forces does not necessarily lead to accessibility and affordability of telecommunication infrastructures.

Judging from the growing participation of the private sector in telecommunication negotiations and the increase in market-opening commitments, the conclusion is that more and more countries believe that liberalizing their telecommunication markets is beneficial to them. The real political issue is no longer whether countries will liberalize but when they will do so. Yet opinions continue to differ, as the ITU's *World Telecommunication Development Report* (1997) observes: "Market access, for example, will be viewed by some as an opportunity, while others that are attempting to develop their own domestic telecommunication service industry might see it as a challenge and a threat to nascent local operators" (p. 102). In some countries, revenues for domestic operators will increase as a result of liberalization, but in other countries, most revenues may accrue to foreign entities. As the ITU report rightly notes, "There will be winners and losers" (p. 106).

As part of the opening up of their markets, many countries have also begun to privatize their public telecommunication operators (PTOs). Whereas liberalization can be defined as the opening of markets to competition, privatization refers to the transfer of state-owned institutions or assets to various degrees of private ownership. These two processes can be in conflict with each other. Liberalization may clash with the desire of governments to get the highest price for their monopoly PTOs, and privatization may conflict with market liberalization when the incoming operator wants monopoly control for an initial period.

Governments pursue privatization and/or liberalization policies for quite different reasons. These policies—especially in poorer countries—may be more related to troublesome economies than to the desire to improve and upgrade telecommunication services. They may be related to the political wisdom of the day (for example, neoliberalism) or to the hope of getting technology transferred in the process. The new policies are neither an unequivocal recipe for disaster nor a guarantee of successful economic and technological performance. Results will be different in different countries, and much more study is needed to establish what social conditions determine benefits and costs.

Privatization has been implemented in a fairly large number of countries; 44 PTOs were privatized between 1984 and 1997 (ITU, 1997, p. 2). These privatizations have raised some $159 billion. The 12 major privatizations in 1996 raised more than $20 billion. These investments were roughly 50 percent domestic and 50 percent foreign. The overall trend has been that more than 30 percent of the invested capital comes from foreign sources. As the ITU reports, the PTOs themselves are usually the most active investors. However, in 1997, majority shares in 29 of the top 40 international carriers were still owned by states: "Rather than full privatization, it is corporatization of state-owned telecommunication companies that has instead proceeded across all regions" (ITU, 1998a, p. 9). Also, liberalization has not proceeded so as to create competitive markets across sectors in all countries. In many countries, basic telecommunication services are not open to competition. Most liberalized are markets for mobile telephony, but even in this sector, several countries do not yet allow competition.

The arguments used to support privatization point to the expansion and upgrading of networks, the improvement of services, and the lowering of tariffs for access and usage of networks. Experiences are varied, however. One of the results of privatization often is the expansion of the telecommunications network. In several countries (for example, Peru and Panama in 1997), privatization considerably improved teledensity. According to the ITU (1998b), "One reason is that network expansion targets have increasingly been made a requirement of privatization concessions" (p. 71). The added telephone lines of course benefit those users who can afford the service. The privatization scheme does not enlarge the group of citizens who have the purchasing power required for the use of telecommunication networks.

In several countries, tariffs have gone down but mainly for big corporate users, whereas the telephone bills for ordinary consumers have hardly benefited. Experiences with the provision of services are also differentiated. This is partly because the expectation of more competition and more choice as a result of privatization was not always fulfilled. As a matter of fact, in smaller and less advanced states, national telecommunication operators have lost against big global coalitions, the new monopolists. It is highly questionable whether markets controlled by a few global operators will actually benefit the consumer. It remains dubious how much competition will remain in the end. The reduction of prices and the increase in investments for technological innovations tend to shake competitors out of the market, and as a result, market liberalization almost everywhere tends to reinforce market concentration. This follows the historical experience that free markets inevitably lead to the formation of monopolies because competitors will shake contenders out of the market or will merge with each other.

The WTO Telecommunication Treaty

In 1994, the Marrakech Agreement Establishing the World Trade Organization (WTO) completed the eighth round of multilateral trade negotiations held under GATT (Uruguay Round). Part of the final treaty was a General Agreement on Trade in Services (GATS). The most elaborate annex concerned the trade in telecommunications. The annex defined basic telecommunication services and networks as follows:

- Public telecommunications transport service: any telecommunication transport service required, explicitly or in effect, by a Member to be offered to the public generally
- Public telecommunication transport network: the public telecommunication infrastructure that permits telecommunications between and among defined network termination points.

Of the 125 signatory countries of the Marrakech Agreement, some 60 made commitments to open their markets for telecommunication services, although most did not commit themselves on the issue of basic telecommunications. The commitments ranged from full competition for all telecommunication services to exceptions for basic telecommunication services, cellular services, or local services.

The Marrakech meeting established the Negotiating Group on Basic Telecommunications (NGBT), which was to deal with telecommunication services and conclude its work by April 1996. The NGBT failed to reach agreement by this date. Several issues remained inconclusive, such as the liberalization of satellite services and the settlement arrangements for international telecommunication rates. The negotiations did lead, however, to an agreement on some basic rules provided in a so-called Reference Paper, which deals with competitive safeguards, interconnection, universal service obligations, transparency of licensing criteria, independence of the regulator, and allocation and use of scarce resources.

A new group, called the Group on Basic Telecommunications, continued the work after July 1996. The main mandate of the group, which was open to all WTO member states and held monthly meetings, was to stimulate more countries to make commitments, to deal with the issue of liberalizing satellite services, and to solve a number of issues related to the provision of telecommunications services.

The new series of negotiations focused on the matter of restrictions on foreign ownership, among other things. The U.S. government pushed particularly hard for allowing maximum foreign ownership in domestic telecommunications. In making their commitments, restrictions on foreign ownership were fully waived by many countries; others, however, retained 25–80 percent of domestic control. Whereas some countries consider foreign ownership an opportunity to attract necessary foreign investment (ITU, 1997, p. 102), others perceive it as a threat to national sovereignty. Although national governments have full control over the scope, the phasing, and the timing of their commitments, once they have made those commitments, they cannot change their concessions in the future. A complex matter for the negotiations became the issue of mobile services provided through satellites. Although the allocation of satellite frequencies is the responsibility of the ITU, a trading aspect arises when national governments use national procedures for spectrum allocation as barriers to trade. Following the provisions of the GATS, such procedures should not be discriminatory.

On February 15, 1997, the Fourth Protocol of the General Agreement on Trade in Services was signed by 72 WTO member states (representing some 93 percent of the world trade in telecommunication services). On February 5, 1998, the protocol entered into force. This World Telecommunications Agreement demands that participating states liberalize their markets. They are allowed some leeway to implement universal access in ways they deem desirable, but significant qualifications in the agreement seriously limit national political space.

The agreement has far-reaching implications for the governance of the basic infrastructures of telecommunications. On the issue of universal service, it states, "Any member has the right to define the kind of universal service obligation it wishes to maintain. Such obligations will not be regarded as anticompetitive per se, provided they are administered in a transparent, nondiscriminatory and competitively neutral manner and are not more burdensome than necessary for the kind of universal service defined by the member" (WTO, 1998). This seriously limits the space for independent national policy making on access.

Since foreign industries cannot be placed at a disadvantage, the national standards for universal service have to be administered in a competitively neutral manner. They cannot be set at levels "more burdensome than necessary." If a national public policy would consider providing access to telecommunication services on the basis of a cross-subsidization scheme rather than on the basis of cost-based tariffs, this might serve the interests of the small users better than those of telecommunication operators. Foreign market entrants could see this obligation as "more burdensome than necessary." As a consequence, the policy would be perceived as a violation of international trade law. It would be up to the largely obscure arbitration mechanisms of the WTO to judge the legitimacy of the national policy proposal.

The focus of the agreement is on the access that foreign suppliers should have to national markets for telecommunication services, rather than on the access that national citizens should have to the use of telecommunication services. The simplistic assumption is that these different forms of access equate. As a result, social policy is restricted to limits defined by the commercial players.

Trade interests rather than sociocultural aspirations determine national tele-communication policy. By 2004, most trading partners had agreed to liberalize their domestic markets. The establishment of worldwide free markets for any type of services does not, however, necessarily imply the availability of such services or the equitable use of these services for all who could benefit from them.

Governments pursue privatization and/or liberalization policies for quite different reasons. These policies may—especially in poorer countries—be more related to troublesome economies than with the desire to improve and upgrade telecommunication services. They may be related to the political wisdom of the day (for example, neoliberalism) or the hope to get technology transferred in the process. The new policies are neither an unequivocal recipe for disaster nor do they guarantee successful economic and technological performance. Results will be different in different countries, and much more study is needed to establish what social conditions determine benefits and costs. The arguments used to support privatization point to the expansion and upgrading of networks, the improvement of services, and the lowering of tariffs for access and usage of Networks.

Changing the Account Rate Settlement System

An important component of global telecommunication politics is the so-called account rate system. Traditionally, the telecommunication system was based in bilateral relations between telecom carriers. The general regulatory framework for the settlement of charges between carriers (often the monopoly telecom operators) was provided by the International Telecommunication Regulations, a treaty administered by the ITU and last revised at the World Administrative Telegraph and Telephone Conference (WATT-C) in 1988. Over the past years with the innovations in technology, the drive toward liberalization, and privati-zation, this regime came under severe pressure. Not only will more and more private commercial companies today be the operators in both countries of origin and destination, they will also offer new services (such as phone cards or Internet telephony) that bypass the settlement system.

One of the essential motives of telecommunications regulation as it was enacted in the first International Telegraph Convention (1865) was to find an adequate system for the division of revenues from international calls among countries of origin, transit, and destination. Basically, the PTO in the country of origin would charge the customer a certain price, then the PTO in the country of destination and the PTO in the country of origin would agree to a price for the services by the destination PTO (providing international lines and switching and delivering calls to local customers). This is called the *account rate*. This amount forms the basis for the charges of operators in destination countries to operators in originating countries. These charges are called *account settlement rates*.

The general recommendation by the ITU has been to divide the charges on a 50/50 basis between carriers. This worked well in situations where monopolies dealt with other monopolies and where international telecommunications was seen as a jointly provided service. This is all changing with the availability of more private operators, more competition, and more technical options to bypass the existing system.

For some time now, a reform of the existing account rate settlement system has been discussed by the OECD (since 1991), by the ITU (since 1992), and by the WTO. In the past, the existing system has served the interests of developing countries well. Since developing countries have usually applied relatively high charges for the completion of international calls at their end, the account rate settlement was an important source of foreign exchange. According to the ITU, each year up to $10 billion may go to developing countries in net payments. This income can—at least in principle—be used to support access to the telecom infrastructure for people in rural areas who would otherwise remain disconnected.

When negotiations about reform did not progress quickly enough, the U.S. administration decided to announce its preferred solution. The Federal Communications Commission in the United States has argued that the country loses billions of dollars each year in payments to other countries. It has therefore introduced (in November 1996) the Notice of Proposed Rulemaking, which went into force in January 1998. Herewith, a revised system was proposed that determines how much U.S. operators can pay operators in foreign countries. This would, on average, be half of what was paid in the past. The European Commission is inclined to follow the U.S. example. The shape of future politics on account rates will undoubtedly have a critical impact on issues such as accessibility of telecommunication in poor countries, since lowering the account rate payments will lead to an increase in costs to local customers in those countries.

The Domain of Intellectual Property Rights

At present, the essential governing institutions in the field of intellectual property rights are the World Intellectual Property Organization and the World Trade Organization. The WTO plays an increasingly important role because it oversees the execution of the legal provisions of the agreement on Trade-Related Intellectual Property Rights (TRIPS). This global agreement emerged under the GATT negotiations (as Annex 1C to the General Agreement on Tariffs and Trade in the Uruguay Round of multilateral trade negotiations, 1993). TRIPS contains the most important current rules on the protection of intellectual property rights (IPRs). It is implemented within the WTO regulatory framework. In this agreement, the economic dimension of IPR protection is reinforced. As Venturelli (1998) correctly summarizes, "The balance has tipped entirely toward favoring the economic incentive interests of third-party exploiters and away from both the public access interests of citizens and the constitutional and human rights of creative labor" (p. 63). As IPRs have achieved a prominent place among the world's most important tradable commodities, the current trade-oriented IPR regime favors corporate producers (publishers, broadcast companies, music recording companies, advertising firms) over individual creators. The provisions of the TRIPS agreement protect the economic rights of investors better than the moral rights of creative individuals or the cultural interests of the public at large. For the dissemination of their products, performing artists, writers, and composers increasingly transfer their rights to big conglomerates with which they sign contracts. Ultimately, these companies determine how creative products will be processed, packaged, and sold.

One of the serious problems with the current trend in IPR protection is that the emerging regulatory framework stifles the independence and diversity of creative production around the world. The regime is particularly unhelpful to the protection of the "small," independent originators of creative products. It establishes formidable obstacles to the use of creative products because it restricts the notion of fair use, under which—traditionally—these products could be freely used for a variety of educational and other purposes. The narrow economic angle of the current trend focuses more on the misappropriation of corporate property than on the innovation of artistic and literary creativity.

A particularly worrying phenomenon is that the current rules provide that once knowledge in the public domain is put into electronic databases, it will come under IPR protection. This will imply a considerable limit to freely accessible sources. Moreover, the present system of governance threatens to transform the new global forum that cyberspace potentially offers (through new digital technologies) into a marketplace where a controlled volume of ideas will be traded.

The one-dimensional emphasis on the commercial facets of copyright protection is reinforced by the progressive shifting of negotiating forums from the WIPO to the WTO. In this process, the protection of intellectual property becomes part of the global free-trade agenda. This implies that the public interest is secondary to the economic interest of the largest producers of intellectual property.

The social value and common benefit of cultural products are not on the transnational corporate agenda. These products (such as knowledge) tend to be seen as commodities that can be privately owned. A different point of view would contest this and propose that knowledge is part of the common heritage of humankind and cannot be the exclusive property of a few members of the community. The emphasis in the emerging system is rather exclusively on the rights of knowledge producers and almost completely bypasses the duties of rights holders. Such duties include the obligation of disclosure—the obligation to provide information and supporting documents concerning corresponding foreign applications and grants. The rights holder can be obliged to work a patent in the country where the patent was granted and can be required to refrain from engaging in abusive, restrictive, or anticompetitive practices.

Current intellectual property rights tend to benefit only the industrial nations, but they can also stimulate free innovation in poorer nations. Rather than strengthening the control of transnational corporations over technology and reinforcing the monopolistic rights of technology providers, the technological capabilities in the developing countries could be strengthened. The pressure to create a uniform global system of IPR protection constrains the flexibility that developing countries need in order to adapt the IPR system to their specific needs and interests. One can expect that in the years to come the domain of intellectual property rights will continue to be a crucial battlefield of conflicting interests.

Recent developments related to the control over works in digital form underline this. The use of protective technologies (such as encryption and copy protection codes) strengthens the monopoly control of owners of intellectual property rights. Because consumers are likely to develop and apply circumvention technologies to undermine this control, the U.S. administration and U.S. motion picture industry have effectively lobbied the World Intellectual Property Organization to incorporate in its 1996 Copyright Treaty a legal provision against circumvention technologies. This provision (in Article 13 of the Treaty) has meanwhile been enacted in the U.S. Digital Millennium Copyright Act of 1998 and in the EU Copyright Directive of 2001. These new legal measures could make it impossible for people who buy perfectly legal items to make extra copies for private use. It may also become impossible to play copyrighted items—even if legally purchased—on different platforms (not on your CD player but alone on your PC)!

The Domain of Mass Media

The main issues in relation to mass media concern concentration of ownership and the trade in media products. The mega-media mergers of the 1980s and early 1990s renewed concerns in many countries about media concentration. On the international level, only minimal concern is being expressed. The essential guideline for policy makers seems to be the deregulation of the marketplace. The common argument in favor of an unregulated marketplace in the provision of information is that it guarantees creative and competitive forums that offer a diversity of contents. Abundant empirical evidence, however, suggests that concentration in the mass media promotes market control by a few companies that tend to produce a limited package of commercially viable contents only. The World Trade Organization's rules, for example, stress the need for competition.

However, the major concern is that public policies should not be anticompetitive in the sense of hampering free access to domestic markets. Current competition rules mainly address the dismantling of public services and the liberalization of markets, not the oligopolization of markets or the conduct of the dominant market parties.

The WTO Basic Telecommunications Agreement of February 15, 1997, governs market access but has little to say about the conduct of parties on the market. It does not guarantee effective, open competition between commercial actors. The nondiscrimination principle that provides for most-favored nation treatment of foreign competitors is inadequate to secure competition on domestic markets.

The WTO provisions on anticompetitive practices do not exclude the possibility that local media markets would be controlled by only three or four foreign suppliers. The lack of a serious competition policy supports unhindered market concentration and reinforces foreign ownership of essential market domains, particularly in developing countries.

One of the main policy issues is the question of whether the info-com market is substantially different enough from markets for other commodities (such as automobiles or detergents) that it should be treated in a different way. Should public intervention for cultural products be different from that for food products? Could it be that even if the shopping mall functions best when the state does not intervene, this does not necessarily apply if the mall is the main provider of information and culture? Moreover, is a genuine international competition policy (Holmes, Kempton, & McGowan, 1996) that governs anticompetitive conduct of market parties a realistic option? Such a policy would imply more regulation and would thus clash with the predominant concern of the major market players to reduce regulation.

Serious global governance to curb the formation of cartels will in any case be difficult. The approaches to cartels differ widely across national legal systems and traditions, and most free trade supporters believe that free markets will eventually create open competition and that anticartel rules create trade barriers.

In an economic environment where mega-mergers are almost natural and are loudly acclaimed by financiers and industrialists, the tendency toward public control is likely to be minimal. The European Commission does indeed prohibit industrial mergers but in a limited and modest way. The commission may propose demands that make companies decide not to merge. According to Jean Paul Marissing (of Caron & Stevens/Baker & McKenzie), who is a legal expert on mergers, out of several thousands of mergers that have been registered with the commission, only 10 were really prohibited (*NRC Handelsblad,* 1998).

One factor for low rate of merger prohibition is that mergers are considered serious problems only when consolidated companies may control more than 40 percent of a market. European regulation can prohibit abuse of monopoly positions but not the development of market monopolies. Equally, in U.S. regulation a merger is considered a threat to competition only if the two companies after their merger control more than 60 percent of a market.

The phenomenon of media concentration is generally acknowledged, but its implications are not of universal concern. Political, industrial, and academic positions on the issue are widely divergent. Scientific research on concentration, for example, tends to focus on the question of effects of media concentration on media contents. Such research often finds it "very difficult to demonstrate any link between the two" (McQuail, 1992, p. 125). This would be relevant if media contents were the core issue. It is, however, more important to question whether consolidation of media ownership guarantees sufficient independent locations for media workers, enough channels for audience reception and/or access, adequate protection against price controls on oligopolistic markets, and opportunities for newcomers in media markets. Even if the oligopolist could demonstrate quality, fairness, diversity, critical debate, objectivity, investigative reporting, and resistance to external pressures in offerings to the marketplace, there would still be reason to provide regulatory correction because the marketplace would effectively be closed for newcomers and thus not constitute a free market.

The players that argue for multilateral regulation of the issue constitute a heterogeneous collective of politicians, academicians, and professionals. They have a variety of motives for the conclusion of a multilateral accord. One motive is to protect the labor conditions of employees in the media industries. This motive addresses both employment opportunities and the quality of work in the media.

The freedom of the workers on the information market is heavily dependent upon the strength of the agreements they can negotiate with their employers. Generally, in cases of market concentration the freedom of their professional position is under threat. The need to accommodate the commercial purposes of the company and the political idiosyncrasies of the ownership inevitably implies forms of direct and indirect censorship.

Another motive is constitutional. Several U.S. Supreme Court decisions, for example, have asserted that the freedom of the press is undermined because the media have become so oligopolistic that censorship powers lie in private hands.

An important motive addresses the extent of independence in information provision and cultural production. Industrial concentration inevitably implies the establishment of power. The mega-companies are centers of power that are at the same time subject and object of media exposure. Moreover, the information industry as power center is linked into other circuits of power, such as financial institutions, military establishments, and the political elite. A specific problem is posed in situations in which mass media that provide news and commentary are part of an industrial conglomerate.

The conglomerate may engage in activities that call for critical scrutiny by the media, but the controlling actors may prefer to protect those activities against exposure. The concern about concentration is also motivated by the threat that oligopolization erodes the diversity of informational and cultural production. In cases where consolidation occurs as vertical integration, meaning that the same actors control production and distribution, the real danger exists that they will exclusively offer their own products to the market. A common example is the newspaper that, as part of a conglomerate, places mainly reviews of its own books.

The growing influence of institutional investors and commercial interests not genuine to the information sector tends to lead to an emphasis on the profitability of the commodity, rather than on its sociocultural quality. As a result, products that can be rapidly sold on mass markets are preferred. Illustrative is the tendency among film production companies and recorded music producers to concentrate on blockbusters. This "Rambo" and "Madonna" tendency reinforces a homogenization of markets, as the less profitable products are avoided.

On the issue of media concentration, the positions taken are conflicting. The preference for strict regulation clashes with the preference for no regulation at all. The pro-regulation position is defended with the following arguments: Antitrust legislation in the media field is defensible because concentration diminishes competition, and as a consequence, diversity on the information market is affected negatively. Moreover, anticartel–type measures promote competition, diversity, and freedom. Against this position is the oft-repeated suggestion that mergers lead to stronger companies with more power to protect information freedom. However, mergers are not always successful. They often occur without careful weighing of assets and liabilities. They may be motivated by the personal interests of top management or the short-term interests of small stockholders. On average, of 10 major acquisitions, 4 or 5 will be sold again. Often the aims that a merger is expected to achieve are not met. It is quite possible that, after the consolidation, profits do not increase, market segments do not expand, and the innovative potential of the firms may even diminish. As a result of unsuccessful mergers, companies may collapse and disappear.

Oligopolization in the information industry may also undermine the civil and political fundamental right to freedom of expression. This is the case when concentration actually diminishes the number of channels that citizens can use to express or receive opinions. In oligopolistic markets, the controlling interests may more easily refuse to distribute certain opinions. For example, in such situations, refusing certain forms of advertisement is easier.

Oligopolists always have the tendency to use their market power to price gouge consumers. This may easily mean that access to information and culture becomes dependent upon the level of disposable income. It can be attractive for the oligopolist to bring competing products on the market. This is, for example, quite common in such sectors as cosmetics or detergents. The implication of this intrafirm diversity is that it erects quite effective obstacles against the entry of newcomers into the market. This outcome is important because often a considerable contribution to market diversity originates with new entrants, although large firms may support loss-making operations by compensating for the losses elsewhere in the company accounts. In this way, newspapers, for example, that otherwise would have disappeared can be maintained. However, the length of time this compensation will be acceptable to shareholders (and in particular institutional investors) is limited. Moreover, losses accumulate over time, and in the middle to longer term, products that are not profitable will have to be removed.

The key arguments against attempts to regulate media concentration are the following: There is no empirical proof that concentration has indeed such negative effects. On the contrary, it can be argued that strong consolidated companies can offer much more diversity and can mobilize more independence in their dealings with governments than smaller companies can. Moreover, strong media can "rescue" loss-making media that otherwise would disappear, and thus their contribution to diversity is retained. It is also argued that more competition does not guarantee more diversity because competitors may all try to reach the largest share of the market with a similar product. Even if regulatory measures against industrial consolidation were successful in stimulating more competition, an increase in product diversity is not guaranteed. Markets tend inevitably toward identical, though marginally distinct, products because, of necessity, they address the largest possible number of buyers. A problem is that allowing competition on the marketplace does not necessarily lead to more diversity. There is some evidence that the deregulated, competitive broadcast systems of Western European countries reflect less diversity in content than the formerly regulated public monopolies. This type of situation occurs largely because the actors in a competitive market all try to control the largest segment by catering to rather similar tastes and preferences of that market segment.

The trading of media services has become global business with an expanding and profitable market. In the years ahead, the international media market is generally expected to reach the $3 trillion mark. This expanding market is to a large extent due to the concurrent processes of deregulation of broadcasting and the commercialization of media institutions. These developments imply a growing demand for entertainment. The related important process is globalization—in terms of markets but also in terms of products and ownership.

Worldwide, a clear trend toward an increasing demand for the American-brand entertainment is seen. An important feature of the trend toward globalization is that the trading by the mega-companies is shifting from the international exchange of local products to production for global markets. Concerns with regard to the world market in media services have been expressed in connection with the 1986–1993 Uruguay Round of multilateral trade negotiations. The special focus of these concerns are television programs and films, and the existing and/or potential constraints to trading them across the world. The concerns focus on forms of national regulation that restrict imports of media services or national policies that protect national media industries. Other concerns focus on trade constraints related to the structure of the international media market, particularly to the large share of market control held by only a few transnational operators.

Perspectives on the issue of traded media services diverge. Some players assert that this trade should be unhindered and that foreign markets should be freely accessed. Others are concerned that, without restrictions on media imports, local cultural industries cannot survive, and local cultural heritage gives way to McDonaldization. The leading media production companies, their associations (such as the Motion Pictures Export Association), and governments of exporting countries (especially the United States) have been concerned about barriers to media trade. The concern about the lack of controls is largely articulated by small producers and by governments of importing countries (Third World countries, Western European countries, Canada). Their preference for import restrictions is largely motivated by the desire to economically and culturally protect their own media industry. This desire is reinforced by the fear that transnational control over local distribution and exhibition mechanisms will exert a decisive influence on what cultural products are locally available.

The contending positions are liberal-permissive claims versus protectionist-restrictive claims. The liberal position prefers an arrangement that permits total liberalization of market access for media services. The more protectionist position favors levels of protection from media imports as instruments to support local media industries or to protect local culture.

One of the complexities of addressing media services in a trade context is that not all of them have commercial purposes. A part of mass media production is typically oriented toward noncommercial, educational, artistic, or sociocultural goals. Although this is recognized in Article IV of the GATT accord, the big media exporters define their product in terms of a commercial commodity only. This implies the collision of the claim to the opportunity to increase markets for a profitable commodity with the claim to rightfully regulate media imports and protect national media markets for a variety of reasons.

For developing countries, another problem with the liberalization claim is that because media products are finished products, it is not likely that liberalization increases labor or technology inputs for them. Contrary to, for instance, tourism, media services do not bring employment or training. That market access is likely to be a one-way street is also a problem. The economic realities of media production and distribution allow for little chance of exports from the Third World countries.

At present it looks as if the most-likely provisions to emerge for the world trade in media services are GATT rules pertaining to traded services and intellectual property rights. The emerging practice of multilateral trade cooperation will be based upon a binding and robust GATT accord. The question remains, however, as to the appropriateness of such an arrangement, given the distinctions between media services and services at large. First, the production of a film or television program resembles manufacturing. An actual physical product is generated, composed of labor- and capital-intensive inputs. So, in comparison with services such as tourism or construction, where employment occurs and value is added at the final destination of the service, films and television programs are finished products that are merely distributed at their final destination. The distancing of production and distribution in these industries virtually eliminates possibilities for technology transfer or highly skilled employment at the point of distribution. In comparison with some services in which developing countries could compete on the basis of a comparative labor-cost advantage, the manufacture of media products is organized in such a way that almost all labor inputs—and certainly all skilled labor inputs—occur in centralized locations far removed from the distribution point.

Second, all the costs in making the product are incurred in turning out the first copy of the film or the television program. Additional copies can be produced very inexpensively. So, profitability in this sector depends on timing and strategic control of the release of the film or program, a process that has become more complicated as the number of different types of potential distribution outlets has multiplied worldwide. This constraint on potential profit intensifies the need to control distribution tightly, for example, ownership of distribution networks (Christopherson & Ball, 1989).

Another complication is that film and television programs are both a good and a service. Contents may be transmitted in tangible formats but also through intangible media such as airwaves. Moreover, as several studies have noted, it is quite difficult to measure in any reliable manner the actual trade volume (Guback, 1969; Widman & Siwek, 1988). Also, whether or not a GATT arrangement would permit certain trade barriers in the light of cultural policies remains to be seen. This process is allowed in the OECD Code of Liberalization of Current Invisible Operations (Annex IV to Annex A of the code), which provides, "For cultural reasons, systems of aid to the production of printed films for cinema exhibition may be maintained provided that they do not significantly distort international competition in export markets" (OECD, 1992). The GATT accord that was concluded in mid-December 1993 did not include the sector of audiovisual services. The most powerful players were divided among themselves and clashed on a free-trade perspective promoted by the United States and a cultural-policy perspective defended by the European Union. The discord is only of marginal significance. The opponents have no basic disagreement about the commercial nature of culture and information as marketable commodities.

European politics has established for some time that broadcasting, for example, is a traded service and is subject to the rules on market competition of the European Economic Community (EEC) Treaty. The European desire to exempt culture from international trade rules is not motivated by deep principles. In the bargaining, at some point a deal is likely to be struck, and a global trade agreement might emerge. For the time being, the major players have agreed to disagree. In February 1994, key U.S. actors (such as the MPEA) and the European Commission both indicated a desire to reconcile their divergent positions on the issue of traded media services.

For the trade negotiations at the WTO Seattle conference (November 1999), the U.S. government proposed the removal of broadcasting and audiovisual products from the exemptions to the existing agreements on the liberalization of telecommunications. The current exemptions are part of the Fourth Protocol of the General Agreement on Trade in Services. The European public broadcasters rejected this proposal. Their position was considerably strengthened by the protocol on public service broadcasting that was appended to the European Union Amsterdam Treaty of June 1997. The EU agreed that public service broadcasting is related to democratic, social, and cultural needs and to the need to preserve media pluralism. The social and cultural significance of public broadcasting was acknowledged by allowing it to function outside the regime of free market funding. In the WTO negotiations, the issue of traded media services continues to be controversial.

LESSONS FROM A KEY PROJECT IN THE DOMAIN
OF GLOBAL MASS MEDIA POLITICS

During the 1970s, a coalition of politicians, media activists, and communication researchers committed itself to the creation of a new international information order (NIIO), also referred to as the new international information and communication order or new world information and communication order (NWICO).

This concept is described in more detail elsewhere in this book. The coalition aspired toward a new order that would be democratic, support economic development, enhance the international exchange of ideas, share knowledge among all the people of the world, and improve the quality of life. This aspiration was first publicly expressed through a meeting of non-aligned heads of state in 1973 at Algiers. This meeting started a project that—after several years of much commotion and anger and little concrete achievement—would again disappear from the world's political agenda. Among the various factors that contributed to the NIIO failure, the most critical one was the lack of participation.

The effort to democratize communication in the 1970s was never a very democratic process. The debate was mainly an exchange among governmental and commercial actors. Ordinary people were not on the playing field. Political and intellectual elites engineered the whole project. Little or no attention was given to people's interests or even to the need to involve ordinary people in the debate.

The NIIO debate was firmly rooted in the realist paradigm of international relations. This paradigm conceived the world as a state-centric system and failed to take serious account of the numerous nonstate actors that had become essential forces in world politics. As a result, the NIIO debate never explicitly promoted the notion that the effective protection of democratic rights could not be guaranteed under the conventional nation–state system. A critical problem was that the realist paradigm glossed over the internal dimension of state sovereignty while focusing on external factors. As a result, the nation–state was seen as protecting the liberties of its citizenry against external claims made by other states. However, the outwardly sovereign state tends also to appropriate sovereign control over its citizens in the process. This follows the vision of the philosopher Thomas Hobbes (1638–1709), who proposed that only the absolute sovereignty of the state (which he referred as the Leviathan) can control the eternal strife among civil actors. This position ignores the fact that state sovereignty represents more than the emancipation from the powers of emperors, popes, and nobility.

The development of legitimate sovereign states went with the development of egalitarianism, in which subjects became citizens. The French Revolution and the American Revolution gave birth both to independent nation–states and to citizens with basic civil rights. As a matter of fact, the French Revolution recognized the primacy of the people's sovereignty. This recognition was not taken up in the NIIO project. It was not a people's movement. Insofar as it aspired toward a democratic order, it was a "democratization from above." Just like the NIIO project, today's popular project for the construction of a global information infrastructure (GII) is steered by the interests and stakes of governments and corporations. It is the bilateral playing field of "princes" and "merchants," and ordinary people are occasionally addressed as citizens or consumers, but they play no essential role.

A concern for the GII elite is actually that people may not be as excited about the digital future as the elite themselves are. It may be that ordinary men and women are not eagerly waiting to believe that virtual reality can resolve the problems of their daily lives. Therefore, many of the official reports on the information society stress the need to promote awareness among consumers. A key concern of the constructors of the information superhighway is that consumers may be hesitant about adding digital services to the present media supply, certainly if they have to pay for them.

The GII project therefore needs to persuade people that the information society will bring them great improvements in lifestyle, comfort, and general well-being. This makes people important targets for propaganda and marketing. However, no serious involvement of people's movements is present in the making of the GII. No trilateral negotiations are taking place between governments, industrialists, and social movements to share decision making on our preferred common future. Like the project of the 1970s, the GII project is about "democratization from above" and is unlikely to be effective in making world communication more democratic.

GLOBAL COMMUNICATION POLITICS TODAY

Current global communication politics is dominated by a set of eight essential issues that will largely shape the future of global communication. The governance of these issues is complicated because the political agendas in the world community are strongly divided and conflicting and define these issues in very different ways. The neoliberal political agenda is commercially oriented and market-centered.

This agenda proposes the liberalization of national markets, the lifting of trade restrictions, and the strengthening of the rights of investors. Opposed to this, one finds a humanitarian political agenda that puts the interests of citizens at the center of global policy making and that wants human rights to be taken as seriously as property and investment rights in global communication politics.

Access

The neoliberal agenda perceives people primarily as consumers and aspires to provide them with access to communication infrastructures, so they can be integrated into the global consumer society. The humanitarian agenda perceives people primarily as citizens and wants them to be sufficiently literate so that communication infrastructures can be used to promote democratic participation.

Knowledge

On the neoliberal agenda, knowledge is a commodity that can be processed and owned by private parties, and the property rights of knowledge producers should be strictly reinforced. On the humanitarian agenda, knowledge is a public good that cannot be privately appropriated.

Global Advertising

The neoliberal agenda has a strong interest in the expansion of global advertising. This implies, among other things, more commercial space in media (mass media and the Internet), new target groups (especially children), more sponsorships (films, orchestras, exhibitions), and more places to advertise (the ubiquitous billboards).

The humanitarian agenda is concerned about the ecological implications of the worldwide promotion of a consumer society and the growing gap between those who can shop in the (electronic) global shopping mall and those who can only gawk. Moreover, the humanitarian agenda has a strong interest in defending public spaces against their commercial exploitation.

Privacy

The neoliberal agenda has a strong interest in data mining: the systematic collection, storage, and processing of data about individuals to create client profiles for marketing purposes. The humanitarian agenda has a strong interest in the protection of people's privacy and the creation of critical attitudes among consumers to guard their personal information more adequately.

Intellectual Property Rights

The neoliberal agenda has a strong interest in the strict enforcement of a trade-based system for the protection of intellectual property rights (IPR) that provides a large degree of freedom for the transnational commercial rights owners to exploit those rights. Equally, these IPR owners have an interest in expanding the period of protection as well as the materials that can be brought under this protection.

The humanitarian agenda is concerned that the present system sanctions the grand-scale resource plunder of genetic information (biopiracy) from poor countries and serves the interests of corporate owners better than the interests of local communities or individual artistic creators. This agenda has a strong interest in protecting the interests of communal property of cultural resources and in protecting resources in the public domain against their exploitation by private companies.

Trade in Culture

The neoliberal agenda has a strong interest in the application of the rules of international trade law to the export and import of cultural products. Under these rules, countries are not allowed to take measures that restrict cultural imports as part of their national cultural policy. The humanitarian agenda is interested in exempting culture from trade provisions and in allowing national measures for the protection of cultural autonomy and local public space.

Concentration

The neoliberal agenda has a strong interest in creating business links (acquisitions, mergers, joint ventures) with partners in order to consolidate controlling positions on the world market and wants to create a sufficiently large regulatory vacuum in which to act freely. The humanitarian agenda is concerned that today's global merger activities have negative consequences for both consumers and professionals in terms of diminishing diversity and creating the loss of professional autonomy.

The Commons

The neoliberal agenda wants the private exploitation of such commons as the airwaves and promotes the auctioning of these resources to private parties. The humanitarian agenda wants to retain the public property of the human common heritage so that public accountability and community requirements remain secure.

Civil Advocacy

At present, the battle between these two conflicting agendas is fought with inequality of arms. The commercial agenda is supported by a strong constituency of the leading members of the WTO and powerful business lobbies (such as the Business Software Alliance and the Global Business Dialogue). The humanitarian agenda, although increasingly active in the economic arena, is still in search of an active constituency in the global communication arena. Although civil advocacy would be up against formidable opponents, a global movement could pose a serious political challenge. It would represent the interests of democratic citizenship and thus present a stronger claim to credibility than business firms. Because it would be inspired by such fundamental notions as universal human rights, it would have a moral authority, which is superior to those who are driven by commercial interests. It could use the court of public opinion more effectively than corporations can and use this to get major concessions from its commercial opponents. A global civil movement would be made up of citizens who at the same time are consumers and thus clients of the media industries, which would make them a forceful lobby.

On December 20, 2000, the *International Herald Tribune* used for one of its articles the following lead: "Small Advocacy Groups Take Big Role as Conscience of the Global Economy." In the same way, it should be possible to state: "Small Advocacy Groups Take Big Role as Conscience of Global Communication Politics." The intervention by public interest coalitions in the arena of global communication politics will not come about spontaneously. It demands organization and mobilization. A modest beginning has been made to achieve this through the Platform for Cooperation on Communication and Democratization. The platform that was established in 1995 is at present made up of AMARC, APC, Article 19, CENCOS, Cultural Environment Movement, GreenNet, Grupo de los Ocho, IDOC, International Federation of Journalists, IPAL, International Women's Tribune Center, MacBride Roundtable, MedTV, OneWorld Online, Panos, People's Communication Charter, UNDA, Vidéazimut, WACC, WETV-Global Access Television, and Worldview International Foundation. Members of the platform have agreed to work for the formal recognition of the right to communicate. They emphasize the need to defend and deepen an open public space for debate and actions that build critical understanding of the ethics of communication, democratic policy, and equitable and effective access.

The right to communicate is also the central concern of the so-called People's Communication Charter (http://www.pccharter.net). The People's Communication Charter (PCC) is an initiative that originated in 1991 with the Third World Network (Penang, Malaysia), the Centre for Communication & Human Rights (Amsterdam, the Netherlands), the Cultural Environment Movement (United States), the World Association of Community Radio Broadcasters (AMARC), and the World Association for Christian Communication. The charter provides the common framework for all who share the belief that people should be active and critical participants in their social reality and capable of governing themselves. The PCC could be a first step in the development of a permanent movement concerned with the quality of our cultural environment.

Eventually this movement could develop into a permanent institution for the enforcement of the PCC, perhaps in the form of an ombudsperson's office for communication and cultural rights. This idea largely follows a recommendation made by the UNESCO World Commission on Culture and Development, chaired by Javier Pérez de Cuéllar, in its 1995 report *Our Creative Diversity*. The commission recommended the drawing of an International Code of Conduct on Culture and—under the auspices of the UN International Law Commission—the setting up of an International Office of the Ombudsperson for Cultural Rights (World Commission, 1995). As the commission writes,

> Such an independent, free-standing entity could hear pleas from aggrieved or oppressed individuals or groups, act on their behalf and mediate with governments for the peaceful settlement of disputes. It could fully investigate and document cases, encourage a dialogue between parties and suggest a process of arbitration and negotiated settlement leading to the effective redress of wrongs, including, wherever appropriate, recommendations for legal or legislative remedies as well as compensatory damages. (p. 283)

Ideally, the proposed ombudsperson's office would have full independence both from governmental and from commercial parties, and as an independent agency it would develop a strong moral authority on the basis of its expertise, its track record, and the quality of the people and the organizations that would form its constituency. Given the growing significance of the global communication arena and the urgency of a humanitarian agenda for its politics, the building of this new global institution constitutes one of the most exciting challenges in the 21st century.

The World Summit on the Information Society

In 1996, the Executive Board of UNESCO explored the possibility of convening an International Conference on Information and Communication for Development to be held in 1998 jointly with other UN agencies, such as the ITU. Unfortunately, this conference never took place as the international community resolved to plan for a world summit on the information society that would be administered by the ITU. In the process, a concrete topic for international negotiations was replaced by the nebulous and contested concept of the "information society," and the UN organization with a broad mandate in the field of culture and communication and with much experience with nonstate actors (the UNESCO) was replaced by the UN organization that champions the "information society" mainly in terms of a technologically determinist view of the global future (the ITU). It will come as no surprise to any critical observer that the Clinton–Gore U.S. administration that propagated universal access to the global information infrastructure played a crucial role in these developments.

When the UN announced the World Summit on the Information Society (WSIS) in 2001, there was criticism of the lack of careful reflection before the UN rushed into this third major global diplomatic event in the politics of global communication. The first event had been the 1948 UN conference on the Freedom of Information, and the second event had been the UN involvement with the 1970s debates on a new international information order. Both earlier projects had largely failed for different reasons. This should have raised a warning flag for the third attempt in the early 21st century. Even so, there also was the positive and constructive expectation—both among diplomats and civil advocates—that the WSIS might provide a global forum to address the most burning issues of communication politics, and moreover there was the aspiration that this global gathering could become a genuine multistakeholder exercise.

After a series of preparatory committee meetings (so-called Prepcoms), the first phase of the WSIS took place in December 2003 in Geneva. It turned out to be a summit that was only partly different from earlier UN summits. There was massive input from well-organized and highly motivated civil movements, particularly under the umbrella of the Communication Rights in the Information Society (CRIS) campaign. However, the WSIS remained largely an interstate diplomatic gathering with no participation of nonstate actors in the final decision-making process. The summit ended with two separate declarations: the Declaration of Principles by states (www.wsis.org); and the civil society declaration, Shaping Information Societies for Human Needs (www.wsis-cs.org). Moreover, the two most burning global issues were not resolved and were referred to the second phase of the summit, to be held in November 2005, in Tunisia. The unresolved issues were the financing of efforts to bridge the global digital divide and the global governance of the Internet. If one takes a positive attitude toward the outcome of the WSIS process, one might conclude that, for the first time, global civil movements were effectively mobilized to address the key issues of the politics of global communication. Since many of the civil advocates see the WSIS as an ongoing process, these issues will remain on the public agenda and will hopefully attract the political attention from citizens worldwide, as well as from their elected representatives in national parliaments and supranational institutions, such as the European Parliament.

> For more information on the topics that appear in this chapter, use the password that came free with this book to access InfoTrac College Edition.
> Use the following words as keyterms and subject searches: global communication, International Telecommunication Union, intellectual property rights, international relations, human rights, Commission on International Trade Law, communication and politics, telecommunication.

QUESTIONS FOR DISCUSSION

1. By and large, the core issues of today's communication politics are the same as a century ago. What new dimensions have technological developments added to these issues?

2. The arena for global communication politics has considerably expanded over the years. Which actors have entered the arena in addition to nation–states?

3. Are the recent shifts in global communication politics also reflected in the national communication politics of your country?

4. The new international information order (NIIO) was a project of "democratization from above." How feasible today is a project to democratize global communication from below?

5. Could you design a future Global Ombudsperson's Office for Cultural Rights? What, in your opinion, should be its main tasks, and how should it operate?

6. Discuss whether or not the WSIS process could evolve into a genuinely democratic multistakeholder arena for the politics of global communication.

REFERENCES

Christopherson, S., & Ball, S. (1989). Media services: Considerations relevant to multilateral trade negotiations. In *Trade in services: Sectoral issues* (pp. 249–308). Geneva: UNCTAD.

Convention Establishing a General Union for the Protection of the Rights of Authors in their Literary and Artistic Works. (1886). Berne, Switzerland.

Guback, T. H. (1969). *The international film industry*. Bloomington: Indiana University Press.

Holmes, P., Kempton, J., & McGowan, F. (1996). International competition policy and telecommunications: Lessons from the EU and prospects for the WTO. *Telecommunications Policy, 20*(10), 755–767.

ITU. (1997). *World telecommunication development report 1996/97: Trade in telecommunications*. Geneva, Switzerland.

ITU. (1998a). *General trends in telecommunication reform 1998: World* (vol. 1). Geneva, Switzerland.

ITU. (1998b). *World telecommunication development report: Universal access*. Geneva, Switzerland.

League of Nations. (1924). International Convention for the Suppression of the Circulation of and Traffic in Obscene Publications, Geneva.

League of Nations. (1933). Convention for Facilitating the International Circulation of Films of an Educational Character. Geneva.

League of Nations. (1938). International Convention Concerning the Use of Broadcasting in the Cause of Peace. Geneva.

McQuail, D. (1992). *Media performance: Mass communication and the public interest*. London: Sage.

NRC-Handelsblad. (1998, July 22). Rotterdam.

OECD. (1992). *Code of liberalization of current invisible operations*. Paris.

Venturelli, S. (1998). Cultural rights and world trade agreements in the information society. *Gazette, 60*(1), 47–76.

Widman, S. S., & Siwek, S. E. (1988). *International trade in films and television programs.* Cambridge, MA: Ballinger.

World Commission on Culture and Development. (1995). *Our creative diversity.* Paris: UNESCO.

WTO. (1998). *World telecommunications agreement.* Geneva.

11

Global Communication and Propaganda

RICHARD C. VINCENT

Richard C. Vincent (PhD, 1983, University of Massachusetts-Amherst) is Professor of Communications at Indiana State University. His previous position was at the University of Hawaii, Manoa. He is author of five books and monographs, and numerous articles and chapters. His research has been an exploration of various aspects of communication equity or freedom, including the construction of meanings and alternate meaning in communication practices. Such work has centered on the eras of International Development and Post-Development. He does political economic analyses and the measure of applied communication practices. Vincent is past president of the MacBride Round Table, an international communication rights advocacy group, and was a delegate at the UN World Summit on the Information Society (WSIS), 2003–2005. He was a Fulbright Scholar at Dublin City University, Ireland, during 1994–1995. He has addressed audiences in more than 20 different countries.

> American traditions and the American ethic require us to be truthful, but the most important reason is that truth is the best propaganda and lies are the worst. To be persuasive we must be believable; to be believable we must be credible; to be credible we must be truthful. It is as simple as that.
>
> – EDWARD R. MURROW,
> (USIA DIRECTOR, U.S. CONGRESSIONAL TESTIMONY, MAY 1963)

 For additional online resources, access the Global Media Monitor website that accompanies this book on the Wadsworth Communication Cafe website at http://communication.wadsworth.com.

> . . . the cosmopolitan turned on his heel, leaving his
> companion at a loss to determine where exactly the fictitious
> character had been dropped, and the real one, if any, resumed.
> –HERMAN MELVILLE in *THE CONFIDENCE MAN* (1857)

Propaganda is one of the oldest terms that we associate with global communication. It has been in use for centuries and affects communication both domestically and abroad. With advances in communication technologies, propaganda has become increasingly important, even dangerous, in this modern day.

Propaganda has to do with the use of communication channels, through known persuasive or manipulative techniques, in an attempt to shape or alter public opinion. In international communication spheres, propaganda is used in three ways. First, government leaders, with intent to mold public opinion on international issues that have bearing on a country and its people, often use its techniques. The second use of propaganda is in attempts to influence matters abroad, normally to reinforce a country's public actions or policies, or perhaps to change or reinforce perceptions of a country, its citizens, or its reputation among individuals elsewhere in the world. Finally, nongovernmental entities may seek access to global communication channels in order to sway public opinion or affect public policy formation.

Sometimes the term *propaganda* is a bit deceiving. When we hear the word *propaganda,* it is likely we think of dominant, devious world leaders who spread a campaign of lies and intimidation, so they might manipulate or brainwash a public. The horrors that were possible under the reigns of Stalin, Mussolini, and Hitler may quickly come to mind. Yet, rarely would we think of our own country and its leaders and institutions being equally cunning and scheming in the management of its information campaigns. All nations conduct propaganda campaigns, however, on both the international and domestic levels. We are all affected, and it happens much more than we may realize. Highly persuasive messages are designed to support public policies, nurture feelings of patriotism, or just convince us that certain activities, situations, or products will serve our best interests if engaged in, consumed, or embraced.

The term *propaganda* is not that simple to define, nor is it always easy to identify. Activities traditionally referred to as propaganda today may further be labeled as public relations efforts, image consulting, the news, and information sharing by organizational spin doctors. Even advertising may be considered propagandistic in nature. Simply put, the purpose of propaganda is to persuade and convert by using intentionally selective and biased information. Examples of propaganda use are widespread and include Napoleon's use of the press, paintings, and even his image on china in the early 19th century; efforts to dissuade U.S. entry into World War II because of extensive business holdings with Germany; false news items placed in the international press by both the CIA and KGB during the Cold War; dropping leaflets behind enemy lines during military conflicts; use of a professional golf pro to ease relations between the United States and South Africa during Apartheid; the hiring of a public relations firm to help sway U.S. public opinion in favor of Kuwait during the

Persian Gulf War; and the very recent employment of high-profile news commentators in the United States to promote a number of presidential initiatives without disclosure that public money had been used to build and disseminate such persuasive campaigns. Most of these examples will be discussed later in this chapter.

ORIGINS OF PROPAGANDA

The origins of the term *propaganda* may be traced to the 17th century. At that time, many people were leaving the church. A group of cardinals was given control over all Catholic Church missions abroad (*Congregatio de Propaganda Fide; Society for the Propagation of Faith, the Jesuits*) by Pope Gregory XV in 1622. The purpose was to supply a unifying effort over the church's foreign mission activities and doctrine. A propagation of the faith was the result. To more fully understand the period, also recall that it was during this time that Galileo was convicted of heresy because of his thesis that the earth was round. The church was trying to standardize its teachings and beliefs in light of the emerging Reformation period. Within a century, the term *propaganda* was used in condemnation of clandestine organizations that attempted to undermine or influence foreign affairs. It was not used to refer to communication media per se until the 20th century.

Propaganda is thought of negatively in that it involves a determination of what degree of truth shall be shared. While the perpetuator of propaganda believes the ends justify the means, the mere fact that someone makes a conscious decision for others underlines the sensitive and potentially questionable nature of propaganda. In the end, it may depend on your personal political, social, and economic beliefs as to whether you find a given propaganda campaign acceptable or not.

When compared to other countries, propaganda came rather late to the United States. The prevailing feeling is that it emanated from Europe where rulers were engaging in what appeared to be constant war. Propaganda was used to recruit the large armies necessary for fighting in World War I, for example, and United States government officials also became concerned about the potential impact if some crazed European leader was to turn his trickery on Americans. The newfound power of motion pictures and radio contributed to the notion that the United States had to become more involved in this new war of words.

After World War I, communications researchers such as Walter Lippmann and Harold Lasswell pioneered the study of propaganda techniques. They suggested that manipulation was necessary for managing individuals in democratic societies. Lippmann (1922) argued that leaders must master the knowledge of consent creation so they might alter every political calculation and modify every political persuasion. Lasswell went further in *Propaganda Technique in the World War* (1927), detailing how exactly such manipulations might be implemented and noting that public opinion control was essential to support demands for justice and majority rule. He was essentially discussing propaganda's use during wartime. Later (1941), he clarified some of these thoughts. Lasswell summarizes that "[t]he enemies of America will wage war for the capture of American opinion, and we may safely predict that this campaign will proceed by other measures than frontal attack" (p. 175). He therefore rationalized the use of propaganda in order to mold public opinion for the support of a democratic society. Someone from a different political persuasion, obviously, might well conclude just the opposite, pointing to the inherent danger implicit in any propagandistic message. Consequently, propaganda is a phenomenon of media discourse guidance or coercion that is not always immediately recognized as harmful.

SEEKING A DEFINITION

Propaganda is not easy to define. Some hold it must involve a specific individual or group. Others contend it must comprise an activity that is secretive, sinister, or deceitful. Doob (1948) concluded, "Propaganda can be called the attempt to affect the personalities and to control behavior of individuals towards ends considered unscientific or of doubtful value in a society at a particular time" (p. 390). Linebarger (1948), on the other hand, posits that "propaganda consists of the planned use of any form of public, or mass-produced communication designed to affect the minds and emotions of a given group for a specific purpose, whether military, economic or political" (p. 39).

As noted earlier, public opinion theorist Harold Lasswell (1941, p. 16) argued that control of public opinion was essential to support the essence of "justice and majority rule." Lippmann (1927) echoes similar feelings when he notes that ". . . the public must be put in its place . . . so that each of us may live free of the trampling and roar of a bewildered herd. Only the insider can make decisions, not because he is inherently a better man but because he is so placed that he can understand and can act. The outsider is necessarily ignorant, usually irrelevant, and often meddlesome" (p. 47).

Someone from a different political persuasion or in a different time might have very well concluded just the opposite, pointing to the inherent danger implicit in any propagandistic message. Consequently, propaganda is a phenomenon of public discourse guidance or coercion that is not always immediately recognized as harmful by everyone. Propaganda might be spread through movies, comics, leaflets, broadcasting, or the Internet. It is found in everyday coverage of events in the national media, conservative talk radio hosts, commonplace broadcast and print media advertising, and radical hate group publications.

Our definition of propaganda was noted at the outset of this chapter, but we repeat it here within this broader discussion. Propaganda has to do with the use of communication channels, through known persuasive or manipulative techniques, in an attempt to shape or alter public opinion.

PROPAGANDA AND PUBLIC RELATIONS

In the United States today, the term *propaganda* has become unpopular in daily rhetoric. Instead of *propaganda,* many prefer to use terms such as *public relations* (PR), *publicity, promotion, marketing, public affairs,* and *advertising.* These are often no more than modern-day synonyms. With a tendency to frame propaganda as something more palatable and acceptable, a great deal of confusion has emerged over what exactly comprises a propagandistic campaign. Further, the constant use and misuse of the term has led to further confusion so that today the term has diminished importance and impact.

It was the German philosopher Georg Hegel who was among the first to demonstrate that even democratic societies might be controlled through hidden persuaders and manipulators. In *The Philosophy of Right* (1821), he noted that influence by commercial interests was a form of public manipulation.

During World War I, Edward L. Bernays, an entertainment industry publicist and nephew of Sigmund Freud, did propaganda pamphlet development for the Committee on Public Information. The group was lead by George Creel. Bernays' 1928 book, *Propaganda,* maintained that propaganda was in fact a useful tool for democratic government. As he observed, it was only natural, after the war ended, that intelligent persons should ask whether it was not possible to apply a similar approach to the problems of peace.

Bernays is credited as the father of public relations. His earlier work, *Crystallizing Public Opinion* (1923), set forth the philosophical foundations for public relations. "If we understand the mechanisms and motives of the group mind, it is now possible to control and regiment the masses according to our will without their knowing it" (p. 83, as qtd. in Ewen, 1976). Today, public relations is a huge industry that does more than $1 trillion in business annually and is estimated to influence some 40 percent of everything that Americans see or read. Bernays' greatest achievement is said to have been a campaign to convince American women they could "emancipate" themselves by smoking Lucky Strike cigarettes, a product he promoted as "torches of freedom."

Writing in the *New Republic,* however, John Dewey (1928) questioned underlying assumptions that propaganda could be camouflaged as news. "Paternalistic care for the source of men's beliefs, once generated by war, carries over to the troubles of peace" (pp. 9–10). Dewey made a particularly strong case that the same type of information manipulation was evident in news coverage found in post-Revolutionary Russia. Similar sentiments were expressed by others of the day.

Interestingly, at the start of 2005, United States President George W. Bush came under fire for excessive White House use of public relations firms to promote administration agendas. The administration was reported to have spent at least $88 million in fiscal 2004 alone. In early 2005, *USA Today* broke the story that the Education Department paid conservative commentator Armstrong Williams some $240,000 to promote president's No Child Left Behind education campaign. Shortly after, *The Washington Post* reported that syndicated columnist

Maggie Gallagher, received $41,500 for work in support of the White House marriage initiative, although she claimed the government work did not influence what she wrote in her columns (Kurtz, 2005). In this case, the White House sought to redirect welfare funds to premarital counseling and abstinence education. More recently, the Defense Department acknowledged it had almost 3,000 PR contracts, according to its response to a FOIA (Freedom of Information) request (Eggerton, 2005). While no laws were broken, these incidents once again fueled the debate over how appropriate such expenditures of taxpayer dollars may be and whether such blatant use of propaganda techniques are appropriate at this level. In fact, estimates show that public relations personnel activities are very pervasive and may in fact account for 30–40 percent of what we see, hear, or read as "news." Clearly, the definition of propaganda often depends on the perspective of the beholder.

These matters, of course, involve White House domestic issues. Nonetheless, with indication of such widespread management of public opinion formation in the domestic market, we are reminded of how fine a line exists between propaganda and public relations efforts generally. Next we will see how the United States has recast efforts to massage certain international relations activities by recasting the notion of propaganda in more positive terms.

PUBLIC DIPLOMACY

One area of government communication campaigns that raises questions today is that referred to as *public diplomacy*. This term is closely related to propaganda and originated as a more acceptable alternative for some. Essentially, public diplomacy refers to so-called truthful propaganda. The key here is the communicator's intent in such a process. Public diplomacy is therefore nothing other than public relations.

The term itself first appeared in the 1960s and was used by then-Dean Edward A. Gullion of the Tufts University Fletcher School of Law and Diplomacy. Writing in 1967, Gullion noted:

> Even beyond the organ of the Government set up to handle information about the United States and to explain our policies, what is important today is the interaction of groups, peoples, and cultures beyond national borders, influencing the way groups and peoples in other countries think about foreign affairs, react to our policies, and affect the policies of their respective governments. To connote this activity, we at the Fletcher School tried to find a name. I would have liked to call it "propaganda." It seemed like the nearest thing in the pure interpretation of the word to what we were doing. But "propaganda" has always had a pejorative connotation in this country. To describe the whole range of communications, information, and propaganda, we hit upon "public diplomacy." (p. 31)

While the term *propaganda* does not address the truthfulness of a matter or position being espoused, public diplomacy, at least in principle, does. Since the term *propaganda* has in recent years increased in terms of negative connotations, this further fueled the move to embrace "public policy" in place of "propaganda." In fact, in 1948, driven by the concern that the U.S. public might fall victim to propaganda produced by Washington, Congress passed the Smith-Mundt Act, forbidding the domestic dissemination of its government's materials designed for audiences abroad.

Public diplomacy became very closely associated with activities emanating from the United State Information Agency (USIA) since that organization used the term when describing its mission. Its activities included production of informational and educational films plus international interactions, including academic exchanges such as the esteemed Fulbright scholarship program as well as other academic and business community interactions. The late Senator J. William Fulbright, after whom the scholarship program was named, often defended the program as a vehicle for increasing mutual understanding between the United States and other countries rather than as another act of propaganda. In 1999, the USIA was disbanded; however, the concept of public diplomacy continued and is largely embraced in the United States Department of State.

The objectives of those involved in public affairs communication are to inform and influence public opinion internationally. At times, this is referred to as the effort to "win the international public's hearts and minds." The Department of State still uses publications, broadcasts, and cultural exchanges to cultivate goodwill toward America generally, as well as its interests and policies. Public diplomacy abroad also involves monitoring global opinion and engaging in dialogues with international audiences. Essentially, these activities seek to influence key international audiences as an extension of traditional diplomacy in order to advance U.S. interests and security and provide "the moral basis for U.S. leadership in the world." The Department of State continues educational and business exchanges previously orchestrated under the USIA.

RESEARCH ON PERSUASION

Propaganda research originated near the end of the First World War and was concerned with understanding the effects of mass media propaganda upon populations subjected to it. As such, propaganda research can be said to be the first major body of work concerned with mass media/mass communications research.

In persuasion studies, the literature tends to be differentiated between one-sided messages that offer arguments in favor of the perspective being promoted and two-sided messages where both favorable and bipolar sides of an argument are given. Many of the early studies were on films used in the American and Japanese soldier studies conducted under the leadership of Hovland (Hovland, Lumsdaine, & Sheffield, 1949).

Research found that communication campaigns could indeed have a positive effect regarding general knowledge on the war. The research did not necessarily follow through in support of U.S. involvement and its justifications for war, however.

Specifically, two-sided arguments were found to be more effective than one-sided approaches when the communication recipients were initially opposed to the viewpoint or if they would likely be exposed to counterarguments at a later point in time. If the subject already held a point of view, and that opinion was positive, one-sided approaches worked best as reinforcement to the held position.

One important finding was that prolonged and repeated exposure to specific forms of propaganda might have a marked effect on basic core values held by subjects (Lumsdaine & Janis, 1953). This notion was further advanced by Gerbner's (1976a) enculturation research many years later.

Another conclusion drawn by researchers is that when subjects possessed greater knowledge on a topic, the one-sided and two-sided approaches were both less effective in enacting attitude change. Regarding education levels, those with lower education were most influenced by one-sided messages, whereas two-sided campaigns were most efficient with the better educated.

Regarding the advertising literature, we find that when subjects possess greater knowledge on a topic, both the one-sided and two-sided approaches are less effective in producing attitude change. However, if a subject was already the user of a competing brand, a two-sided ad was still effective, particularly when repeated a number of times. Overall, greater change could be expected with either argumentative approach with smaller everyday purchases as opposed to more expensive occasional buys (Faison, 1961; Whitehead, 1968; Sawyer, 1974; Rogers, 1975; Cook & Flay, 1978).

Several later propaganda theories should also be mentioned here. One is Berlo's Hypodermic needle theory that is additionally at times referred to, after Schramm (1982), as the Silver Bullet Model. This theory espouses the notion that the mass media are so powerful that they can inject messages into an audience who then fall down as if hit by a bullet. Bullet theories therefore argue that subjects cannot resist the mass mediated manipulation because of its innate appeal. In essence, it is an acknowledgement that media messages can produce phenomenal change and essentially get us to do whatever they wish. Because of its fatalistic view, media theorists have never widely embraced this as a theory per se, and it has been relegated more or less to the level of folk belief. Nonetheless, often when an unusually grotesque crime occurs, politicians and the general public will center debate on the excessive sex and violence found in the mass media. Appeals for greater control of media and its output then typically ensue. Folk theory or not, this serves as a good example of how individuals are motivated by a truly stunning media event.

This research often suggests that media has a powerful and direct effect on the public. The magic bullet or hypodermic needle theory is a fairly basic stimulus-response approach to media influence. Because of its latent assumptions and subsequent fears that audiences were helpless when faced with media campaigns, this audience was at the mercy of the mass media. Later theories tended to focus directly on individuals such as opinion leaders, who reinforced the status quo.

Social context became significant in work by Klapper (1949, 1960). He proposed a model of so-called limited effects where social relationships proved more influential than direct psychological influences. According to Klapper, this constituted the environment in which an individual lives as well as relationships to the groups to which she or he belongs. In such a context, attention is directed to items the individual finds interesting, and this then leads to reinterpretations of messages vis-à-vis one's held attitudes, experiences, and knowledge.

Since 1967, George Gerbner has been involved in research on the impact of media, particularly the long-term effects of television violence. His Cultural Indicators project (Gerbner & Gross, 1976a, 1976b; Gerbner, Gross, Morgan & Signorelli, 1986). Concerned with tracing ways the mass media depicts the U.S. cultural environment, has been a study of more than 3,000 television programs and 35,000 characters. His research has demonstrated that individuals grow up with an unprecedented diet of violence that has severe consequences. This "mean world syndrome" as he calls it, reinforces the worst fears and apprehensions and paranoia of people. Gerbner concludes that those who consume greater levels of television tend to believe the violence portrayed on television is normal and that it is a good and effective way to solve problems. He further believes that heavy exposure to television desensitizes viewers, and they lose the ability to understand the consequence of violence, as well as the ability to empathize, to resist, and to protest its occurrences. Finally, Gerbner argues that the result of heavy television viewing is a pervasive sense of insecurity and vulnerability that results in individuals who are more likely to be afraid to go out on the street in their communities, especially at night. They fear strangers and meeting other people and lose the ability to be kind to strangers.

Gerbner's research offers a twist on the traditional propaganda perspective. Propaganda customarily was attributed to state players or at least those working for government entities. With Gerbner, we have a media industry, part of the much larger transnational industry structure, crafting its messages for the maximization of profits and industry control. Gerbner argues that transnationalism or big business is extremely powerful and spreads its clout internationally by attempting to homogenize culture through its Western dominated film and television programming (Gerbner, Mowlana & Schiller, 1996; Gerbner, 2001). More recently, Gerbner has been critical of both sex and violence in our media (2001).

Noam Chomsky along with Edward Herman (Herman and Chomsky, 1988) make comparable arguments but, instead of sex and violence, argue that certain media entities "propagandize on behalf of, the powerful societal interests that control and finance them" (p. xi). They refer to the elite media, arguing that the other outlets simply follow their lead. The entire process where media accepts the government framework and supports its policies is one they call "media subservience."

Here and elsewhere (Chomsky, 1994; Herman & Chomsky, 1988), Chomsky argues that U.S. media's ultimate purpose is to divert public attention away from important political issues. This is done through media programming that places a high priority on promoting essentially mindless entertainment. Chomsky thus acknowledges an even greater role of the political–military–economic complex, suggesting its real goal is to marginalize the citizenry in national dialogues and decision making. He further fuels this argument by going back to positions expressed by some of the country's founding fathers: John Jay, for one. Unconscious participation in support of the system may involve activities by stakeholders who are just trying to preserve the institution that they work in and embrace. This is typical behavior in an institution or organization. Conscious participation involves more direct forms of collusion between industry and governance. Chomsky considers U.S. media responsible at various levels, including what he considers to be the press's poor record when covering world issues.

When Chomsky discusses media's control of issues as well as its news flow record, he incorporates ideas commonly associated with both the gatekeeping theory of news (McCombs & Shaw, 1972) and agenda setting (White, 1950). Gatekeeping refers to decisions concerning which stories are covered by the media, which are not, and ultimately who makes the decisions for inclusion or exclusion. It acknowledges that news organizations constantly filter news events and determine which stories are appropriate for their given audiences. Agenda setting acknowledges that issues become a part of the public agenda and that their importance is essentially ranked when covered by the media as to perceived importance. The top story in a news broadcast or front page positioning, as indicated by being placed above the fold or at top of the program, are ways the media assigns importance. In other words, agenda setting tells us what we as viewers should "think about." Issue awareness is only possible, obviously, when issues are covered, and this loops matters back to the realization that gatekeeping is a pervasive force of power brokering by the news industry.

Gerbner and Chomsky each embrace a modified version of the hypodermic model or magic bullet theory. Nonetheless, unlike the earlier research, both Gerbner and Chomsky argue that such effects may be combated through greater awareness and public activism. Under such perspective, the media industry or the larger political–military–economic complex is only effective when individuals fail to be aware of the system and attempt to do nothing about it. Progressivism is the key to combating potential effects as citizens take back their society through proactive behavior. This research generally embodies the principles of civil society that relate to the writings of Locke (1728), Rousseau (1755, 1985), and Mill (1860, 1862), as well as more contemporary thoughts on social empowerment and communication by Habermas (1970, 1979, 1984, 1987, 1989), Foucault (1988), and Giddens (1981, 1984, 1987, 1990).

WARTIME PROPAGANDA

In support of a nation's wartime effort, the use of propaganda was fairly simple. According to Lasswell (1927, reprint 1938), propaganda was important to (1) mobilize hatred of the enemy; (2) preserve friendship of allies; (3) procure the cooperation of neutral nations, if possible; and (4) demoralize the enemy. In

Propaganda Technique in the World War (1927), Lasswell closely analyzed propaganda campaigns used by Central and Allied powers during the First World War. The blatant use of propaganda had become widely practiced by World War II, with many countries, including Germany, Japan, Great Britain, the United States, and Australia, producing extremely effective documentary films promoting national agendas.

The highly nationalistic and persuasive documentaries and newsreels by German filmmakers, like *Die Deutsche Wochenscha* (*The German Weekly Newsreel*), the anti-Semitic *Der Ewige Jude* (*Eternal Jew*) (1940) directed by Fritz Hippler, the *Marsch zum Fuhrer* (*March with the Fuhrer*) (1938, 1940) on the Hitler Youth movement, and *Fuehrer schenkt den Juden eine Stadt* (*The Fuehrer Gives a City to the Jews*) (1944), that attempted to portray Jews as well-treated in German concentration camps, are examples of the Nazi propaganda effort.

One of the most frightening of these films was Leni Riefenstahl's *Triumph des Willens* (*Triumph of the Will*) (1934), the official record of the Nuremberg Party Rally of 1934, as well as her much more subtle *Olympia: The Festival of Beauty* (1936–1938), a very artistic portrait of the Berlin Olympics. Whether her films were of Nazi Rallies or the Berlin Olympiad, she always provided skillfully crafted films glorifying Hitler and Germany.

In response, some of the United States' best film directors, such as Frank Capra, John Huston, John Ford, William Wyler, John Sturges, Walt Disney, Chuck Jones, Theodor Geisel (Dr. Seuss), and others, joined the war effort for their country. Capra's *Why we Fight* series (1943–1945) were poignant films that helped spread propaganda for the allied effort. Great Britain and others also produced highly effective documentaries and entertainment films during the period.

Among the titles found in United States–produced films of the period were Bugs Bunny in *You're a Sap, Mr. Jap* (1942) and *Bugs Bunny Nips the Nips* (1944). Other titles included *Daffy the Commando* (1943) and *Fifth Column Mouse* (1943), all by Warner Brothers' Chuck Jones. Walt Disney's *Donald Gets Drafted* (1942), *Private Pluto* (1943), and *Commando Duck* (1944) are other titles produced for the war. Among the live action films were *Japanese Relocation* (1943), the official U.S. documentary that played down the internment of some 110,000 Japanese, mostly U.S. citizens; and Otto Brower and John Ford's *Sex Hygiene* (1942) and *Pickup* (1944), titles that warned military personnel about the dangers of venereal diseases.

These titles were often produced for screening to U.S. troops. Most soldiers were not well versed on public affairs and were therefore perceived to be in need of attitude and motivation change. Hence, a film such as *Jap Zero* (1943), starring Ronald Reagan, proved very popular and effective. The films were also directed to the general public, and these addressed the need to accept sacrifices of consumer goods such as nylons and tires, when raw materials were needed for the war machine. Furthermore, civilians, particularly women, were encouraged to join the war effort. One cartoon had Bugs Bunny singing in *Any Bonds Today?* (1942), and live-action dramas included *You, John Jones!* (1944) that starred James Cagney, Ann Sothern, and Margaret O'Brien in a promotion for homefront patriotism and duty. Many other Hollywood stars, such as Lucille Ball, Henry

Ford, George Reeves, Lionel Barrymore, Walter Brennan, Katharine Hepburn, Bing Crosby, Bob Hope, Alan Ladd, Barbara Stanwyck, Humphrey Bogart, and track star Jesse Owens, were recruited for the campaign. World War II marked a true sophistication in psychological warfare.

The Second World War was the last time we saw such a strong public consensus in the United States for a national war effort. Researchers such as Carl Hovland's Yale University team (Hovland, Janis, & Kelley, 1953; Janis, 1967) spent vast time and energy studying the mass media campaign, particularly as directed to soldiers. The research found marked gains in transmission of factual material, although a lesser impact on attitudinal and motivational levels. The focus of the research activities was largely based on interests in the medium's power of mass persuasion rather than any considerations for larger audience ramifications.

STRATEGIES OF A PROPAGANDA CAMPAIGN

The year 1937 saw the creation of the Institute for Propaganda, performing analysis headed by Edward Filence and designed to educate Americans about propaganda techniques, particularly the dangers and pervasiveness of political propaganda. While the Institute released a series of books, *The Fine Art of Propaganda,* edited by Alfred McClung Lee and Elizabeth Briant Lee (1939), was perhaps most influential. While there are many techniques of propaganda, the book identified seven frequently found devices, or "tricks of the trade." These seven common "devices" were so artfully articulated that they are taught in schools and used in communication textbooks to this day. The seven instruments in the "ABCs of propaganda analyses" are *name calling, glittering generality, transfer, testimonial, plain folks, card staking,* and the *band wagon effect.* We review these seven concepts here.

Name Calling

Name calling involves the use of labels to project an idea in a favorable or unfavorable light. The latter is likely the scenario most recognize, however. Its purpose is also to discourage individuals from examining substantive evidence on an issue.

One frequent use of name calling comes when stereotyping is employed to paint a negative image of the opposition or enemy. The intent may be to suggest major political or ideological differences, real or imagined. Name calling employs emotional reactions and encourages the public to draw hasty conclusions with only a cursory examination of issues.

Individuals, ethnicities, and national groups have often been disparagingly labeled. In modern society, many examples abound. During the Cold War, Ronald Reagan called the Soviet Union an "Evil Empire." In the course of recent Gulf Wars, President Bush labeled Saddam Hussein another Hitler, and Hussein painted the United States as the "Great Satan." Several countries were named as members of the "Axis of Evil." In other conflicts, the enemy has been called "Commie," "Gooks," "subversive," "Pinko," and "Red." Today the opposition are often labeled "terrorists." In fact, when launching the Crusades in 1095, Pope Urban II is said to have referred to the Muslim nation as "despised," an "accursed race," "unclean nations," and one people that worship demons (Sardar & Davies, 2002, p. 147). Whether in conventional or terrorist war, or simply a war of words, painting the opposition in a derogatory manner provides vast power.

In 1951, the new democratically elected president Arbenz of Guatemala announced a program for land reform by returning large tracts to the people. One large landholder was the U.S.-owned United Fruit Company (UFA) (known as United Brands since 1975) that stood to lose a portion of land it never developed. This land was valued at $525,000 in its own tax statements, but UFA insisted it be paid $16 million. UFA flooded media with their version of the facts and data and began circulating a report that Guatemalan activities were "Moscow-directed." UFA also arranged for trips for U.S. journalists and lobbied members of Congress. Using UFA vessels and facilities, the CIA was sent to overthrow the legitimately elected government. A violent civil war ensued, and the situation remains problematic to the present day, claiming more than 100,000 lives since it began. Furthermore, right-winged repression continues, along with gross imbalances in national wealth (McCann, 1976).

Recently we saw another orchestration of public opinion. This time it came in the days just prior to the U.S.-led Allied involvement during the First Persian Gulf War. Soon after Iraq invaded Kuwait, the PR firm Hill & Knowlton was hired, with funding almost exclusively coming from the Kuwaiti government (MacArthur, 1992; Pratt, 1994). The agency was charged with helping to improve Kuwait's image in the United States. An existing image at the time was that young Kuwaitis had fled to Cairo and were dancing away in its discos (Kunczik, 1997). The firm organized a variety of media interviews and other information programs to counter the image of a mass exodus (Trento, 1992). The most controversial story, though, involved a report that Iraqi soldiers were going into Kuwaiti hospitals and throwing babies onto the floors to die as they took the incubators back to Baghdad. President George H. W. Bush even referenced this allegation in a speech. Hill & Knowlton orchestrated testimony of an alleged 15-year-old Kuwaiti girl, Nayirah, relaying the incidents. Testimony took place before an October 1990 U.S. Congressional Human Right's Caucus hearing, and media, including ABC's *Nightline,* were persuaded to run the story. In retrospect, it was discovered that Congress and audiences were never told that the girl, who said she volunteered at al-Addan hospital and witnessed the atrocities, was in fact the Kuwaiti ambassador's daughter and was living in Washington at the time of the alleged incidents. Because Nayirah's surname was withheld, supposedly to protect her family back in Kuwait, Nayirah's whereabouts were never questioned and collaboration was not sought. In defense of the interview, Hill & Knowlton responded that the testimony was true in substance and that the use of Nayirah as a witness was stylistic in nature. The firm Hill & Knowlton had been previously associated with defending human rights records in Turkey and Indonesia.

As noted, the name-calling spin may be positive or negative. Yitzhak Shamir was a guerrilla fighter against the British and was dubbed a Freedom Fighter in Israel. He later became Israeli Prime Minister. Likewise, Northern Ireland's Gerry Adams was labeled a terrorist by the British and Unionists but later was named leader of the Republican arm party, Sinn Féin, and he became a lead negotiator in Ulster peace talks. Throughout history, name calling has often been used as a one-sided attempt to dismiss the opposition on the basis of emotionally laden but logically unsound arguments.

Glittering Generality

The tendency to associate an issue or image with a noble or virtuous term is known as a *glittering generality*.

This use of vague terms, typically with high moral connotations, is the key to the glittering generality. The device is intended to arouse both faith and respect in listeners or readers. The exact meanings of these glittering terms as presented are literally impossible to define, hence the vagueness of the generalities.

When former President George H. W. Bush announced his "new world order," he was using a glittering generality. The difficulty was that there was never great clarity of exactly what the world order was. John Steinbruner (1991) likened the Bush-inspired new world order to Voltaire's sarcastic remarks on the "Holy Roman Empire," "neither holy, nor Roman, nor an empire" (p. 20). The best Bush could do was the following:

> What is at stake ... is a big idea—a new world order, where diverse nations are drawn together in common cause to achieve the universal aspirations of mankind: peace and security, freedom, and the rule of law. Such is a world worthy of our struggle, and worthy of our children's future ...
>
> The world can therefore seize this opportunity to fulfill the long-held promise of a new world order—where brutality will go unrewarded, and aggression will meet collective resistance. (George H. W. Bush, State of the Union address, January 29, 1991)

The difficulty is that his new world order evolved into nothing more than a euphemism for political supremacy, where issues of democracy and human rights have gone largely ignored. In recent years, the make-up of a new world order appears to have meant that certain nations and people were at the top, while a system of second-class societies and economies was still perpetuated. The so-called "new world order" advocated by the president and promoted by late-20th-century United States, Western, and even United Nations policies failed to provide many answers that were initially expected of the staggering label. In the post–Cold War era, a new world order is essentially a world system largely led by the one remaining superpower.

The terms *freedom* and *democracy* are also examples of this propaganda approach and in fact are cited in the same Bush address.

For two centuries, America has served the world as an inspiring example
of freedom and democracy. For generations, America has led
the struggle to preserve and extend the blessings of liberty. And today,
in a rapidly changing world, American leadership is indispensable.
Americans know that leadership brings burdens, and requires sacrifice.
(George H. W. Bush, State of the Union address, January 29, 1991)

As has been noted elsewhere, one person's freedom may very well be
another person's idea of slavery. Consider that even in the United States, freedom
is not always the same. The liklihood of criminal imprisonment and harsher penal
sentences is much greater for the lower classes, as the more affluent can afford
effective legal defenses. We also see a decline of personal freedoms in the post-
9/11 United States, particularly for those of Arab descent. In the post-9/11
environment, many were glad to sacrifice long-held human and personal rights
in favor of promises for greater security and safety. The question remains,
however, as to whether the risks were ever real or were simply manufactured
rhetorically by political leaders seeking other objectives.

Robert Gates, Deputy National Security Advisor during the First Gulf War,
has confirmed that when it was time to end that short battle and announce a
cease-fire, General Schwarzkopf requested the decision to end the war be
extended several hours in order to allow for the label, the "hundred-hour
war." The reported purpose was so that it might play better on American
television. Furthermore, intentional or not, Israel launched a memorable military
activity in 1967 that is labeled the "Six Day War" after increasing terrorist attacks
by Syria over the Golan Heights and the armies of Egypt, Jordan, Syria, and
Lebanon were poised at Israel's borders, directing their sights on Sinai. While the
Israeli victory was quite a surprise to the world community and thus holds
meaning, the brief encounter in Iraq has seemingly much less meaning, given
the grossly outmatched opposition encountered by the United States.

Finally, Gerbner (1996, 2000) has pointed out that certain communication
industry terms, such as *broadband,* or the Clinton–Gore campaign promoting the
construction of an *information superhighway,* are in themselves all meaningless
terms. The debate around them, argues Gerbner, essentially hides the content
standardization campaign that industry or government leaders wish to assert over
the public's communication channels.

We would add the most unfortunate term, *collateral-damage,* that came out of
the Vietnam War and has the effect of playing down, even eradicating, the
terrible notion that innocent civilians are injured and killed as a result of being
in the general area of an attack or because our weapons systems and "smart
bombs" are not as sophisticated as we may pretend. The use of *collateral damage* is
at times likely used as a way of circumventing issues of misdirected attacks where
weapons totally miss their intended mark.

Both of the Gerbner-cited terms, *broadband* and *information super highway,* plus
smart bombs and *collateral damage,* are examples of glittering generalities. Such
generalities tend to be accepted placebos by the communicators, the media,
and the audience. These short yet captivating phrases reduce matters to systematic

maneuvers, thus creating a level of comfort and audience acceptance of information. They can be a powerful tool by maintaining a semblance of valid information flow.

These generalities present information with minimal details camouflaging contentious ideas and possibly distorting facts. These may be used too by people who seek to muzzle freedoms and democratic governance.

Image Transfer

When one takes the power, respect, or good reputation bestowed on an existing entity or concept, and then attempts to share these positive qualities through association with a product, individual/group, or position/program, the perpetrator is hoping to benefit through the phenomenon known as *image transfer*.

In transference, the use of images is the key. The cross seen in Christian churches is omnipresent and immediately symbolizes Christianity along with the many teachings and the power of the church. The use of the cartoon character Uncle Sam represents a consensus of public opinion by Americans. Both symbols stir emotions. Immediately one thinks of a complexity of feelings we have with respect to church or nation.

One example of transference involved an internationally renowned professional golfer and a heart surgeon. During the 1970s, South African leaders wished to boost their international image and to combat effects of apartheid. Several public relations firms were employed for the task. One result was that Dr. Christian Barnard was used as a go-between in a labor dispute between South Africa and the American AFL-CIO. Barnard argued for compassion, and his presence is attributed as having led to a solution to the problem via new South African business opportunities. And, during the same period, golfer Gary Player was asked to write letters to U.S. corporate executives concerning declining interest in continued investments in South Africa. Player wrote to Bank of America, McDonnell Douglas, and Union Carbide offering corporate officers a week with him in South Africa. The notion of playing golf with Player was attractive. Player, in turn, was compensated for the time he wasn't on the pro golf tour. While both Barnard and Player were critical of apartheid, they allowed themselves to be used in their country's propaganda campaign.

Another area where transference often takes place is in advertising. At the global level, product country of origin often affects image. This is the case with U.S. cultural products today. For motion pictures, television programs, rock music, and fashion, American-style has become somewhat of a fascination among young people worldwide and dominates many cultural and commercial trends.

We saw criticism against the United States, however, as cultural hegemony was being threatened by this global spread of culture. The sheer dominance and glamour associated with U.S. images are often too much to handle as countries see their national traditions falling prey. Countries such as Egypt had long fought the entry of MTV into their marketplace but acquiesced in an attempt to avoid isolationism. Yet, it is the fear of encroachment by U.S. culture that is one of the principal reasons for Middle Eastern hatred of the West today.

Concern about transborder data flow is not limited to Arab countries, of course. The French have long fought to keep the English language out of their culture by banning many English words. *Cookie* was one of those words banned. Frankly, the term *chocolate chip biscuit* does not convey the same image for many, even though this was the required term in France when a specialty bakeshop was to be established in Paris over a decade ago.

This is one reason that French farmers have targeted McDonald's restaurants when they protested U.S. trade policies in recent years. The protesters feared Western economic policies would jeopardize their agrarian livelihoods.

Historically, U.S. products such as Coca-Cola, IBM computers, and Ford cars have been quite successful in Japan. Throughout the world, English has become the dominant business language and controls some 65–80 percent of the world's Internet content. We can see the anger levied toward largely American, almost always Western, transnational corporations and in the Western-led International Monetary Fund (IMF) and World Bank protests staged in Mexico, Switzerland, Britain, Australia, Canada, New Zealand, Taiwan, South Korea, Norway, and the Czech Republic, and at the World Trade Organization (WTO) meeting in Seattle in late 1999. The corporate symbols of these huge transnationals have been transformed into cultural icons and represent more than just the commercial products they were originally designed to promote. They represent the Occident or West, and everything that is good or bad about it. In some ways, corporate image building was so good and so effective that these corporate symbols now represent something far beyond the original intent. Consequently, image transfer may not always serve the purposes of the marketer. While good reputation is the goal of marketers and public relations pundits, unintended negative associations may evolve almost by accident.

Testimonial

A *testimonial* is when a distinguished or recognized but highly unpopular person is used to cast a product, individual/group, or position/program in either a positive or negative light.

On March 14, 2002, accompanied by U2 rock musician Bono, President George W. Bush relied on success testimonials to support his development aid campaign in a speech delivered to the Inter-American Development Bank. Bush cited recent economic development successes in Mozambique, Uganda, and Bangladesh to support his plan to provide increased relief efforts to countries that embraced his standards of just rule, investing in people, and encouraging economic freedom. He went on to acknowledge that "successful development also requires citizens who are literate, who are healthy, and prepared, and able to work." He also promised that the United States would increase development assistance by $5 billion in its new Millennium Challenge Account. In this global development and self-investment address, Bush cited data he says demonstrates that a dollar of foreign aid attracts two dollars of private investment. While embracing free-market objectives that some have challenged as not universally appropriate, the speech was an inspiring one that showed new levels of international concern from the U.S. administration. The argument certainly acquired greater power through the use of Bono's testimonial.

In another incident, this time a CNN interview with George H. W. Bush on relations with the Soviets following the fall of the Berlin Wall, the senior Bush acknowledged that the administration had

> . . . tried hard to co-operate . . . to understand the pressures
> on Gorbachev and not stick our fingers in Gorbachev's eye . . . Who knows
> how they would have *had* to react. And we didn't do that. And there were
> a lot of examples where we tried to understand his position, tried to be
> restrained, probably as good an example was the Baltic states we never
> recognized in the U.S., the Soviet occupation or the takeover of the Baltic
> states . . . this wasn't that all problems weren't behind us, and surely they
> weren't all behind us in terms of arms control and exactly how we
> negotiated cuts in conventional forces, nuclear wet forces. But having
> said all that I think it was a breakthrough (Bush, 1999, March 28).

Hence, the administration's foreign policy approach with the Soviets is spun quite favorably and the White House appears to have been very wise in retrospect.

Going back to U2 and Bono, recently the controversial Department of Defense and Iraq War architect, Paul Wolfowitz, became the White House nominee for World Bank president. Once again, Bono was sought for endorsement to defuse some criticism of the candidate. Not only was the earlier Bush affiliation with Bono an example of the use of image transfer, as noted earlier, but it also enters into the realm of testimonial by association. In Wolfowitz's case, the Americans were trying to defuse criticisms against the nominee, particularly those emanating from Europe.

Worldwide, we often see images of politicians and government officials visiting sites of battle or memorials to war victims. U.S. officials, including the president, sometimes made surprise visits to troops in Iraq. Likewise, British Prime Minister Margaret Thatcher visited the Falklands Islands in January 1983, in the aftermath of that war. For Thatcher, the 1982 war attributed to a dramatic change in her political image, leading to a landslide victory in the 1983 elections and eight additional years in office. When Prince Charles visited the region in March 1999, he was photographed placing a wreath at the 2nd Parachute Regiment memorial in Goose Green, the East Falklands. Besides serving official duties expected of public office holders, officials also benefit through association with wartime events and memories, particularly the gallantry and sacrifice that others gave in support of a national cause.

To further exemplify testimonial usage, we turn to advertising, where celebrity affiliations may be arranged. Business activities benefit from arranged ties with personalities, events, or venues. In 1996, the first television commercial shot in outer space featured Pepsi in the MIR space station. In 2000, a space launch featured the new Pizza Hut logo. Furthermore, popular music is often used as background narrative for broadcast commercials. As promotions company Entertainment Marketing Communications International (EMCI) (2005) advises: "Stand next to a celebrity, event or lifestyle property to help accomplish corporate or brand marketing objectives."

As we so often see, the use of personal experience, whether resulting in success or failure, is often used to lend credibility in campaigns.

Plain Folks

The use of *plain folks* comes in when a communicator wishes to convince others that they or their ideas are good or valid since they are similar to everyone else, just everyday ordinary people.

In recent U.S. presidential elections, various candidates have run on the "regular guy" or "plain folk" image. John Kerry was often labeled an elite in his election bid against George W. Bush. It is somewhat ironic when the highest elected office in the land resorts to bashing of opponents who are painted as too well educated or having too high a business or political stature.

Jimmy Carter, the former peanut farmer, often wore blue jeans in the Oval Office. He also ran as a Washington outsider, undamaged by the Watergate scandal, further reinforcing his everyman appeal. Yet Carter's outsider position also presented problems for him once he was in office. This happened despite his many accomplishments, particularly on the international front. It was during the Clinton candidacy that the regular folk image was truly manipulated. Bill Clinton's penchant for cheeseburgers, Big Macs, and French fries was a positive for him when it came to public-image building. Even George W. Bush was quite successful with his bus trips into the American heartland, stopping to eat pancake breakfasts and chatting with the electorate, although admission to the latter events was normally controlled and participants hand-picked. Comparable examples are found in other countries.

As Bush once pronounced, "I am not an imperial president." Yet political leaders with regular-guy images must still demonstrate the ability to achieve, particularly in the international domain. This sometimes produces problems for elected officials.

This regular-guy approach may also work when it comes to crafting a positive image with a country's military personnel stationed abroad. Such was the case for recent leaders such as Ronald Reagan and the two Bush presidents. The junior Bush used the technique when he arranged his "Mission Accomplished" photo-op by landing in a Navy S-3B Viking jet on the aircraft carrier *USS Lincoln* as it returned from Iraqi duty on May 1, 2003. The image sought was that of a commander in chief fully in control. When Mike Dukakis attempted a photo-op riding in an Army tank in 1988, during his campaign against the senior Bush, the similar attempt backfired. John Kerry also was not very successful when he was seen wearing a camouflage jacket and carrying a 12-gauge shotgun while goose hunting during his 2004 Ohio campaign. Vice President Dick Cheney quipped that the Second Amendment (right to bear arms) was more than just a photo opportunity. The regular-guy approach then does not always give a distinct advantage.

In Britain, Prince Andrew served as a helicopter pilot aboard the *HMS Invincible* during the 1982 Falklands War. Pictures of him helped fuel the image of the British royal family and their involvement in the country's military affairs, just as did photos of Prince Charles training as a Royal Navy pilot in September 1971, where he followed in the footsteps of his father, grandfather, and both great-grandfathers. Additionally, images of Fidel Castro, Yasser Arafat, Yitzhak Shamir, Gerry Adams, and others as freedom fighters earlier in their careers certainly helped fuel political aspirations years later.

Despite the success of George W. Bush as a regular-guy at home, his difficulty with Europe's leaders may in part be a result of low image credibility. We saw such fallout in October 2004 when citizens of 8 out of 10 nations (Russia and Israel not included) were reported to prefer Kerry to Bush, according to a poll initiated by Canada's Quebec-based *La Presse* newspaper (Travis, 2004). Even Prime Minister Tony Blair's strong support for Bush did not translate into an endorsement of the U.S. leader in Great Britain. This was the case despite the more than $1 billion annually that the administration was spending to improve its international image, according to a September 14, 2003 article in *USA Today* (Weiser, 2003). A Globescan-PIPA poll conducted at the University of Maryland found that international citizens with higher education and income levels felt more negatively about Bush and U.S. influence in general in late 2004 (Kull & Miller, 2004; BBC, 2005). Bush's strong moral character honed at home was not as effective on the international stage, where many expressed displeasure with his poor stance on the environment and military coalition building.

Card Staking

Card Stacking occurs when a presentation uses a selection of facts and distortions, elucidations and confusions, and both logical and illogical statements. Put another way, the propagandist stacks cards against the truth. It is also the most difficult to detect, for not all information has been provided, through distortion or omission, for the audience to make an informed decision.

The "Big Lie" was a label used to characterize disinformation campaigns in Nazi Germany. Adolf Hitler was known to espouse this approach when attributing Germany's First World War loss to Jewish influence on the media:

> From time immemorial, however, the Jews have known better than any others how falsehood and calumny can be exploited. Is not their very existence founded on one great lie, namely, that they are a religious community, whereas in reality they are a race? (Hitler, 1923, 1971. *Mein Kampf,* p. 134)

Statements such as this were used to generate hatred of Jews that later fed support of genocide. Plus, while never verified, it was Joseph Goebbels, Hitler's minister of propaganda, who has been credited with having said that if a lie is repeated enough times, it would become widely accepted as truth.

A more contemporary case also involves the activities of Germany in World War II, this time as promoted by British writer David Irving. Irving considers himself a historian, and he challenges the very existence of a Holocaust (Libstadt, 1993; *Irving v. Penguin Books,* 1996; Charny, 2001). He concludes that it is nothing more than "an ill-fitting legend." While Irving acknowledges that many

Jews died, he claims they were not killed in gas chambers under direct orders from Hitler. Irving contends the killings were no different than any other atrocious deed we would find in war. Deborah Lipstadt (1993) counters that while familiar with historical evidence, Irving "bends it until it conforms with his ideological leanings and political agenda" (p. 47). Richard Evans (2002), Cambridge professor of modern history, goes on to add that Irving's work is fraught with deep duplicity in treatment of historical sources and that his misuse of these sources results in mistakes that appear to be calculated and deliberate.

In recent years, we have seen similar distorions of truth in U.S. foreign policy issues. In one such case, the Bush administration asked news networks to refrain from playing tapes from Al-Qaeda and Osama bin Laden yet could not supply direct evidence as to why it would be harmful. Instead the justifications were vague and amounted to card stacking, as we see in the following briefing by Condoleezza Rice:

> [L]et me just say that I think the networks have been very responsible in the way that they have dealt with this—my message to them was that it's not up to me to judge news value of something like this, but it is to say that there's a national security concern about an unedited, 15- or 20-minute spew of anti-American hatred that ends in a call to go out and kill Americans. And I think that that was fully understood. We are still concerned about whether there might be some signaling in here, but I don't have anything more for you on that yet. (October 15, 2001)

This use of suppression of opposing points of view clearly falls under the heading of card stacking. Furthermore, consider that the media were regularly provided with information on weapons of mass destruction (WMD), the "Axis of Evil," and suicide bombers. It therefore is not difficult to understand how Americans may widely conclude that all Arabic and Muslim people are likely terrorists. Such selective omission forms the basis of U.S. stereotypes against all Arabics. We consequently see racial stereotyping or profiling at airports, or for that matter at any public gathering place. During many special events, law enforcement officials have increased their surveillance, and charges that Muslims are being singled out are common. Stereotypes clearly have been perpetuated by a marked absence of news showing Arabs in a favorable light. Therefore, by implying that an opponent is evil or guilty of reprehensible acts, the emphasis has shifted to an emotional one, and reasonable discussion has been curtailed.

Bandwagon Approach

The *bandwagon approach* involves utilization of a notion that "Everybody is doing it," or "We are all doing it," so that group members are encouraged to just join or follow the crowd.

In post-9/11 United States, it became difficult for anyone to speak out against U.S. foreign policy generally or the Bush administration specifically. To not support the administration's war on terror was likened to nonpatriotism, even though many aspects of the Homeland Security legislation and its ultimate implementation were blows to civil rights for both citizens and visitors. Racial profiling was just one of the practices used by law enforcement officials as thousands were unjustly detained or imprisoned. The country paid a major price in areas of personal freedom and expression when it sacrificed many long-fought battles for civil liberties.

To assert that everyone must join the fight against terrorism is a clear bandwagon technique. So too were the criticisms levied against lawmakers who failed to support the administration as it entered a war based on the presupposition that weapons of mass destruction were being held by the Iraqis. In fact, it now appears that Iraq may have been in general compliance with UN sanctions.

"You're either with us or against us" is the battle cry often heard in times of national crisis when criticism of the status quo is being discouraged. Such was the mentality when war protesters against the Vietnam War were faced with the criticism, "America, love it or leave it" during the 1960s and 1970s. Another slogan based on strong feelings of nationalism is "My country, right or wrong." Such a reaction denies the very foundations upon which the republic had been established. British journalist G. K. Chesterton (1902) observed " 'My country, right or wrong' is a thing no patriot would ever think of saying except in a desperate case. It is like saying 'My mother, drunk or sober.' " While we all would want our motherlands to remain free, open, and beyond reproach, it is the ability to withstand doubt that may be the greatest test of its freedoms (Loory, 2004).

The slogan "Four out of five dentists use this toothpaste" is a form of bandwagoning. Bandwagoning also appeals mostly to those who are "joiners"; they join "because everyone else is." Additional examples are the profuse use of flags, "support our troops" bumper stickers, or magnetic pro-troop and anticancer ribbons that people place on their automobiles. These and similar campaigns appeal for individuals to join the groundswell of public opinion and activity on the rationale that "everybody else is joining." The methods are not really scrutinized, and winning is thought to be everything. The bandwagon technique additionally appeals to sentiments of loyalty and nationalism.

MODERN USE OF PROPAGANDA

The propaganda landscape has become much more complicated today. The long-running Cold War was often central to activities as we saw governmental efforts to produce propaganda continue in the aftermath of the Second World War. Let us look at some domestic media campaigns from the period.

In one short postwar production, *The House I Live In* (1945), actor Frank Sinatra sings the title song and talks with street kids in an effort to address racism and anti-Semitism. Other social guidance films sought to educate the postwar population in areas of social education. Among these was *Ask Me, Don't Tell Me* (American Friends Service Committee, 1961), about the lives of San Francisco youth gangs and how work projects might serve as a preventative measure for juvenile delinquency. Other films sought to council teenagers in areas of daily life, including *Contents: Cheating* (1952), where John gets Mary into trouble when he tricks her into giving him Algebra test answers. *How Much Affection?* (1958) considers the limits of affection when teens are going steady, and when and how to say "no" to drinking, smoking, and petting. Another film, *Measure of a Man* (1962), specifically addresses how to avoid social pressures and avoid being lured into a drink of that "demon beer."

We saw political sentiments such as anti-Communism addressed by a variety of films, some of which are considered quite humorous in present-day context. Among these was *Red Nightmare* (1962), an account of what might happen if Communists gained access to a typical small American town. The film starred Jack Webb and included an enactment of how a "typical" American would respond if his wife, children, and friends rejected him for a Communist lifestyle: The film portrayed a mock exercise where a local police chief pretended to be a Communist official and shut down the local media. In another film, *The Truth About Communism* (1962), Ronald Reagan hosts and narrates a heavily skewed account on the development of the Communist movement and its then-present state of operations. Other titles include R. G. Springsteen's *Red Menace* (1949); George V. Allen's *Yankee Go Home: Communist Propaganda* (1950); and the four-film series, *You Can Beat the A-Bomb* (1950); *One Plane, One Bomb* (1954); *Warning Red* (1956); and *The House in the Middle* (1954).

These concerns spread to other domestic situations as seen in the film *Communists on Campus* (1970) that warns against student protest activities on campuses, including activities of Students for a Democratic Society (SDS), the Black Panthers, and student protestors against the Vietnam War. Another film produced by the United States Department of Defense, *Why Vietnam?* (1965), attempts to explain U.S. policy on South Vietnam through an address by President Lyndon B. Johnson and remarks by Secretary of State Dean Rusk and Secretary of Defense Robert McNamara.

The youth counterculture was addressed in *The Hippie Temptation* (1967), a lifestyle study of Haight-Ashbury district (San Francisco) hippies narrated by Harry Reasoner. The film purports to examine the reasons why youths become hippies and their dependence on drugs, particularly experimentations with LSD. Another film, *Reefer Madness* (1936), is today often cited as a very one-sided and highly inaccurate antimarijuana film.

While there are many more genres, one particular interest is the gay-agenda group with documentaries offering opinions on gay rights and how gay men and lesbians live lifestyles that may damage American culture, including its moral values and civil liberties. One of these, *Gay Rights, Special Rights: Inside the Homosexual Agenda* (1993), a Southern Baptist Convention production, includes testimonials by "recovered" gay men and lesbians who have renounced the gay lifestyle and become Christians. All of these represent subtle or sometimes not-so-subtle forays in propaganda.

On the world scene, parties have sought to employ various media channels to present their messages and viewpoints. Just as with the many social issues just described, these too are often not balanced in terms of viewpoint, and little, if any, attempt may be made to engage in objectivity of message delivery. As a result, both print and electronic media have been employed to deliver messages to individuals and nations on a plethora of social and political issues. And just as the United States engages in public diplomacy campaigns, we must assume that many, if not most, of these international efforts often reflect similar inaccuracies found in their domestic information sharing methods. Whether labeled truthful propaganda, public diplomacy, or something else, the legitimacy of such messages rests in the eye of the beholder or, in this case, message sender.

Put a different way, we note that the history of documentary film and video is peppered with questions of realism and degree of manipulation by the documentarian. This goes back to the early days of newsreels and such early film classics as Robert Flaherty's work—*Nanook of the North* (1922), *Man of Aran* (1934), *Louisiana Story* (1948)—that has been heavily criticized for the manipulation of reality. Newsreels such as *March of Time* had long used actors to recreate assorted news events, and rarely was such footage identified as a recreation. So, when the outcry came during the summer of 2004 regarding the Michael Moore documentary film, *Fahrenheit 9/11,* some were surprised when critics challenged the motion picture for its editorial stance against George W. Bush and the war in Iraq. There is no wide agreement among scholars that objectivity ever has been considered a prerequisite for documentaries. Others charge that Western consumer and industry pressures on the U.S. news media often encourage news reporting to seek tight but limited narrative structures and a format that favors entertainment value over adequate information sharing.

Thus, when Ted Koppel was criticized for airing names of U.S. military killed in Iraq or when the Voice of America was criticized for running an interview with the Taliban's Mullah Mohammed Omar, these should just be considered tests of a system and its ability to embrace its constitutionally guaranteed freedoms of expression. Russian television repression of videos showing its country's missiles misfiring, moreover, was not an admirable act of journalism. While potential government embarrassment is one reason Vladimir Putin argued for further controls over television news, given recent Chechnyan events, it is exactly such coverage that lends credibility to the journalistic process and upholds the surveillance or watchdog function of the mass media. That is to say that such press coverage, while potentially uncomfortable for certain government leaders, is also a way to ensure oversight over these same democratically elected officials. The events should not be misread as disloyalty. They are in fact the highest form of patriotism.

As a result, the very foundations of a fair and objective press may be in question for most of our mainstream media at the most basic levels. Within such a milieu, it may be more appropriate to question the objectives of Western journalism rather than the presence or absence of bias in a particular documentary film title.

TERRORISM AS PROPAGANDA

Governments continue to be major users of propaganda in the delivery of messages, but another player has emerged that has found propaganda quite effective for its campaigns and as a tool in public opinion formation. This category of propaganda is known as *terrorism*. When engaged in by governments, we normally call it state terrorism. When the message emanates from a non-governmental group, it is called nonstate terrorism. Today, nonstate terrorism is carried out by a collection of social and political players and propaganda as a channel for alternative diplomacy. Sometimes, smaller state actors may become involved but normally in clandestine ways. The players at the forefront are almost always nonstate entities that feel terrorism is an effective way to counter better-equipped state or multinational industry interests. This, in reality, is a continuation of the old North-South communication impasse where entities of the developing world see or believe that industrialized countries and their interests are unwilling to dialogue. The players need not be located in the developing world, however, for groups located in the industrialized world also may feel disenfranchised and sometimes resort to acts of terrorism. While we would hope that all alienated groups, regardless of their global location, would choose nonviolent means to express their differences or displeasures, we must acknowledge that the number of groups and individuals who condone violent propaganda campaigns appears to be on the rise. In this case, these propagandists resort to terrorism to place both military and civilian populations at risk because of what they perceive or rationalize as a potentially more effective means to achieve certain gains. This behavior is typically justified by a higher political and/or social purpose.

As noted earlier in this chapter, parties have sought to employ various media channels to present their messages and viewpoints. Newspapers; newsletters; audio and videocassettes; films; posters, handbills, and flyers; bumper stickers; tee shirts; and even political pin backs and buttons have been used to oppose actions, distribute messages, and sway public opinion. For years, a very effective form of antiestablishment communication was the labor union newsletter and newspaper. During the Berkley free speech period of the 1950s and 1960s, underground newspapers were quite popular. At times, unfortunately, groups have taken to more violent actions in order to publicize an agenda and convince the status quo to reconsider its position or actions. Guerilla warfare and sometimes terrorism were in fact a twist on conventional military tactics used by American colonists when fighting the British almost two and a half centuries ago. Nevertheless, guerilla warfare normally targets a conventional military force or operations. Terrorists often target nonmilitary populations, activities, and infrastructures.

Sometimes a bona fide military uprising may be called an act of terrorism. Clearly, the rebels found in the early American Colonies saw themselves as freedom fighters, whereas the British perceived them as something akin to irritating terrorists. This can be definitely said of the "Indians" involved in the Boston Tea Party. As noted earlier, "One man's terrorist is another man's freedom fighter." As Rourke (1999) has observed:

> It is easy to condemn such [terrorist] activities when countries or groups
> with which you disapprove conduct them. What about assassination
> and other such actions by a country with which you may have
> sympathy? . . . Those who question the legitimacy of such acts [Reagan's
> strike against Qaddafi and Clinton's strikes in Somalia and Afghanistan]

argue that what constitutes terrorism is often in the eye of the beholder and, in this case, killing civilians with a bomb dropped on a building by a warplane is no different than killing civilians by planting a bomb in a building. (pp. 346–47)

The term *terrorism* first entered into European languages after the French revolution of 1789. In early years, it was largely through violence that French governments tried to impose a radical new order on a suspicious and reluctant public. Consequently, from the very beginning, we find that terrorism was acknowledged as a form of control that could be imposed by a dictatorial government against its own subjects.

In the 19th century, the term *terrorism* became associated with nongovernmental movements. One group of Russian revolutionaries of Narodnaya Volya (the people's will), in 1878–1881, believed in the targeted killing of "leaders of oppression," specifically Tsarist Russia. They assassinated Tsar Alexander II on March 13, 1881, believing such an attack would serve as a catalyst to a revolution. For many years, terrorism continued mostly through the assassination of leaders, such as the killing of Austrian Archduke Ferdinand by a 19-year-old Bosnian Serb student in Sarajevo on June 28,1914.

In the 20th century, terrorism expanded beyond assassination of political leaders and heads of state. European colonial powers saw pressure to withdraw from colonies, such as that which happened in Ireland. The Easter Rebellion on Easter Monday, April 24, 1916, marked the uprising of Irish nationalists against the British. Some 16 men were executed by the British immediately or soon after the rebellion. Sinn Féin became the dominant political party in Ireland, worked the parliamentary election in 1918, and pushed for cutting ties with Great Britain. They also sought to end the separatist movement in Northern Ireland and establish an Irish republic. Turmoil continued until January 1919, when the Sinn Féin party assembled in Dublin as the Dáil Éireann, or national assembly, and proclaimed themselves independent. The Anglo-Irish Treaty of 1921 gave independence to 26 Irish counties yet allowed 6 largely Protestant counties the option of remaining part of Great Britain. The 6 Northern counties were referred to as Ulster. Greater instability was seen in Ulster from the 1960s onward. The violent sabotage of a peaceful civil rights march in 1968 by the Royal Ulster Constabulary (RUC) marked the beginning of the so-called "troubles." The British sent troops to Derry and Belfast in August 1969. Viewed as a tool of the Protestant majority, the Irish Republican Army (IRA) resurfaced and began to attack both British and Protestants interests. In response, London withdrew the North's parliamentary independence, although a 1985 agreement allowed Dublin to become involved as a consultant. Northern Ireland and Britain both have seen a continuation of killings. Although catastrophic terrorist events abated for a few years following those that occurred in the United States on September 11, 2001, recently, acts of terrorism have reccurred in Ulster, indicating "the troubles" are not over.

Another form of terrorism evolved as indigenous populations began looking for leverage in their support for leadership claims in emerging post-colonial states. In one case, Malaya (now Malaysia) saw a terrorism campaign launched by

Communists in 1948, but this failed due to continuity of British military opposition as well as an organized program stressing political reform for cultivating a climate of political independence. After the withdrawal of European control, terrorism continued in many places, personified in the killing of police and local officials, aircraft hijackings, hostage taking, and bombings. Causes championed by terrorists rested on revolutionary socialism and nationalism as well as religion.

A number of airplane hijackings occurred from 1968 onward, often ending in the explosion of the aircraft after landing at Middle East destinations. In February 1970, three terrorists attacked El Al passengers in an airport transit bus traveling from the airport terminal to the aircraft in Munich, Germany. In May 1972, three members of the radical Japanese Red Army (JRA) group arrived on an Air France flight and then used automatic weapons in the arrival lounge, killing 26 people at the Tel Aviv Airport. Earlier hijackings focused on the Israeli-Palestine issue, and in September 1972, 11 Israelis were killed in a Palestinian attack on Israeli athletes at the Olympic Games in Munich, Germany. Public horror intensified. In other incidents, in December 1973, 5 Palestinian terrorists began shooting in the terminal lounge at the Rome Airport, killing 2; captured an American Airlines plane; killed all 29 people aboard; herded additional hostages into a Lufthansa jetliner; killed an Italian customs policeman and a hostage; and were later flown to an unknown destination after releasing their remaining hostages in Kuwait. In December 1985, 4 terrorists entered the check-in area of El Al, TWA, and Panama at Rome's Leonardo da Vinci Airport, began firing with submachine guns, and threw grenades. Eleven people were killed and 70 injured. The same month at Vienna's Schwechat Airport, 3 terrorists attacked waiting passengers at the El Al lounge with machine guns and hand grenades, killing 2 and injuring 47. Some airport incidents also occurred in the United States. Terrorism was not limited to airports either. In 1985, 4 Palestinians hijacked the Italian cruise ship *Achille Lauro* as it traveled with over 400 passengers and crew, including 19 Americans, in waters off Egypt. The hijackers demanded that Israel free Palestinian prisoners. After a two-day siege, the hijackers surrendered in exchange for a pledge of safe passage. An Egyptian jet tried to fly the hijackers to freedom, but U.S. Navy F-14 fighters intercepted the plane and forced it to land in Sicily, where the Palestinians were taken into custody. Egypt's President Hosni Mubarak decorated the EgyptAir 737 pilot and demanded an apology from the United States, which President Reagan refused to do. Later, thanks to U.S. pressure, the United Nations General Assembly scrapped a proposal to invite Yasser Arafat to speak at the UN's 40th-anniversary celebration. Arafat had condoned the hijacking of the *Achille Lauro* and accused Reagan of an "act of piracy" by intercepting the EgyptAir 737. Then, in 1981, some 52 American hostages held at the U.S. embassy in Tehran for more than 14 months were released. The ordeal began in November 1979, when a group of radical Iranian students, angered by U.S. support for the Shah, stormed the American embassy in Tehran. They had backing of the Iranian government, led by Ayatollah Khomeini. It is important to note that in many of these incidents, other countries were known to support terrorist activities but typically maintained an air of public deniability.

Terrorism continued in the Middle East as a way to battle Israeli occupation of the West Bank and Gaza. The Israelis often resorted to heavyhanded attacks on Palestinian interests that they claimed were necessary, but this then further fueled Palestinian acts of terrorism. The United States has been historically supportive of the Israeli position, but many other countries, including most Middle East neighbors, have been quite critical. At the moment, Israel continues to defend its position of aggression, even when not carried out in direct retaliation toward Palestinian terrorist events. Conversely, the high levels of Palestinian terrorism that were first seen in the late 1960s and 1970s again surfaced in 2001 and continue unabated, although the return of the Gaza Strip and West Bank to Palestinian control in late 2005 may become an important step in ultimately resolving the conflict.

The close of the 20th century saw a new form of religious/cultural-based terrorism emerge under the direction of Osama bin Laden. The Arab-born freedom fighter, who had once been trained by the United States for battle against the Soviets in Afghanistan, became leader of a fairly small Islamic group known as Al-Qaeda (The Base). Al-Qaeda Muslim extremism provided an interpretation of Islam that arguably rationalized the killing of military, government officials, and civilians. Targets generally became those the group saw as oppressive Western forces seeking to dominate Muslim countries, particularly those in the Middle East. Al-Qaeda is credited with killing hundreds in bombings of American embassies in Africa in August 1998, the attack on the USS Cole in October 2000, and the widespread damage inflicted on the World Trade Center and Pentagon on September 11, 2001. Observers have noted that since Al-Qaeda's intensions are hazy and seek catastrophic damages, there is little room for compromise or negotiations. The group's objectives appear to be for total compliance with their demands for a full-scale Western withdrawal, and their ultimate power rests in the unpredictable nature of attacks. In many ways, fear has become a much greater weapon than the attacks themselves.

Elsewhere, we have seen terrorism as part of numerous international conflicts and incidents. In 1995, members of Aum Shinrikyo, a Japanese cult based on a combination of Hindu and Buddhist thought and obsessed with an apocalyptic agenda, released deadly sarin nerve gas in the Tokyo subway system. Twelve people were killed and some 5,000 people hospitalized during the Monday morning rush-hour attack. Sarin is a highly toxic nerve agent developed by the Nazis in the 1930s. Sarin gas is said to be 500 times more toxic than cyanide.

Radical Muslim terrorists have surfaced in other countries. From 1969 to today, Muslim rebel groups in the Southern Philippines have been seeking autonomy from the mostly Christian Philippines. One rebel group, the Abu Sayaf Group, is believed to be linked specifically to Osama bin-Laden's Al-Qaeda. Another group, the Communist New People's Army (along with the rival Alex Boncayao Brigade [ABB]); seeks to overthrow the Philippine government and wishes to install a Marxist-type rule. In recent years, the Indonesian island of Sulawesi has seen violence between Muslims and Christians. Activity increased in 2001, when thousands of fundamentalist Muslim militia members called Laskar Jihad, from the island of Java, joined the fight.

In other terrorist uprisings, we find that since 1958, the Basque Fatherland and Liberty rebel group (ETA) has fought an urban guerrilla battle against the Spanish government. The ETA is fighting for independence of the Basque region of northern Spain and southwestern France. Some 800 deaths have been attributed to the terror campaign to date.

Elsewhere, the Islamic Salvation Front won the Algerian national elections in 1992, but this was voided by the military. This resulted in a bloody rebellion by the military wing, the Islamic Salvation Army (AIS). The fighting has been particularly harsh on journalists: Some 60 have been assassinated since the start of the conflict. While the AIS surrendered in June 1999, other groups continue to battle the government.

In Kashmir, a land divided between India and Pakistan, border clashes have continued since 1991 and have threatened several times to become full-fledged war. Kashmiri terrorists attacked the Indian Parliament in December 2001. Security forces killed the militants before they could enter the Parliament building. The result was a violent confrontation along the line of control (LOC) in Kashmir between Indian and Pakistani armies. Both countries are considered to be nuclear powers, thereby raising the stakes of any ensuing conflict.

In Sudan, on the other hand, we have seen a backlash against a government dominated by Muslin Arabs, a war that has swelled largely on racial, religious, and regional differences. War has been levied against the government, as the country's southern portion is still predominantly black Christian.

And, while Russia had seen a variety of terrorist operations, today it faces increasingly visible terrorism from the Chechnya guerilla war resistance. Chechnya is located in the mountainous Caucasus region and has long lacked favor from the Russian leadership. Among the resistance are a small number of Islamist militants who hail from outside Chechnya and reportedly may have links to Al-Qaeda. In rhetorical retaliation, Russia attempts to paint a picture that all Chechens are Islamist terrorists, thereby justifying harsh retaliatory measures placed on the Chechen resistance. Tens of thousands of Chechens and Russians have already been killed or wounded in the two Chechen wars. Among the recent Chechen terrorist attacks was an October 2002 attack on a Moscow theater, where some 700 people were taken hostage. A highly criticized commando raid by Russian special forces using a gas to incapacitate the terrorists left over 120 hostages and terrorists dead. One of the most radical of the Chechen terrorist leaders, Shamil Basayev, took credit for the attack. Prior to the Moscow theater attack, some 41 people, including many children, were killed in a bomb blast during a military parade in May 2002 in the southwestern town of Kaspiisk. Two separate Moscow incidents, the 1999 bombings of a shopping arcade and apartment building, left 64 dead. In August 2004, two separate Russian airline flights (Tu-134 and Tu-154) exploded minutes apart, and it was later found that two Chechnyan women roommates boarded the separate flights and are believed to have been responsible. Ninety people aboard the two aircraft were killed, and traces of the explosive Hexogen were found in both wreckages. Then, to the horror of the world, more than 1,200 hostages were taken in a school in the southern Russian city of Belsan. More than 335 hostages and 30 attackers were killed, and 700-plus were wounded. Not a single Chechen was found among the dead gunmen, according to Sergei Ivanov, Russia's defense minister. Fueling the case for state terrorism, the Strasbourg-based European court of human rights found Moscow guilty of killing Chechnyan civilians.

Perhaps the most troubling aspects of terrorism—as it is now widely practiced—is a belief that a few acts of violence, often against symbolic targets, will prove highly persuasive and that the trend to attack innocent civilians will underline the incompetence of the government and political leaders. Sometimes this is indeed true. As Rourke (1999) counters:

> However, much one may condemn the acts themselves, it is also
> accurate to say that over the years Palestinian terrorists almost certainly
> played a role in increasing the willingness of Israel to deal with them,
> in enhancing the global awareness of and concern with the Palestinian
> cause, and in bringing pressure on Israel by the international community
> to reach an agreement with them. (p. 350)

We have seen that in some societies, terrorism may become part of the culture and actually stands in the way of continuing development efforts (Roberts, 2002).

While the notion that the United States is a rogue state that shares in the blame may be highly offensive to many Americans, what we really must do is look beyond our emotions and examine tactics used. The narcissistic cyclical application of patriotism and terrorism has initiated and perseverated problems globally.

There appears to be little debate over whether the treatment of Afghani prisoners at Guantanamo Bay, Cuba, involves questionable and abusive practices. Rather than address the charges, the Untied States chooses to argue the technicalities of the internment and whether terrorists are covered by international laws on the treatment of war prisoners. A similar situation exists in the so-called "administrative arrests" carried out, without the opportunity of trial, by Israel against many Palestinians during the past decade or two. In addition, Chinese attempts to quell uprisings by Muslim separatists in the western Xinjiang region is yet another example of potential state terrorism. While some may see all of these groups as freedom fighters, each respective government justifies its actions by labeling those groups as rebels or criminals. Even as criminals, these detainees are often denied certain basic rights, further complicating issues.

Bodies such as the European Union and United Nations have drafted statements and policies defining terrorism. They agree that terrorism is a deliberate act by an individual or group against a country, its institutions, or its people. The intent is to damage its economic, political, and social configurations. Under such a rubric, terrorism is that which is directed against countries. Other uses are conveniently sidestepped.

We have already acknowledged that when governments are the aggressors, this is called state terrorism. So, terrorism may emanate both from state and nonstate players. It appears to come down to how an event is spun and who is doing the spinning.

Throughout the ages, governments have indeed participated in terrorist acts, although at the time they may not have been considered as such. The German air blitz on London and the resulting U.S. and British bombing of German cities are just two examples of the use of terror to demoralize citizens. The Allied attack on Dresden, an art and cultural center with almost no military importance, serves as a key example of state terrorism. As insinuated previously, most Western definitions of terrorism make no attempt to address such actions, nor do they separate attacks on civilians versus military/security targets.

Regardless of the final outcome of current world struggles, serious questions are being raised. It ultimately may rest on which side prevails and who writes the histories. But public sentiment in the meantime will be influenced by rhetoric, and there is little debate that all sides are trying to influence world opinion. Since status quo nations generally have greater access to the traditional media, groups that perceive themselves as marginalized may continue to seek to employ non-traditional form of persuasion. For this reason, incidents of terrorism have been increasing in recent years and will likely continue as long as it appears to be a viable option and most terrorists are never captured.

ADDRESSING TERRORISM

During the U.S. occupation in the post-Iraqi war, beginning in 2003, the world has been horrified by media images such as kidnapped British aid worker Margaret Hussein, a convert to Islam; and the beheading of U.S. construction worker Nick Berg. Are these acts of terrorism? Of course they are. Is it propaganda? Absolutely.

As already suggested, another way to frame these events is as strategic, perhaps desperate, attempts to sway public opinion. Even President Bush conceded during a December 20, 2004 press conference, "Car bombs are effective propaganda tools." Likewise, the terrorists involved in planning and carrying out the attacks of 9/11 undoubtedly counted on the extensive playtime on televisions and presence on the front pages of newspapers worldwide.

Terrorists have long relied on media coverage in response to their gruesome deeds. It is through such coverage that these acts gain enormous power. Recognizing this power, the British government long ago made it illegal for any broadcaster to air interviews with IRA members or their families.

The greatest problem we appear to face today is the continuing spread of terrorism and the perception that it is an effective substitute for traditional diplomacy. Terrorism has become endemic in particular countries and regions, and the United States has become one of the biggest, if not the largest, target. According to a Rand study, the number of terrorist acts worldwide have been increasing because (1) some terrorists believe attention is becoming harder to obtain, (2) past experience has proved profitable, (3) states have been taking an active role, (4) it has been motivated by religious imperatives, and (5) the ease of access to information has lead to increased attempts by amateur terrorists (Hoffman, 1999).

Since there are common factors, it ought to be possible to define and put a stop to terrorism. In the 1960s, the UN General Assembly embarked on such a mission. Initially little progress was made, in part because some states saw terrorism as a response to legitimate grievances, thereby believing terrorism might be justified. The Jewish extremist group Irgun and its 1940s campaign in Palestine, the Viet Cong activities in South Vietnam from the late 1950s to the mid-1970s, and the Provisional IRA in Northern Ireland from the late 1960s onward were all cited as valid terrorist campaigns.

The UN emphasis, consequently, was on limited practical measures. International conventions from 1963 to 1999 addressed specific terrorist acts, such as aircraft hijacking and diplomatic hostage taking, and drew policies so that these were specifically condemned. As terrorism concerns escalated, the UN General Assembly took further steps to define and outlaw such acts.

The newer view of terrorism as mass murder has had marked effects on the debate. Terrorism, after all, targets civilian populations as opposed to the historical notion of war in which armies just fight other armies. In justification of modern trends, many terrorists argue that civilians share in the guilt of their governments by complicity. Taking the Middle East as example, terrorists believe attacks on both Israeli soldiers and innocent civilians are justified as necessary because indigenous people are fighting to free their land. Hamas argues that those Jews who settled on Palestine territory share in the guilt. While many would not accept the argument, it nonetheless serves to demonstrate the complexity of issues and the difficulty in bringing an end to the conflict. As noted, however, recent Gaza Strip and West Bank pullouts are a recent admirable gesture.

Nonetheless, the events of 9/11 brought strong international condemnation and have markedly changed the debate. Thus, when the United States proposed a military response to Taliban forces amassed in Afghanistan, none of the 189 member states voted in opposition.

At the global level, we see changing sentiments as countries previously said to harbor terrorists have begun working with Western governments to bring terrorism under control. The Sudanese government, for example, which previously offered a haven for Al-Qaeda, has increased cooperation with the U.S. intelligence community. Jordan and Egypt have tightened controls, increased security, and are detaining Islamic militants. Jordan has been specifically restricting activities by Hamas and the Islamic Jihad.

Al-Qaeda has also been increasingly linked to terrorist activities around the world. The Philippines has engaged more aggressively with militant Islamic groups, and this includes the Abu Sayyaf, believed to have close Al-Qaeda ties. The group is further thought to be involved in attacks against U.S. forces in Mogadishu, Somalia, an operation that began as support of safe passage of humanitarian aid. Forces were pressed into combat with Somali warlord, General Mohammad Farah Aideed, whose operations are believed to have been planned by a chief military strategist of Al-Qaeda. With Al-Qaeda links also rumored in the Chechnyan fight against Russia, plus attacks on civilian railroad commuters that killed 200 people in Madrid, Spain, critics have become more vocal and sentiment against terrorism appears to be on the rise. In fact, it is believed that terrorists led by Al-Qaeda have plotted terrorist actions against several countries, including Britain, France, Germany, Iraq, and Italy, as well as the Spanish and

Russian incidents. Other Al-Qaeda operations in Jordan, Israel, and the United States reportedly have been thwarted.

Al-Qaeda may suffer from its own success. Its ability to launch terror strikes may now be limited. Yet, through the use of modern communication media, bin Laden has reached a level of influence that few countries have ever been able to achieve. This demonstrates the power of the so-called "fear factor," for if bin Laden never commits another terrorist act, the world will continue to fear his actions. Even if he is ultimately captured, his power continues through sleeper cell activity that may have been set in motion years ago. The 9/11 attacks were planned for six years; the 1998 attacks on U.S. embassies in Africa for five.

The real solution to terrorism is to address the heart of the problem: global inequities and the imbalance of power. While other terrorist groups will undoubtedly emerge, the likelihood of this occurring might diminish if we turn our attention to the promotion of equitable governance policies and eradicating poverty, improving health care resources, increasing access to communication technologies, and providing people worldwide with the opportunity to decide their own futures through participatory governance. Africa, for example, is considered a potential breeding ground for fundamentalism. The rise of Al-Qaeda cells in Kenya, Somalia, and Ethiopia, among others, provides further evidence that terrorism often follows when living conditions are perceived as deplorable and injustices prevail. If poverty and inequality provide a climate for terrorism to develop, then addressing these basic human needs may be essential to finding a solution to the escalating wave of terrorism. Otherwise, we may see the spread of atrocious and savage terrorism that shows no respect for human life. Terrorism is a form of propaganda. Sowing good will may be an even stronger weapon in bringing terrorism to an end.

CONCLUSIONS

Propaganda is a long-established communication technique employed for public opinion manipulation. It has been in use for centuries and affects communication both domestically and abroad. Advances in communication technologies have made propaganda even more pervasive today.

Government leaders, to mold public opinion on international issues in domestic circles or to influence matters abroad, often use propaganda. It also has been used by nongovernmental entities seeking to access global communication channels for the purpose of public opinion formation or manipulation.

Not only governments, or those attempting to sway opinion making of governments, use propaganda, but public relations practitioners who may serve as agents of these parties use it as well. In modern times, these public relations campaigns have become more complicated under the rubric of public diplomacy as governments make efforts to sway public opinion through less obvious and sometimes coercive techniques of opinion "management." Advertising, too, is a form of opinion manipulation, and while this falls outside our discussions on propaganda per se, its many methods are ultimately linked to the larger body of knowledge employed by the propagandist.

We have seen how the notion of propaganda has evolved, from its origins during the 17th century to the 20th century, when the power of contemporary media was recognized and governments began to tap its potential for public manipulation and control. War efforts were a natural setting for propaganda campaigns, which expanded as other government information programs sought to influence public opinion for higher national purposes. One of the concerns is how far government or societal leaders may go in utilizing the schemes of media persuasion in efforts to mold public opinion. This may be particularly the case when some of their campaigns or policies may not be considered in the best interests of the public at large, as has been hinted at recently in propaganda campaigns at both domestic and international levels.

Of further concern are issues raised by contemporary theorists George Gerbner and Noam Chomsky. Gerbner argues that market forces vying for our media attention are molding a dangerous climate of insecurity and vulnerability from the "scary world" depictions found in U.S. media. Chomsky proposes that media propagandize on behalf of powerful societal interests, which control and finance them. Each of these authors demonstrates the dangers of big media, as operators of many communication channels in the modern world. These modern stimulus-response approaches to media influence reinforce earlier work by Berlo (1960) and Schramm (1963) posit that subjects cannot resist the mass-mediated manipulation because of its innate appeal.

Communication has become more sophisticated. When we consider the words of Lippmann that "the public must be put in its place," we acknowledge the rather cynical side of propaganda and the fine line between its constructive uses versus its many abuses. It is telling that international terrorists seek access to many of the same communication channels that governments have traditionally sought for opinion manipulation. Some outside the societal mainstream have created catastrophic crimes against humanity and then used the media to fashion their own messages of rebellion and disorder. Marginalized groups likely will continue to seek out such nontraditional forms of persuasion, as they feel disenfranchised by mainstream global governance processes and our social and economic institutions.

As we have argued, a solution to terrorism may rest in our willingness to address global inequities and international power imbalances. Terrorism may diminish if we turn our attention to equitable governance policies and eradicating poverty, improving health care resources, increasing access to communication technologies, and providing people worldwide with an opportunity to decide their own futures through participatory governance.

It also would serve us well if we all engaged in more-straightforward communication with our global neighbors. Deceitful communication renders little respect once discovered. A much more solid foundation results when communication is built on a bedrock of honesty and mutual respect.

Propaganda may further benefit from increased public discussion on its nature and abuses, and how mass opinion exploitation may work against the very goals of a democracy and the freedoms of choice and expression it espouses. Just as we discuss the implementation of various economic, social, and political policies in our countries today, so too might we expand these discussions into areas of political and corporate control of media, and the use of public funds to intentionally mislead individuals at both domestic and international levels. A true democratic system involves active participation by its many members. Using communication media to manipulate or marginalize public involvement goes against the very keystone upon which a democracy is constructed.

Along with the need for greater awareness and dialogue comes a corresponding responsibility for our media to become more aggressive and look to lead, not follow, our governments and their actions. Government and institutional surveillance is one of the basic functions that media provides in our modern societies. The failure to perform such watchdog activities is an embarrassment to us all. If our republics are truly solid, then they should be able to withstand the scrutiny of criticism. Questioning our institutions and leaders is not unpatriotic but rather our duty in a democratic system. Without such accountability, we all suffer. A civil society cannot exist when its elected officials succeed in marginalizing citizens and restricting participation.

For more information on the topics that appear in this chapter, use the password that came free with this book to access InfoTrac College Edition. Use the following words as keyterms and subject searches: disinformation, propaganda, public opinion, public manipulation, political persuasion, public relations, advertising, public diplomacy, propaganda techniques, modern propaganda, international conflicts, national identity, image and perception.

QUESTIONS FOR DISCUSSION

1. How do Magic Bullet theories influence propaganda theory? How do Magic Bullet theories conceptualize the mass media audience? Are Magic Bullet theories irrelevant today?

2. Can you name the seven different approaches outlined in the Institute for Propaganda's ABCs of propaganda strategies? Which do you think are the most dangerous?

3. How is it that the modern theories of Gerbner and Chomsky are considered propaganda theories?

4. Name several ways in which our media have failed us by propagating propaganda, and what might they do to begin to reverse such trends?

5. Taking what you now know about propaganda, name some recent events that would be considered propaganda on the domestic or international level.

REFERENCES

BBC World Service Poll. (2005, January 19). *In 18 of 21 countries polled, most see Bush's reelection as negative for world security.* Washington, DC: Program on International Policy Attitudes (PIPA) and Globescan. ·

Berlo, D. K. (1960). *The process of communication: An introduction to theory and practice.* New York: Holt, Rinehart, & Winston.

Bernays, E. L. (1923). *Crystallizing public opinion.* New York: Liveright Publishing Corporation.

Bernays, E. L. (1928). *Propaganda.* New York: Liveright Publishing Corporation.

Bush, G., (U.S. President (1991, January 29). *State of the union address.* United States of America, The White House.

Bush, G. H. W. (1999, March 28). Interview: The wall comes down. In *CNN cold war series,* National Security Archives, George Washington University. Retrieved April 1, 2005, from http://www.gwu.edu/~nsarchiv/

Charny, I. W. (2001, July 17). The psychological satisfaction of denials of the holocaust on other genocides by non-extremists or bigots, and even by known scholars, *IDEA: A Journal of Social Issues, 6*(1). Retrieved April 1, 2005, from http://www.ideajournal.com/articles.php?id=27

Chesterton, G. K. (1902). *The defendant* (2nd ed.). London: R. Brimpley Johnson, Project Gutenberg EBook (EBook #12245). Retrieved September 10, 2005.

Chomsky, N. (1994). *World orders, old and new.* London: Pluto Press.

Cook, T. D., & Flay, B. R. (1978). The persistence of experimentally induced attitude change. In L. Berkowitz (Ed.), *Advances in experimental social psychology* (vol. 3, pp. 166–224). New York: Academic Press.

Dewey, J. (1928, December 5). Impressions of Soviet Russia. *The New Republic,* pp. 65–66. Reprinted in Dewey, J. (1929). *Impressions of Soviet Russia and the revolutionary world.* New York: New Republic. Retrieved September 10, 2005, from http://www.geocities.com/deweytextsonline/isr.htm

Doob, L. W. (1948). *Public opinion and propaganda.* New York: H. Holt.

Eggerton, J. (2005, March 20). DOD's big flack attack. *Broadcasting & Cable.* Retrieved September 12, 2005, from http://www.citizensforethics.org/press/pressclip.php?view=127

Entertainment Marketing Communications International (EMCI). (2005). Corporate World Wide Web site. Retrieved April 1, 2005, from http://www.emcionline.com/

Evans, R. (2002). *Lying about Hitler: History, holocaust and the David Irving trial.* New York: Basic Books.

Ewen, S. (1976). *Captains of consciousness: Advertising and the social roots of the consumer culture.* Toronto: McGraw Hill.

Faison, E. W. (1961). Effectiveness on one-sided and two-sided mass communication in advertising. *Public Opinion Quarterly, 25,* 68–69.

Foucault, M. (1988). Technologies of the self. In L. Martin, H. Gutman, & P. Hutton (Eds.), *Technologies for the self: A seminar with Michel Foucault* (pp. 16–49). Amherst: University of Massachusetts Press.

Gerbner, G. (1996). *Invisible crises.* Boulder, CO: Westview Press.

Gerbner, G. (2000). *The future of media: Digital democracy or more corporate control?* New York: Seven Stories Press.

Gerbner, G. (2001, April 3). Lecture, *Telling all the stories: Media, markets and mayhem.* Carbondale: Southern Illinois University.

Gerbner, G., & Gross, L. (1976a). Living with television: The violence profile. *Journal of communication, 26,* 172–199.

Gerbner, G., & Gross, L. (1976b). The scary world of TV's heavy viewer. *Psychology today, 10*(4), 41–89.

Gerbner, G., Gross, L., Morgan, M., & Signorelli, N. (1986). Living with television: The dynamics of the cultivation process. In J. Bryant & D. Zillman (Eds.), *Perspectives on media effects* (pp. 17–41). Hillsdale, NJ: Lawrence Erlbaum Associates.

Gerbner, G., Mowlana, H., & Schiller, H. I. (1996). *Invisible crises: What conglomerate control of media means for America and the world.* Boulder, CO: Westview Press.

Giddens, A. (1981). *A contemporary critique of historical materialism, vol. 1: Power, property and the state.* London: Macmillan.

Giddens, A. (1984). *The constitution of society: Outline of the theory of structuration.* Berkeley: University of California Press.

Giddens, A. (1987). Structuralism, post-structuralism and the production of culture. In A. Giddens & J. Turner (Eds.), *Social theory today* (pp. 73–108). Cambridge, MA: Polity Press.

Giddens, A. (1990). *The consequences of modernity.* Stanford, CA: Stanford University Press.

Habermas, J. (1970). Toward a theory of communicative competence. In H. P. Dreitzel (Ed.), *Recent sociology No. 2* (pp. 114–148). New York: Macmillan.

Habermas, J. (1979). *Communication and the evolution of society.* Boston: Beacon Press.

Habermas, J. (1984). *The theory of communicative action, vol. 1: Reason and the rationalization of society.* London: Heinemann.

Habermas, J. (1987). *The theory of communicative action, vol. 2: Life-world and system: A critique of functionalist reason.* Cambridge, MA: Polity.

Habermas, J. (1989). *The structural transformation of the public sphere: An inquiry into a category of bourgeois society.* Cambridge, MA: The MIT Press.

Hegel, G. W. F. (1821, 1991). *The philosophy of right.* Reprint: *Elements of the Philosophy of Right,* A. W. Wood (Ed.), H. B. Nisbet (trans). Cambridge: Cambridge University Press.

Herman, E. S., & Chomsky, N. (1988). *Manufacturing consent: The political economy of the mass media.* Pantheon: New York.

Hitler, A. (1923, reprint 1971). *Mein kampf* (R. Manheim, Trans.). Boston: Houghton Mifflin.

Hoffman, B. (1999). *Countering the new terrorism, chapter two: Terrorism trends and prospects.* Santa Monica, CA: Rand, Policy Resources for Congress series.

Hovland, C. I., Janis, I. L., & Kelley, H. H. (1953). *Communication and persuasion: Psychological studies of opinion.* New Haven, CT: Yale University Press.

Hovland, C. I., Lumsdaine, A. A., & Sheffield, F. D. (1949). *Experiments on mass communication: Studies of social psychology in World War II.* Ann Arbor, MI: Association for Consumer Research.

Irving v. Penguin Books & Lipstadt (1996). 1996-1-III3. London: Queen's Division Bench.

Janis, I. (1967). Effects of fear arousal on attitude change: Recent developments in theory and experimental research. In L. Berkowitz (Ed.), *Advances in experimental social psychology* (vol. 3, pp. 166–224). New York: Academic Press.

Klapper, J. (1949). *The effects of mass media.* New York: Bureau of Applied Social Research.

Klapper, J. (1960). *The effects of mass communication.* Glencoe, NY: The Free Press.

Kull, S., & Miller, D. (2004, September 8). *Global public opinion on the U.S. presidential election and U.S. foreign policy.* Washington, DC: Program on International Policy Attitudes (PIPA) and Globescan.

Kunczik, M. (1997). *Images of nations and international public relations.* Mahwah, NJ: Lawrence Erlbaum Associates.

Kurtz, H. (2005, January 26). Writer backing Bush plan had gotten federal contract. *Washington Post,* p. C01.

Lasswell, H. D. (1927; reprint 1938). *Propaganda technique in the World War.* New York: Peter Smith; London: Broadway House.

Lasswell, H. D. (1941). *Democracy through public opinion.* Menasha, WI: George Banta Publishing Co. and Chi Omega Fraternity.

Lee, A. M., & Lee, E. B. (Eds.). (1939). *The fine art of propaganda: A study of Father Coughlin's speeches.* New York: Harcourt Brace and Company.

Linebarger, P. M. A. (1948). *Psychological warfare.* Washington, DC: Infantry Journal Press.

Lippmann, W. (1922). *Public opinion.* New York: Harcourt Brace and Company.

Lippmann, W. (1925). *The phantom public.* New York: Harcourt Brace and Company.

Lippmann, W. (1927). *Public opinion.* New York: MacMillan.

Lipstadt, D. E. (1993). *Denying the Holocaust: The growing assault on truth and memory.* New York: The Free Press.

Locke, J. (1728, 1988). *Two treatises of government* (5th ed.). London: Printed for A. Bettesworth in Pater-Noster-Row, J. Pemberton in Fleetstreet, and E. Symon in Cornhill. Reprint: Cambridge: Cambridge University Press.

Loory, S. H. (2004). My country, right or wrong. *Global Journalist Magazine,* No. 2. Retrieved January 19, 2005, from http://www.globaljournalist.org/2004-2/final-word.html

Lumsdaine, A. A., & Janis, I. L. (1953). Resistance to "counterpropaganda" produced by one-sided and two-sided "propaganda" presentations. *Public Opinion Quarterly, 17,* 311.

MacArthur, J. R. (1992). *Second front: Censorship and propaganda in the Gulf War.* Berkeley, CA: University of California Press.

McCann, T. (1976). *An American company: The tragedy of United Fruit.* New York: Crown.

McCombs, M., & Shaw, D. L. (1972). The agenda-setting function of mass media. *Public Opinion Quarterly, 36,* 176–187.

Melville, H. (1857, 1967). *The confidence man.* Indianapolis, IND: Bobbs-Merrill.

Mill, J. S. (1860, 1909). *On liberty.* Reprint: Harvard Classics, Volume 25, P. F. Collier & Son.

Mill, J. S. (1862). *Considerations on representative government.* New York: Harper & Brothers, Publishers, Franklin Square.

Pratt, C. B. (1994). Hill & Knowlton's two ethical dilemmas. *Public Relations Review, 20*(3): 277–295.

Roberts, A. (2002, Spring). Counter-terrorism, armed force and the laws of war. *Survival (Quarterly Journal of IISS), 44*(1), 7–32.

Rogers, R. W. (1975). A protection motivation theory of fear appeals and attitude change. *Journal of Psychology, 91,* 93–114.

Rourke, J. T. (1999). *International politics on the world stage* (7th ed.). New York: McGraw-Hill.

Rousseau, J.-J. (1755, 1909). *Discourse on the origin of inequality among mankind and is it authorized by natural law?* Reprint: The Harvard Classics.

Rousseau, J.-J. (1985, 1987). *On the social contract.* In D. A. Cress (Ed.) (Trans.), *Jean-Jacques Rousseau: Basic political writings* (pp. 139–752). Indianapolis, IN: Hackett Publishing Co.

Sardar, Z., & Davies, M. W. (2002). *Why do people hate America?* New York: Disinformation Co.

Sawyer, A. G. (1974). The effects of repetition: Conclusions and suggestions about experimental laboratory research. In G. D. Hughes & M. L. Ray (Eds.), *Buyer/consumer information proceedings* (pp. 190–219). Chapel Hill: University of North Carolina Press.

Schramm, W. (ed.) (1963). *The Science of* Human Communication. New York: Basic Books.

Schramm, W. (1982). *Men, women, messages and media.* New York: Harper & Row.

Steinbruner, J. (1991, June). The rule of law. *The Bulletin of the Atomic Scientists, 47*(5), 20.

Travis, A. (2004, October 15). Poll reveals world anger at Bush. *The Guardian.* Retrieved September 12, 2005, from http://www.guardian.co.uk/uselections2004/viewsofamerica/story/0,15221,1327568,00.html

Trento, S. B. (1992). *The power house: Robert Keith Gray and the selling of access and influence in Washington.* New York: St. Martin's Press.

Weiser, C. (2003, September 14). $1 billion international image campaign isn't enough to buy U.S. love. *USA Today.* Retrieved September 10, 2005, from http://www.usatoday.com/news/washington/2003-09-14-prawar-gns_x.htm

White, D. M. (1950). The gatekeeper: A case study in selection of news. *Journalism Quarterly, 27,* 383–390.

Whitehead, J. L. (1968). Factors of source credibility. *Quarterly Journal of Speech, 54,* 59–63.

12

Global Advertising and Public Relations

DEAN KRUCKEBERG AND MARINA VUJNOVIC

Dean Kruckeberg (PhD, University of Iowa) is an APR, Fellow PRSA, and Professor of Public Relations in the University of Northern Iowa's Department of Communication Studies. He is coauthor of the books *Public Relations and Community: A Reconstructed Theory* and *This Is PR: The Realities of Public Relations*. A recipient of several national awards, he is a cochair of the Commission on Public Relations Education and a former board member of the Public Relations Society of America. Kruckeberg's teaching and consulting have included work in the United Arab Emirates, Latvia, Russia, and Bulgaria.

Marina Vujnovic (MA, University of Northern Iowa) is a PhD student in mass communications, the School of Journalism and Mass Communication, the University of Iowa. She is a former newspaper journalist, political columnist, and public relations practitioner in her native Croatia, and she has taught communication at the University of Zagreb and was an administrative assistant for the Croatian Communication Association.

Newsom, Turk, and Kruckeberg (2004) say that public relations practitioners are intermediaries between the organizations that they represent and all of their organizations' publics. They note, "As a management function, public

For additional online resources, access the Global Media Monitor website that accompanies this book on the Wadsworth Communication Cafe website at http://communication.wadsworth.com.

relations involves responsibility and responsiveness in policy and information to the best interests of the organization and its publics" (p. 2). They further define public relations as "the various activities and communications that organizations undertake to monitor, evaluate, influence and adjust to the attitudes, opinions and behaviors of groups or individuals who constitute their publics" (p. 400). Noting that the strategy of advertising is to create desire and to motivate demand for a product, the authors say that designing advertisements, preparing advertisements' messages, and buying time or space for their exposure are the tasks of advertising. They further observe, "Advertising has been defined as paid-for time or space, except in the case of public service announcements (PSAs) where the time and space are donated to a nonprofit organization" (p. 258).

Both advertising and public relations—when examined on a global scale—must be comparatively considered within a context that includes historical and evolutionary factors that have influenced their development regionally. Full appreciation must be given for the diverse cultural, governmental/regulatory, economic, geographic, and technological factors that have differently influenced the development of advertising and public relations in various parts of the world, as well as the range of dominant ideological beliefs that have mitigated their development and contemporary practice.

Advertising and public relations are changing rapidly throughout the world, arguably becoming more global in their practice. Such globalism is partly in response to rapidly developing transnational media and global communication systems that are both creating and becoming increasingly dependent upon global markets to sustain them, as well as in response to a corresponding multiculturalism—all of which have come about because of previously unimaginable technological advances that are changing how and why people communicate.

This chapter provides a brief historical analysis and a prognosis of the continuing development—and role—of advertising and public relations worldwide, together with the implications of this development as well as of the future challenges in the mission, role, and function of both advertising and public relations.

BRIEF HISTORY OF ADVERTISING AND PUBLIC RELATIONS WORLDWIDE

Incorrectly so, laypeople in the United States oftentimes associate advertising and public relations solely as (1) Western, if not U.S., in origin; and (2) corporate in purpose, that is, representing primarily wealthy and powerful corporations that sell consumer products and services, increasingly to a global market. Too, laypeople often associate both advertising and public relations as (3) manipulative in their role, function, and intent.

These assumptions not only are simplifications but indeed in themselves constitute gross inaccuracies. However, more credence can be ascribed to the common contentions that both advertising and public relations are (4) democratic in their traditions, and (5) capitalistic in their heritages.

Western in Origin?

Campbell, Martin, and Fabos (2005) note that advertising has existed in the Middle East since 3000 B.C., when Babylonian shop owners began hanging signs outside their stores. Early Egyptian merchants hired criers to announce the arrival of ships, and the walls of ancient Pompeii had advertisements painted on them; by 900 A.D., town criers in European cities were directing customers to stores. English booksellers used brochures, bills, and posters to announce new books in the 1470s, and advertisements in English newspapers began appearing in 1622.

In public relations, Kruckeberg, Badran, Ayish, and Awad (1994) make compelling arguments that the public relations role and function in the Middle East date at least as far back as Mohammed, and popular U.S. public relations textbooks point to public relations–like activities throughout the world that extend back into antiquity.

Indeed, although public relations in its contemporary sense is frequently regarded as a 20th-century U.S. phenomenon, a German organization had—if not the first—at least one of the earliest internal public relations departments. By 1890, Alfred Krupp's company had a "news bureau" composed of as many as 20 staff members ("The German Public Relations Business," 1987).

However, Mallinson (1991) notes that U.S. public relations was exported to post–World War II Europe primarily through Great Britain, in great part because of the two countries' historical and linguistic ties but also as an outcome of the U.S.–British military alliance in World War II that had preceded this postwar U.S. overseas investment.

Nevertheless, although no corner of the globe can exclusively claim the origins of public relations, and while sophisticated public relations in its most contemporary sense is being practiced throughout the world, Kruckeberg (1999) observes,

> The common presumption is that North American public relations
> is most sophisticated and thereby most deserving of emulation. Not only
> are North American strategies, tactics and techniques held in global
> esteem, but base cultural and ideological assumptions of North American
> public relations are unquestioningly accepted as normative to modern
> public relations practice, i.e., contemporary public relations practice
> is assumed to be predicated on specific North American social, political
> and economic ideologies. Public relations practice in North American
> society extends from philosophical foundations that hold in particular
> reverence the right to expression of public opinion and to freedom
> of the press, as well as a social tradition that is far more individualistic

than historically has been that of many indigenous cultures in other parts of the world. Finally, public relations is based on—and inherently assumes—a sophisticated communication infrastructure that has evolved in North America, both politically and technically.

Despite the apparent widespread emulation of U.S. public relations practice elsewhere in the world, Ovaitt (1988) argues that public relations may be even more culture-bound than is either marketing or advertising—making it harder to conduct public relations programs based on concepts that extend across international boundaries.

For example, Tsetsura (2000a) observed that by 2000, public relations in Russia had existed for little more than 15 years but nevertheless was well on its way to achieving respect in that country. She noted that especially during recent years, many specialized public relations agencies had been established in that country, and internal PR departments also had been created in many Russian companies. Furthermore, Russian scholars were actively examining the theories and practice of public relations, and the author's research indicated that American public relations theory had had a significant impact on Russian public relations theory.

However, Tsetura's research found the following:

> In general, American textbooks were more theoretically oriented than the Russian textbooks. Russian textbooks, in their turn, were primarily written for practitioners and students who are, most likely, unfamiliar with the public relations phenomenon at all. . . .
>
> Another tendency that should be noticed is a high concentration on political relations and election campaign strategies. Today, for many practitioners and even scholars, public relations is associated only with politics . . . or with integrated communications. (p. 60)

Significantly, Tsetsura's research found that Russian public relations textbook authors either were not familiar with—or chose to ignore—some major theoretical concepts of contemporary American theory. They tended to focus more on practice than on theory and on suggestions for practical suggestions, tactics, and practical tips rather than on theoretical explanations. Tsetsura (2000b) further suggests that misleading explanations of the goals of public relations in the past, which had been promulgated in the early 1990s by Russian scholars who were not educated in public relations, had contributed to a negative image of public relations in Russia.

Al-Enad (1990) sees a difference between Western practice of public relations and what is appropriate practice in less-developed countries (LDCs). He contends that public relations practice in Third World nations might also apply to Europe's less-developed former Eastern Bloc countries. Al-Enad observes that whereas Western public relations literature places public relations between an institution and its publics or environment, public relations in developing nations is located between material and nonmaterial aspects of the culture.

Regardless of diverse regions' historical or contemporary influence, Kruckeberg (1994) concludes,

Suffice it to say, there is growing appreciation for public relations professional practice worldwide. Countries previously unfazed—or at least unmoved —by negative public opinion are becoming cognizant of the benefits of good public relations to fulfill increasingly obvious needs. Aggressively, a range of public and private organizations and institutions are seeking both the knowledge and the means to enable these countries' total infrastructures to practice "good public relations." (p. 2)

Advertising, if not "global" in its commonality of strategies and tactics and in the availability of like media worldwide, most certainly is used extensively throughout the world. However, it is often tailored to indigenous—rather than global—tastes and perspectives; indeed, some advertising would be questionable, if not disastrous, if used elsewhere. For example, Vietnamese television viewers who were watching the Euro 2000 soccer matches saw a commercial for Binh Tien Consumer Goods Company's shoes, an advertisement produced by Chicago advertising agency Leo Burnett Company that contrasted the footwear of Vietnamese soldiers in the "American War"—that is, sandals made of tires—with the latest athletic shoes made by the Vietnamese manufacturer.

Burnett's headquarters says its partnership with a Vietnamese advertising agency was not trying to exploit a painful chapter in the history of Vietnam and the United States; it was just trying to sell shoes using images familiar to Vietnamese. "Anyone who has seen the ad realizes it does not exploit the war," said a Burnett representative. "Rather, it employs historical achievements that have meaning to the Vietnamese people" (Flagg, 2000, p. A19). Although the advertisement was well-received in Vietnam, its use in the United States would have been unthinkable.

One campaign of Swedish furniture company Ikea in the United Kingdom featured "hapless Ikea employees who are forced to sniff a colleague's armpit." Another commercial employed tattooed thighs to help sell the company's furniture (Beck, 2001). A British advertising agency caused an uproar by using Holocaust images to promote an Imperial War Museum exhibit, with one poster reading, "Come and see what man can achieve when he really puts his mind to it" (Ellison, 2000b). In 2004, Coca-Cola was pleased to learn that its "Buddies" TV ad had scored higher among teenagers for brand awareness, persuasion, and likeability than had any other Coke ad during the past decade. In the commercial, which was designed to air during the National Collegiate Athletic Association basketball tournament, a friend holds a refrigerated Coke can next to several parts of his body, including his armpit, to cool himself down after a game of hoops. He then gives the can to his friend, who does not know where his Coke had been. Reportedly, some company executives complained that the ad was "lowbrow" and was certainly not suitable for an older audience, such as those viewing a golf tournament. In 2000, the same soft drink company had run a commercial in Germany showing a woman donning a pair of frozen panties, although Coca-Cola had pulled another German ad that depicted a couple groping one another (McKay & Terhune, 2004).

The importance of understanding international strategies and tactics and of appreciating indigenous sensitivities becomes quickly evident to advertising agencies whose clients themselves have obtained their resources globally, including tapping into a worldwide labor pool. Such clients want an advertising agency that can provide services worldwide and that is sensitive to the nuances of regional markets throughout the world.

Effective advertising today must operate in a multicultural world that is unforgiving of marketers' cultural insensitivity to and lack of understanding of cultures other than their own. For example, John Hancock Financial Services aired a television spot in July 2000 that featured two Caucasian women at an airport holding an Asian baby. Although viewers could not positively identify the baby's ethnicity from this advertisement, adoption agencies nevertheless protested—fearing that Chinese government officials would assume that the child was from China and that the implied homosexuality of the two female parents was being tolerated by American adoption officials, an attitude the Chinese government did not share concerning prospective adopting parents (Gubernick, 2000).

Nike pulled a magazine advertisement for a running shoe after disabilities rights groups objected to the advertisement's reference to people having such challenges as being "drooling and misshapen" (Grimes, 2000)—a characterization that one might hope would be a faux pas in any culture. The 2000 Super Bowl commercial that showed a walking Christopher Reeve brought derision for its perceived exploitation of a celebrity tragedy (O'Connell, 2001), although this advertisement's perceived tastelessness was certainly eclipsed by Janet Jackson's halftime wardrobe malfunction during the 2004 Super Bowl that offended millions of Americans while perhaps not being remarkable to those in other parts of the world.

Wives from perhaps all or most of the world could nevertheless sympathize with a German wife, who accused her husband of unfaithfulness when a postcard arrived at their home from "Your Sweetie" that thanked her husband for the flowers; days later, a second postcard revealed that the mailing was an advertising campaign from the German flower industry (Aalund, 2000). A study by a global advertising agency found that many Europeans were put off by a proliferation of technical advertisements designed to encourage consumers to purchase these products; instead of enticing Europeans to enter this market, however, new product announcements were persuading them to wait until the onslaught of technology development had slowed to a manageable pace (Ellison, 2000c).

Families of murder victims objected to Benetton's 2000 "We, on Death Row" advertising supplement that featured pinups and in-depth interviews with inmates awaiting execution. The advertising campaign was designed to raise consciousness about the death penalty as well as awareness about the Benetton label of fashion clothing (Dumenco, 2000). Kraidy and Goeddertz (2003), however, concluded that discourse by the U.S. prestige press about the Benetton campaign instead demonstrated a lost opportunity for meaningful global dialogue about capital punishment, leaving unfulfilled any civic potential of advertising because of the U.S. media's hostile coverage that the authors said exposed the instability of hegemonic ideologies in mass-mediated public discourse.

Some companies, for example, Nokia, are attempting a global advertising campaign to create a more-unified identity worldwide; however, while creating a standardized message, the company is nevertheless relying primarily on visual images and is designing different ads for different regions to include actors and settings consistent with the regions where the ads are being placed (Matthews & Pringle, 2004).

In sum, it is highly naive to think of advertising and public relations as Western phenomena, either in their evolution and development or especially in their effectiveness in a global but nevertheless highly multicultural world.

Corporate in Purpose?

Seemingly compelling evidence suggests that advertising has been strongly—if not overwhelmingly—corporate in purpose, that is, accompanying the growth of large corporations as national and global institutions and enjoying the steady growth of consumerism as a worldwide social and economic phenomenon. Major clients of advertising agencies disproportionately include large corporations that sell goods and services, not only within the borders of their own countries but increasingly also to international markets. Although many corporations have marketed their products and services globally throughout most of their histories, others are now looking more closely to find opportune niches in international sites. For example, Unilever PLC launched a skin lotion for black women in Brazil, a nation that North Americans might be surprised to learn has the world's largest black population next to Nigeria, although members of this population do not necessarily identify themselves as being black (Ellison & White, 2000a). Procter and Gamble sends out 4.5 million copies of its promotional magazine *Avanzando Con Tu Familia* (Getting Ahead with Your Family) to Hispanic families in the United States (Porter & Nelson, 2000). Advertising figures from 2003 showed that ad spending in Hispanic magazines had grown 24 percent over the previous year, while advertising spending in general during that time had grown only 8.6 percent (Jordan, 2004).

Public relations has not been restricted to primarily supporting corporations that sell products and services. Popular U.S. textbooks point to governmental and nongovernmental organizations' social programs that were promoted in the 20th century through public relations. Nevertheless, Heath (2000) observes that "from its birth, public relations has been seen as a tool used largely by corporate managements to get their way" (p. 70).

Indeed, while both advertising and public relations historically have been widely used by corporations, U.S. governmental and nongovernmental organizations have also long used advertising, as well as public relations. Historically, patriotic World War II posters from the U.S. government come readily to mind, as do the various "poster" causes of charities and other nongovernmental organizations.

Of course, political campaigning and agendas throughout the world, both in democratic and totalitarian countries, have included both advertising and public relations techniques. For example, consider the propaganda of wartime Germany under propaganda head Paul Joseph Goebbels (Boehm, 1989). Furthermore, scholars today contend that professional public relations practice in particular should be available for all publics.

Contemporary scholars see historic inequities that can be corrected through the use of public relations. Grunig (2000), for example, argues that a set of principles must be developed to overcome the problem of a possible imbalance in power between clients of public relations practitioners and the publics with whom they communicate. Further, considerable attention today is being paid to public relations for activist groups. Indeed, Holtzhausen (2000) contends,

> The fact that public relations as activism receives so little attention
> supports the theory that public relations has become part and parcel
> of the maintenance of metanarratives and domination in society. In fact,
> activists are often portrayed as the enemy of organizations and government,
> although they are actually the real voices of democracy. (p. 100)

The advertising industry in recent years has paid increasing attention to the concept of "relationship marketing," which has much potential, not only for corporations' relationships with customers and other publics but also for a variety of governmental, nongovernmental, and charitable organizations. As an example, Hollywood has responded to charges that the entertainment industry is marketing violence to children by airing, on network television, public service announcements against youth violence (Bravin, 2000). KFC has had to respond to charges of cruelty to its chickens, not only in the United States (Koenig, 2004) but in such distant locations as Taiwan (Associated Press, 2003).

Manipulative in Their Role, Function, and Design?

Manipulative is a pejorative word, but there is little question that advertising—both consumer advertising to sell products and services, and public relations–oriented "institutional" advertising to sell ideas or to garner support for an organization—is most commonly persuasive in nature. The role, function, and design of public relations, however, are more complex. Grunig (2000) acknowledges that most people seem to view public relations as a "mysterious hidden persuader working for the rich and powerful to deceive and take advantage of the less powerful" (p. 23), and he further observes that some critical scholars and many practitioners view public relations as "a manipulative force in society" (pp. 23–24). However, Grunig contends that most scholars and professionals believe that public relations plays an essential role in a democratic society. He argues,

> Public relations will have its greatest value to client organizations,
> to publics, and to society if it views collaboration as the core of its
> philosophy and makes collaboration the focus of research to develop
> a body of knowledge to guide public relations practice. Furthermore, . . .
> public relations brings an essential element of collectivism into the
> commonly individualistic world view of most Western organizations
> and . . . collaboration, as the core of what political scientists call societal
> corporatism, is the key element of democratic societies. (p. 25)

Contemporary advertising and marketing executives, particularly those engaged in "relationship marketing," appreciate that satisfactory relationships with customers and others, developed through quality products and service tailored to individual needs as well as through responsible corporate citizenship, have proven far more effective than crude attempts at manipulation.

Democratic in Tradition?

Both advertising and public relations are highly democratic in tradition, the former because advertising by its nature suggests the availability of consumer choice—that is, a marketplace democracy and the ultimate consumer determination of the relative benefits of these choices—and the latter because of an inherent supposition of the importance and value of public opinion within democratic forms of government.

Holtzhausen (2000) argues that the role of public relations should be to continuously demystify the client organization and its practices, transforming it into a more democratic institution for both internal and external publics. She notes that "a democratic institution will consistently communicate openly with its publics and will be prepared to change itself in that process" (p. 105).

Sriramesh and White (1992) address democratic requisites by linking societal culture and public relations in these two propositions:

Proposition 1: Societal cultures that display lower levels of power distance, authoritarianism, and individualism, but have higher levels of interpersonal trust among workers, are most likely to develop ... excellent public relations practices....

Proposition 2: Although such occurrences are rare, organizations that exist in societal cultures that do not display these characteristics conducive to the spawning of excellent public relations programs also may have excellent public relations programs if the few power holders of the organization have individual personalities that foster participative organizational culture even if this culture is atypical to mainstream societal culture. (p. 612)

Capitalistic in Heritage?

Both advertising and public relations are steeped in the capitalistic tradition. Holtzhausen (2000) says that public relations in the Western world is a product of both modernism and capitalism, originating to maintain the status of private and public organizations that have participated in the capitalist system. "The organization itself is an ideological vehicle for capitalism. And the public relations practitioner is part of the ideological message. The purpose of ideologies, like all metanarratives, is to make people think alike and so assert power over society; therefore, the purpose of all ideologies is political" (p. 100).

However, Kruckeberg (1996) argues that although a democratic culture and government are important to the ideology of public relations, nothing inherently restricts implementation of public relations practice in nations having other than purely capitalistic economic systems.

In sum, arguments can be made that contemporary advertising and public relations are not solely Western (or U.S.) in their origin, nor can they be practiced effectively through an exclusively Western perspective; that they do not historically or inherently represent exclusively corporate interests but rather have served well, and can continue to serve well, many organizations—including governments and nongovernmental organizations and charities—and these organizations' causes throughout their histories; and that they are not solely (nor are they best practiced as being) manipulative in nature. However, both advertising and public relations have strong democratic traditions and capitalistic heritages. Given all of this, what can be anticipated and what should be expected from today's advertising industry and from contemporary public relations practice in the postmodern, postmillennial, post–Cold War era of transnational media and global communication in the age of an information revolution?

Postmodern, Postmillennial, Post–Cold War Era

Although the 20th century unquestionably gave birth to the most extraordinary achievements in world history, its 100 years also were the most bloody and—arguably—the most dysfunctional for many elements of society worldwide. Although much that occurred in the 1900s was good, a fundamental belief and premise must be accepted that humankind must do far better in the third millennium for society even to continue. Basic questions that must be addressed and adequately resolved for the 21st century include these: What does it mean to be human and to be part of humankind in postmodern global society? What moral fields must be developed or modified to ensure this humanity, this humanness? What ethos—that is, moral and spiritual character—must be developed or modified in global society to nurture this humanness? After late 20th-century victories of democracy and capitalism in former Eastern Bloc countries, what new forms of democracy and capitalism can or must be developed, not only regionally but also within a global ethos? Can and should democracy be culturally specific, and should culturally specific capitalism be embraced in different parts of the world according to societal tradition and heritage? Indeed, some social problems must be recognized as being so overwhelming, so critical, that all available resources must be allocated to address them in the new century.

ENVIRONMENTAL CHALLENGES, POPULATION GROWTH, POVERTY AND HUNGER, WAR

Kennedy (1993) notes not only new and increasingly critical environmental challenges but also a corresponding increase in the world's population—replete with rising demographic imbalances between rich and poor countries. Perhaps most alarming of these is the population explosion. He observes, "From the viewpoint of environmentalists . . . the earth is under a twofold attack from human beings—the excessive demands and wasteful habits of affluent populations of developed countries, and the billions of new mouths born in the developing world who (very naturally) aspire to increase their own consumption levels" (p. 33).

The Office of Population, Bureau for Global Programs, Field Support and Research, of the U.S. Agency for International Development (1996), before the millennium, reported that while the *rate* of the world population growth was continuing to fall nearing the turn of the century, actual population numbers still were increasing and were expected to total 7.6 billion persons by the year 2020. Further, the share of the population represented by the more developed countries had declined from 27 percent of the world total in 1970 to 20 percent in 1996. More recent data do not dispute these basic projections. If present trends continue, the more developed countries will make up only 16 percent of world population in little more than two decades. Andrew Belsey and Ruth Chadwick (1992) remind us that one-fifth of the world's population—1 billion people—remain in dire physical need.

An inhospitable—perhaps irreversibly damaged—global environment, together with resultant poverty and hunger and war, can be ill afforded in the third millennium. All of the world's resources, and its people's best minds, must give priority to threats to the environment, to responsible management of the world's population, and to the elimination of poverty, hunger, and war. Advertisers would be naive to view such a growing population simply as increased markets, and public relations practitioners must consider the challenges that such 21st-century demographics pose in creating mutually beneficial relationships with culturally diverse publics, as well as with global society at large.

Nevertheless, advertising and public relations practitioners can help address social problems that will occur through practitioners' expertise not only in communication but also in societal problem solving. In the 1980s, India had advertising billboards reminding, "A baby boom is the nation's doom." Increasingly, "social marketing" skills and public relations community- and relationship-building efforts of practitioners will need to reach "markets" and publics worldwide with messages that do far more than support the sale of products and services, many of which a majority of the world's population may not be able to afford and some of which may be harmful. These missions are more profound and far more difficult to achieve than advertising executives and public relations practitioners' simple attempts to sell products and services and justify the existence of their organizations within society.

THE MANAGEMENT OF CHANGE

Rapid change must be not only acknowledged but also proactively managed. Technology is advancing geometrically, and time and space are being compressed in ways that would have been unfathomable in past generations.

We must appreciate that we do not presently know where technology is going, that we do not know the societal effects of emerging technology, and that it is likely that this technology will affect different societies and cultures in different ways, that is, technology in less-developed countries might well have different social outcomes from those in First World western societies. Technology with often unfathomed and possibly unfathomable ramifications includes unfettered and unregulated satellite radio (McBride & Pasztor, 2004); influential, if biased and sometimes misleading, blogs that are replete with advertising (Lillkvist, 2004); and TiVo—for example, the day after the 2004 Super Bowl, TiVo announced that more people had replayed the Janet Jackson incident than any other event in the history of this digital video recorder. TiVo knew this because it has the technology to track the viewing habits of all of its users— certainly a sober implication for those who assume or are concerned about privacy (Wingfield & Saranow, 2004). Meanwhile, Kodak has chosen to shift its future into digital technology, finding its film business in the maturity stage of the product life cycle (Bandler, 2003).

Carey (1989) notes Innis's observation that culture is fundamentally affected by communication technology, which can alter the structure of interests (the things thought about) by changing the character of symbols (the things thought with) and by changing the nature of community (the arena in which thought is developed).

Referring to the technological age, Kruckeberg (1995–1996) observes,

> Life is more like taking [a] drive down a crowded avenue at 90 miles per hour. Response to feedback must be made far more quickly than many people may be able to "drive" comfortably and safely. The opportunity for prolonged deliberation in decision-making and feedback no longer exists, given the pressures of instantaneous transmission of communication and the accompanying expectations of those with whom one is communicating. (p. 36)

Holtzhausen (2000) looks forward to a postmodern age in which technology will not dominate humanity but rather will serve it. The ethically responsible society, Holtzhausen says, will support science and technology but will also emphasize imagination, sensitivity, emotion, humanity, and an appreciation of differences.

Such change has direct implications for the advertising and public relations industries. For example, in just four years, Internet advertising had grown from virtually nothing into a $5 billion business (Alsop, 2001). In London, several companies developed technology to allow motion-picture advertisements to be projected onto the walls of subway tunnels (Ellison, 2001). "Cuecats"—small hand-held scanners that plug into personal computers to read bar codes on products as well as "cues" printed alongside ads and articles in newspapers, magazines, and catalogs—can automatically call up web pages related to the products (Mossberg, 2000).

The head of the sensory-design research lab at Britain's Central St. Martin's College, explaining "sensory marketing," has extolled the benefits of reaching new shoppers and steady customers through their sense of smell. British Airways' first-class and business-class lounges at London's Heathrow Airport and New York's Kennedy Airport have spritzed scent into the air to enhance British Airways' brand image (Ellison & White, 2000b).

Employers concerned about productivity will have to consider an additional threat: advertisers' view of the workplace as a place to target potential customers through the Internet. One United Kingdom advertising executive said, "Most advertisers concede there is a growing recognition that workers are spending more time taking care of personal business and are acting like consumers at the office" (Ellison, 2000a, p. B13). More important questions about change, however, must address how transnational media and global communication in the age of information revolution will affect society itself.

TENSIONS FROM TECHNOLOGY, GLOBALISM, AND MULTICULTURALISM

Technology is significant not only in and of itself but has become the major intervening variable affecting the two other critical variables of the future—globalism, and its converse, multiculturalism. The interaction of these three variables will create dynamic tensions in the future that will need examination and resolution. On behalf of the organizations that they represent, advertising executives and public relations practitioners will need to address many of these tensions.

GOVERNMENTS, CORPORATIONS, AND PRIVATE CITIZENS

Fundamental changes will certainly occur in the relationships among governments, corporations, and private citizens. Schiller (1995) said that, among the 37,000 companies that have predominated globally, the largest 100 transnational mega-firms were the global power wielders.

> This world corporate order is a major force in reducing greatly the influence of nation states. As private economic decisions increasingly govern the global and national allocation of resources, the amount and character of investment, the value of currencies, and the sites and modes of production, important duties of government are silently appropriated by these giant private economic aggregates. (p. 21)

Schiller (1995) argued that these corporations promoted deregulation and privatization of industry worldwide, notably in the telecommunications sector. One effect of this large-scale deregulation and massive privatization, Schiller said, was the increasing ineffectualness of national authority.

Corporations may have become more powerful and influential than many nation–states. Corporations are capable of making unilateral decisions because these transnational organizations can cross frontiers with impunity to accomplish their goals. Further, it cannot be assumed that decisions made by transnational corporations will be within the moral field of Western culture or in the best interest of others. Governments will not be able to protect citizens' rights if governments' power—and the power of their citizens—pales in comparison to unaccountable corporations whose missions and goals can be totally self-serving.

Related issues of concern in the 21st century include tensions between indigenous cultures' sense of individualism and collectivity, traditions of egalitarianism versus authoritative governmental philosophies and infrastructures, conflicting worldviews among those in different societies, the changing nature of mass societies, and questions of ethics of the majority versus the ethics of the dominants.

NATIONALISM VERSUS GLOBALISM

The idea of a homogenous global culture—whether through a neocolonial cultural imperialism or through a melding of what is good (or bad) in many or all cultures—can be assumed no more than can a revamped nationalism and metaphorical (if not literal) "ethnic cleansing," which latter scenario in the contemporary age some have likened to the pre–World War I Balkans. Bell (1988) observed pessimistically:

> As we approach the twenty-first century, the problems of color,
> of tribalism, of ethnic differences—in Southeast Asia, the Middle East,
> the fratricidal hatred in the Muslim world—all bespeak an agenda
> of issues that contemporary sociology, least of all Marxism, is ill prepared
> to understand. We see, particularly in Marxism, how much our
> sociological categories were framed within the context of Western
> society, and how the themes of the Enlightenment, rationality,
> industrialization, consciousness, class development, the idea of "historic
> nations" and social evolution, became our prisms of understanding.
> And how irrelevant Marx, and even Weber and Durkheim, may
> be. (p. 441)

Merrill (1996) foresaw a future era of conformity and authoritarianism, as had been described by Karl Mannheim. Mannheim talked of a historical cycle reminiscent of Nietzsche and Comte and distinguished three stages of development—the medieval man in collective solidarity, the post-Renaissance man in individual competition, and the presently emerging man steeped in "group solidarity." It is this third category toward which we are presently drifting, Merrill says, and it applies equally to humans in communist, fascist, and liberal-capitalist cultures, for the factor that Mannheim saw as uniting them all "is the phenomenon of Great Society which the industrial revolution has brought into being." Merrill says, "The pull of organizations . . . largely accounts for this drift toward conformity and authoritarianism" (Merrill, 1996, p. 61).

Gilder (1992), however, predicted a new age of individualism that "will bring an eruption of culture unprecedented in human history." He continued,

"Every film will be able to reach cheaply a potential audience of hundreds of millions of people around the world" (p. 54).

Stephen (1995) viewed fragmentation of the self as follows:

> The fragmentation of society has been mirrored by a fragmentation of self. In navigating the complex external world, the modern individual by necessity differentiates between the private or personal self and the public self. The public self, a kind of *Gesellschaft* personae . . . is tailored specifically to withstand the travails of presentation in multiple epistemic contexts. (p. 14)

And Bell (1988) early observed the rise of national tensions in almost every part of the world, as much in the (former) communist world as anywhere else, as was greatly evidenced in the Balkans in the 1990s.

PAST VERSUS FUTURE

Tensions will remain between modern and traditional societies, as well as within the traditional societies themselves, particularly when the latter face overwhelming pressures to modernize. Stephen (1995) noted two characteristics that differentiate modern and traditional societies:

> The first dimension is pluralism. In traditional societies beliefs are consensual and communication functions mainly to convey information and to coordinate action. Modern societies are highly pluralistic. Beliefs are up for grabs and communication is used to create shared constructions of reality—local pockets of consensus—that provide stability and bridge existentially isolated individuals. . . .
>
>   The second dimension is egalitarianism. If a society is predominantly hierarchical rather than egalitarian—as may more often be the case in traditional societies—interpersonal interaction occurs predominantly between individuals of unequal social power. (p. 16)

TENSIONS AMONG THE FIRST, SECOND, AND THIRD WORLDS

Although the Cold War may have been effectively won, the categorizations of the First, Second, and Third World may not yet be obsolete. However, with the effective removal of Marxist ideologies throughout much of the world, problems between the First World and the Third World may in fact have been clarified.

Bellah, Madsen, Sullivan, Swidler, and Tipton (1991) noted,

> Now that East–West tensions are sharply diminishing, we can better understand that the deepest chasm is between the rich and the poor

nations. . . . We have a long way to go before we understand the cultural dynamics of rapid social change and the terrible price that it has exacted in individual souls and in societies all over the globe. (p. 250)

Problems articulated in the 1970s regarding the flow of news and the balance of information between nations remain (Emery & Emery, 1988). World economic interdependence still places the heaviest economic burdens on the world's poorest nation–states (Bellah et al., 1991).

CLASS STRATIFICATION

Bell (1988) noted that less cooperation and solidarity have occurred within the international working class in recent times than in the past 100 years. However, many social scientists see social class issues remaining in the 21st century. Brook and Boal (1995) warned about the contemporary technological age:

Automation in the name of progress and "inevitable" technological change is primarily to the benefit of that same class that not so long ago forced people off the land and into factories, destroying whole ways of life in the process: "labor-saving" devices have not so much reduced labor as they have increased profits and refined class domination. (p. viii)

Neill (1995) predicted that computerization of schools will not contribute to "high wages" or "good jobs," but in fact the U.S. class hierarchy will be intensified.

Kruckeberg (1995) questioned who will buy computers for the underclass of people and what Third World peasants—with unfulfilled needs for food and fiber—will have to say to one another electronically.

Or, will there be only increasing alienation and anomie—both for those availing themselves of communication technology and for a global underclass of people who cannot or will not accept telecomputers, powerbooks, electronic note pads, digital computer-linked cameras, portable faxes, cellular telephones with cameras and satellite uplinks? (p. 78)

Stephen (1995) noted that modern societies are characterized by a formal egalitarianism, but they are in fact stratified. Indeed, one characteristic of modernity, he says, has been the gradual unfolding of forms of behavior that enunciate class distinctions.

CONTROL OF TECHNOLOGY

Many of these dynamic tensions will be affected directly by policies related to the control of technology and its development and implementation. Will such control rest exclusively or predominantly with corporations and the marketplace in which they compete and influence, with governments, or with world citizenry?

Will influence and decision making related to development and implementation come primarily from the technologists and the corporations they represent and be market driven? Or will they come from the sundry professionals using (consuming) this technology or from global citizenry at large? How will issues of privacy versus access be addressed? Indeed, how will fundamental issues of education, not only of global leaders but also of the world's citizens, be addressed? That is, will generations of technocrats and their corresponding worldview replace or challenge the very foundations of society as held in trust by the liberal arts? Will global culture be a culture of technology, and will this culture imperialistically predominate in all areas of global society? For example, in early 2001, Microsoft centralized its marketing effort with a $200 million advertising campaign—the beginning of a nearly $500 million global marketing campaign (Buckman, 2001).

AN IDEOLOGICAL FOUNDATION
FOR ADVERTISING AND PUBLIC RELATIONS

To suggest that advertising and public relations can ameliorate the 21st-century problems identified in this chapter would be naive and presumptuous, although both can do much—independently and together—by contributing to the resolution of these problems. Kruckeberg (1995–1996) predicted,

> Organizations will need "keepers and reconcilers" of their values
> and belief systems up to and including their base ideologies. Those
> professionals will be critically needed who can examine, maintain
> and modify as necessary traditional organizational and societal values
> and beliefs that will be challenged in a McLuhanesque "global village"
> in which the values and belief systems of peoples throughout the world
> will ideologically confront one another. (p. 37)

He says that professionals will be critically needed who can examine, maintain, and modify, as necessary, indigenous organizational and societal values and belief systems in an age and communication milieu in which values, beliefs, and ideologies will be continually challenged. Tomorrow's public relations practitioners must define themselves globally as professionals through examination and articulation of their own values, belief systems, and ideology as a professional community.

Kruckeberg (2000) has argued that public relations practitioners must "professionalize" on a global scale to provide a succinct definition of their role and function within global society as well as an articulate description of their worldview (that is, their ideology, values, and belief systems), and the same argument is made for advertising. This "professionalization," he says, will take practitioners away from the functionary role of a corporate "gunslinger" or "Samurai warrior," providing this specialized occupation with the necessary philosophical foundation to develop a "professional" worldview.

Grunig (2000) has argued for a set of socially acceptable values for public relations, as well as a set of principles that can overcome possible power imbalances between the clients and publics of public relations practitioners.

Vujnovic (2005) argues that public relations practitioners must remain independent of their organizations' dominant coalitions to keep from becoming a minority voice who will become coopted and assimilated into the values and worldviews of others in these coalitions, who are neither educated nor sensitive toward public relations, their organizations' publics, and their organizations' social responsibility toward society-at-large. She argues that the "power" of public relations practitioners in organizations comes from the very nature of public relations practitioners' work.

Vujnovic advocates that the major role in organizational culture belongs to public relations practitioners and that, as a symbol-producing members of their organizations, public relations practitioners participate in the creation and interpretation, as well as the change and implementation, of organizational culture. Therefore, public relations practitioners' values and worldviews play an essential part in influencing organizational culture.

She concludes that public relations scholars and practitioners must challenge the status quo of traditional mainstream public relations literature in the 21st century; that is, they must critically examine even the most basic assumptions of the role and function of public relations practitioners in their organizations and the ultimate impact that they have on their organizations, their organizations' publics, and society-at-large.

The same advice would hold for advertising scholars and practitioners because the challenges of the 21st century are such that our most basic premises must be continually retested and re-evaluated in a rapidly changing world.

CONCLUSION

Advertising and public relations are hardly a panacea for the social or global problems in the 21st century, but both can be used effectively to ameliorate some of the problems that we face. As powerfully persuasive and informative processes, advertising and public relations affect people of the world in many ways, especially in the advanced nations. However, if these professions become more readily accessible to all peoples and nations; if they are practiced humanely, not manipulatively, they may result in improved international relations and international communication. Ideally, both advertising and public relations should operate collaboratively with social, political, economic, and global organizations according to democratic principles and in tune with traditional values of a given society.

For more information on the topics that appear in this chapter, use the password that came free with this book to access InfoTrac College Edition. Use the following words as keyterms and subject searches: international public relations, international advertising, advertising agencies, public relations agencies, media corporations, propaganda, capitalism, nationalism, multiculturalism.

QUESTIONS FOR DISCUSSION

1. In what ways could historical and evolutionary factors differently affect how advertising and public relations are practiced in a given region or society? For example, how could cultural, governmental/regulatory, economic, geographic, and technological factors—as well as dominant ideological beliefs— influence the role, function, and strategies of public relations and advertising?

2. Is Kruckeberg (1996) correct that nothing inherently restricts implementation of public relations practice in nations having other than purely capitalistic economic systems? Why or why not?

3. Should democracy be culturally specific, and should culturally specific capitalism be embraced in different parts of the world according to societal tradition and heritage? Defend your answer, and discuss your answer's implications for advertising and public relations practice in those societies.

4. In what ways can advertising and public relations practitioners help address social problems that will occur in the 21st century? What implications would your answer have for the role of advertising and public relations and for the education of its practitioners?

5. Will the 21st century bring the evolution of a homogenous global culture or accentuate more pronounced multicultural differences among the world's peoples? What relationships exist among technology, globalism, and multiculturalism, and how will these variables affect the practice of public relations and advertising?

REFERENCES

Aalund, D. (2000, October 9). Is that lipstick I see on your collar, or just another flower ad? *Wall Street Journal,* p. B1.

Al-Enad, A. H. (1990). Public relations' roles in developing countries. *Public Relations Quarterly, 35*(1), 24–26.

Alsop, S. (2001, January 22). Give commercials a break. *Fortune, 143,* 50.

Associated Press. (2003, November 27). Animal rights activists in Taiwan protest KFC's treatment of chickens [electronic version]. *Associated Press Worldstream.* Retrieved September 24, 2005, from http://web.lexis-nexis.com/universe/document? _m=9768b84a8ba0e5005bb66a1dcafea0ea&_docnum=106&wchp=dGLbVlb-zSkVb&_md5=ce1a8200a1fb95942e80692261b7c8cd

Bandler, J. (2003, September 25). Kodak shifts focus from film, betting future on digital lines. *Wall Street Journal,* p. A1.

Beck, E. (2001, January 4). Ikea sees quirkiness as selling point in U.K. *Wall Street Journal,* p. B12.

Bell, D. (1988). *The end of ideology.* Cambridge: Harvard University Press.

Bellah, R. N., Madsen, R., Sullivan, W. M., Swidler, A., & Tipton, S. M. (1991). *The good society.* New York: Vintage Books.

Belsey, A., & Chadwick, R. (1992). Ethics and politics of the media: The quest for quality. In A. Belsey & R. Chadwick (Eds.), *Ethical issues in journalism and the media* (pp. 1–14). London: Routledge.

Boehm Ed. (1989). *Behind enemy lines: WWII Allied/Axis propaganda.* Secaucus, NJ: Wellfleet Press.

Bravin, J. (2000, September 14). Hollywood launches messages of peace. *Wall Street Journal,* p. B17.

Brook, J., & Boal, I. A. (1995). Preface. In J. Brook & I. A. Boal (Eds.), *Resisting the virtual life: The culture and politics of information* (pp. vii–xv). San Francisco: City Lights.

Buckman, R. (2001, January 22). Microsoft ads push big-business software. *Wall Street Journal,* p. B9.

Campbell, R., Martin, C. R., & Fabos, B. (2005). *Media & culture: An introduction to mass communication.* Boston: Bedford/St. Martin's.

Carey, J. W. (1989). Space, time, and communications: A tribute to Harold Innis. In J. W. Carey (Ed.), *Communication as culture* (pp. 142–172). Boston: Unwin Hyman.

Dumenco, S. (2000, December 18–25). Keyword: Sell. *New York, 33,* 54, 57.

Ellison, S. (2000a, October 9). U.K. advertisers focus online campaign on at-work Web surfers. *Wall Street Journal,* p. B13.

Ellison, S. (2000b, November 2). Ads for a Holocaust exhibit in London cause a stir. *Wall Street Journal,* pp. B1, B4.

Ellison, S. (2000c, December 14). Europeans await tech-ad onslaught to abate. *Wall Street Journal,* p. B6.

Ellison, S. (2001, January 10). Subway tunnels become latest frontier for ads. *Wall Street Journal,* p. A19.

Ellison, S., & White, E. (2000a, November 24). Marketers discover black Brazil. *Wall Street Journal,* pp. A11, A14.

Ellison, S., & White, E. (2000b, November 24). When there's more to an ad than meets the eye. *Wall Street Journal,* pp. A11, A14.

Emery, M., & Emery, E. (1988). *The press and America: An interpretive history of the mass media.* Englewood Cliffs, NJ: Prentice Hall.

Flagg, M. (2000, October 17). In today's Vietnam, the war is a selling point. *Wall Street Journal,* p. A19.

The German public relations business has not yet declared itself essential for industry and it still has to prove itself. (1987, April). *PR World,* p. 8.

Gilder, G. (1992). *Life after television.* New York: W. W. Norton & Co.

Grimes, A. (2000, October 26). Nike rescinds ad, apologizes to disabled people. *Wall Street Journal,* p. B20.

Grunig, J. E. (2000). Collectivism, collaboration, and societal corporatism as core professional values in public relations. *Journal of Public Relations Research, 12*(1), 23–48.

Gubernick, L. (2000, September 14). Hancock ad raises alarm in adoption community. *Wall Street Journal,* p. B1.

Heath, R. L. (2000). A rhetorical perspective on the values of public relations: Crossroads and pathways toward concurrence. *Journal of Public Relations Research, 12*(1), 69–91.

Holtzhausen, D. R. (2000). Postmodern values in public relations. *Journal of Public Relations Research, 12*(1), 93–114.

Jordan, M. (2004, March 3). Hispanic magazines gain ad dollars. *Wall Street Journal,* p. B2.

Kennedy, P. (1993). *Preparing for the 21st century.* New York: Vintage Books.

Koenig, D. (2004, July 26). Pilgrim's Pride stock falls again after animal-cruelty charges [electronic version]. *The Associated Press State & Local Wire.* Retrieved September 24, 2005, from http://web.lexis-nexis.com/universe/document?
_m=14ea8036ec54c7a7bbea5a27ce3d8261&_docnum=76&wchp=dGLbVlb-zSkVb&
_md5=22af43d74c1521e76357a348290f965a

Kraidy, M. M., & Goeddertz, T. (2003). Transnational advertising and international relations: U.S. press discourses on the Benetton "We on Death Row" campaign. *Media, Culture & Society, 25,* 147–165.

Kruckeberg, D. (1994, August). *A preliminary identification and study of public relations models and their ethical implications in select internal public relations departments and public relations agencies in the United Arab Emirates.* Paper presented at the meeting of the Association for Education in Journalism and Mass Communication conference, Atlanta, GA.

Kruckeberg, D. (1995). International journalism ethics. In J. C. Merrill (Ed.), *Global journalism: Survey of international communication* (pp. 77–87). New York: Longman.

Kruckeberg, D. (1995–1996, Winter). The challenge for public relations in the era of globalization. *Public Relations Quarterly, 40*(4), 36–38.

Kruckeberg, D. (1996, September). Answering the mandate for a global presence. *International Public Relations Review, 19*(2), 19–23.

Kruckeberg, D. (1999, August). *Overlaying First World public relations on Second and Third World societies.* Paper presented at the meeting of the Association for Education in Journalism and Mass Communication conference, New Orleans, LA.

Kruckeberg, D. (2000). Public relations: Toward a global professionalism. In J. A. Ledingham & S. D. Bruning (Eds.), *Public relations as relationship management: A relational approach to the study and practice of public relations* (pp. 145–157). Mahwah, NJ: Lawrence Erlbaum Associates.

Kruckeberg, D., Badran, B. A., Ayish, M. I., & Awad, A. A. (1994). *Principles of public relations.* Al-Ain: United Arab Emirates Press.

Lillkvist, M. (2004, March 15). Blogs grow up: Ads on the sites are taking off. *Wall Street Journal,* p. B1.

Mallinson, B. (1991). A clash of culture: Anglo-Saxon and European public relations. New versus old, or just dynamic interaction? *International Public Relations Review, 14*(3), 24–29.

Mathews, A. W. (2000, October 12). Advertisers find many Web sites too tasteless. *Wall Street Journal,* pp. B1, B14.

Matthews, R. G., & Pringle, D. (2004, September 27). Nokia bets one global message will ring true in many markets. *Wall Street Journal,* p. B6.

McBride, S., & Pasztor, A. (2004, March 1). Decency push, satellite radio is poised to grow. *Wall Street Journal,* p. B1.

McKay, B., & Terhune, C. (2004, June 8). Coke pulls TV ad after some call it the pits. *Wall Street Journal,* p. B1.

Merrill, J. C. (1996). *Existential journalism.* Ames: Iowa State University Press.

Mossberg, W. S. (2000, October 12). New ad scanner fails to prove itself helpful or convenient to use. *Wall Street Journal,* p. B1.

Neill, M. (1995). Computers, thinking, and schools in the "New World Economic Order." In J. Brook & I. A. Boal (Eds.), *Resisting the virtual life: The culture and politics of information* (pp. 181–194). San Francisco: City Lights.

Newsom, D., Turk, J. V., & Kruckeberg, D. (2004). *This is PR: The realities of public relations.* Belmont, CA: Wadsworth.

O'Connell, V. (2001, January 11). Edgy spots stir controversy, and results. *Wall Street Journal,* p. B13.

Office of Population, Bureau for Global Programs, Field Support, and Research, U.S. Agency for International Development. (1996, July). *World population profile: 1996.* Washington, DC.

Ovaitt, F., Jr. (1988). PR without boundaries: Is globalization an option? *Public Relations Quarterly, 33*(1), 5–9.

Porter, E., & Nelson, E. (2000, October 13). P&G reaches out to Hispanics. *Wall Street Journal,* p. B1.

Schiller, H. I. (1995). The global information highway: Project for an ungovernable world. In J. Brook & I. A. Boal (Eds.), *Resisting the virtual life: The culture and politics of information* (pp. 71–83). San Francisco: City Lights.

Sriramesh, K., & White, J. (1992). Societal culture and public relations. In J. E. Grunig (Ed.), *Excellence in public relations and communication management* (pp. 597–614). Hillsdale, NJ: Lawrence Erlbaum Associates.

Stephen, T. (1995). Interpersonal communication, history, and intercultural coherence. In F. R. Casmir (Ed.), *Communication in Eastern Europe: The role of history, culture, and media in contemporary conflicts* (pp. 5–25). Mahwah, NJ: Lawrence Erlbaum Associates.

Tsetsura, E. Y. (2000a). *Conceptual frameworks in the field of public relations: A comparative study of Russian and United States perspectives.* Unpublished master's thesis, Fort Hays State University, Hays, KS.

Tsetsura, E. Y. (2000b, March). *Understanding the "evil" nature of public relations as perceived by some Russian publics.* Paper presented at the meeting of the Educators Academy of the Public Relations Society of America, Miami. FL.

Vujnovic, M. (2005, March). *The public relations practitioner as ombudsman—A reconstructed model.* Paper presented at the 8th International Public Relations Research Conference, Miami, FL.

Wingfield, N., & Saranow, J. (2004, February 9). TiVo tunes in to its users' viewing habits. *Wall Street Journal,* p. B1.

13

Communication and Culture

CHRISTINE L. OGAN

Christine L. Ogan (PhD, University of North Carolina) is Professor of Journalism and Informatics at Indiana University, Bloomington. Her teaching and research have spanned the area between communication technologies and international communication. Her most recent book, *Communication and Identity in the Diaspora: Turkish migrants in Amsterdam and their Use of Media,* examines the impact and use of satellite television from Turkey in the lives of the migrants in the Netherlands. Some of Ogan's current work focuses on gender and information technology in higher education.

WHAT IS CULTURE?

We may use the term *culture* in our everyday speech and expect that other people have the same understanding of it that we do. It is so common a concept that we often don't take the time to think about what we mean by it. Culture defines what it means to be a human being. It is all our behavior summed up, our whole life experience. Perhaps because it is so all encompassing, Raymond Williams (1983) has called it "one of the two or three most complicated words in the English language" (p. 87).

In a good summary of the problem of duality of meaning in the concept as it is used today, Scannell, Schlesinger, and Sparks (1992) say the following:

On the one hand there is a concern with artistic expression and creative, aesthetic, representational activity, and on the other with ways of living,

For additional online resources, access the Global Media Monitor website that accompanies this book on the Wadsworth Communication Cafe website at http://communication.wadsworth.com.

the organization and nature of social activity. In both there is a concern
with the transmission and reception of values and meanings,
but the focus of attention and methods of approach are very different.
The study of the arts as culture, drawing on literary and aesthetic traditions
tends to a top-down view of culture embodied in the division between
high and low culture. The study of culture as a way of life draws more on
social history, anthropology and sociology and focuses on the structures
of everyday life and its forms of interactions—"popular" culture. (p. 1)

In its use as a concept referring to a "way of life," we speak of culture at all
levels and for all types of social collectives. Here, we will identify a few of those
that will be important to the subsequent discussion in this chapter. At the
broadest level, we could speak of human culture, but that is so vague as to be
impossible to grasp. More frequently, we refer to national culture, as if all of
the people living within a particular nation–state share the same culture. Of
course, culture existed before nations were formed. And many nations, such as
those in Africa formed out of colonial boundaries, were created with artificial
borders that included multiple cultures while dividing other cultures from
one another.

Mass media are key components in any nation's culture. For some, they
represent a low cultural form and are thus not worthy of serious study. People
who think this way would not value a sitcom on television as much as an opera.
Others, however, believe that the media, as popular cultural forms, must be
examined because they are so pervasive and touch so many people. Lord David
Putnam (1998), filmmaker and British Junior Minister of Education, in an
introduction to a speech by the Canadian Minister of Heritage to a European
media conference, argued that one must look at the audiovisual industry as an
important component of a nation's culture.

Stories and images are among the principal means by which societies
transmit their values and beliefs, from generation to generation,
and community to community. As an industry we have developed
the creation and marketing of these images to a point at which they
confront us, intellectually and emotionally, in every aspect of our daily
lives . . . Culture is an essential element of the lifeblood of any nation.
It sustains the conscience and vitality of a society. One measure of any
community wishing to regard itself as truly civilized, is the quality and
depth of its cultural achievement. It's that which defines our personal
and our national identity.

CULTURE INDUSTRIES

The term *culture industries* was coined by Theodor Adorno and Max Horkheimer.
These men were part of a group who formed the Frankfurt Institute for
Social Research in 1923 in Germany. Before World War II, the Nazis exiled

the group to the United States, but following the war most of them, including Adorno and Horkheimer, returned to Germany. They developed an approach to scholarship called "critical theory" that was based on Marxist philosophy. Adorno (1991) said, in an essay published in English more than 20 years following his death in 1969, that he and Horkheimer had first coined the term *culture industries* in their 1947 work, *Dialectic of Enlightenment*. It was used to refer to "products which are tailored for consumption by masses, and which to a great extent determine the nature of that consumption, are manufactured more or less according to plan" (1975, p. 12). The two believed that the real purpose of mass media was to provide ideological justification for the capitalistic societies where these industries developed. Mass culture (a term they chose not to use because it had an "agreeable" interpretation) was developed as a tool of capitalism for the social control of society, according to Adorno and Horkheimer.

Though scholars today do not dismiss the idea that the mass media are instruments of capitalism, the term *culture industries* carries a more positive meaning today. The United Nations Educational, Scientific, and Cultural Organization (UNESCO) (1999) describes culture industries as important national economic resources that allow expressions of creativity to be "copied and boosted by industrial processes and worldwide distribution." UNESCO includes publishing, music, audiovisual technology, electronics, video games, and the Internet in the category of cultural industries.

Other Cultural Groupings

We may think of culture as the way of life of all human beings, or of nations, or of ethnic groups within or across national boundaries. But there are other specific types of cultures too. Businesses have cultures, and each business has its own set of cultural characteristics. Since global corporations employ people all over the world, it is likely that the culture of the corporation will conflict with the culture of the society where the employees live. If the society values harmonious family and personal relationships over personal achievement and the transnational corporation established in this society values individual achievement and loyalty to the company for all its employees, then it is likely that some cultural conflict will arise in this environment.

Other groups have cultures too. Any organization to which we belong develops a culture if it manages to survive. An organization's culture is the glue that keeps people attached to it and allows members to identify with it. It is the set of meanings the members of the group share. We all belong to multiple groups, each with its own characteristic culture. These include schools, religious organizations, civic groups, and even neighborhood groups. And certainly each family has a culture that distinguishes it from other families. Each family has a set of traditions, a way of living and interacting. We have learned from animal behaviorists that many animal groupings also have cultures.

TRANSMISSION OF CULTURE

How is it we come to understand, articulate, and accept the culture of any group to which we belong? We know that it must be learned. We are born into a family, a community, a nation, but must learn the culture of those groupings before we can become an integral part of them.

Clifford Geertz (1973) defined culture as "an historically transmitted pattern of meanings embodied in symbols, a system of inherited conceptions expressed in symbolic forms by means of which men communicate, perpetuate, and develop their knowledge about and attitudes toward life" (p. 89). The primary symbolic system used to transmit culture is that of language. Michael Schudson (1994) notes that "the importance of language as an aspect of culture can scarcely be overestimated. Language is the fundamental human mass medium. It is the mass medium through which all other media speak" (p. 29).

Benedict Anderson (1983) described the way "print capitalism" in the form of newspapers created "imagined communities" in the late 18th century where people came to believe that they shared a culture with people whom they may never have met face-to-face. The newspaper allowed people to read about others who lived in their nation who were culturally like themselves. Ulf Hannerz (1996) noted that this awareness made people also realize that there was something beyond their local culture. While writing and print allowed people to develop a sense of we-ness, "simultaneously, it would have underlined a sense of cultural discontinuity which was very congruent with the political ideal of the nation–state. As you are a citizen of one country and not another, and as territory belongs to one state but not the other, you identify with either one language or the other" (p. 21). So while written language increased the power to transmit one culture, thereby bringing people together, it differentiated people and nations from other cultures, thereby separating them. Silvio Waisbord (2004) says that this linguistic bond in contemporary society is achieved through television. Television helps perpetuate national cultures "by spreading a vernacular and reinforcing linguistic bonds among populations" (p. 374).

Families used to be nearly the only transmitters of culture to young children by teaching the symbolic system, or language, to their children. And until the children learned to read in their native language, few outside cultural messages came through to the children. That all changed when first radio, then television entered the household. Joshua Meyerowitz (1985) articulates this view in his book, *No Sense of Place*.

> Unable to read, very young children were once limited to the few
> sources of information available to them within and around the home:
> paintings, illustrations, views from a window, and what adults said
> and read to them. Television, however, now escorts children across
> the globe even before they have permission to cross the street. (p. 238)

Whether those cultural influences are detrimental or not is open to question, but television certainly sends messages that can conflict with the family culture. So children learn to negotiate multiple cultures from an early age.

This issue becomes more complicated when multiple languages are spoken. That can occur in the home when a family has migrated from a place where a different language is spoken and when multiple languages are spoken in the same country, as in Switzerland and Canada, for example.

Richard Collins (1990) believes that although language has played an important role in preserving the cultural distinction of the francophone citizens of Quebec, such small linguistic communities are always vulnerable to influences by the dominant language group through the mass media.

> Many in Quebec fear that modern communication technologies, particularly television, threaten the continued existence of their community, and thus francophone society in North America. They argue (and their fears are shared by many in metropolitan France who believe the world francophone community is vulnerable to the pressures of English) that Quebec's anticipated fate is representative, and that larger and larger distinct societies will be threatened with loss of identity and assimilation as the "mass" embraced by mass communication expands with technical change; as the mass embraced by modern communication becomes larger and larger, so the critical mass required for a community's linguistic and cultural survival also increases. (p. 192)

Transnational television stations now surrounding the globe expand this issue. In almost every country of the world, it is possible to receive one or more (usually many more) television channels of news, entertainment, and sports that are broadcast in English and delivered locally via satellite. Some people fear that the existence of so much English-language broadcasting brings us ever closer to English being the only world language for business, science, scholarship, and now news and entertainment. The pervasiveness of English is believed to threaten many other cultures. That may be changing, however, as currently only about 35 percent of the content on the Internet is said to be in English ("Internet Users," 2005). The dramatic increase in Asian users, particularly Chinese users, has also been marked by an increase in websites written in several Chinese languages to about 600,000 in 2003. People who speak a Chinese language constitute about 14 percent of the world's total users in 2005 ("Internet Users," 2005).

In some countries, like Germany and Turkey, all imported audiovisual media are dubbed into the local language. If the dubbing is of high quality, some viewers have trouble distinguishing a local from an imported product. In other countries, like the Netherlands, English-language imports are subtitled instead. When audiences can hear the English spoken by the actors in the program, the Dutch believe viewers will improve the quality of their spoken English.

HOW THE WEST DOMINATES IN PRODUCTION OF CULTURE

You may have heard it said that the United States is imperialistic when it comes to cultural products, specifically when it comes to films and television programs. No matter where you go in the world, you may find that Hollywood films dominate the screens of local cinemas and that U.S. sitcoms and soap operas fill a big part of the schedules of local television stations. And you may wonder why that is.

The easy answer to why so many U.S. films and television programs are aired internationally is that the United States produces more of them than any other country in the world. What's more, these programs and films are popular the world over. People really like the content. So why is that such a problem? Some scholars have conducted research on this issue.

As early as 1969, when Herbert Schiller, an American mass communications scholar, published *Mass Communication and the American Empire,* the U.S. domination of the world's media was noted. Schiller claimed in that book that the military-industrial complex in the United States was using its television programs and films to obtain world dominance in cultural products. In 1971, two Finnish scholars, Kaarle Nordenstreng and Tapio Varis (1974), decided to document the flow of television programs in the world by sending out questionnaires to program directors at television stations throughout the world. They asked people to calculate the number of domestically produced and imported television programs broadcast to audiences in their countries. Later they expanded the study to examine the international systems of sales and exchange. From the more than 50 countries included in the study, they determined that the international flow of television programs was overwhelmingly one way, from the United States (and to a lesser extent Western Europe) to the rest of the world. The authors found that the flow was dominated by entertainment content. Nordenstreng and Varis also concluded that the one-way flow was based on historical conditions related to the introduction of television and economic resources and demographic characteristics of the exporters and importers of programs. Television was an offshoot of the existing broadcast and film industries, and it developed first in the industrialized nations. Later, television hardware and software were exported to less-developed countries. Though the poorest countries tended to be more dependent on foreign production, it did not explain all of the flow. For example, India produces more than 1,000 films a year, the greatest number of feature-length films in the world and at least twice the number that Hollywood produces, yet it exports these films at a much lower rate than does the United States.

> There are thus other factors besides the economy of a nation which influence the extent of inflow of TV material. The population size is naturally of crucial importance, since it largely determines such marketing conditions as the size of the TV audience, the general dominance of a national culture, and usually also a common or unifying language. (Nordenstreng & Varis, 1974, p. 54)

Tapio Varis (1985) replicated the study in 1983, and the general conclusion was that no major changes in the international flow of television programs and news had occurred since 1973. Varis did find a trend toward more regional exchanges in the second period, however. But the increased transnational concentration of media ownership and the unknown effect of direct broadcast satellites on program exchanges led Varis to be concerned that the flow of media products would continue to be one way.

In 1977, Jeremy Tunstall, a professor at the City University London, produced *The Media Are American,* another major publication that influenced thinking about the role of the United States in the world's media. Tunstall added historical context and economic and cultural analysis to reach his conclusions about American media domination. Though he dismissed Schiller's notion of an imperialist plot to subjugate the world, his research supported the finding of U.S. media dominance in the world. And he expressed concern about the extent of influence the exported news and entertainment might have.

> The central thesis of the present book, however, is that the media are not just one more example of any general thesis. The media are about politics, and commerce and ideas. This is a strange enough combination even when the media stay at home. But as an item of international trade the combination is even more unusual. When a government allows news importation it is in effect importing a piece of another country's politics—which is true of no other import. The media also set out to entertain and intrigue—to make people laugh or cry—they have an emotional appeal unlike other products. And because the media also deal in ideas, their influence can be unpredictable in form and strength. (p. 263)

Other scholars also influenced the discussion of media and cultural imperialism at the time. Ariel Dorfman focused attention on the cultural messages contained in U.S. cartoon strips when he wrote *How to Read Donald Duck* in 1975. Arman Mattelart (1979) wrote about advertising and the commercial control of media industries. Still others, like Oliver Boyd-Barrett (1980) and Alan Wells (1972), wrote more theoretically about the concept of cultural and media imperialism. The trend in the literature of the period from the early 1970s to the mid-1980s was to view the United States as the destroyer of world cultures and world media economies. But most of the evidence brought to bear on the topic was economic evidence, not cultural proof. This is a problem, says John Tomlinson in his book, *Cultural Imperialism* (1991).

> Because of the constant tendency to revert to an economic account, where cultural "effects" of media imperialism are posited, they are invariably problematic. Either they are simply assumed and allowed to function in the discourse as a self-evident concomitant of the sheer presence of alien cultural goods, or else they are inferred using fairly crude interpretative assumptions. (p. 34)

That happened because it was relatively easy to examine program schedules and determine how much imported content a station would broadcast. It was also relatively easy to count the number of foreign films screened at local theatres and compare them with the number of domestic films produced in a given year. It was even easy to determine profits or losses from film and television production over time. What was more difficult was trying to figure out if people were somehow personally affected by the cultural messages contained in the television programs and films.

In Tomlinson's view, we could assess blame to specific institutions—the mass media, the United States, or multinational capitalists—when accounting for the economic aspects of cultural imperialism. But dealing with cultural domination is not so easy. Here, "it is not individual practices we are blaming, but a contextualizing structure: capitalism, not just as economic practices, but as the *central (dominant) positioning of economic practices* within the social ordering of collective existence" (Tomlinson, 1991, p. 168). And there are no agents to blame for this situation. Instead, the "cultural discontents have complex multiple determinations that have arisen over time and thus that no *present* agent is 'responsible' in any full sense" (p. 169).

Perhaps what we are dealing with is a redefinition of the cultural context for individual nation–states and communities. The focus on economic development—generally under the umbrella of multinational capitalism—becomes the guideline for every autonomous system, and economic interdependence becomes the key to survival in the global system, while the strategies for preserving important elements of the cultures of the societies around the world have received much less attention.

We have little information, concerning the individual effects of the consumption of Western cultural products. We know something about the effect on people's health when McDonald's and KFC become the preferred meals in cultures where the local diet is relatively free of animal and other fats. It would be nice to so easily measure the effects of hip-hop music on the teenagers of a particular country where traditional music was based on a different tonal system and was not amplified so highly that conversation became impossible in a room where it was played. Or it would be even better if we could attach electrodes to people's heads when they watch *Desperate Housewives* or the latest Steven Spielberg film to determine if attitudes and behavior are changed as a result of exposure.

Most researchers have to resort to asking people questions about their reactions to certain imported content and draw conclusions from what those people *say* about their attitudes and behavior surrounding that content. The alternative is to conduct ethnographic studies through observation of small samples and draw conclusions about what relationship the researcher thinks a given behavior has with the consumption of imported media. Perhaps because of the major limitations in available methodologies, few studies have even focused on the issue. Empirical work has been limited to a few studies of the impact of the old television program *Dallas* on groups of Israeli Arabs, immigrants to Israel from Morocco and Russia, Israeli Kibbutz residents, second-generation Americans in Los Angeles, and Japanese citizens (Katz & Liebes, 1985). A second study was based on a self-selected sample of responses to an ad in a Dutch newspaper requesting information from people about why they liked *Dallas* (Ang, 1985). The Liebes and Katz study (1990) is the most extensive empirical study, but it included only 40–80 people selected nonrandomly from each community.

It would be wonderful to be able to both analyze the texts of cultural products and the reception of those texts by audiences in countries where charges of cultural imperialistic practices have been made, but alas, the enormity of this task makes it impossible. We are forced, instead, to limit our focus to particular programs, such as the internationally popular soap, *The Young and the Restless,* or to try to determine the overall impact of the volume of imported products through in-depth survey. Or we could analyze the volume of texts exported from the United States and Europe on film or in television programs for the dominant cultural meaning. Though each of these methods taken alone is unsatisfactory, the accumulation of studies with limited focus could add to our understanding of the effects of imported cultural fare and could indeed help us to determine whether cultural imperialism exists and at what level.

The tentative conclusion from the limited research of the empirical work is that "audiences are more active and critical, their responses more complex and reflective, and their cultural values more resistant to manipulation and 'invasion' than many critical media theorists have assumed" (Tomlinson, 1991, pp. 49–50). So if Americans do export a large amount of media products, from news on television to feature-length films, we just don't know exactly what the cultural impact of consuming those products might be.

Marian Bredin (1996) believes that the power of the media to bring cultural change to any ethnic group is quite limited. In the study of the role of communication technologies in aboriginal communities in remote regions of northern Canada, Bredin concludes that patterns of "local resistance and cultural persistence" prevent imported media from having powerful effects. Bredin says that such power cannot be attributed to imported media because such a conclusion ignores "the historical processes of contact and change which aboriginal groups have previously negotiated. These include 'prehistoric' intertribal contact, migration and cultural diffusion, engagement in trade with Europeans, adoption of Christianity and syllabic literacy and the transition to permanent settlements and exposure to formal education. Taking these factors into account, it is clear that media cannot be isolated as the sole or even primary cause of cognitive, affective or behavioral changes among aboriginal people...." (p. 165).

Despite our inability to understand exactly how U.S. media may affect people in other countries, the worries about U.S. dominance have not diminished. In fact, they have expanded to concerns about transnational control. In a reissue of his 1969 book, *Mass Communications and the American Empire,* Schiller noted in the 1992 retrospective that his description of cultural imperialism and those responsible for it had changed. The companies involved in the spread of cultural imperialism had grown into conglomerates that were not only based in the United States but also in Germany, Japan, France, Brazil, and England.

It is the globalized audiovisual and Internet environment that now generates most concern. In the years since, satellite and cable television have extended the reach of national channels and privately owned transnational channels to television markets in every part of the world. The European Audiovisual Observatory attributes this phenomenon to three factors in the European member countries: the effect of deregulation; the advance of digital technology; and the overcapacity of European satellite systems ("Transfrontier Television," 2004, p. 6). The research that the Observatory prepared for the

Council of Europe found that 1,100 national or transnational television channels are available or originate in the European Union but that more than 200 of these channels are aimed at nonnational markets. In other words, they are global channels that also appear in other parts of the world without any acknowledgement of local cultures.

WHAT CULTURES DO TO DEFEND CULTURAL AUTONOMY

The international diffusion of television programs, films, and other media to countries is not a new phenomenon. Hollywood films have been popular in countries outside the United States for as long as they have been made. In the silent film era, it was even easier to export films because language was not a factor. Countries with large domestic markets for their cultural products always had an advantage as they could pay for the production costs at home and look to the export markets as mostly profit. This enabled the big countries to charge less for those programs when selling them abroad and be very competitive with other countries' exports. Small countries were at a disadvantage because they could not afford to produce many films or television programs and often had trouble covering costs because of the size of their domestic markets. They became vulnerable to the imported products, finding them cheaper than producing their own films and television programs. The research by the European Audiovisual Observatory illustrates that this issue persists. The organization's study found that while less than 1 percent of the audience in countries like the United Kingdom and France spent much time with transnational channels, 84 percent of the total audience in Luxembourg and 46 percent of the audience in Ireland were regularly exposed to such channels ("Transfrontier Television," 2004).

Several strategies have been taken by countries with low production of films or television programs to protect their own cultural products. Those strategies include:

- Quotas
- Subsidies and grants
- Regional alliances, including co-productions
- Adaptations of programs produced in other cultures
- Resistance measures

Quotas

The most significant policy for supporting domestic television production is that of the European Union. Drafted in 1984 (but adopted as policy in 1989 and revised in 1997) in a green paper titled "Television Without Frontiers," the European Union adopted a directive for its then-15 member countries that called for all television stations to devote more than half of their schedules to European programs. The directive excluded news, sports, advertising, games, teletext, and teleshopping from consideration. France, the country that keeps the closest watch on the preservation of its culture, was the strongest proponent of the adoption of this directive. France's protectionist cultural policy covers everything from cultural products like television and film to attempts at preventing foreign words from creeping into the French language. It is the only country in Europe to require television stations and film distributors to import European products. France also requires that no more than 40 percent of films screened in the country come from outside Europe. It also requires that 40 percent of the output on French broadcasting stations be French. Of late, however, France has had more trouble in maintaining sufficiently high amounts of French fiction on television or at the cinema. The Global News Wire noted that French state protectionism had erected barriers that excluded nonprofits, such as the programs created by the Public Broadcasting System in the United States. The article concluded that the situation where the "commercial and the mediocre often crowd out the excellent is most commonly caused by the restrictions on cultural trade imposed by the governments, not the forces of globalization" ("Making a Case," 2004).

Collins (1999) cites a document from researchers in France that says that French fiction (produced only by France or in coproduction with other countries) used to account for 49 percent of broadcast fiction on three major channels but in 1996 only accounted for 25 percent. That decline has continued. A press release from the European Audiovisual Observatory found that 626 hours of fiction were produced for broadcast in 1996, but only 592 hours were produced in 2003—the lowest in the five largest countries in Europe ("European TV Fiction," 2004). And though the numbers of French films increased from 97 in 1995 to 148 in 1998, the French share of France's domestic film market dropped from 35 percent in 1995 to 27 percent in 1998. More current data show some improvement. In 2003, the reported market share for French films in France was 34.8 percent but down from 35 percent in 2002 ("French Cinemas Suffer," 2004).

After the strong showing of the hit *Amelie* in 2001, ticket sales abroad for French films declined, with a 12 percent box office drop worldwide ("French Cinemas Suffer," 2004). French film critics have been blamed for being overly critical of domestic films while they praise American products (Riding, 1999a, p. E1).

The United States has taken the position that cultural products should be treated like any other goods traded in the market. In international trade talks, the United States has opposed the setting of quotas on film and television imports, viewing such quotas as trade barriers. However, other countries have been successful in obtaining a "cultural exception" for audiovisual products in the General Agreement on Tariffs and Trade (GATT), claiming that these are expressions of national identity and should be preserved. If no protection for these cultural expressions is provided, say those countries whose films and television programs are being threatened by imports, those industries might not survive. The World Trade Organization, consisting of 148 members in 2005, was created in 1995, successor to the 1947 GATT. The current GATT serves as the rule book for the WTO.

"Television Without Frontiers" was implemented in 1989 before direct broadcast satellite and pay TV options existed. Today there is less agreement on the degree to which broadcast stations comply with the quotas in Europe and how effective the quotas really are in maintaining a European identity in broadcasting content. As Feigenbaum (2004) put it, "There is very little a country can do to prevent DBS transmissions that do not respect quotas. Technically, this would probably require jamming and employing such a technique would immediately associate those jamming the signal with a practice only associated with non-democratic governments" (p. 255).

Subsidies

The United States also opposes the use of government subsidies provided for development of films and television programs. But many countries take the position that without subsidies, their audiovisual sector will totally succumb to foreign imports. The 15 countries of the European Union are trying to harmonize their national subsidies to work together to increase protection for all of their film and television industries. But according to an analysis in *Screen Digest*, "a European film industry only exists as a political ideal and has no concrete existence in reality" ("Towards a Single European Market," 1999, p. 261). The article concludes that unless all of the countries open up their national subsidy and incentive mechanisms to all European producers, a single market will never develop. Yet even with subsidies, European-made films are not the most popular in their own markets. For example, in 2003, the 20 most popular films in France included 16 made abroad (most in the United States), only 3 produced in France and 1 in Germany (Lichfield, 2003).

Italy is a country internationally known for its films, and in 1998, for the first time ever, a foreign film won the Academy Award for best picture. That was the Italian film, *Life is Beautiful*. Subsidies have helped keep the Italian film industry afloat too. In 1999, the state invested $94 million in 70 films. And recently, the government announced support of 74 million Euros (about $95 million) for 2005. Since the 1998 international success, Italian film production has fallen dramatically. In 2003, it produced 90 films, but in 2004 that number dropped to 25, with only 14 of those passing the Italian standards for minimum box-office take of 1 million Euros (Adler, 2005).

The European Union has been supplying grants for new production projects under a program called MEDIA (Measures to Encourage Development of the Audiovisual Industry). Now in its third five-year program under MEDIA II, the program's aim is to provide training and to "stimulate the distribution and development of European audiovisual works and to boost production companies" (Media Plus, 2005). Feigenbaum (2004) believes that subsidies offer the most promise for boosting production of cultural products, and he argues that government aid to film and television production should not have to be justified on an economic basis. "Culture is its own reward," he says (pp. 260–261).

Regional Alliances including Coproductions

National subsidies are usually carefully guarded and opened up only in the case of coproductions ("Towards a Single European Market," 1999, pp. 261–262). Coproduced films, usually ones that combine the talents and resources of two film production companies in two countries, have several advantages. They have a larger domestic market, that of two or more countries. They have appeal across cultures, not just within a particular culture. They usually have wider name recognition of principle actors, director, and so on. There is some evidence to support their economic success

The European MEDIA project is a regional alliance. Though loans and subsidies are its main means of supporting local projects, the fact that it exists as a regional organization displays moral support for local ventures.

In early 2004, EU regulators announced a plan to restrict European governments' ability to link industry subsidies to domestic production. The rule change required that national governments could only require that up to 50 percent of a subsidized film be made in the home country rather than the previous rule that allowed 80 percent to be made in that country. This move was expected to force filmmakers to co-produce a larger percentage of films with European and other partners (Stern, 2004).

Some bilateral agreements also favor coproductions. One such deal was struck between India and Canada. The two countries expected that the agreement would generate nearly $200 million to start and would take advantage of Bollywood's popularity and filmmaking expertise (Nag, 2004).

In 2005, in talks at UNESCO, about 100 European, Latin American, African, and Asian nations called for an international agreement that would allow state subsidies and import taxes on films, music, books, and television programs (Godoy, 2005). As might be expected, the United States, Japan, Mexico, and India opposed such an agreement. If it is accepted, the UNESCO agreement would override any other agreements before the World Trade Organization (Godoy, 2005).

Adaptations

For countries with smaller markets or fewer resources, film and television program production is too expensive to release many new products. In general, audiences prefer programs produced in their own language and set in their own cultural environment. In other words, they like local programs. The compromise that has been struck to address this dilemma is increasingly popular. It amounts to buying the rights to an imported television series or film and adapting it to the local culture and language. The producers, directors, writers, and actors are local. Only the format and the production values are imported. Soap operas travel particularly well when repackaged. *Good Times, Bad Times,* an Australian soap that has been remade for several European markets, accounted for nearly two-thirds of the German station RTL's advertising revenues in 1999 (Sacirbey, 1999). Game shows like *Jeopardy* and *Family Feud* have also done well in European adaptations.

In the last several years, we have all noticed a trend toward increased proportions of program schedules devoted to a genre referred to as "reality television." This format has become popular because of its low cost. But it is also a format that is easily exportable and can fit nicely into any cultural environment through local adaptation. Waisbord (2004) sees "format television," of which reality programs are only one type, as a way to appeal to local preferences for programs that culturally and linguistically match with audiences in every part of the world. He emphasizes that "language remains a pillar of cultural distinctiveness and national identities in a globalized world" and that the links between language and nation are in some cases "fundamental to an understanding of processes of cultural unification and difference" (p. 372).

Format television programs have also been imported by the U.S. television networks, less for cultural reasons than economic. *Who Wants to Be a Millionaire,* which originated in the United Kingdom, was one of the first big hits of the 21st century. Many of the reality-based television programs appearing in the United States, including *Survivor* and *Big Brother,* had their beginnings in Europe. The BBC game show, *The Weakest Link,* was adapted for U.S. viewing by NBC, but it retained the British host of the program, Anne Robinson, known for her mistreatment of guests on the show. When the program aired in the United States, the prizes increased dramatically to about $1 million from the UK version, which pays out about 10,000 pounds maximum. The program did not last long after 9/11 and lost its sharp-tongued host in syndication.

Another British program, *Pop Idol,* became fabulously popular in the United States as *American Idol* and then was picked up all over the world. This format program was ideally suited to local cultures as every nation could choose contestants to perform local music in the local language. When the program was aired in Lebanon as *Superstar,* it included contestants from several Arab countries—making it a regional production. But when a Jordanian singer won the Beirut-based contest and the people celebrated her victory in the streets of Amman, The Islamic Action Front in Jordan accused the Jordanian government of promoting the singer and the contest to "distract the masses" with nonsense (Abdallah, 2003). Some local spokespeople commented that the popular program allowed the citizens to be distracted from the serious public issues in the country. When the program aired in India as *Indian Idol,* Abhijeet Sawant, the winner, was besieged by parents wanting him to accept marriage proposals on behalf of their daughters. An estimated 48 million Indians watched the final round ("American Modeled," 2005).

Resistance

Some cultural groups try to resist being deluged by products from abroad by producing more products about themselves. This is a little different than offering subsidies or forming regional alliances, though the result may be the same. An example of how this has happened in Brazil might help explain the process. Brazil has a large television production and distribution system called TV Globo. It produces most of the television programs for the local market but also exports many programs to other countries. Within Brazil are groups of indigenous cultures that were there before Europeans arrived in the country to settle it. Today most of these native groups live in the Amazon rain forest, much as they did hundreds of years ago. As major parts of the forest are destroyed and settled by outsiders, the local residents see their way of life and their environment disappearing. They also feel their cultural heritage will disappear unless they do something about it. One of these groups, the Kayapo Indians, have resisted the dominant culture and its media with their own media. Armed with video cameras, the Kayapo have been documenting their own cultural traditions by recording their stories, dances, history, and ceremonies on video tape. The older Kayapo had become concerned as younger ones had abandoned the hunting and gathering culture of their ancestors for work in the lumber and mining industries. They also worried as they watched their children gaze at television in the evenings rather than listen to elders pass on culture through storytelling, details of ancestral customs, dream interpretation, and comments on changes in nature and the events of the day. So they began making an electronic record to resist being overpowered by the mass media of Brazil.

But recording one's own video is not the only way to resist mass media. Marie Gillespie (1995) found that Punjabi families in Southall London used prerecorded Indian films in their homes for a similar purpose. British television and films did not focus much attention on their culture, so to pass on the cultural heritage to their children, parents regularly used the Indian films as a focus of family gatherings. The BBC has recognized the need to attend to minority culture media interests. In developing new digital radio and television channels, the corporation had plans for dedicating stations focused on black and Asian listeners (Ward, 2001). An analysis by the BBC's marketing division in 2004 had this to say about the response to programs dedicated to minority interests: "White and South Asian viewers feel that the BBC is the best at ethnic minority representation on TV according to a report commissioned by the CRE in 2003. Whilst black viewers give Channel 4 and BBC ONE equal first place [sic]" ("Audiences: Ethnic Minorities," n.d.).

Television delivered by satellite is available to accomplish the same goal. U.S. satellite subscribers can pay a monthly fee to receive television channels from Arab countries, India, or other countries alongside their U.S. channels. DirecTV and Dish TV, the two major suppliers of direct broadcast satellite services in the United States, offer foreign language programming in at least 18 different languages and sell it in packages based on a world region or language.

In Israel, the Mizrahi Jews, an ethnic minority made up of Sephardic Jews and their descendants, now have their own television channel (Briza) that is delivered along with a package of several domestic and imported channels on the "Yes" satellite network. The channel offers music from the Middle East; drama from Egypt, India, Turkey and Spain; and local content that appeals to this minority group who believe their interests are not well served on the Israeli national channels (Sappir, 2001). Briza's director, Ron Cahlili, said he is not bothered by the imports on his channel. He sees them as "an alternative to McDonald's—the American and English-dominated culture" (Sappir, 2001).

Resistance can come in other forms too. For Canada, it came through legislation to keep Canadian advertisers from spending their money in split-run editions of U.S. magazines. Canada has a bigger problem than most countries in maintaining a unique culture. Sharing a 2,000-mile border with the United States as well as a common language, it is barraged by American television stations' signals that spill over the border. And American films dominate the Canadian box office. Of the box-office receipts in Canadian theaters, 91 percent come from U.S. films, with only 1 percent of those receipts derived from Canadian-made English-language films; Canadian primetime television programs are 70 percent American made ("Canada's Film Industry," 2005). American magazines also circulate widely across the border, constituting four out of five titles on the newsstands ("Culture Wars," 1998). Bill C-55 was created to keep Canadian advertising dollars in Canada supporting Canadian magazines. In 1998, the Minister of Canadian Heritage proposed a bill that would make it a criminal offense for Canadians to buy advertising in U.S. magazines produced predominantly for the American market. It went into effect in 1999.

Policies that resist foreign media domination have been developed in other countries too. Both China and India have a ban on direct broadcast satellite and the associated subscription fees. Though Asia was once thought to be an economic boom market for satellite television, international satellite television broadcasters like Rupert Murdoch have found that they have to supply programming free to domestic cable television companies and hotels, relying on advertising revenues for profits ("Asian Restrictions and Censorship," 1999).

NOT ALL POP CULTURE IS AMERICAN

From the evidence presented, it would seem that the media really are American, and aside from a few pockets of resistance, there has been little success in battling with Hollywood or U.S. television producers and satellite broadcasters. But audiences around the world still prefer their local cultures and their local cultural products to those that are imported. Current trends seem to show that local production is regaining dominance in television content. In India, Japan, Russia, and Brazil, domestic production accounts for between 70 and 96 percent of market share ("Making a Case," 2004).

Music sales provide even more optimism. Germany is the world's third-largest music market, following the United States and Japan. There, local performers earn nearly half of the $3.5 billion in annual sales. More than half of music sales in Spain are generated by Spanish and Latin American artists. And about half of French sales go to French rock groups ("Culture Wars," 1998). In the United States, much international music is sold; specifically, Spanish and Latin American artists are most popular.

Musical comedy, originally an American cultural form, has been looking to England for some of its best musicals since the mid-1970s; *The Phantom of the Opera, Joseph and the Amazing Technicolor Dreamcoat, Les Miserables,* and *Jesus Christ*

Superstar are among them. The latest example is the 2005 Broadway opening of *Monty Python and the Search for the Holy Grail,* reinvented as the musical *Spamalot.*

Much of the magazine and book publishing in the United States is also owned by foreign companies. The biggest U.S. publisher, Random House, is owned by a German company, Bertelsmann AG, for example. Harper-Collins is owned by Australian Rupert Murdoch, who became a U.S. citizen in order to purchase broadcast stations in this country.

ROLE OF JOURNALISTS IN PRODUCTION OF CULTURE

Culture is at the core of what journalists do. Though it is now widely recognized to be unachievable and probably undesirable, the goal of objectivity was the aim of news production for decades. Journalists were expected to produce news without bias, as if they could detach themselves somehow from what they wrote. If that had been possible, perhaps we could think of news as a culture-free product. The news event occurs; the journalist shows up on the scene and writes down the facts of the event. If it is a televised event, the camera records the details of the event or the interviews with the experts on videotape. The journalist then writes the story and the next day it appears in the newspaper or it is aired that evening on television. If news were really produced that way, theoretically it could be translated into other languages and disseminated to audiences throughout the world and be understood in exactly the same way. The event would be understood as it actually happened.

But as John Fiske (1987) points out in his writing about television news culture, the empiricist concept of objectivity that has been under attack for most of this century does not exist. The concept of objectivity assumes that there is a single truth, but Fiske says that " 'truth' exists only in the (television) studio, yet that 'truth' depends for its authenticity upon the eyewitness and the actuality film, those pieces of 'raw reality' whose meanings are actually made by the discourse of the studio, but whose authenticating function allows that discourse to disguise its productive role and thus to situate the meanings in the events themselves" (pp. 288, 289). In other words, the television news producer deceives herself that truth exists and the production of the news story is just a matter of organizing it for easy consumption by the audience.

Herbert Gans (1980), a sociologist who wrote a highly regarded book about the culture of news production based on an ethnographic study of CBS, NBC, *Newsweek and Time,* said that "enduring values are built into news judgment; as a result, most values and opinions enter unconsciously" (p. 182). Those enduring values spring from the cultural orientation of the journalist. Gans groups the enduring values into eight clusters: ethnocentrism, altruistic democracy, responsible capitalism, small-town pastoralism, individualism, moderatism, social order, and national leadership (p. 42). While some of these values travel across national and cultural boundaries, others are firmly grounded in American culture.

News culture is also revealed in news formats. As U.S. news has traveled the globe, first through international newspapers and news magazines, and later through television news, U.S. news formats have been picked up and copied by news organizations around the world. CNN, which appears in more than 200 countries, has perhaps had more influence on international broadcast news formats than any other single U.S. news organization. The use of stand-ups, voiceovers, outtakes, and sound bites has become ubiquitous in national television news programs everywhere. Whether we like it or not, this is another way that U.S. media culture has been adopted in other countries.

MANAGING CULTURAL CONFLICT

We are all well aware that cultures of the world do not always get along. Nations go to war with other nations; ethnic minorities within nations do battle with the dominant culture of the nation; and religious and racial differences reveal themselves in many different places. Our concern is what role the media play in ameliorating or exacerbating such conflicts internationally.

As the media become increasingly global, circulating news, information, and entertainment across borders, we might think that they would be able to help smooth out the differences between various cultural groupings. Benjamin Barber (1995), a political scientist, thinks that we need to understand two opposing trends in the world to understand what is happening on this front: globalization vs. fragmentation. Or as his book title says it, *Jihad vs. McWorld*.

> The first scenario rooted in race holds out the grim prospect of a retribalization of large swaths of humankind by war and bloodshed: a threatened balkanization of nation-states in which culture is pitted against culture, people against people, tribe against tribe, a Jihad in the name of a hundred narrowly conceived faiths against every kind of interdependence, every kind of artificial social cooperation and mutuality: against technology, against pop culture, and against integrated markets; against modernity itself as well as the future in which modernity issues. The second paints that future in shimmering pastels, a busy portrait of onrushing economic, technological, and ecological forces that demand integration and uniformity and that mesmerize peoples everywhere with fast music, fast computers and fast food—MTV, Macintosh, and McDonald's—pressing nations into one homogenous global theme park, one McWorld tied together by communications, information, entertainment, and commerce. Caught between Babel and Disneyland, the planet is falling precipitously apart and coming reluctantly together at the very same moment. (p. 4)

In a multicultural world where only about 20 of the world's states are homogeneous, many cultural groups feel they are buried by global culture and global corporations. Barber (1995) claims that the search for local identity, "some set of common personal attributes to hold out against the numbing and neutering uniformities of industrial modernization and the colonizing culture of McWorld" (p. 9), may end up as an open rebellion against a dominating group that seeks to wipe out that identity. If that is true, then the global media merely encourage cultural conflict by sending the message that we are all alike, we are all consumers, and nothing makes us unique.

And just as the media have become more global, they are simultaneously taking on an increasingly local character. Cable television has acquired the technical ability to deliver hundreds of channels to our home, and satellite dishes allow the reception of an equally large number of channels. The Internet provides millions of sites for media consumers. And as the cost to address smaller and smaller target audiences comes within reach, it is possible for people to tune out the global media and tune in media that address only our particular ethnic, religious, political, linguistic, and racial interests. So we stop learning about others and focus only on ourselves and those who are like us, allowing us more opportunity to feed our prejudices and ignorance.

One example of the role of television in this regard is that of MED-TV, later known as Medya TV. Medya was a Kurdish-language television station broadcast from several different European countries, ending up in France until the French courts closed it in 2004. The Kurds are a minority group who populate portions of Turkey, Iraq, and Iran, and who have never had a nation–state. They have been denied various rights in all three countries where they live. In Turkey, they were not permitted the right to schooling or mass media in their native language until the Turks allowed Kurdish language broadcasting in 2004. Otherwise, they have full rights as citizens of Turkey. The primary media in Turkey—both print and broadcast—are disseminated in Turkish. Ataturk, the founder of modern Turkey, believed that everyone who lived within the borders of the Turkish Republic should be identified as Turks. That included the Kurdish population. The Kurds, for their part, have wanted to publicly express their unique cultural and linguistic identity. For about 16 years, the PKK, a Kurdish revolutionary group, waged a separatist war in southeastern Turkey. In 1994, MED-TV was established as a broadcasting voice to the Kurdish peoples wherever they live. Because Turkey would not grant permission for such a station, the organizers began broadcasting via satellite from London. The Turks said the British should close the station because it was owned by the PKK and was airing revolutionary messages. The Kurds denied any direct PKK connection with the station. The managers said they only wished to be able to transmit the Kurdish language and culture to their people. In April 1999, the Independent Television Commission in Britain agreed that the station had been broadcasting programs that might encourage acts of violence in Turkey (Kinzer, 1999) and closed down the station. The station's director, Hikmet Tabak, claimed that the decision was made following pressure by the Turkish government to close it down. The station was located in other European cities following its closure in the United Kingdom. Of late, several other Kurdish stations have sprung up in Europe to serve the international Kurdish community.

This case is clearly complex but not unusual. Television may have been used to exacerbate a conflict between some Kurdish citizens in Turkey and the

Turkish government. It might have encouraged a prolongation of the violence and acts of terror. The station claimed it was doing no such thing. It was merely enriching the cultural experience of the Kurdish people by broadcasting in their language about subjects of interest to their cultural group. The Kurds have claimed the national television stations in Turkey do not articulate their interests or celebrate their culture.

To further the communication about topics related to the Kurds, several websites have been opened. This is also a common practice for other minority groups, especially when they feel that their voices are being suppressed by mainstream national or global media.

The Kurdish example is representative of the way cultures struggle to preserve a distinctive identity. In doing so, however, they may create more conflict with other cultural groups, rather than creating a climate for mutual cultural understanding.

HYBRID CULTURES AND THE MEDIA

In the United States, perhaps more so than in any other nation, a variety of ethnic groups have come together to live in the same geographic space. Here it has been called a "melting pot," though the term has been frequently criticized. The melting pot referred to the concept of bringing a variety of cultural groups together. As people migrated to the United States, each group lost some of its unique characteristics while it acquired characteristics of other cultures—mostly of the dominant or "American" culture. The melting pot concept also brought a promise of a better life for immigrants. In exchange for giving up some of their cultural distinctiveness and assimilating into the dominant culture, they were given the same democratic rights and freedoms as other Americans, whether born here or naturalized citizens.

Of course, none of these groups ever became totally assimilated. They held onto the traditions of their cultural roots, some even keeping their language over generations. And the media helped them preserve those ties. Newspapers in a variety of languages circulated in the big cities. Blocks of time were purchased for radio or television broadcasting in other languages. Even whole television stations broadcast in other languages, particularly in areas where large numbers of immigrants from a particular culture lived. In recent times, Spanish-language broadcasting has been the most popular. Hispanics constituted more than 14 percent of the U.S. population at the end of 2004 and are both the fastest-growing and largest minority population in the country ("Hispanic Trends," 2005). So, the United States has a large audience for Spanish language media. Univision Communications, a Spanish-language media company, claims to broadcast to 97 percent of Hispanic households through its 32 broadcast stations and its cable affiliates and cable company, Galavision ("Univision to Launch," 2005).

While immigrants may hold onto their cultural roots when they settle in another society, they also modify their traditions and behaviors in what has been called variously a process of hybridity, creolization, or glocalization.[1] Cultural identity is not fixed but rather is fluid and dynamic, and that is true for everyone, whether immigrant or native in a particular place. As Stuart Hall (1992) has put it, several consequences for cultural identity are related to the process of globalization. As national identities decline and local identities are strengthened through resistance to globalization, new identities of hybridity also take the place of the old national identities.

> Cultural identities come from somewhere, have histories. But, like everything which is historical, they undergo constant transformation. Far from being eternally fixed in some essentialized past, they are subject to the continuous "play" of history, culture and power. Far from being grounded in a mere "recovery" of the past, which is waiting to be found, and which, when found, will secure our sense of ourselves into eternity, identities are the names we give to the different ways we are positioned by, and position ourselves within, the narratives of the past. (Hall, 1997, p. 52)

Hall was writing primarily about the experience of migrants who live in the diaspora. They bring their histories with them when they migrate, but those histories change and develop as they blend with the culture where they find themselves and with their day-to-day experiences. Thus, the terms *hybridity* or *creolization* refer to the mix of cultural frames for all of us. The dominant culture also takes on characteristics and traditions from the migrants to that culture. That is especially revealing as we look in a telephone directory for a list of restaurants in any given community. The world's cuisines are available in even small-town settings. And the term *fusion* has come to be applied to the mix of ingredients and cooking styles from two or more cultures to form new dishes.

Robertson (1994) writes that this process of fusion or glocalization occurs in the world's media too. He disputes the notion of media imperialism, arguing that (1) cultural messages sent from the U.S. to other cultures are differentially received and interpreted according to the local cultural context; (2) U.S.–produced films and television programs tailor their products to a global market because they need the international market to be profitable; (3) seemingly national cultural resources, like Shakespearean plays, end up being interpreted and consumed in a local way and no longer belong to the culture where they originated; and (4) ideas and cultural products flow from the "periphery" to the "center" (or from the Third World to the West) far more often than we have thought (p. 46).

---

1. These terms have been developed in discussions of cultural identity by several authors. See Ulf Hannerz, *Transnational Connections,* London: Routledge, 1996, for a discussion of creolization; Roland Robertson, "Globalisation or Glocalization," *The Journal of International Communication, 1*(1), 1994, pp. 33–52 for a discussion of glocalization; and Homi K. Bhabha *The Location of Culture, London, Routledge, 1994, for a discussion of hybridity.*

Because it makes good business sense, many television program producers and filmmakers include characters from a variety of ethnic backgrounds, set plots in other cultural environments, and include story lines that deal with ethnic issues. Minority cultures form audiences too. And they buy products. It therefore becomes important to satisfy their interests and lure them to the box office, to tune in the channel, or to buy the newspaper or magazine. If media executives have come a little late to this realization, they are certainly catering more to minority interests today.

WHAT WE CAN CONCLUDE

So in trying to sum up the issue of global culture as it is presented through the media, it is hard to make generalizations. We have seen that the United States dominates in the production of films and television programs. Journalism, American-style, is also exported around the globe in broadcast and print formats. And yet, as powerful as the United States is in the global place of its cultural products, people in other countries have been able to preserve their own cultures and even do some influencing of their own. We are all born and raised into a nation, a community, and a family. And what we learn to value in these cultural environments sticks with us for life. Even if we leave our family, our community, and our nation, we never fully leave those cultures behind. No matter how many television programs or films we watch, or how many books we read in our own language or other languages, we never totally abandon the cultures into which we were socialized. Rather, we learn to value new cultures and add them to the mix of what we already know. That's why it is so hard to understand and write about communication and culture. I often think that my life experiences in different cultures have caused me to leave little pieces of myself in various parts of the globe. And when I return to a certain place, I remember what it is I enjoyed about that place: the music in an Irish pub, the coffee in a little street café in Paris, the weekly market in any Turkish town or village. But also, the farmer's market in Blooming-ton, Indiana. Re-experiencing the things I like in a particular culture reminds me that different personal needs are satisfied in different places by different cultures.

For more information on the topics that appear in this chapter, use the password that came free with this book to access InfoTrac College Edition. Use the following words as keyterms and subject searches: glocalization, globalization, cultural identity, culture industries, cultural products, cultural norms, cultural dominance, cultural imperialism, intercultural communication, media influence, cultural conflicts, hybrid cultures, acculturation, indigenous cultures.

QUESTIONS FOR DISCUSSION

1. In this chapter, our mass media have been described as *culture industries*. Does the use of that term make you uncomfortable? What problems are raised by

the combination of business and culture? Is there a way we could have cultural products without making money from them?

2. This chapter has discussed several ways in which countries try to protect their cultural products. Why might that not be a good idea? What would change if countries took the opposite position and instead were happy to send and receive cultural products, such as books, television programs, and films, more freely? A plan by the BBC to market television programs to users via Internet download is in a trial stage. Should it be successful, what impact might that have on audiences around the world?

3. How easy is it to change people's minds by exposing them to films or television programs with a different cultural perspective or set of values?

4. How might the media be used to resolve cultural conflict instead of exacerbating it?

5. How likely is it that the process of globalization might lead someday to one global culture with little or no local or regional variation on that culture? Is "format television" moving the world in that direction? If that should happen, what might our mass media look like?

REFERENCES

Abdallah, S. (2003, August 19). Islamists blast government role in TV show. United Press International. Retrieved September 20, 2005, from LexisNexis online database (News library). Adler, T. (2005, February 23). Cinefund expects to launch before summer 2005. *Screen Finance*. Retrieved September 20, 2005, from http://www.gii.co.jp/sample/pdf/fi6685.pdf

Adorno, T. W. (1975). Culture industry reconsidered (A. G. Rabinbach, trans.). *New German Critique, 6,* 12–19.

Adorno, T. W. (trans.). (1991). *The Culture Industry.* London: Routledge.

American modeled "Indian Idol" hunted by fathers with marriage proposals. (2005, March 19). Agence France Presse—English. Retrieved September 20, 2005, from LexisNexis online database (News library).

Anderson, B. (1983). *Imagined communities: Reflections on the origin and spread of nationalism.* London: Verso.

Ang, I. (1985). *Watching Dallas: Soap opera and the melodramatic imagination.* London: Methuen.

Asian restrictions and censorship of internet and television. (1999, October 16). *The Economist.* Retrieved from Lexis-Nexis online database. (News library).

Audiences: Ethnic minorities. (n.d.) Retrieved September 22, 2005, from http://www.bbc.co.uk/commissioning/marketresearch/audiencegroup7.shtml

Barber, B. (1995). *Jihad vs. mcworld.* New York: Times Books.

Bhabha, H. (1994). *The location of culture.* New York: Routledge.

Boyd-Barrett, O. (1980). *The international news agencies.* London: Constable.

Bredin, M. (1996). Transforming images: Communication technologies and cultural identity in nishnawbe-aski. In D. Howes (Ed.), *Cross-cultural consumption: Global markets local realities* (pp. 161–177). New York: Routledge.

Canada's film industry enjoys considerable success in the shadow of a cultural giant [electronic version]. (2005, Winter). *Canada World View 24.* Retrieved September 20, 2005, from http://www.dfait-maeci.gc.ca/canada-magazine/05-title-en.asp

Collins, R. (1990). *Culture, communication and national identity: the case of Canadian television.* Toronto: University of Toronto Press.

Collins, R. (1999). European Union media and communication policies. In J. Stokes & A. Reading (Eds.), *The media in Britain: Current debates and developments* (pp. 158–169). London: MacMillan.

Culture wars. (1998, September 12). *The Economist,* p. 97.

Dorfman, A. (1975). *How to read Donald Duck: Imperialist ideology in the Disney comic.* Translation by A. Mattelart. New York: International General.

European TV fiction down. (2004, October 1). European Audiovisual Observatory. Strasbourg. Retrieved September 20, 2005, from http://www.obs.coe.int/about/oea/pr/mipcom2004.html

Feigenbaum, H. (2004). Is technology the enemy of culture? *International Journal of Cultural Policy. 10*(3), 251–263.

Fiske, J. (1987). *Television culture.* New York: Methuen.

French cinemas suffer 5.6 percent box office drop in 2003. (2004, January 14). Agence France Presse. Retrieved September 20, 2005, from LexisNexis online database (News Library).

Gans, H. J. (1980). *Deciding what's news: A study of CBS Evening News, NBC Nightly News, Newsweek and Time.* New York: Vintage Books.

Geertz, C. (1973). *The interpretation of cultures.* New York: Basic Books.

Gillespie, M. (1995). *Television, ethnicity and cultural change.* London: Routledge.

Godoy, J. (2005, February 17). Culture: U.S.–Europe battle erupts over protecting the arts. IPS-Inter Press Service. Retrieved September 20, 2005, from Lexis-Nexis database (News library).

Hall, S. (1992). The question of cultural identity. In S. Hall, D. Held, & T. McGrew (Eds.), *Modernity and its futures* (pp. 272–316). Cambridge, UK: Polity Press in association with The Open University.

Hall, S. (1997). Cultural identity and diaspora. In K. Woodward (Ed.), *Identity and difference* (pp. 51–59). London: Sage.

Hannerz, U. (1996). *Transnational connections: Culture, people, places.* New York: Routledge.

Hispanic trends: A people in motion. (2005). *Pew Hispanic Center.* Retrieved September 20, 2005, from http://pewhispanic.org/reports/report.php?ReportID=40

Internet users by language. (2005). *Internet World Stats.* Retrieved September 20, 2005, from http://www.internetworldstats.com/stats7.htm

Katz, E., & Liebes, T. (1985). Mutual aid in the decoding of *Dallas*: Preliminary notes from a cross-cultural study. In P. Drummond & R. Paterson (Eds.), *Television in transition: Papers from the first international television studies conference* (pp. 187–204). London: British Film Institute.

Kinzer, S. (1999, April 29) Kurds are determined to restore TV station shut by the British. *The New York Times,* p. A13.

Lichfield, J. (2003, December 27). Boom turns to bust for French film-makers. *The Independent,* p. 12.

Liebes, T., & Katz, E. (1990). *The export of meaning: Cross-cultural readings of* Dallas. New York: Oxford University Press.

Making a case for cultural globalization. (2004, September 9). Global News Wire-Europe Intelligence Wire. Retrieved September 20, 2005, from Lexis-Nexis online database (News library).

Mattelart, A. (1979). *Multinational corporations and the control of culture: The Ideological apparatuses of imperialism.* Translated by Michael Chanan. Sussex: Harvester Press.

Media plus: Third phase of the Media Programme (measures to encourage the development of the audiovisual industry) (2005) ... Retrieved September 20, 2005, from http://europa.eu.int/grants/grants/media/media_en.htm

Meyerowitz, J. (1985). *No sense of place.* New York: Oxford.

Nag, A. (2004, January 12). India brews up Canadian showbiz co-prod'n treaty. *Daily Variety,* p. 58.

Nordenstreng, K., & Varis, T. (1974). *Television traffic—a one-way street?* Paris: UNESCO.

Putnam, D. (1998, April 6). Introduction, *Proceedings of Audiovisual Conference.* Luxembourg: Office for Official Publications of the European Communities.

Riding, A. (1999a, December 14). *French fume at one another over U.S. films' popularity,* p. E1.

Riding, A. (1999b, December 15). The world trade agreement: The French strategy. *The New York Times,* p. D19.

Robertson, R. (1994). Globalisation or glocalisation? *The Journal of International Communication, 1*(1), 33–52.

Sacirbey, O. (1999, October 27). Germans want home-grown TV ... with U.S. look. *The Christian Science Monitor,* p. 1.

Sappir, S. L. (2001, January 15). Satellite TV's spicy dish. *The Jerusalem Report,* p. 40.

Scannell, P., Schlesinger, P., & Sparks, C. (Eds.). (1992). Introduction. In *Culture and power* (pp. 1–14). London: Sage.

Schiller, H. (1969). *Mass communication and the American empire.* New York: A. M. Kelly.

Schiller, H. (1992). *Mass communications and American empire.* Boulder, CO: Westview.

Schudson, M. (1994). Culture and the integration of national societies. In D. Crane (Ed.), *The sociology of culture* (pp. 21–43). Cambridge, MA: Blackwell.

Stern, A. (2004, January 12). EU regulators reveal new subsidy plan. *Daily Variety,* p. 58.

Television without frontiers: Green paper on the establishment of the common market for broadcasting, especially by satellite and cable. (1984). Brussels: Commission of the European Communities.

Tomlinson, J. (1991). *Cultural imperialism: A critical introduction.* Baltimore, MD: The Johns Hopkins University Press.

Towards a single European market in film. (1999, October). *Screen Digest,* 261–268.

Transfrontier television in the European Union: Market impact and selected legal aspects. (2004, March 1–3). Background paper prepared by the European Audiovisual

Observatory. Dublin and Drogheda. Retrieved September 20, 2005, from http://www.obs.coe.int/medium/radtv.html.en

Tunstall, J. (1977). *The media are American.* London: Constable.

UNESCO. (1999). Cultural industries: UNESCO sector for culture. Retrieved September 20, 2005, from http://www.unesco.org/culture/industries/index.html

Univision to launch first full power Spanish language television station in North Carolina. (2005). *Univision.* Retrieved September 20, 2005, from http://www.univision.net/corp/en/pr/Raleigh_30042003-2.html

Varis, T. (1985). *International flow of television programmes.* Paris: UNESCO.

Waisbord, S. (2004). McTV: Understanding the global popularity of television formats. *Television & New Media, 5*(4), 359–383.

Ward. A. (2001, January 19). BBC claims public support as it plans to invest Pounds 300m in digital TV and radio. *Financial Times,* p. 4.

Wells, A. (1972). *Picture-tube imperialism? The impact of U.S. television on Latin America.* Maryknoll, NY: Orbis.

Williams, R. (1983). *Keywords* (2nd ed.). New York: Oxford.

14

Patterns in Global Communication: Prospects and Concerns

LEO A. GHER

Leo A. Gher (MS, Southern Illinois University Carbondale) is Associate Professor at Southern Illinois University–Carbondale. A long-term media executive of broadcasting, television distribution, and cellular companies, Gher continues to serve as the chairman of the board of Avery Media International, whose clients include Arab Radio and TV, Egyptian Radio and Television, ENOKI—Japan, Lithuanian Broadcasting, and others. He is the author of *The Art & Science of Media Management – Volume I: Sales & Sales Management,* and coeditor (with H. Amin) of *Civic Discourse and Digital Age Communications in the Middle East.* Professor Gher is the founder of the Global Fusion Consortium, which presents annual international conferences, and is a two-time Fulbright Fellow to Croatia and China.

At the end of the 20th century, the United States Congress passed a laissez-faire Communications Act, which was the manifest beginning of a new world order for media around the world. This American legislation, however, was not the democratizing transformation of the information

For additional online resources, access the Global Media Monitor website that accompanies this book on the Wadsworth Communication Cafe website at http://communication.wadsworth.com.

age envisioned by the writers of the 1980 *MacBride Report,* but it was a sign of things to come. In the era of 20th-century broadcasting, traditional networks dominated the distribution systems of most sovereign nations. CBS was the model in the United States; the BBC, in the United Kingdom; Gostelradio, in the Soviet Union; and in such countries as China, India, Finland, and Egypt, among others, communications networks were ruled or regulated by governmental institutions. Although it is true that certain programs from one country were often aired on other nations' systems, the content control was always held within state bureaucracies or by the citizen-owners of the nation. But as the new millennium began, a de facto free marketplace of media had been established consisting of global networks accountable only to corporate stockholders or the chief executive officers of international conglomerates. In recent years, unique superplayers have emerged on the world stage, and media cartels have been formed to secure capital or dominate a marketplace. Telephone companies have joined with television networks, entertainment giants have merged with online powerhouses, banking conglomerates have united with cable operators, and computer software interests have partnered with satellite distributors. Other companies have forged horizontal alliances to control specialized business sectors.

The *information revolution,* in any case this generation's information revolution, seems to have come to an end, or at the very least a maturation. Some future historian will probably place its life span within the last 25 years of the second millennium of the Christian calendar. It has been called the driving force behind globalization, but of course all information revolutions (newspaper, telegraph, telephone, cinema, radio, television) have had a significant global impact. That this revolution, or any of its forerunners, will have had a greater impact on humanity than Gutenberg's printing press is highly unlikely. But this generation's information revolution has indeed had profound effects on the world community, and recent changes in entertainment and information services have occurred at a faster pace than ever before. Societies everywhere are now faced with four critical questions about the meaning of such change: Is humanity better off as a result of the transformation? Who are the winners and the losers? What immediate concerns should industry leadership address? And what are the prospects for the future development of media and communication in a new world order?

The purpose of this concluding chapter is threefold. First, the current status of the communication industry's global infrastructure will be reviewed; second, issues of privacy and information warfare will be examined; and third, the interdependent connections of global economics, transnational media corporations, and vanishing national culture in 21st-century media will be explored.

THE STATUS OF INFRASTRUCTURE
IN THE COMMUNICATIONS INDUSTRY

The term *information revolution* is often misunderstood, and to many people it is intrinsically confusing. Different writers have called this period of change "the communications age" or "the era of new media." Some authors have dubbed it the "computer generation," and of course, there's the popular designation, the "information superhighway." Nicholas Negroponte probably described it most appropriately when he called it a "digital revolution" because the fundamentals of this latest paradigm shift may be found in the transformation from mechanical and analog information processing to digital processing. No matter what industry sector is examined—radio or television, Internet or intranet, telephony, hobby games, ipods, e-commerce, or computerization—a majority of communication businesses are now supported by a digital infrastructure. One of the most important developments of the digital revolution has been wireless technology, first achieved through the use of global satellites. These space-based systems are now the established infrastructure of the modern global communications industry.

The Global Satellite System

In 1965, the first commercial satellite was launched into orbit. With the rollout of services, that initial geosynchronous satellite (GEO) could handle only 240 voice circuits at a single time. Orbiting satellites now carry approximately 40 percent of transnational voice traffic and virtually all television exchange among countries. Throughout the late 1990s and into the 2000s, numerous personal communications satellite systems were launched, using low earth orbits (LEO), which minimize transmission delays. More satellites were launched during this period than in the industry's entire 40-year history. Currently, more than 50 percent of the world's in-orbit transponders are C-band transponders, but the Ku-band frequency is the preferred frequency for future projects because launch protocols are simpler and less costly. At the beginning of the new millennium, geostationary satellites and low-earth-orbit satellites encompassed the planet, constituting a global infrastructure fully capable of providing direct voice, data, radio, and television services to the 6 billion citizens of the planet (Ricardo's Geo-Orbit, 2000). By 2003, there were 261 GEO commercial communication satellites in orbit and 49 more under construction ("Via Satellite's Global Satellite Survey," 2004). The sizeable swell in capacity suggests a virtual glut of space segments available today and underlies the exceptionally competitive market for satellite operators, as well as launch providers and spacecraft manufacturers (Boeke, 2002).

Asia–Pacific Rim

A number of prominent satellites have been established to serve the Asia–Pacific region. They include AsiaSat, InSat, KoreaSat, NStar, Palapa, APStar, MeaSat, Thaicom, IntelSat 801, ChinaStar, SinoSat, and Telkom, among others. Satellite providers in Asia have had a good idea of where the industry is heading. But the business model is not new in every instance, and there has been concern about the ability to move quickly when new opportunities arise across multiple markets. The main prospects for satellite services in Asia are in digital TV and broadband transmission. Direct-To-Home (DTH) services have been available only recently in a few countries but are growing. There is now a trend toward open markets, which is sweeping through telecommunications and broadcasting sectors (Brown, 2003a). Bandwidth demand in the Asia–Pacific region has spurred new business development, especially with terrestrial fiber companies (the "soft alliance") who may explore possibilities in working more closely with the satellite sector ("Asian Economic Tigers," 2001).

Furthermore, the development of hybrid networks may take the place of some global satellite services. A hybrid network combines both space and terrestrial connections to deliver customer signals efficiently and economically. BT Broadcast Services (BTBS) is one of the pioneers in hybrid satellite/terrestrial networks. It carries the Hallmark Channel's Asian feed by fiber optic cable from Denver to Hong Kong. It then uplinks this feed through BTBS's Hong Kong teleport, which relays the Hallmark Channel to millions of viewers across Asia. Such hybrid solutions serve the needs of a dynamic and growing Asian market ("Hybrid Networks," 2004).

The Middle East

Much progress in satellite services is being made in the Middle East, especially in selling broadband Internet access by satellite and direct broadcast satellite television (DBS). With Ku-band satellites centrally stationed over the region, the Arab Satellite Communications Organization (ArabSat) is one of the Middle East's most important service providers. Arab countries have, of course, participated in IntelSat for many years ("The Middle East Satellite Market," 2002). Moreover, NileSat, Amos 1, and the ArabSat DBS platforms have added considerable capacity to information and entertainment offerings in recent years.

As part of providing complete satellite services to the region, the Riyadh, Saudi Arabia–based ArabSat supports digital/analog TV and radio, and provides transmission facilities for most Arab countries' television programming. ArabSat members are Algeria, Bahrain, Djibouti, Iraq, Jordan, Kuwait, Lebanon, Libya, Mauritania, Morocco, Oman, Qatar, Somalia, Sudan, Syria, Tunisia, the Palestine Liberation Organization, the United Arab Emirates, Yemen, South Yemen, Saudi Arabia, and Egypt.

At the end of 2003, ArabSat provided platforms for its 21 member countries with four spacecraft offering broadband, telephony, and broadcast services. Industry research indicates that the Arabic pay-TV market consisted of 400,000 households, with growth expectations to reach 500,000 within the next few years, and experts say there is considerable room for growth in specialized TV channels and international programming aimed at non-Arab nationals living in the Middle East. ArabSat's newest spacecraft, ArabSat 2D, has been transmitting three digital bouquets since early 2003. It carries 30 TV digital programs in addition to private TV broadcasting of some of Arab states. The broadband availability within the Middle East is in a growth cycle. The number of broadband users grew 88 percent between April 2001 and September 2002 (Mitsis, 2003).

Africa

With the exception of some major cities, Africa's terrestrial communications infrastructure is scarce at best and nonexistent at worst ("Africa: Unexpected Land," 2004). There is no question that Africa is potentially a very big market. The International Telecommunication Union (ITU) estimates that Africa will experience a 64 percent increase in all telecom traffic by 2005, while Internet users in the region almost doubled in the period from 1995 to 2000 (Brown, 2003b). Players within the continent have been stimulated by PanAmSat's PAS 4 satellite, which began beaming programming from its high-powered Ku-band downlink to South Africa. Africastar now offers DTH digital audio to the continent, and organizations or companies like IntelSat and PanAmSat are currently providing Africa with better and more high-power transmissions services. Satellite systems also play an important role in Africa's cellular telephone platforms. In 2004, the largest growth for Anacom's satellite transceivers on the continent was for new GSM (mobile telephone) installations ("Africa: Broadband," 2005). With the expanding requirements for broadband applications, South Africa's Telkom SA recently launched a broadband service designed to provide always-on Internet access and data services for business/government users. According to industry reports, there are only 3 million Internet users within the continent's population of more than 700 million. Historically, Africa has been a trial for satellite companies to profitably expand their business, even though satellite footprints cover the continent. Problems are two-fold. The mixture of authoritarian regimes, government troubles and intermittent warfare has made the continent a perilous land for investors, and Africa's economic challenges and environmental catastrophes have produced a consumer base that would like to have communications services but cannot afford them (Careless, 2005).

Europe

Europe has always been the pioneer in the fields of DBS and DTH transmission services, and those services are flourishing throughout the continent. SES Global is targeting several applications, including DTH services, cable packages, occasional use, and governmental services. Eutelsat, another European satellite player, is fine-tuning its market presence by increasing its package offerings to its client bases. With the acquisition of the Atlantic Bird 3 satellite and the launch of Atlantic Bird 1, Eutelsat completed its goal of developing a fleet of satellites—its Atlantic Gate (Mitsis, 2002). Currently, the European broadcasting marketplace is entering a new and particularly vibrant phase, after a 3-year lull from 2002 to 2004. The focus of industry talk is centered on HDTV (high-definition TV) technologies and new consumer electronics devices such as the personal video recorder (PVR). Satellite pay–TV operators, such as BSkyB in the United Kingdom, Canal Satellite, and TPS in France, are already deploying successful PVR strategies. In terms of HDTV, the emergence of Euro 1080, the first European HD channel, is perhaps an indication of things to come (Holmes, 2004).

South America

Latin America is sustained by a variety of trans–Atlantic satellites, including IntelSat and PanAmSat, and thanks to the continued deregulation of the telecommunications sector, Argentina is becoming the region's satellite center. For the most part, individual users are permitted access to IntelSat directly, which is a growing trend for several countries on the continent. This enlightened policy is making life easier for entrepreneurial corporations in the satellite industry, which provides financial growth and business opportunity for the nations involved. A surge in satellite operators began in the late 1990s with privatization of international satellite companies and the advancement of satellite technology entering the first decade of the 21st century. One example is Intelsat's 907, which is now orbiting above South America at 27.5 degrees west. The satellite was built by Loral (SS/L), and is equipped with a payload of 98 transponders, 76 C–band and 22 Ku–band, in 36 MHz equivalents. PanAmSat's newest bird, Galaxy 3C is located in orbit at 95 degrees west, just above the equator and west of Colombia and Ecuador. Built by Boeing Satellite Systems, the 702 spacecraft supports a payload of 76 transponders.

Three major players, in numbers of transponders and/or estimated revenues, are Intelsat, PanAmSat, and SES Global, which appear to have accumulated 70 percent of the market in the region. South America has experienced remarkable growth in the market for satellite services, which has grown 20 percent annually from 1998 though 2003 ("Latin America: Big Challenges," 2003).

North America

The North American satellite scene has been changing rapidly and is undergoing a dramatic transformation in the opening years of the new millennium. The often–discussed World Trade Organization agreement has opened up the telecommunications market for a variety of services from different countries, and the formation of a Pan-American market for satellite services has emerged. United States and Latin American operators are forming partnerships; Canadian companies are offering services to U.S. businesses, and U.S. satellites have been authorized to cover Canada at the same time. The United States, nevertheless, continues to monopolize the North American satellite market and claims more geosynchronous satellites and more C–band and Ku–band transponders than any other country.

Compressed digital satellite technology has become the true success story of the communications revolution. Where transoceanic cables once provided the industry's primary infrastructure, orbital satellite systems currently dominate.

As Boeke and Fernandez (1999) report, "Satellites are blanketing all areas of the world, both developed and developing. In this sense, satellites already do and will continue to provide backbone telecommunications connectivity around the world" (p. 5).

HDTV and digital video recorders (DVRs) signify the leading themes for the DBS sector, and the broadband sector began enlarging its activities with the launch of Telesat's Nimiq 2 in 2002. DVRs are the core of News Corp's strategy for the future of DBS in North America. HDTV will become visible on the scene via Ku-band and Ka-band. Major players such as Boeing, General Dynamics, and Lockheed Martin are progressing to their launch and satellite businesses, but the smaller players such as Virginia-based Orbital Sciences are making noteworthy advances as well. In the coming years, DTH television services will continue to be strong drivers for satellite revenues in North America, and Ka-band business and two-way Internet services hold remarkable potential for the future. The greatest growth potential, however, will be found in direct-to-consumer services such as DBS, digital audio, and two-way broadband access ("The North American Satellite Market," 2003).

More satellites will be launched in the second decade of the 21st century, but the industry is entering a period of maturation in which second- and third-generation technologies are being implemented. Additionally, businesses are experiencing a transformation from geostationary-based systems to low-earth-orbit constellations, and many governmental operators are exiting the market, either by auctioning off, privatizing, or not replacing existing satellites. As a result, the market for space-based telecommunications services will become highly commercialized, providing ubiquitous coverage around the world.

Global Internet Services

The Internet is undeniably bound to national telephone systems, which are, of course, unevenly distributed around the globe, and attempts to measure this infrastructure are problematic at best. The *preeminent economies*[1] of such nations as the United States, Canada, England, Japan, and Germany have perfected sophisticated fiber-optic telephone (and cable) infrastructures, which support high-speed connectivity and full penetration of the market. Digital wireless systems are, moreover, becoming increasingly popular in all developed countries.

---

1. This writer favors redefining such expressions as *First World, Second World,* and *Third World;* and *industrialized, developing,* and *underdeveloped* for characterizing the economies of the today's sovereign nations. The decision is not motivated by political correctness but because the terms are antiquated and lack meaning in the 21st-century economic world. More useful descriptors might be as follows:

- *Preeminent economy*—a dominant world power in terms of gross domestic product (GDP), upon which other nations depend for commercial trade, market leadership, international security, and government stability. Examples are the United States, the United Kingdom, Germany, and Japan.

- *Developed economy*—a significant world leader in terms of GDP, upon which regional partner nations rely for commerce, authority, constancy, and defense. Examples

In 2004, according to Computer Industry Almanac Inc. (2004), the global population of online users of the Internet had reached 935 million. The United States and China accounted for almost 285 million users, or 30 percent of the online population. Japan, Germany, and India make up the other 3 of the 5 highest-ranked wired nations of the world, and the next 10 ranked countries include the United Kingdom, South Korea, Italy, France, Brazil, Russia, Canada, Mexico, Spain, and Australia. This group of 15 accounts for 99 percent of the online universe (Computer Industry Almanac Inc., 2004). In other words, the remaining 200 sovereign nations' online population is negligible. Efforts to systematically gauge the size and status of the Internet at any specific moment are tricky—the mere act of stopping to measure causes inaccuracies in the measurement. Down through the years, the growth of the Internet was estimated at a somewhat steady 10 percent per month. But in 1994, Internet growth exploded. Given a comparable sustained growth rate, aggregate worldwide users of the Internet should exceed 1.21 billion by the end of 2006 (ClickZ Stats, 2005).

With the implementation of personal communication services (PCS) technology in 1997, maximized penetration of telephone and television services, and the utilization of computer convergence technology, the United States has become the first fully integrated digital telecommunication market in the world. However, the picture is far different for both *expectant* and *base economies* of the world. Investment in communication infrastructure is considerably slower, and the growth of the essential components (computer accessibility, telephony networks, new media technology, and Internet connectivity) to give their citizenry access to online services is far behind countries with preeminent or *developed economies*. Statistics derived about such economies are stark. Nearly 85 percent of all websites worldwide are in English, yet less than 10 percent of the global population speaks English. The United States has more computers than the rest of the world combined, and the cost of a computer in the United States is less than one month's wages. In Bangladesh, a computer costs the average Bangladeshi more than eight years' income. In several African countries, the average monthly cost of Internet connection and services runs as high as $100 (USD), compared to $10 in the United States (Women's Learning Partnership, 2004).

Nonetheless, some expectant economies have had balanced growth in the number of people linking to the Internet. In the Middle East, 12 million people, or 3.4 percent of that region's population, are now online. By the end of 2004,

---

include the original members of the European Union, Canada, France, Scandinavian states, and the Asian Tigers.

- *Expectant economy*—a serious regional principal, with an uneven but normally upward-trending GDP, often dominant in a specialized, business sector; administrative policy is frequently fluid. Examples are Poland, India, Mexico, Brazil, Saudi Arabia, and China.

- *Base economy*—a nation whose gross domestic product is stagnant or shrinking and that relies on the international community for aid; governmental institutions are unstable. Examples include most nations of sub-Saharan Africa, Afghanistan, Iraq, Cuba, the breakaway states of Indonesia, and Russia.

Arab states had an average of 7.2 telephone lines per 100 inhabitants, which is approximately 13 percent of the average in North America (Community Tele-service Centres, 2005). Most Arab states rely heavily on coaxial-cabled telephone lines to link computer owners to the Internet. Many regions of the world are like the Middle East, where communications infrastructure progress has been piece-meal, growing only at an arithmetical pace (World Bank, 1999). This unhurried tempo is a problem and will cause a sharp economic crisis for expectant or base economies because nations with preeminent or developed economies are grow-ing at geometrical speed, and obviously, the gap is widening moment by moment.

Nations with base economies are another matter altogether. Most sub-Saharan Africa countries and much of Asia, excluding Pacific Rim nations and India, are without up-to-date telephone infrastructure. Living standards and the quality of life in some African countries are even now regressing. Low incomes for unskilled workers and high unemployment rates remain the situation. The income gap between the rich and the poor has never been so great (Larsen, 2001). Countries with base economies are now confronted by inexorable worldwide dynamics. The poorest countries are frequently described as being left behind by globalization. They receive little investment or private capital from abroad (Gher & Amin, 1999). In Africa, with a population of over 700 million people, there are fewer than 14 million telephones (Women's Learning Partnership, 2004). On the other hand, some signs of optimism may be found. Once low-earth-orbit satellite systems become fully operational, both expectant economies and base economies will be able to bypass the enormous build-out costs of land-based communica-tions infrastructure and will be capable of entering the new world order with one quantum leap to space-based communications systems.

To say the least, global telecommunications has been transformed. Devel-oped nations, world news services, and international business conglomerates have taken advantage of digital technologies and are far ahead of most other countries. The communication revolution is no longer a revolution—it has, in fact, reached a state of maturation. Electronics manufacturers, of course, will build better toys, terrestrial broadcasters will implement high-definition television, Microsoft and Apple will redesign computer operating systems over and over, and marketers will create a never-ending demand for new products—but the basics of com-pressed, digital technologies are now well established and widely accepted.

PRIVACY AND INFORMATION WARFARE

With maturation, the communications industry faces two intriguing and pointed issues: privacy and information warfare. In a 1928 judgment, Justice Louis Brandeis wrote, "The evil incident to invasion of the privacy of the telephone is far greater than that involved in tampering with the mails." The transformation from analog to digital, or from wired to wireless technologies, does not lessen the concerns about privacy and information warfare.

In the 1990s, the Federal Bureau of Investigation (FBI) initiated several programs that would not only ensure access to digital infrastructures but would also increase the government's ability to capture communications of all kinds. The earliest projects were designed to inspect digital telephone and pager communications, but later activities have been extended proportionately with the increased use of the Internet. Many U.S. lawmakers were appropriately cautious about institutionalizing such projects, but European governmental and police groups took up the idea quickly (Rogers, 1999).

Governmental Intrusion

For more than a decade, news sources have informed the public about a surveillance system called Echelon, which has been cooperatively operated by the security services of the United States, the United Kingdom, Canada, Australia, and New Zealand. Under a covenant known as UKUSA, the system entitles these countries to observe and analyze telephone, fax, email, and Internet communications. Echelon is, of course, able to monitor email and e-commerce from any part of the world, but the huge volume of messaging makes it impossible to scrutinize individual messages. To solve the problem, Echelon employs special computer programming known as a "dictionary." The dictionary is programmed by security services to search communications for key words, special phrases, or names of senders and recipients. Currently, the five governments use different dictionaries, each with its own specialized set of parameters. When a communication is flagged for its content by any of the dictionaries, it is automatically singled out for detailed analysis.

Echelon monitoring terminals are located around the world. The New Zealand and Yakima, Washington, stations oversee trans-Pacific satellite traffic; while the Sugar Grove, Virginia, station, along with Morwenstow in Britain, watches the Atlantic region. The Geraldton, Australia, station monitors the southern Asia region and some trans-Pacific satellite communications; and the Shoal Bay, Darwin, station oversees most of the Southeast Asian territories. All Echelon terminals monitor geostationary satellites in the Clark Belt above the equator quite easily, but it is more difficult for the terminals to observe low-earth-orbit satellites such as those used in Iridium, Globalstar, and Orbcomm fleets. Furthermore, domestic law that forbids government spying on its own citizenry has been one barrier for the Echelon group to overcome. Member nations circumvent this problem by simply spying for each other, then handing over intriguing data to partner nations. Because much of the process is automated, the system is open to abuse. It is estimated that 80 percent of the intercepted communications at the Geraldton station are forwarded to the CIA (Central Intelligence Agency) or NSA (National Security Agency) in Washington DC, without ever being examined locally.

Initial funding for Echelon was authorized during the Cold War era, when the Soviet Union was seen as an eminent danger to Western democracies. That threat, of course, has greatly diminished, but the system was expanded in the 1990s and then again after 9/11 when organized crime, drug cartels, and terrorist organizations were targeted for investigation. The end of the Cold War has moved national attention from the capitalist–communist ideological war to the economic battlefront, in which information is the new currency. There is evidence that much of the surveillance being carried out by the UKUSA group is now economic in nature and that the sharing of data is selective. Countries, organizations, and even individuals not within the Echelon alliance are at risk and are subject to abuses of privacy law.

The U.S. government, meanwhile, has been in the process of establishing a 21st-century electronic surveillance system called FIDNet (Federal Intrusion Detection Network) that would monitor government computer systems and communications networks for any signs of international terrorist hacker attacks. Data assembled would be sent to the FBI, which would then thwart the hacker attacks, a process that could easily be extended to the private sector (DIT-net, 1999).

Invasion of privacy in the digital age is not the exclusive franchise of governments; corporations are just as culpable. Recently, Microsoft began shipping communication software that permitted their operators to chat with America Online (AOL) users. AOL immediately revised its software to limit messages from hacker attacks. AOL and Microsoft redesign their software on an hour-to-hour basis—AOL to impede, Microsoft to circumvent. Cisco Systems, in another part of cyberspace, carelessly let it be known that their QoS (quality of service) programming could be sorted to block access to particular Internet activities. Open access groups are worried that anti–open access groups might use Cisco's QoS software to block cable modem users from seeing specific websites.

In another interesting development, Wink Technologies has been partnering with dozens of broadcast, satellite, cable, and television companies that plan to include Wink technology in future consumer products. The reason these companies are attracted to Wink is that its software has the capacity to monitor user behaviors: viewing habits, online surfing actions, and even purchasing trends. After monitoring, Wink programming directs the data back to the company paying for the service. The idea is to focus highly targeted advertising or direct marketing to online users. In sum, the federal government hopes to spy on its population to protect it from transnational crackers and al-Qaeda-like terrorist networks; AOL wants to safeguard its online customers from Microsoft programmers and constricted access to websites by Cicso Systems hackers; and Wink Technologies is creating software that makes it simple for content providers to gather information on everyone (Rogers, 1999).

International Information Warfare

For the citizens of the 21st century working in a global network of electronic commerce and online information, future war is not likely to come from a nuclear bomb, environmental disaster, or terrorist attack but by email. Computer hackers can spread cyber viruses that strike without warning, destroying a company's sensitive files, and cyber terrorists can scatter propaganda around the world in microseconds using the World Wide Web. In both the near term and the long term, cyber attacks will be the price paid for the freedom to surf the information superhighway. It is not a case of whether it *will* happen but *when*. Unlike the 9/11 attack against the World Trade Center, an individual or group hoping to cause damage now has the capability to incapacitate or cripple society without firing a shot or launching a single missile.

For many years, techno-evangelists have been hyping the benefits of the digital age, but they have steadfastly turned a blind eye to its hazards, and recently the online community has been visited by the dark side of the World Wide Web. With premeditation, crackers have constructed viruses that have disrupted and damaged governments and businesses on a planetary scale. In the summer of 2000, the innocuous "Love Bug" virus attacked computers on every continent. After a worldwide investigation to find the perpetrators of this electronic disease, it was determined that the program's creators posted the virus on the World Wide Web by accident, an accident that caused $10 billion in damage to businesses and individuals everywhere (Ewing & Kunii, 2000).

Showing off for their peers by breaking into secured targets is the initial goal of most computer hackers, but many malevolent crackers in cyberspace are out to do serious damage. The United States may be the world's only superpower, but it has been particularly susceptible to cyber attacks. The U.S. Department of Defense registers more than 80 attacks every week, and the U.S. government, as a counter-measure, has committed more than $2.3 billion a year to protect its computer networks from sabotage (Rogers, 1999). Most developed nations of the world are following the U.S. lead, and many experts now suggest that the next e-market boom will be driven by corporations specializing in e-security, rather than those focusing on e-commerce, operating systems providers, or software programming.

International Debate Concerning Free Access to New Media

In many expectant and base economies, information cannot be freely exchanged via the Internet. While claiming to protect the public from pornography or cultural invasion, many of these nations tightly control the right of entry to modern entertainment and information services. The governments of Saudi Arabia, Tunisia, Bahrain, Iran, and the United Arab Emirates, for example, block access to some foreign television channels and websites. Iraq and Libya have not yet linked to the Internet, and Syria, the only country in the Middle East that has made physical connection to the World Wide Web, has prohibited local access to its citizens.

But the outgrowth of tools to counter censorship and defeat surveillance—tools such as encryption, anonymous remailing, anticensorship proxy servers, and wireless communications—seems to be outpacing the machinery of government control. Moreover, many people in countries where media censorship is enforced are already using the Internet to overcome restraints on information. Local organizations are disseminating news more effectively than ever, newspapers are posting stories online that were censored in print editions, and cybercafes are appearing everywhere in nations that restrict home access to the Internet.

GLOBAL ECONOMICS, TRANSNATIONAL MEDIA, AND VANISHING CULTURE

During the past 25 years, many changes have occurred that require fresh thinking about the new world order in the communication industry and about global economics and cultural identity. Humanity is entering a post–communications revolution period, a time filled with punctuated uncertainties. Ideas and beliefs, organizations and institutions are being metamorphosed. They shift, they crack, and they break apart, and it is natural for people to feel great stress and a desire to return to the past, when the old certainties were the foundations of society, economics, and government. But in this new millennium, the community of nations cannot rebuild the past. As we enter this period, societies are being driven in two opposing directions. A constricting force drives people into isolation, and an expanding force drives economies toward globalization. The dynamics of constriction are created by the ethnocentric and populist themes of lost cultural identity and a return to traditional values, while the dynamics of expansion are being powered by transnational commercialism and a new media environment.

The breakup of the Soviet Union in 1989 may be seen as a case study of the constricting force at work. Such countries as Estonia, Latvia, Lithuania, and Poland, among others, wished to break away from their domineering commonwealth to revitalize a lost national unity and to rediscover their cultural identity. At the end of the 1990s, Yugoslavia followed a similar pattern, when such countries as Slovenia, Croatia, Bosnia-Herzegovina, and Albania severed their relationship with another overlord to reinstitute their own national character. In the summer of 2000, native Fijians insisted that Fiji be governed only by the indigenous peoples of the islands, Isatubu peoples sought independence from the Solomon Islands, Tamil tribes fought for freedom from Sri Lanka, and other comparable battles were waged in many regions of the world. It is an easily recognizable and very old pattern of society—it is the reawakening of tribalism.

Cultural Impact

Concerns expressed by peoples outside of Western civilization about the digital age are genuine and valid. As seen through their eyes, the consistent flow of pop culture media from the West is a threat to their culture and traditions. Although such tensions have existed for hundreds of years, the sudden and addictive impact of videogames, music CDs, computer software, stereotyping films, racial profiling, and Western television programming has intensified the defensiveness of societies in many countries. Such societies are notably protective of old traditions, religious proprieties, and conservative values, and are justifiably proud of their cultural legacies, preserved through the use of language, customs, culture, and their own media (Schleifer, 1992). Numerous countries have responded to this infiltration, imagined or real, through severe rules of censorship. In the West, freedom of expression is a basic right, protected by constitutional authority. But in many nations outside the Western sphere of influence, this type of censorship is easily tolerated, even expected, as a form of civic responsibility within a legitimate social framework.

For peoples of non-Western heritage, stereotyping in film and television continues to be a source of cultural, religious, and ethnic degradation. Although such stereotyping itself is intrinsically harmful, the larger problem can be seen only in the context of American entertainment dominance. Nearly 90 percent of films and television programs exhibited worldwide are American in origin, and these entertainment products are the main perpetrators of stereotyping imagery. No peoples are exempt, but Arabs, Iranians, and Turks have been particularly villainized in American action-adventure films.

Economic Impact

Global economics and digital communications systems encourage sovereign states to expand their reach outward and to create external partnerships to compete in the contemporary economy. It has not always been that way, however. In the Cold War era, economics and politics were bipolar—the mainstay in the West was the United States; and in the East, it was the Soviet Union. Both superpowers were willing to accept the responsibility of being the wellspring for international economics. In recent years, many business experts have envisioned three major trading blocs (the European Union, NAFTA, and Pacific Rim partners) as substitutes for the old bipolar system. These trading blocs would be large enough to support expectant and base national economies, but the tripolar powers would have to be willing to finance the process, just as the United States and the Soviet Union did after World War II. This has not occurred. To its credit, Germany has taken up the responsibility of resurrecting the East German economy, but Japan has been entirely unwilling to accept any negative balance of trade, however limited it might be. In their turn, Europe, Japan, the Asian Tigers, and now China have all used the American market to jump-start their economic and national development. But without easy access to global markets and modern communication systems, economic progress and growth are difficult, if not impossible, for countries with expectant or base economies. However, it should be obvious to all that the American market, as big as it is, cannot be the world's sole source of economic energy much longer.

At this time in history, the fundamental assets of capitalism—land, labor, natural resources, and cash—are entirely fungible; resources are moved unhindered and virtually instantly from country to country as needed. In a free market economy, any nation or consortium can compete if its fundamentals are in place, and the most important fundamental for creating economic wealth in today's economy is human brainpower. Such manmade brainpower industries as electronic computing, information management, and telecommunications are already dominant in world marketplaces. All sovereign states must make key structural changes to meet the challenges of the coming brainpower revolution. No peoples are exempt—not those of Britain, Germany, Japan, Estonia, Fiji, India, Kenya, Egypt, Brazil, Vietnam, Russia, or America.

What is required for the manmade brainpower economy of tomorrow? Free enterprise, an open market, an educated population, superior communications infrastructure, and 10,000 public- and private-sector partnerships are the key ingredients. This type of partnering is the linchpin for survival in future times.

CONCLUSION

As humankind enters the 21st century, it is facing a civilization with one super-power and numerous transnational media consortia, which are responsible to no sovereign state or world body. There are 3 preeminent economic powers and about 20 nations with developed economies—the clear winners of the information revolution. Some 50 sovereign states with expectant economies must make institutional or structural adjustments if they expect to compete in the market-places of the new world order. This leaves an estimated 150 nations with base economies as the undeniable losers of the information revolution, and with the constricting force fully active in the world, that number will increase over time as jingoistic groups break away from their current federal affiliations.

Civilization is changing, recreating itself at a geometrical pace, and the time lapse between each reconstruction is shrinking dramatically. At one time, the period of reconstruction proceeded at a millennium's pace, then in hundreds of years, then in decades, and now it has shrunk to less than a human life span. The next revolution will probably take less than 10 years to complete. Obviously, the kingdom of 1950s television has completely disappeared, and the "Tiffany net-work" of Walter Cronkite news has splintered into hundreds of information channels. The way individuals use entertainment and information services has changed forever.

In the meantime, as a direct result of digital technology, individuals have given up a great deal of privacy, and nations have lost a considerable measure of security and sovereignty. It is clear that the utopian hopes for this recent information revolution have been only partially fulfilled. However, some won-derful advancements have been made. The planet has been encased by fleets of space-based satellites that have the capacity to provide entertainment and information services to the earth's entire population, and compressed digital technology makes it cost effective for any nation or consortium to compete for commercial, financial, and industrial resources.

To be successful, the next revolution must build upon the infrastructure of the global electronic media now in place. The coming change will be a brain-power revolution, in which manmade resources will be used in every part of the world, not just in the West. Such a change will take leadership—a higher-level leadership—and institutional commitments from all to build a system of public-access computer networks. This goal can be achieved by making sure that digital telecommunication access is available everywhere. Individually owned or leased computer hardware would no longer be required; only a link to the public-access computer networks would be necessary. Online computing services would be priced as tiered rates of the telephone company. But such a system must be seen as a public commitment, not a private one, because the supply-demand protocols of free enterprise capitalism will not normally commit to long-term structural investments.

Building roads, constructing sewers, laying telephone lines, launching satellites, and educating the population are the public responsibilities of local, national, and, in the near future, world governments. With such advanced communication networks, the job of educating "the other half" of the world's population may begin.

For more information on the topics that appear in this chapter, use the password that came free with this book to access InfoTrac College Edition. Use the following words as keyterms and subject searches: MacBride Report, information revolution, global satellite system, global Internet services, information warfare, privacy, access to media, global village.

QUESTIONS FOR DISCUSSION

1. Do you think that Marshall McLuhan's concept of the global village is achievable in a post–9/11 world? Why or why not? Cite evidence from this chapter.

2. In what ways are Western media organizational strategies similar to or contrary to those of other regions of the world?

3. What economic growth patterns and telecommunication infrastructure support systems can you identify among the various regions of the world?

4. How have privacy rights and communications security been compromised at the beginning of the third millennium? Make two forecasts about the resolutions to these critical problems.

5. What are the cultural and religious repercussions of acquiring new electronic technology and media in developing countries?

REFERENCES

Africa: Broadband and telephony services hold most promise. (2005, February 1). *Via Satellite, 20*(2).

Africa: Unexpected land of opportunity. (2004, February 1). *Via Satellite, 19*(2).

Asian economic tigers re-awaken, satellite industry pounces on market potential. (2001, April 10). *Via Satellite, 16*(4).

Boeke, C. (2002). Via satellite's global satellite survey Trends and statistics. *Via Satellite, 17*(7).

Boeke, C., & Fernandez, R. (1999, July). Satellite trends and statistics, 1998. *Via Satellite, 14*(9), 18–29.

Brown, P. (2003a, January 1). Access Asia: Open markets mean more opportunities. *Via Satellite, 18*(1).

Brown, P. (2003b, July 1). Africa: Pairing customers with capabilities. *Via Satellite, 18*(7).

Careless, J. (2005, March 1). AFRICA: Broadband and telephony services hold most promise. *Via Satellite, 20*(2).

ClickZ Stats. (2005). Population explosion! Retrieved January 31, 2005, from http://www.clickz.com/stats/sectors/geographics/article.php/3455061

Community Teleservice Centres. (2005). Impact of Community Teleservice Centres (TTSCs) on rural development. Retrieved February 2, 2005, from http://pressroom.com/~screenager/broadband/MIntl.html

Computer Industry Almanac Inc. (2004, September 3). Worldwide Internet users will top 1 billion in 2005. USA remains #1 with 185M Internet users. Retrieved February 2, 2005, from http://www.c-i-a.com/pro0904.htm

DITnet. (1999). Retrieved June 2000, from http://www.ditnet.co.ae/

EPIC warns that FBI surveillance plan marks the return of cold war mentality. (1999, August 2). *Multimedia Week, 8*(29).

Ewing, J., & Kunii, I. M. (2000, May 22). DoCoMo rising. *Business Week—European Edition,* p. 18.

Gher, L. A., & Amin, H. Y. (1999, February). New and old media access and ownership in the Arab world. *Gazette, 61*(1), 61.

Holmes, M. (2004). European broadcasting: Satellite players ready for a new era. *Via Satellite, 19*(9).

Hybrid networks: A winning partnership for satellite. (2004, January 1). *Via Satellite, 19*(1).

Larsen, F. (2001). Globalization and the poor countries: Viewpoint of the IMF. Retrieved February 14, 2005, from http://www.imf.org/extenal/np/vc/2001/010101.htm

Latin America: Big challenges for satellite operators. (2003, May 1). *Via Satellite, 18*(5).

The Middle East satellite market: Gaining ground gradually. (2002, February 1). *Via Satellite, 17*(2).

Mitsis, N. (2002). Broadcasting in Europe: Changing the landscape. *Via Satellite, 17*(12).

Mitsis, N. (2003). The Middle East: Broadcasting, broadband and business growth. *Via Satellite, 18*(10).

The North American satellite market: What lies ahead. (2003, November 1). *Via Satellite, 18*(11).

Ricardo's Geo-Orbit. (2000, May). Global GEO satellites. Retrieved June 2000, from http://www.geo-orbit.org

Rogers, G. K. (1999, July 22). Security versus privacy. *Bangkok Post.*

Schleifer, S. A. (1992). *Global media, the new world order, and the significance of failure: Media in the midst of war.* Cairo, Egypt: Adham Center Press.

Via Satellite's global satellite survey. (2004, July 1). *Via Satellite, 19*(7).

Women's Learning Partnership. (2004). *Facts and figures*: Technology. Retrieved February 2, 2005, from http://learningpartnership.org/facts/tech.phtml

World Bank. (1999, September). *Middle East/North Africa Status Report, 1999.* Retrieved June 2000 from http://wbln0018.worldbank.org/mna/mena.nsf

List of Acronyms

ABC American Broadcasting Company

ABU Asia–Pacific Broadcasting Union

AFP Agence-France Presse

AFRTS U.S. Armed Forces Radio–Television Service

ANR All News Radio

AP Associated Press

APC Association for Progressive Communication

APTN Associated Press Television News

ArabSat Arab Satellite Communications Organization (members are the 22 nations of the Arab League)

ARAMCO Arab-American Oil Company

ASBU Arab States Broadcasting Union

ASCO Arab Satellite Communications Organization

ASEAN Association of Southeast Asian Nations

AT&T American Telephone and Telegraph

BBC British Broadcasting Corporation

BBG Broadcasting Board of Governors

CANA Caribbean News Agency

CARICOM Caribbean Community

CBS Columbia Broadcasting System

CBU Caribbean Broadcasting Union

CCTV China Central Television

CIA Central Intelligence Agency

CIS Commonwealth of Independent States

CMC computer-mediated communication

CNN Cable News Network

CNNfn CNN Financial Network

CNNI CNN International

CNN/SI CNN/Sports Illustrated

COE Council of Europe

COMSAT Communication Satellite Corporation

COPUOS U.N. Committee on the Peaceful Use of Outer Space

CRIS Communication Rights in the Information Society

CSCE Conference on Security and Co-operation in Europe

DBS direct broadcast satellite

DJN Dow Jones Newswires

DPA Deutsche Press Agency

DTH direct-to-home

DVD digital video disc

DVR digital video recorder

DW-TV Deutsche Welle Television

EBU European Broadcasting Union

EC European Community

EEC European Economic Community

EU European Community

EutelSat European Telecommunications Satellite Organization

FAO Food and Agriculture Organization

FCC Federal Communications Commission

FDI foreign direct investment

GATS General Agreement on Trade in Services

GATT General Agreement on Tariffs and Trade

GDP gross domestic product

GII global information infrastructure

GNN Global News Network

GNP gross national product (total amount of goods and services produced within a country)

HDTV high-definition television

IANS India Abroad News Service

IBI International Broadcast Institute

IBU International Broadcasting Union

IC international communication

ICAO International Civil Aviation Organization

IGOs international governmental organizations, or intergovernmental organizations

IIC International Institute of Communication

ILO International Labor Organization

IM Instant Messenger

IMF International Monetary Fund

IMO International Maritime Organization

INGOs international nongovernmental organizations

INS International News Service

IntelSat International Telecommunications Satellite Organization

IPI International Press Institute

IPR intellectual property right

ISDN Integrated System Digital Networks

ISPs Internet service providers

ITAR-TASS Information Telegraph Agency of Russia–Telegraph Agency of the Soviet Union

ITU International Telecommunication Union (a U.N. specialized agency)

LDCs less-developed countries

LECs local exchange carriers

LEOs low earth orbits

MDCs more-developed countries

MENA Middle East News Association

MSO multiple system operator

MTV Music Television

NAFTA North American Free Trade Agreement

NAM Non-Aligned Movement

NATO North Atlantic Treaty Organization

NBC National Broadcasting Company

NGBT Negotiating Group on Basic Telecommunications

NGOs nongovernmental organizations

NHK Nippon Hansai Kyoki (Japan Broadcasting Corporation)

NICs newly industrialized countries

NIIO new international information order

NSF National Science Foundation

NTIA National Telecommunications Information Administration

NWEO new world economic order

NWICO new world information and communication order

NWIO new world information order

NWO new world order

OECD Organization for Economic Cooperation and Development

OIRT Organization for International Radio and Television

OPEC Organization of Petroleum Exporting Countries

OPECD Organization for Economic Cooperation and Development

PAHO Pan American Health Organization

PanAmSat Pan American Satellite

PCC People's Communication Charter

PCS personal communication services

PR public relations

PRSA Public Relations Society of America

PSA public service announcement

PTO public telecommunications operator

PTT Post, Telegraph, and Telephone

PVR personal video recorder

QoS quality of service

RASCOM Regional African Satellite Project

RFE/RL Radio Free Europe/Radio Liberty

SNTV Sports News Television

TASS Telegraph Agency of the Soviet Union

TDF transborder data flow

TNC transnational corporation

TNMC transnational media corporation

TNT Turner Network Television

TRIPS Trade-Related Intellectual Property Rights

UCC Universal Copyright Convention

UN United Nations

UNCITRAL United Nations Commission on International Trade Law

UNCTAD United Nations Conference on Trade and Development

UNDP United Nations Development Program

UNESCO United Nations Educational, Scientific, and Cultural Organization

UNICEF United Nations Children's Fund

UNIDO United Nations Industrial Development Organization

UPI United Press International

UPU Universal Postal Union

USAID United States Agency for International Development

USIA United States Information Agency

VCR video cassette recorder

VOA Voice of America

VOIP Voice-Over Internet Protocol

WAP wireless application protocol

WARC World Administrative Radio Conference

WHO World Health Organization

WIPO World Intellectual Property Organization

WSIS World Summit on the Information Society

WTN World Television Network

WTO World Trade Organization

Suggested Readings

Allan, S., & Zelizer, B. (Eds.). (2004). *Reporting war: Journalism in wartime*. New York: Routledge.

Akwule, R. (1992). *Global telecommunications: The technology, administration, and politics*. Boston: Focal Press.

Albarran, A. B. (1998). *Global media economics: Commercialization, concentration, and integration of world media markets*. Ames: Iowa State University Press.

Albarran, A. B., & Goff, D. H. (Eds.). (2000). *Understanding the Web: Social, political, and economic dimensions of the Internet*. Ames: Iowa State University Press.

Alexander, A., Owers, J., & Carveth, R. (Eds.). (1998). *Media economics: Theory and practice* (2nd ed.). Mahwah, NJ: Lawrence Erlbaum Associates.

Alger, D. (1998). *Megamedia: How giant corporations dominate mass media, distort competition, and endanger democracy*. Lanham, MD: Rowman & Littlefield.

Allen, D. (Ed.). (1996). *Women transforming communications: Global intersections*. Thousand Oaks, CA: Sage.

Alleyne, M. D. (1995). *International power and international communication*. New York: Saint Martin's Press.

Alleyne, M. D. (1997). *News revolution: Political and economic decisions about global information*. New York: St. Martin's Press.

Altschull, J. H. (1994). *Agents of power: The media and public policy,* (2nd ed.). Boston, MA: Allyn and Bacon/Longman.

Ammon, R. J. (2001). *Global television and the shaping of world politics: CNN, telediplomacy, and foreign policy*. Jefferson, NC: McFarland & Company.

Anokwa, K., Lin, C.A., & Salwen, M.B. (Eds.). (2003). *International Communication: Concepts and Cases*. Belmont, CA: Wadsworth.

Artz, L., & Kamalipour, Y. R. (Eds.). (2005). *Bring 'Em On: Media and politics in the Iraq war*. Lanham, MD: Rowman & Littlefield.

Artz, L., & Kamalipour, Y. R. (Eds.). (2003). *The globalization of corporate media hegemony*. Albany, NY: State University of New York Press.

Bagdikian, B. H. (2004). *The new media monopoly* (5th ed.). New York: Beacon Press.

Berenger, R. (Ed.). (2004). *Global media go to war: Role of news and entertainment media in the 2003 Iraq war*. Spokane, WA: Marquette Books.

Barker, C. (1999). *Television, globalization, and cultural identities*. London: Open University Press.

Barnouw, E., & Barnouw, E. (1998). *Conglomerates and the media*. New York: New Press.

Barsamina, D., & Chomsky, N. (2001). *Propaganda and the public mind*. Cambridge, MA: South End Press.

Becker, T. D., & Slaton, C. D. (2000). *The future of teledemocracy: Visions and theories—Action experiments—Global practices*. Westport, CT: Greenwood.

Boyd, D. A. (1999). *Broadcasting in the Arab world: A survey of the electronic media in the Middle East* (3rd ed.). Ames: Iowa State University Press.

British Broadcasting Corporation. (1982). *Voice for the world: The work of the BBC external service*. London: BBC.

Broad, R. (Ed.). (2002). *Global backlash: Citizen initiatives for a just world economy*. Lanham, MD: Rowman & Littlefield.

Browne, D. R. (1999). *Electronic media and industrialized nations: A comparative survey*. Ames: Iowa State University Press.

Browne, R. B., & Fishwick, M. W. (1998). *The global village: Dead or alive?* Bowling Green, Ohio: Bowling Green Popular Press.

Burniske, R. W., & Monke, L. (1999). *Breaking down the digital walls: Learning to teach in a post-modern world.* Albany: State University of New York Press.

Burns, R. (1998). *Television: An international history of the formative years.* Edison, NJ: Institute of Electrical Engineers.

Cambridge, V. C. (2005). *Immigration, diversity, and broadcasting in the United States, 1990–2001.* Athens, Ohio: Ohio University Press.

Campbell, R. (with Martin, C. R., & Fabos, B.). (2000). *Media and culture: An introduction to mass communication.* Boston: Bedford/St. Martin's.

Carey, A., & Lohrey, A. (Eds.). (1997). *Taking the risk out of democracy: Corporate propaganda versus freedom and liberty.* Urbana: University of Illinois Press.

Carruthers, S. L. (2000). *The media at war: Communication and conflict in the 20th century.* New York: St. Martin's Press.

Cate, F. H. (1997). *Privacy in the information age.* Washington, DC: Brookings Institution Press.

Chinoy, M. (2000). *China live: People power and the television revolution* (Updated ed.). Lanham, MD: Rowman & Littlefield.

Chitty, N., Rush, R., & Semati, M. (Eds.). (2003). *Studies in terrorism: Media scholarship and the enigma of terror.* Southbound: Penang, Malaysia.

Chomsky, N. (2003). *Hegemony or survival: America's quest for global dominance.* New York: Metropolitan Books.

Chomsky, N. (2002). *Media control: The spectacular achievements of propaganda.* New York: Seven Stories Press.

Chomsky, N. (1991). *Deterring democracy.* London: Verso Books.

Cooper, K. (1942). *Barriers down.* New York: Farrar & Rinehart.

Cooper-Chen, A., & Kodama, M. (1997). *Mass communication in Japan.* Ames: Iowa State University Press.

Craige, B. J. (1996). *American patriotism in a global society.* New York: State University of New York Press.

Croteau, D., & Hoynes, W. (2001). *The business of media: Corporate media and the public interest.* Thousand Oaks, CA: Pine Forge Press.

DeFleur, M. L., & Ball-Rokeach, S. (1989). *Theories of mass communication* (5th ed.). New York: Longman.

Demers, D. (2001). *Global media: Menace or Messiah.* Cresskill, NJ: Hampton Press.

Derne, S. (2000). *Movies, masculinity, and modernity: An ethnography of men's. Imgoing in India.* Westport, CT: Greenwood.

Diamond, L. (1994). *Political culture and democracy in developing countries: Textbook edition.* Boulder, CO: Lynne Rienner.

Diehl, P. F. (1997). *The politics of global governance: International organizations in an interdependent world.* Boulder, CO: Lynne Rienner.

Dizard, W. P., Jr. (1989). *The coming information age* (3rd ed.). New York: Longman.

Donahue, R. T. (1998). *Japanese culture and communication: Critical cultural analysis.* Lanham, MD: University Press of America.

D'Souza, D. (1996). *The end of racism: Principles for a multiracial society.* New York: Free Press.

Ducatel, K., Webster, J., & Herrmann, W. (Eds.). (2000). *The information society in Europe: Work and life in an age of globalization.* Lanham, MD: Rowman & Littlefield.

Dutton, W. H. (Ed.). (1996). *Information and communication technologies: Visions and realities.* Oxford: Oxford University Press.

Ebo, B. (2001). *Cyberimperialism? Global relations in the new electronic frontier.* Westport, CT: Praeger.

Eckes, A. E., Jr., & Zeiler, T. W. (2003). *Globalization and the American century.* Cambridge, UK: Cambridge University Press.

El-Nawawy, M., & Iskandar, A. (2003). *Al-Jazeera: The story of the network that is rattling governments and redefining modern journalism.* Boulder, CO: Westview Press.

El-Nawawy, M., & Iskandar, A. (2002). *Al-Jazeera: How the free Arab news network scooped the world and changed the Middle East.* Boulder, CO: Westview Press.

Emerson, T. I. (1970). *The system of freedom of expression.* New York: Random House.

Epstein, E. (2000). *News from nowhere: Television and the news.* Lanham, MD: Rowman & Littlefield.

Ess, C. (Ed.). (2001). *Culture, technology, communication: Towards an intercultural global village.* Albany: State University of New York Press.

Eugster, E. (1983). *Television programming across national boundaries: The EBU and OIRT experience.* Dedham, MA: Artech House.

Fardon, R., & Furniss, G. (Eds.). (2000). *African broadcast cultures: Radio in transition.* Westport, CT: Praeger.

Featherstone, M. (Ed.). (2000). *Global modernities.* Thousand Oaks, CA: Sage.

Flournoy, D., & Stewart, R. (1997). *CNN: Making news in the global market.* London: University of Luton Press.

Fortner, R. S. (1993). *International communication: History, conflict, and control of the global metropolis.* Belmont, CA: Wadsworth.

Frederick, H. H. (1986). *Cuban-American radio wars.* Norwood, NJ: Ablex.

Frederick, H. H. (1993). *Global communication and international relations.* Belmont, CA: Wadsworth.

Friedland, L. A. (1992). *Covering the world: International television news services.* New York: 20th Century Fund.

Garnham, N. (1990). *Capitalism and communication: Global culture and the economics of information.* Thousand Oaks, CA: Sage.

George, J. (1994). *Discourse of global politics: A critical (re)introduction to international relations.* Boulder, CO: Lynne Rienner.

Gerbner, G., Mowlana, H., & Nordenstreng, K. (1993). *The global media debate: Its rise, fall, and renewal.* Norwood, NJ: Ablex.

Gershon, R. A. (1996). *The transnational media corporation: Global messages and free market competition.* Mahwah, NJ: Lawrence Erlbaum Associates.

Gher, L. A., & Amin, H. Y. (Eds.). (1999). *Civic discourse in the Middle East and digital age communications.* Norwood, NJ: Ablex.

Gillett, S. E., & Vogelsang, I. (Eds.). (1999). *Competition, regulation, and convergence: Current trends in telecommunications policy research.* Mahwah, NJ: Lawrence Erlbaum Associates.

Ginneken, J. V. (1999). *Understanding global news: A critical introduction.* Thousand Oaks, CA: Sage.

Goldstein, R. J. (Ed.). (2000). *The war for the public mind: Political censorship in 19th century Europe.* Westport, CT: Praeger.

Gross, P. (1996). *Mass media in revolution and national development: The Romanian laboratory.* Ames: Iowa State University Press.

Gudykunst, W. B. (Ed.). (1993). *Communication in Japan and the United States.* Albany: State University of New York Press.

Gudykunst, W. B., & Mody, B. (Eds.). (2001). *Handbook of international and intercultural communication* (2nd ed.). Thousand Oaks, CA: Sage.

Gudykunst, W. B., & Nishida, T. (1994). *Bridging Japanese/North American differences.* Thousand Oaks, CA: Sage.

Gurtov, M. (1999). *Global politics in the human interest* (4th ed.). Boulder, CO: Lynne Rienner.

Hachten, W. A. (1992). *The world news prism: Changing media of international communication* (3rd ed.). Ames: Iowa State University Press.

Hachten, W. A. (1993). *The growth of media in the Third World, African failure, Asian successes.* Ames: Iowa State University Press.

Hafez, K. (Ed.). (1999). *Islam and the West in the mass media: Fragmented images in a globalizing world.* Cresskill, NJ: Hampton Press.

Halbert, D. J. (1999). *Intellectual property in the information age: The politics of expanding ownership rights.* Westport, CT: Praeger.

Hamelink, C. J. (1994). *The politics of world communication.* London: Sage.

Hamelink, C. J. (1995). *World communication.* London: Zed Books.

Hart, M. (2000). *The American Internet advantage: Global themes and implications of the modern world.* Lanham, MD: University Press of America.

Hemer, O., & Tufte, T. (Eds.). (2005). *Media & global change: Rethinking communication for development.* Goteborg, Sweden: NORDICOM.

Herbert, J. (2000). *Practicing global journalism: The effects of globalization and the media convergence.* Boston: Butterworth-Hienemann.

Herman, E., & Chomsky, N. (2002). *Manufacturing consent: The political economy of mass media.* New York: Pantheon.

Herman, E., McChesney, R. W., & Herman, E. S. (1998). *The global media: The missionaries of global capitalism.* Herndon, VA: Cassell Academic.

Hill, K. A., & Hughes, J. E. (1998). *Cyberpolitics: Citizen activism in the age of the Internet.* Lanham, MD: Rowman & Littlefield.

Hilliard, R. L., & Keith, M. C. (1996). *Global broadcasting systems*. Boston: Focal Press.

Holmes, P. A. (1999). *Broadcasting in Sierra Leone*. Lanham, MD: University Press of America.

Inglehart, R. (1990). *Culture shift in advanced industrial society*. Princeton, NJ: Princeton University Press.

International Commission for the Study of Communication Problems. (1980). *Many voices, one world: communication and society, today and tomorrow*. New York: UNESCO.

Jandt, F. E. (1998). *Intercultural communication: An introduction* (2nd ed.). Thousand Oaks, CA: Sage.

Johnston, C. B. (1998). *Global news access: The impact of new communications technologies*. Westport, CT: Greenwood.

Jones, T. D. (1998). *Human rights: Group defamation, freedom of expression, and the law of nations*. Boston: Martinus Nijhoff.

Kamalipour, Y. R., & Snow, N. (Eds.). (2004). *War, media, and propaganda: A global perspective*. Lanham, MD: Rowman & Littlefield.

Kamalipour, Y. R., & Rampal, K. (Eds.). (2001). *Media, sex, violence, and drugs in the global village*. Lanham, MD: Rowman & Littlefield.

Kamalipour, Y. R., & Thierstein, J. P. (Eds.). (2000). *Religion, law, and freedom: A global perspective*. Westport, CT: Greenwood.

Kamalipour, Y. R. (Ed.). (1999). *Images of the U.S. around the world: A multicultural perspective*. Albany: State University of New York Press.

Kamalipour, Y. R., & Carilli, T. (Eds.). (1998). *Cultural diversity and the U.S. media*. Albany: State University of New York Press.

Kamalipour, Y. R. (Ed.). (1995, 1997). *The U.S. media and the Middle East: Image and perception*. Westport, CT: Greenwood/Praeger.

Kamalipour, Y. R., & Mowlana, H. (Eds.). (1994). *Mass media in the Middle East: A comprehensive handbook*. Westport, CT: Greenwood.

Karim, K. H. (2000). *The Islamic peril: Media and global violence*. Montreal, Canada: Black Rose Books.

Kennedy, P. (1993). *Preparing for the 21st century*. New York: Vintage Books.

Keohane, R. O., & Nye, J. S. (1971). *Transnational relations and world politics*. Cambridge: Harvard University Press.

Ku, C., & Diehl, P. F. (Eds.). (1998). *International law: Classic and contemporary readings*. Boulder, CO: Lynne Rienner.

Lai, D. (1997). *Global perspectives: International relations, U.S. foreign policy, and the view from abroad*. Boulder, CO: Lynne Rienner.

Ledbetter, J. (1997). *Made possible by: The death of public broadcasting in the United States*. London: Verso Books.

Lee, C. C. (1980). *Media imperialism reconsidered: The homogenizing of television culture*. Beverly Hills, CA: Sage.

Lee, C-C., Chan, J. M., Pan, Z., & So, C. Y. K. (2002). *Global media spectacle: News war over Hong Kong*. Albany, NY: State University of New York Press.

Lengel, L. B. (Ed.). (1999). *Culture and technology in the new Europe: Civic discourse in transformation in post-socialist nations*. Norwood, NJ: Ablex.

Lent, J. A. (1999). *Women and mass communication in the 1990's: An international, annotated bibliography*. Westport, CT: Greenwood.

Li, H. (1998). *Image, perception, and the making of U.S.–Chinese relations*. Lanham, MD: University Press of America.

Lindahl, R. (1978). *Broadcasting across borders: A study on the role of propaganda in external broadcasts*. Göteborg, Sweden: C. W. K. Gleerup.

Loader, B. D. (Ed.). (1997). *The governance of cyberspace*. London: Routledge.

Lull, J. (2000). *Media, communication, culture: A global approach*. Irvington, NY: Columbia University Press.

McKenzie, R. (2006). *Comparing media from around the world*. Boston, MA: Pearson/Allyn & Bacon.

Mackenzie, H. (1999). *The directory of the armed forces radio service series*. Westport, CT: Greenwood.

Malek, A., & Kavoori, A. P. (Eds.). (2000). *The global dynamics of news: Studies in international news coverage and news agenda*. Westport, CT: Praeger.

Mansell, R., & Wehn, U. (1998). *Knowledge societies: Information technology for sustainable development*. Oxford: Oxford University Press.

McChesney, R. W. (1999). *Rich media, poor democracy: Communication politics in dubious times*. Urbana: University of Illinois Press.

McChesney, R. W., Wood, E. M., & Foster, J. B. (Eds.). (1998). *Capitalism and the information age: The political economy of the global communication revolution.* New York: Monthly Review Press.

McLuhan, M., Fiore, Q., & Agel, J. (1997). *War and peace in the global village.* New York: Wired Books.

McLuhan, M., & Powers, B. R. (1992). *The global village: Transformation in world life and media in the 21st century.* New York: Oxford University Press.

McPhail, T. C. (1987). *Electronic colonialism: The future of international broadcasting and communication.* Newbury Park, CA: Sage.

McPahil, T. L. (2005). *Global communication: Theories, stakeholders, and trends* (2nd ed.). Malden, MA: Blackwell.

McQuail, D. (1992). *Media performance: Mass communication and the public interest.* London: Sage.

McQuail, D. (2000). *McQuail's mass communication theory* (4th ed.). Thousand Oaks, CA: Sage.

McWilliams, W. C., & Piotrowski, H. (1997). *The world since 1945: A history of international relations.* Boulder, CO: Lynne Rienner.

Meadows, M. (2001). *Voices in the wilderness: Images of aboriginal people in the Australian media.* Westport, CT: Greenwood.

Melkote, S. R. (1998). *International satellite broadcasting and cultural implications.* Lanham, MD: University Press of America.

Melody, W. H. (Ed.). (1997). *Telecom reform: Principles, policies, and regulatory practices.* Lyngby: Technical University of Denmark.

Merrill, J. C. (Ed.). (1995). *Global journalism: Survey of international communication* (3rd ed.). White Plains, NY: Longman.

Mickelson, S. (1983). *America's other voice: The story of Radio Free Europe and Radio Liberty.* New York: Praeger.

Mittelman, J. H. (Ed.). (1996). *Globalization: Critical reflections.* Boulder, CO: Lynne Rienner.

Mohammadi, A. (Ed.). (1997). *International communication and globalization.* Thousand Oaks, CA: Sage.

Moore, R. L. (1999). *Mass communication law and ethics* (2nd ed.). Mahwah, NJ: Lawrence Erlbaum Associates.

Moore, R. L., Farrar, R. T., & Collins, E. L. (1997). *Advertising and public relations law.* Mahwah, NJ: Lawrence Erlbaum Associates.

Mostert, A. (n.d.). *A brief history of Radio New York Worldwide.* New York: Radio New York Worldwide.

Mowlana, H. (1990). *The passing of modernity: Communication and the transformation of society.* New York: Longman.

Mowlana, H. (1996). *Global media in transition: The end of diversity?* Thousand Oaks, CA: Sage.

Mowlana, H. (1997). *Global information and world communication.* London: Sage.

Nancy, H. (1993). *The making of exile cultures: Iranian television in Los Angeles.* Minneapolis: University of Minnesota Press.

Nazer, H. M. (1999). *Power of a third kind: The Western attempt to colonize the global village.* Thousand Oaks, CA: Sage.

Neuman, J. (1996). *Lights, camera, war: Is media technology driving international politics?* New York: St. Martin's Press.

Ngwainmbi, E. K. (1999). *Exporting communication technology to developing countries: Sociocultural, economic, and educational factors.* Lanham, MD: University Press of America.

Nohrstedt, S. A., & Ottosen R. (Eds.). (2004). *U.S. and the others: Global media images on "the war on terror."* Göteborg, Sweden: Nordicom.

Nohrstedt, S. A., & Ottosen R. (Eds.). (2006). *Global war—Local views: Media images of the Iraq War.* Göteborg, Sweden: Nordicom.

O'Heffernan, P. (1991). *Mass media and American foreign policy: Insider perspectives on global journalism and the foreign policy process.* Westport, CT: Greenwood.

Olson, S. R. (1999). *Hollywood planet: Global media and the competitive advantage of narrative transparency.* Mahwah, NJ: Lawrence Erlbaum Associates.

Over, W. (1999). *Human rights in international public sphere: Civic discourse for the 21st century.* Westport, CT: Praeger.

Paraschos, E. E. (1998). *Media law and regulation in the European Union: National, transnational, and U.S. perspectives.* Ames: Iowa State University Press.

Perry, N. (1998). *Hyperreality and global culture.* New York: Routledge.

Pettman, R. (1996). *Understanding international political economy, with readings for the fatigued.* Boulder, CO: Lynne Rienner.

Pintak, L. (2003). *Seeds of hate: How America's flawed Middle East policy ignited the Jihad.* London, UK: Pluto Press.

Price, M. E., & Verhulst, S. G. (Eds.). (1999). *Broadcasting reform in India: Media law from a global perspective.* New York: Oxford University Press.

Prosser, M. H. (Ed.). (2000). *Civic discourse and discourse conflict in Africa.* Norwood, NJ: Ablex.

Prosser, M. H., & Sitaram, K. S. (Eds.). (1999). *Civic discourse: Intercultural, international, and global media.* Norwood, NJ: Ablex.

Quester, G. H. (1990). *The international politics of television.* Lexington, MA: Lexington Books.

Qvist, P. O., & von Bagh, P. (2000). *Guide to the cinema of Sweden and Finland.* Westport, CT: Praeger.

Ryan, M. P. (1998). *Knowledge diplomacy: Global competition and the politics of intellectual property.* Washington, DC: Brookings Institution Press.

Said, E. (1988). *Covering Islam: How the media and the expert determine how we see the rest of the world.* New York: Pantheon.

Samovar, L. A., & Porter, R. E. (2001). *Communication between cultures* (4th ed.). Belmont, CA: Wadsworth.

Sassen, S. (1988). *The mobility of labor and capital.* Cambridge: Cambridge University Press.

Sayyid, B. S. (1997). *A fundamental fear: Eurocentrism and the emergence of Islam.* London: Zed Books.

Schlesinger, A. M., Jr. (1992). *The disuniting of America: Reflections on a multicultural society.* New York: W. W. Norton & Co.

Seib, P. (1997). *Headline diplomacy: How news coverage affects foreign policy.* London: Praeger.

Semati, M. (Ed.). (2004). *New frontiers in international Communication theory.* Lanham, MD: Rowman & Littlefield.

Shapiro, M. J. (1997). *Violent cartographies: Mapping cultures of war.* Minneapolis: University of Minnesota Press.

Shaw, M. (1996). *Civil society and media in global crises: Representing distant violence.* New York: Books International.

Sitaram, K. S., & Prosser, M. H. (Eds.). (1998). *Civic discourse: Multiculturalism, cultural diversity, and global communication.* Norwood, NJ: Ablex.

Sitaram, K. S., & Prosser, M. H. (Eds.). (2000). *Civic discourse: Communication, technology, and cultural values.* Norwood, NJ: Ablex.

Smolla, R. A. (1992). *Free speech in an open society.* New York: Alfred A. Knopf.

Sparks, C., & Tulloch, J. (Eds.). (2000). *Tabloid tales: Global debates over media standards.* Lanham, MD: Rowman & Littlefield.

Sreberny-Mohammadi, S., Winseck, D., McKenna, J., & Boyd-Barrett, O. (Eds.). (1998). *Media in global context: A reader.* New York: Oxford University Press.

Stevenson, R. L. (1993). *Communication, development, and the Third World: The global politics of information.* New York: University Press of America.

Stevenson, R. L. (1994). *Global communication in the 21st century.* New York: Longman.

Tanno, D. V., & Gonzalez, A. (Eds.). (1998). *Communication and identity across cultures.* Thousand Oaks, CA: Sage.

Taylor, P. M. (1997). *Global communications, international affairs, and the media since 1945.* New York: Routledge.

Tehranian, M. (1990). *Technologies of power: Information machines and democratic prospects.* Norwood, NJ: Ablex.

Tehranian, M. (Ed.). (1999). *Global communication and world politics: Domination, development, and discourse.* Boulder: Lynne Rienner.

Tehranian, M. (Ed.). (1999). *Worlds apart: Human security and global governance.* London: I. B. Taurus.

Tehranian, M., Hamikzadeh, F., & Vidale, M. (Eds.). (1977). *Communications policy for national development: A comparative perspective.* London: Routledge, Kegan & Paul.

Tehranian, M., & Tehranian, K. (Eds.). (1992). *Restructuring for world peace: On the threshold of the 21st century.* Cresskill, NJ: Hampton Press.

Teich, A. H. (2000). *Technology and the future* (8th ed.). Boston: Bedford/St. Martin's.

Thussu, D. K. (1998). *Electronic empires: Global media and local resistance.* New York: Oxford University Press.

Thussu, D. K. (2000). *International communication: Continuity and change.* New York: Oxford University Press.

Tomlinson, J. (1991). *Cultural imperialism: A critical introduction.* Baltimore: Johns Hopkins University Press.

Turow, J. (1997). *Breaking up America: Advertisers and the new media world.* Chicago: University of Illinois Press.

UNESCO. (1999). *World communication and information report, 1999–2000.* Paris: UNESCO.

Valdivia, A. N. N. (1995). *Feminism, multiculturalism, and the media: Global diversities.* Thousand Oaks, CA: Sage.

Van Belle, D. A. (2000). *Press freedom and global politics.* Westport, CT: Praeger.

Van Dijk, J. (1999). *The network society: An introduction to the social aspects of new media.* Thousand Oaks, CA: Sage.

Veseth, M. (1998). *Selling globalization: The myth of the global economy.* Boulder, CO: Lynne Rienner.

Vincent, R. C., Nordenstreng, K., & Traber, M. (Eds.). (1999). *Towards equity in global communication: MacBride update.* Cresskill, NJ: Hampton Press.

Volkmer, I. (2004). *News in global sphere: A study of CNN and its impact on global communication.* Luton, UK: University of Luton Press.

Wang, J. (2000). *Foreign advertising in China: Becoming global, becoming local.* Ames: Iowa State University Press.

Wark, M. (1994). *Virtual geography: Living with global media events.* Bloomington: Indiana University Press.

Weiss, T. G., & Gordnker, L. (Eds.). (1996). *NGOs, the UN, and global governance.* Boulder, CO: Lynne Rienner.

Wells, A. (Ed.). (1996). *World broadcasting.* London: General Hall Press.

Willis, J. (Ed.). (1999). *Images of Germany in the American media.* Westport, CT: Praeger.

Wilson, K. G. (2000). *Deregulating telecommunications: U.S. and Canadian telecommunication, 1840–1997.* Lanham, MD: Rowman & Littlefield.

Wood, J. (1994). *History of international broadcasting.* Edison, NJ: Institute of Electrical Engineers.

Wood, J. (1999). *History of international broadcasting* (vol. 2). Edison, NJ: Institute of Electrical Engineers.

World Commission on Culture and Development. (1995). *Our creative diversity.* Paris: UNESCO.

Youm, K. H. (1996). *Press law in South Korea.* Ames: Iowa State University Press.

Index

Boldface page numbers indicate material in tables or figures.